Interactive Multimedia in Education and Training

Sanjaya Mishra
Indira Gandhi National Open University, India

Ramesh C. Sharma
Indira Gandhi National Open University, India

IDEA GROUP PUBLISHING
Hershey • London • Melbourne • Singapore

Acquisitions Editor:	Mehdi Khosrow-Pour
Senior Managing Editor:	Jan Travers
Managing Editor:	Amanda Appicello
Development Editor:	Michele Rossi
Copy Editor:	Lori Eby
Typesetter:	Amanda Appicello
Cover Design:	Lisa Tosheff
Printed at:	Yurchak Printing Inc.

Published in the United States of America by
    Idea Group Publishing (an imprint of Idea Group Inc.)
    701 E. Chocolate Avenue, Suite 200
    Hershey PA 17033
    Tel: 717-533-8845
    Fax: 717-533-8661
    E-mail: cust@idea-group.com
    Web site: http://www.idea-group.com

and in the United Kingdom by
    Idea Group Publishing (an imprint of Idea Group Inc.)
    3 Henrietta Street
    Covent Garden
    London WC2E 8LU
    Tel: 44 20 7240 0856
    Fax: 44 20 7379 3313
    Web site: http://www.eurospan.co.uk

Library of Congress Cataloging-in-Publication Data

Interactive multimedia in education and training / Sanjaya Mishra, Ramesh C. Sharma, Editors.
    p. cm.
  ISBN 1-59140-393-6 -- ISBN 1-59140-394-4 -- ISBN 1-59140-395-2
 1. Interactive multimedia. I. Mishra, Sanjaya. II. Sharma, Ramesh C.
  QA76.76.I59I5816 2004
  006.7--dc22

                              2004003752

British Cataloguing in Publication Data
A Cataloguing in Publication record for this book is available from the British Library.

Interactive Multimedia in Education and Training

Table of Contents

Preface

There have been many experiments and innovations in the field of education and training regarding knowledge delivery. From face-to-face to virtual education, different technologies have played great roles at different times. In the last two decades, due to the advent of computer technologies, information delivery has got new meaning. Development, access, and transfer of text, sound, and video data have given a unique face to classrooms, libraries, and training and resource centers, in the form of interactive multimedia programs.

Interactive multimedia as a subject/topic is still in its stage of infancy, which excites and attracts educational technologists. However, design and development of an interactive multimedia program is a complex task involving a team of experts, including content provider(s), multimedia developer(s), graphic designer(s), and, of course, the instructional designer(s), who most of the time plays the role of a project manager as well. This book is not about multimedia development, but the subject matter delves into the complex issue of planning, guiding, and designing multimedia from the instructional perspective. As such, we address pedagogical issues, applications, and effectiveness.

What is Interactive Multimedia?

Multimedia has been defined in a number of ways. It is not our intention here to go into the details of these definitions. But, in order to clarify the use of the term in the context of the book, we would prefer to quote a few of them:

Definition 1: "Multimedia is the combination of a variety of communication channels into a co-ordinated communicative experience for which an integrated cross-channel language of interpretation does not exist" (Elsom-Cook, 2001).

This definition gives way for two approaches—one that is termed the "multiple-media" utilization, and the other in which a combination of different channels acquires unification as a medium. The latter approach leads us to the next definition:

Definition 2: "… multimedia can be defined as an integration of multiple media elements (audio, video, graphics, text, animation, etc.) into one synergetic and symbiotic whole that results in more benefits for the end user than any one of the media elements can provide individually" (Reddi, 2003).

Definition 2 essentially tries to emphasize the second approach of Definition 1 with more clarity and spells out the components of multimedia. Taking a systems theory perspective, it also tells us that the overall effectiveness of multimedia is better than any one component of it. But, neither of the definitions explicitly includes the "interactive" power of multimedia, as in Definition 3:

Definition 3: "The term 'interactive multimedia' is a catch-all phrase to describe the new wave of computer software that primarily deals with the provision of information. The 'multimedia' component is characterized by the presence of text, pictures, sound, animation and video; some or all of which are organized into some coherent program. The 'interactive' component refers to the process of empowering the user to control the environment usually by a computer" (Phillips, 1997).

Though the authors of various chapters use different words and phrases throughout the book, the intentions are invariably in tune with Definition 3 referred to above.

Multimedia has been a favorite area for organizations as a means of training employees. McCrea and others (2000) and Urdan and Weggen (2000) found online training being given preference by organizations, considering that with this method, employees can be trained in less time, with less cost, and more effectively than with other methods. It has been found that integrating multimedia into course delivery certainly adds to the advantages (Najjar, 1996).

Authors of the various chapters in this book critically examine interactive multimedia as a tool for education and training in various settings. Much has already been said in the literature about how-to aspects of multimedia development (Boyle, 1997; Phillips, 1997; Villamil & Molina, 1998; Lachs, 2000; Elsom-Cook, 2001; Low et al, 2003; Reddi & Mishra, 2003). Here, the authors make an attempt to build a theoretical understanding based on experience and re-search. The pictures projected in all these chapters are successful implementa-tion stories of multimedia, and how it is useful as an educational tool. Neverthe-less, there is a huge amount of literature on "no significant difference." Kahn (n.d.), in a short review, questions the effectiveness of multimedia in online training but recommends that it has a place "where visual/ or auditory depiction could enhance the learning experience." Contributors of different chapters share their innovative uses of the potentials of multimedia, and this is expected to further motivate and guide other teachers and readers to use multimedia in their teaching. The chapters in the book are organized in three parts—planning and design considerations, pedagogical issues, and application and case stud-ies.

Planning and Design Considerations

Planning for multimedia is a much broader consideration than the design and development issues. It is important because the implementation of multimedia-enabled teaching and learning has to be integrated into an already existing sys-tem and practice. Moreover, issues such as media mix, choice, and teaching—learning functions should match the requirements of the subject. It is in this context that Patrick Fahy, in Chapter 1, discusses the characteristics of multi-media in relation to basic pedagogic tasks and organizational realities. He em-phasizes that successful implementation of multimedia-enabled teaching and learning includes organizational change, changes in attitudes, and issues related to cost, acquisition of appropriate technologies, and human resources. In Chap-ter 2, Geraldine Torrisi-Steele provides conceptual guidelines and a planning framework for effective use of multimedia in education. Banerji and Scales in Chapter 3 review current developments in performance support systems and recommend use of interactive multimedia based on performance-centered de-sign for teaching and learning. In Chapter 4, Loreen Butcher-Powell provides a theoretical framework for enhancing teaching through the use of Web-based multimedia. In Chapter 5, Yoshii and others discuss the Irvine-Geneva develop-ment strategy for computer-based learning materials that can be adaptable to many languages and cultures. Based on the experiences gained in the develop-ment of a group of software systems, the authors describe software character-istics and tools that can be successfully implemented in global education. In the last chapter of this part (i.e., in Chapter 6), Lisa Gjedde describes a narrative (storytelling) framework for designing multimedia learning environments.

Pedagogical Issues

Learning is primarily the process through which we become the human beings we are, and it takes place through a variety of media, strategies, and processes, of which interactive multimedia is just one. Using these media and technologies, we internalize information and knowledge available in the external world to construct our own experiences. Research into human learning is primarily categorized into three distinctive groups: behaviorism, cognitivism, and constructivism. There are others who also believe in experiential learning and andragogy. All of these have significance for the design and development of interactive multimedia. In this part dealing with theoretical issues, there are six chapters. In Chapter 7, Vassilios Dagdilelis discusses the principles of designing educational software and emphasizes that "construction of educational software should be based on some method; otherwise it is in danger of failing of costing too much or of being greatly delayed." Michael Sankey, in Chapter 8, continues the discussion of multiple representations in multimedia materials raised in the previous chapter. Sankey reviews the issue of multimedia literacy of learners and investigates the learning styles, visual representations, and cognitive constraints experienced by the learners when information is presented in multiple ways. Based on these analyses, Sankey suggests a set of 12 design principles. In Chapter 9, Paul Kawachi discusses a four-stage model for learning critical thinking skills using multimedia. The four stages of Design for Multimedia Learning (DML) model are brainstorming cooperative group learning using synchronous media, lateral-thinking collaborative learning using asynchronous media, hypothesis testing in a collaborative synchronous manner, and experiential learning in cooperative synchronous media. Though this model is more about multiple-media use in teaching and learning, it has a new innovative framework to offer in the context of use of interactive multimedia on the Web. Peter Doolittle and others in Chapter 10 focus on multimedia and the effect of cognitive load on teaching, training, and learning. Based on a review of research, they present seven principles of multimedia design:

Individuals learn, retain, and transfer information better

1. when the instructional environment involves words and pictures rather than words or pictures alone (multimedia principle)

2. when the instructional environment involves auditory narration and animation rather than on-screen text and animation (modality principle)

3. when the instructional environment involves narration and animation rather than on-screen text, narration, and animation (redundancy principle)

4. when the instructional environment is free of extraneous words, pictures, and sounds (coherence principle)

5. when the instructional environment involves cues, or signals, that guide an

individual's attention and processing during a multimedia presentation (signaling principle)

6. where words or narration and pictures or narration are presented simultaneously in time and space (contiguity principle)

7. where individuals experience concurrent narration and animation in short, user-controlled segments, rather than as a longer continuous presentation (segmentation principle)

In Chapter 11, Elspeth McKay examines contextual issues involved in interactivity of multimedia instructional materials and the cognitive style construct as a meta-knowledge acquisition process. From a human–computer interaction (HCI) perspective, she describes a framework applicable in Web-based educational systems. In the next chapter (Chapter 12), Retalis looks into the issue of interoperability of multimedia learning objects. This chapter describes a brokerage system for the exchange of learning resources.

Applications and Case Studies

Interactive multimedia has applications in a variety of situations in education and training, in corporate presentation, in advertising, and in many other areas. In this part, there are six chapters presented as illustrative case studies of the application of multimedia. In Chapter 13, José Rodríguez Illera describes the use of interactive multimedia in AIDS prevention. The design of the multimedia package adopts some of the lessons outlined in Parts I and II of this book, especially the use of role play as narrative and the social construction of meaning that make it a successful program. Katia Tannous in Chapter 14 describes some examples of multimedia use in engineering education that extensively uses the power of simulation. In Chapter 15, Balram and Dragicevic report a new embedded collaborative system for structuring and managing multimedia in cartography teaching and learning. In Chapter 16, Leo Tan Wee Hin and others describe a multimedia system for learning science in an informal setting of a science center in Singapore. The authors present a case of high-quality visualizations, interactivity, immersive experiences, and stereoscopic imagery in the multimedia virtual environment that contributes toward experiential learning and has the significant influence of the constructivist approach. In Chapter 17, Mike Keppell and others describe the use of multimedia in dental and health science courses. Using a case-based learning design and learner-centered approach, the illustrative multimedia examples demonstrate the importance of instructional design. In the last chapter of the book (i.e., Chapter 18), Felicia

Zhang reports on the use of interactive feedback tools to enhance language learning, in this case, Chinese Mandarin.

Conclusions

In education and training settings, interactive multimedia packages have been found to be used as library-based multimedia resources for teachers and students; as supplementary curricular material for a specific course; as a tool for teaching and reinforcing analytic and reading skills and for building an entire course around the use and creation of multimedia materials (Bass, n.d.). In the modern society, where computer and Net technologies are becoming indispensable, the learning technologies are found to be deployed in all sectors: schools, colleges, universities, and industries. The emergence of the knowledge and educational content industry, the emergence of virtual campuses of learning, the availability of new learning and training tools, and the deployment of such tools to meet the diverse needs of learners have greatly influenced education and training systems. The needs for lifelong learning, just-in-time training, and retraining led to the development of widely accessible and reusable digital multimedia content and learning repositories. As the contributors of this book point out, the advantages are multifarious: increased interoperability, reusability, and individualization of digital learning materials. The learners are benefited in terms of increased quality, relevance, and contextualization of their learning.

The primary objective of *Interactive Multimedia in Education and Training* is to document and disseminate relevant theoretical frameworks and the latest empirical research findings and showcase illustrative examples of multimedia applications in various disciplines. The 18 chapters included in this book have attempted to achieve this objective and shall be useful to teachers, researchers, educational administrators, and policy makers as a one-step reference point on innovative use of multimedia, based on sound pedagogical principles. Nevertheless, there are still gray areas, such as the assessment of multimedia packages, their costs, and return on investment (ROI). In spite of this gap, it is expected that this book will encourage teachers/trainers and administrators to plan, design, develop, and implement interactive multimedia in educational settings: in basic, secondary, higher, and further education, and in business and industrial training.

References

Bass, R. (n.d.). A brief guide to interactive multimedia and the study of the United States. Retrieved November 24, 2003 from the World Wide Web: http://www.georgetown.edu/faculty/bassr/multimedia.html

Boyle, T. (1997). *Design for multimedia learning*, London: Prentice Hall.

Elsom-Cook, M. (2001). *Principles of interactive multimedia* (p. 7). London: McGraw Hill.

Kahn, D. (n.d). How effective is multimedia in online training? *E-learning Guru.com White Papers*. Retrieved November 26, 2003 from the World Wide Web: http://www.e-learningguru.com/wpapers/multimedia.pdf

Lachs, V. (2001). *Making multimedia in the classroom*. London: Routledge Falmer.

Low, A. L. Y., Low, K. L. T., & Koo, V. C. (2003). Multimedia learning systems: A future interactive educational tool. *Internet in Higher Education, 6*, 25–40.

McCrea, F., Gay, R. K., & Bacon, R. (2000). *Riding the big waves: A white paper on B2B e-learning industry*. San Francisco: Thomas Weisel Partners LLC.

Najjar, L. J. (1996). *The effects of multimedia and elaborative encoding on learning*. Atlanta, GA: Georgia Institute of Technology.

Phillips, R. (1997). *The developers handbook to interactive multimedia: A practical guide for educational developers* (p. 8). London: Kogan Page.

Reddi, U. V. (2003). Multimedia as an educational tool. In U. V. Reddi, & S. Mishra (Eds.), *Educational multimedia: A handbook for teacher-developers* (pp. 3–7). New Delhi: CEMCA.

Reddi, U. V., & Mishra, S. (Eds.). (2003). *Educational multimedia: A handbook for teacher-developers*. New Delhi: CEMCA.

Urdan, T. A., & Weggen, C. C. (2000). *Corporate e-learning: Exploring a new frontier*. WR+Hambrecht & CO.

Villamil, J., & Molina, L. (1998). *Multimedia: An introduction*, New Delhi: Prentice-Hall of India.

Acknowledgments

The editors would like to express their sincere gratitude and thanks to all those who directly or indirectly helped in the collation and review process of the book, without whose support, the project could not have been satisfactorily completed. Most of the authors of chapters included in this book also served as referees of articles written by other authors. In addition, many others provided constructive and comprehensive reviews on chapters. Some of those who provided the most comprehensive, critical, and illuminative comments include Dr. Som Naidu, University of Melbourne; Dr. Kinshuk, Massey University; Dr. Punya Mishra, Michigan State University; and Dr. Allison Littlejohn, University of Strathclyde—our sincere thanks to all of them.

A special note of thanks goes to all the staff at Idea Group Inc., whose contributions throughout the whole process from inception of the initial idea to final publication have been invaluable. Especially we are indebted to Mehdi Khosrow-Pour, Senior Academics Editor; Jan Travers, Senior Managing Editor; Michele Rossi, Development Editor; Amanda Appicello, Managing Editor; and Jennifer Sundstrom, Assistant Marketing Manager for providing support from time to time and dealing with our queries at a lightening speed. Their special interest in the publication, and professional guidance made it easier for us to complete the editing work on time.

We would like to thank our employer, the Indira Gandhi National Open University, and its staff members for their constant encouragement to do quality work. Dr. Sharma, especially would like to thank his wife, Madhu, and children, Anku and Appu, for their constant support and understanding.

Last but not the least, all the contributing authors of the book deserve special thanks for their excellent contributions, and we are grateful to all of them for having faith on us during the long development process of the book and for meeting the deadlines.

Sanjaya Mishra
Ramesh C. Sharma
Editors

Part I

Planning and Design Considerations

Chapter I

Planning for Multimedia Learning

Patrick J. Fahy, Athabasca University, Canada

Abstract

Multimedia tools, applied with awareness of the realities of organizational culture, structures and finances, have been shown to enhance the performance of learning systems. If some predictable pitfalls are avoided, and proven pedagogical design principles and appropriate vehicles (including the Internet) are used effectively, multimedia can permit greater individualization, in turn fostering improved learning, learner satisfaction, and completion rates.

Introduction

Effective uses of multimedia in open and distance learning (ODL) depend upon various factors, some intrinsic to the media themselves, and others related to the differing pedagogic tasks and organizational environments into which these tools are introduced. For those planning use of multimedia, it may be valuable to consider the likely impacts of these tools on teaching and learning practices and outcomes, and on organizational structures and processes, as they are likely to be different in scope and magnitude from those of traditional instructional innovations.

This chapter discusses some of the characteristics of multimedia in relation to basic pedagogic tasks and organizational realities. The goal is to alert new users to issues that often arise in multimedia implementations and to assist experienced users in assessing their strategies, by outlining some fundamental considerations commonly affecting implementation of multimedia. Both new and experienced technology users will hopefully find the discussion useful for reflecting on options, and anticipating potential pedagogic and administrative challenges, as they move from simpler to more complex combinations of media for teaching.

The chapter begins with a discussion of the term *multimedia*, including a review of some of the characteristics (including common pedagogic benefits and potential issues) of specific media. Based on this analysis, some of the conditions under which multimedia might readily support learning tasks are explored. Finally, the impact of multimedia as an innovation on aspects of organizational culture (including structure and finances) are addressed.

Defining Multimedia

While the term "multimedia" has not always been associated with computers (Roblyer & Schwier, 2003, p. 157), there is no doubt that it is the merging of increasingly powerful computer-based authoring tools with Internet connectivity that is responsible for the growing interest in and use of multimedia instruction, in both distance and face-to-face environments. This trend is encouraged by growing evidence that well-designed online delivery, regardless of the media used, can improve retention, expand the scope and resources available in learning situations, and increase the motivation of users (Fischer, 1997; Bruce & Levin, 1997; Mayer, 2001). For these reasons, the term "multimedia" is now firmly associated with computer-based delivery, usually over the Internet and accompanied and supported by interaction provided via some form of computer-mediated communication (CMC).

Definitions of multimedia vary in particulars but tend to agree in substance. Mayer (2001, p. 1) defined multimedia learning simply as "presentation of material using both words and pictures." Roblyer and Schwier (2003) observed that definition is problematic, because it is increasingly difficult to distinguish multimedia from other tools with which it seems to be converging. They also note that multimedia have sometimes been defined simplistically by the storage devices they employ, e.g., CD-ROM, videodisc, DVD, etc., a practice they regard as clearly inadequate. Roblyer and Schwier offered this definition of multimedia: "A computer system or computer system product that incorporates text, sound, pictures/graphics, and/or audio" (p. 329). They added that the multimedia implies the purpose of "communicating information" (p. 157).

In keeping with the above, in this chapter, the term "multimedia" refers to the provision of various audio and video elements in teaching and training materials. Usually, the delivery of the media is by computer, and increasingly, it involves the Internet in some way, but the storage and delivery devices, as noted above, are secondary to the forms of the stimuli that reach the user. The definition assumes that media are used, but it does not address such design issues as choice of specific media for differing pedagogic purposes and levels of user control.

Basic to considering how specific media contribute to the effectiveness or ineffectiveness of multimedia is a brief discussion of the available research on technology in learning. Multimedia technologies invariably consist of media with effects on learning that have been studied before, making this knowledge pertinent and applicable here (Saettler, 1990).

Media and Learning

Specific Media Characteristics

For some time, media have been used with more traditional delivery methods (lectures, tutorials) to support essential teaching objectives, such as the following (Wright, 1998):

- Clarifying and illustrating complex subjects
- Adapting to individual learning styles
- Improving retention and aiding recall
- Reaching nonverbal learners

Debates have occurred over the precise role of media in learning. The fundamental disagreement between Clark (1983, 1994) and Kozma (1994) about
media and learning is familiar historically and need not be repeated here. It seems
clear that Mayer's (2001) views of multimedia (discussed later) clearly support
one point made in that debate, that of the "interdependence" of presentation
media and delivery methods in certain circumstances, especially in collaborative
situations, and where higher-order learning is an objective (Crooks & Kirkwood,
1988; Juler, 1990; Koumi, 1994). As Berge (1995, p. 23) concluded, and as has
been documented by Mayer (2001), "Some media channels promote particular
interactions, and other channels can hinder that same type of interaction."

While the potential for successful high-level learning outcomes is present in
media use, a persistent problem in multimedia applications has been failure to
achieve more than low-level learning outcomes (Bloom, Englehart, Furst, Hill, &
Krathwohl, 1956). Helm and McClements (1996) commented critically,
"Interactivity in the context of multimedia often refers to the learners' ability to
follow hypertext links or stop and start video clips…. Much of what passes for
interactivity should really be called feedback" (p. 135). These are serious
criticisms, justifying Mayer's (2001) advice, "Instead of asking which medium
makes the best deliveries, we might ask which instructional techniques help guide
the learner's cognitive processing of the presented material" (p. 71).

The varying characteristics of different presentation media and modes, and their
implications for learning, have direct implications for the design of multimedia
strategies and materials. *Sound* can supplement visual information and can be
used to attract attention, arouse and hold interest, provide cues and feedback, aid
memory, and provide some types of subject matter (heart or machinery sounds,
voice clips). *Music* can be used to augment feedback, grab attention or alert
users, and support the mood of a presentation. *Synthetic speech*, while useful
for handicapped users, is less effective if too mechanical sounding. Szabo (1998)
concluded that achievement gains due to audio are "weak or non-existent." He
added that where benefits are seen, they tend to accrue to the more highly verbal
learners. Problems with development costs and bandwidth for delivery of audio
can also be significant (Wright, 1998; Szabo, 1998).

Graphics and color can be used for various purposes, from simple decoration
to higher-level interpretation and transformation (helping the observer to form
valid mental images) (Levin, Anglin, & Carney, 1987). Research has shown that
realism and detail are not critical in graphics and may, in fact, extend learning
time for some users; relevance is more important than detail (Szabo, 1998). Color
may also distract some learners, unless it is highly relevant to instruction. A
significant proportion of individuals (especially men) have some degree of color-
blindness, suggesting that color should be placed under the control of the user
where possible. The best contrasts are achieved with blue, black, or red on white
or white, yellow, or green on black.

Animation can sometimes shorten learning times by illustrating changes in the operation or state of things; showing dangerous, rapid, or rare events; or explaining abstract concepts. For some, animation increases interest and holds attention better than text or audio, and the resulting learning seems to be retained (Szabo, 1998). Overall, however, research indicates that well-designed and imaginative verbal presentations may be capable of producing similar outcomes (Rieber & Boyce, 1990), leading to the conclusion that animation may not possess many unique instructional capabilities.

Video (motion or sequences of still graphics) can be used to show action and processes and to illustrate events that users cannot see directly or clearly in real time. Video, when used skillfully and artistically, can also emotionally move observers and can produce impacts affecting attitudes similar to in-person observation of real events.

Hypermedia is the linking of multimedia documents, while *hypertext* is the linking of words or phrases to other words or phrases in the same or another document (Maier, Barnett, Warren, & Brunner, 1996, p. 85). Hypertext and hypermedia may be difficult to distinguish and increasingly difficult to separate from other applications of multimedia (Roblyer & Schwier, 2003). When paired with plain text, hypertext has been shown to be a cost-effective way to extend text's information-conveying capabilities, especially for more capable learners. Szabo (1998) suggested that hypertext should be used more to provide access to information than for actual teaching, in recognition of the need for hypertext materials to be placed in context for maximum impact (especially for less experienced or less capable learners).

Hypermedia is a particularly promising form of multimedia materials designed for ODL (Maier, Barnett, Warren, & Brunner, 1996, p. 85; Roblyer & Schwier, 2003). With advances in hardware, software, and human–computer interfaces, it is now technically feasible to use hypermedia systems routinely in online teaching. Dozens of hypertext and hypermedia systems exist, with most offering three basic advantages:

- Huge amounts of information from various media can be stored in a compact, conveniently accessible form, and can easily be included in learning materials.

- Hypermedia potentially permit more learner control (users can choose whether or when to follow the available links).

- Hypermedia can provide teachers and learners with new ways of interacting, rewarding learners who developed independent study skills and permitting teachers to be creative in how they interact with learners (Marchionini, 1988, p. 3).

There are potential problems, too, in learning with hypermedia, related to the volume and structure of all information found on the Web. The vast amounts of information available can overwhelm the learner, especially if structure is inadequate or procedures such as searches are not skillfully refined, allowing learners to "wander off" and become engrossed in appealing but irrelevant side topics. Learners who do not have independent study skills may not be able to manage the complexity of hypermedia. This problem may not be immediately evident, however, because they *appear* to be engaged and on task, sometimes deeply so.

Other potential problems in teaching with hypermedia include some unique to this medium and others common to all learning situations that require specific skills or make assumptions about learner attributes and characteristics:

- Hypermedia require basic literacy skills. While this may change as increasing bandwidth makes audio and video available, presently, the Internet and its multimedia products rely heavily on text.

- A related problem is that interacting with hypermedia and multimedia requires keyboard and mouse skills, as well as understanding and manipulating function keys. The computer illiterate, the unskilled, or the physically handicapped may be affected.

- More broadly, accessing hypermedia and multimedia requires computer use, including sitting in front of the machine and making sense of its cues and displays. Those with vision, concentration, coordination, or mobility problems, or those distracted or confused by the intense stimulation of colors, animation, sound, etc., may be penalized.

The above specific features of media have been shown to affect their usefulness for teaching and learning. In addition to the limitations of media, a key point here is the importance of historical media research to the present discussion: multimedia are *media*, and the view taken in this chapter is that knowledge previously gained about their impact on learning is still highly applicable.

Media Characteristics, Teaching Conditions, and Learning Outcomes

When media are used together, their effects can interact, sometimes unpredictably. With media, "more is not necessarily better."

There is as yet little thorough research on multimedia technologies to inform design and implementation decisions; use of previous research may help guide present practice. What follows is a discussion of some key didactic purposes to which media may apply, followed by some remarks about the Internet as a base for multimedia delivery.

Evaluations have shown that a fundamental benefit to students from the best uses of technology in teaching is a more systematic approach to the individualization and customization of instruction (Massy & Zemsky, 1999). Properly designed, a technology-based learning environment provides students with more options than are typically available in traditional learning situations, in content, pace, preparation, and review of prerequisites, and for activities such as collaboration, consultation, and testing/evaluation. These are objectives that have long been recognized as pedagogically essential (Zimmerman, 1972; Mezirow & Irish, 1974; Kemp, 1977; Dede, 1996; Roblyer, Edwards, & Havriluk, 1997). Among the benefits of technology delivery are the potential for less required training time; greater mastery and better transfer of skills; more consistency in delivery of content (a particularly important outcome of skill training); and greater student persistence, completion, satisfaction, collaboration, and self-direction (Grow, 1991; Moore, 1993). In some situations, experience has shown that highly self-directed students may be able to undertake and complete advanced studies with little or no direct assistance or intervention from the institution, increasing efficiency through the "unbundling" of learning from direct teaching (Massy & Zemsky, 1999, pp. 2–3). In the best examples, technologies increase learning, enhance learner satisfaction, stabilize costs, and raise the visibility and appeal of (and potential revenues from) existing programs (Oberlin, 1996).

While positive effects are possible in teaching with media, they are not automatic. Internal consistency of objectives is critical: multimedia technologies must be congruent with the organization's learning model and actual teaching practices, as well as with students' expectations and capabilities for autonomy and self-direction (Grow, 1991). If tools are chosen for their technological capabilities alone, there is a risk of failing to fit with the organizational environment (Helm & McClements, 1996; Mayer, 2001; Welsch, 2002), resulting in potentially disastrous technology implementation "mistakes" (Quinn & Baily, 1994).

Despite differing characteristics, useful online training technologies have in common the effect of bringing the student into timely and productive contact with the tutor, the content, and peers, thereby reducing the "transactional distance" in distance learning, the communications gap or psychological distance between geographically separated participants (Moore, 1989; Chen & Willits, 1998). The differences in how various media accomplish their effects are important to their potential usefulness. Figure 1, for example, compares instruction delivered by human and technological means (Fischer, 1997).

Figure 1: Comparison of characteristics of human- and technology-based instruction

Training element	Human-delivered training	Technology-based training
Planning and preparation	Able to design training to correspond to the training plan; able to monitor consistency	Must be systematically designed to conform to the training plan
Expertise	Presenters hired from industry usually represent the most current knowledge and highest expertise	Must be designed to conform to industry standards; currency with standards must be maintained
Interactivity	Instructors tend to train the group, ignoring individual needs	Able to focus on individual needs in content, pacing, review, remediation, etc.
Learning retention	Retention rates vary	Can be up to 50% higher than instructor-led group training
Consistency	Instructors tend to adapt to the audience, sacrificing consistency	Rigorously maintains standards but may also be designed to adapt to learner's performance or preferences
Feedback, performance tracking	Human instructors especially good at constant, ongoing evaluation, response to trainee performance	Better at keeping records and generating reports, but designing cybernetic systems to adapt instruction based on feedback is costly, complex

Note: Elements: Fisher, 1997 (pp. 29-30).

Illustrated in Figure 1 are some of the trade-offs inherent in the decision to use teaching media, as opposed to traditional forms of delivery alone. If a critical value for a program is met by tutor-based delivery, and resources are plentiful, it may be chosen without regard for cost. Where economy is important, however, the "best" delivery solution may not be affordable; a less costly but still adequate solution may have to be chosen. (This was the purpose of Bloom's [1984] "two-sigma" challenge, to find a teaching medium as effective as one-on-one tutoring. The search, of course, continues with multimedia.) Analysis such as the above may assist in identifying the trade-offs involved in the choice of one medium or technology over another and may suggest compensating strategies to improve the effectiveness of whatever tool is chosen (Wolfe, 1990).

Besides cost and accessibility (Bates, 1995), another issue in selecting media is the type of experience or learning outcomes intended by the training (DeSanctis & Gallupe, 1987). Picard (1999), for instance, sees the key contribution of media as their ability to promote *relationship building*, and not merely *information exchange*, in work or learning.

Figure 2: Relation of data, audio, and video technologies to information exchange and relationship-building outcomes

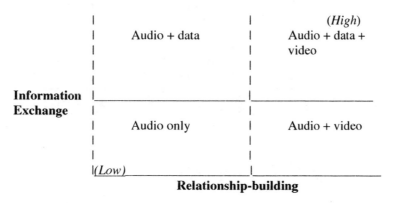

Source: Picard (1999).

From Figure 2, we see the following:

- When relationship-building and information exchange needs are both low, audio media alone may suffice.

- When both relationship-building and information-exchange needs are high, audio, video, and information exchange (including text) should all be present.

- Relationship-building is enhanced by combining audioconferencing and video together with data, especially text. (Text alone has substantial relationship-building capabilities, as anyone who has ever had a pen pal, or exchanged love letters, can attest.)

In relation to learning, technologies have potential directly to address common teaching tasks. In Figure 3, the views of several theoreticians regarding tasks or conditions essential to learning are compared. Two points should be noted in this comparison: (a) there is considerable apparent agreement among authorities on elements essential to effective teaching and learning, and (b) there appear to be obvious roles for multimedia in supporting some of these tasks.

Figure 3: *Comparison of models of effective teaching and learning: roles for multimedia*

Bloom (1984)	Chickering & Gamson (1989)	Gagne (1985)	Joyce & Weil (1980)	Moore (in Garrison, 1989)
Tutorial instruction	Student–faculty interaction	Presenting new material; describing objectives; gaining learner's attention	Presenting stimuli, objectives; sequencing learning tasks	Communicating in an understandable manner
Reinforcement	Student–faculty interaction	Recalling previous learning; enhancing retention and recall	Increasing attention; promoting recall	General support
Corrective feedback	Proper feedback	Providing feedback on performance	Prompting and guiding	Feedback
Cues and explanations	Student–faculty interaction	Learning guidance	Prompting and guiding	Guidance
Student participation	Active learning; student reciprocity and cooperation	Student performance	Evoking performance	Active involvement
Time on task	Time on task; communicating high expectations	Assessing performance		
Assessing and enhancing learner's reading and study skills	Respecting diverse ways of learning			

A broader point in this discussion is made in Figure 3: technologies have capabilities to assist in specific teaching tasks, if used within their identified limitations as presentation and delivery media. The purpose of research on media is to identify characteristics (capabilities and limitations) that can then be applied in the ID phase, thus avoiding use of the wrong tool for a specific pedagogical purpose. Previous media research can be useful in identifying multimedia implementations able to supply or support the following:

- **Instruction**—CAL (computer-assisted learning), including various types of simulations, can be used, supported by varieties of CMC (e-mail, synchronous and asynchronous IP-audio- and IP-videoconferences, text-chat, file exchanges, and data access).

- **Reinforcement, corrective feedback, and cues and explanations**— CAL and, especially, CML (computer-manager learning) can be useful.

- **Participation, engagement, time-on-task**—Strategies for collaboration and cooperation with peers and authorities include various forms of problem-based learning, using Internet-based communications tools. Motivational advantages are gained from the scope of access and the immediacy of interaction provided by the Web.

- **Assessing and respecting diverse learning styles, preferences**— Though not cited by all the authorities in Figure 3, this may be one of the most powerful arguments for multimedia delivery. (As Fletcher [1992] recognized more than a decade ago, individualization is both "a morale imperative and an economic impossibility"—unless, it is argued here, use is made of well-designed multimedia resources.)

As noted earlier, technologies vary in their immediacy and interpersonal impact. For example, video affects the likelihood and, according to some research, the speed with which relationships will grow in mediated interaction, while simple data exchange may do little to promote relationships in virtual work teams (Walther, 1996; Picard, 1999). The objectives of the instruction should dictate the media to be used and must be grounded in the media's demonstrated capabilities; the choice of media thus both affects and reflects the relative emphasis on different desired learning outcomes.

Multimedia and the Internet

Multimedia are increasingly associated with the Internet, which offers both delivery advantages and challenges to users: advantages arise from the Internet's enormous capacity to link and interconnect, but there are potentially serious problems related to lack of inherent structure and tutor control (Thaler, 1999; Stafford, 1999; Campbell, 1999). Advantages of the Internet for teaching, under ideal conditions, include the following (Heinich, Molenda, Russell, & Smaldino, 1996, p. 263):

- *Engrossing:* The opportunity for deep involvement, capturing and holding learner interest.

- *Multisensory:* The incorporation of sounds and images along with text (but see Mayer's [2001] *multimedia principles*, below, regarding the limits of sensory channels).

- *Connections:* Learners can connect ideas from different media sources, for example, connecting the sound of a musical instrument with its illustration.

- *Individualized:* Web structure allows users to navigate through the information according to their interests and to build their own unique mental structures based on exploration.

- *Collaborative creation:* Software allows teachers and learners to create their own hypermedia materials; project-based learning provides opportunities for authentic collaboration.

Some of the more common problems with the Internet for teaching, and as a platform for multimedia delivery, are as follows (Heinich et al., 1996, p. 263):

- *Getting lost:* Users can get confused, or "lost in cyberspace."

- *Lack of structure:* Those whose learning style requires more structure and guidance may become frustrated. Some less-experienced or less well-disciplined users may also make poor decisions about how much information they need.

- *Noninteractive:* Programs may simply be one-way presentations of information with no specific opportunities for interaction or practice with feedback. A further problem is that, due to poor design, what may be intended as *interaction* is sometimes more accurately called *feedback* (Helm & McClements, 1996).

- *Time-consuming:* Because they are nonlinear and invite exploration, hypermedia programs tend to require more time for learners to reach prespecified objectives. Because they are more complex than conventional instructional materials, hypermedia systems require more time to master ("Workers find," 2000).

- *Bandwidth*: This continues to be a critical barrier to Web-based multimedia use for some potential users. While broadband availability is increasing worldwide (*PC Magazine*, 2003), especially outside North America ("Where's the broadband boom?," 2002), online speeds still prevent many users from accessing multimedia efficiently or reliably (Howard, 2001; Miller, 2002).

The above inherent limitations of the Internet as a multimedia delivery tool arise from its very nature. In order for these limitations to change, the Internet would have to become more structured, limiting user choices. This is unlikely, as these changes would make the Web a very different entity from what it is today (Greenaway, 2002).

Planning Issues with Multimedia

Design and Development Principles

The potentials and challenges discussed above underscore the importance of planning and design in the implementation of multimedia. Fortunately, research offers principles that can guide instructional designers and instructors in the development and use of multimedia. Mayer's (2001) work is particularly useful. His examination of the impact of multimedia on learning, based on how the human mind works to process verbal and visual information (p. 4), has produced important insights about media and learning, including the following:

- Words and pictures, although qualitatively different, complement one another and promote learning, *if* learners are successful in mentally integrating visual and verbal representations (p. 5).

- True learning is more a process of knowledge construction than information acquisition (p. 12).

- Deep learning is evidenced by retention *and* transfer (lack of which indicates no learning, or merely superficial rote learning) (pp. 5, 16–17).

In Mayer's model, there are three key assumptions underpinning a cognitive theory of multimedia learning: (a) humans have dual channels for processing input as part of learning, the *visual* and the *auditory*; (b) while the two channels exist in most people, humans are limited in the amount of the information they can process in each channel at one time; and (c) learners must actively process information and experience as part of learning, by a process that includes attending to relevant incoming information, organizing selected information into coherent mental representations and integrating mental representations with other knowledge (p. 44).

Mayer (2001, p. 41) concluded that successful learning requires students to perform five actions, with direct implications for the design of effective multimedia instruction:

1. Select relevant words from the presented text or narration.

2. Select relevant images from the presented illustrations.

3. Organize the selected words into a coherent verbal representation.

4. Organize selected images into a coherent visual representation.

5. Integrate the visual and verbal representations with prior knowledge.

Mayer articulated seven principles useful for guiding the design of multimedia instruction. Under these principles, students have been shown to achieve greater retention and transfer (Mayer, 2001, p. 172):

1. **Multimedia principle**: Students learn better from words and pictures than from words alone.

2. **Spatial contiguity principle**: Students learn better when corresponding words and pictures are presented near rather than far from each other on the page or screen.

3. **Temporal contiguity principle**: Students learn better when corresponding words and pictures are presented simultaneously rather than successively.

4. **Coherence principle**: Students learn better when extraneous words, pictures, and sounds are excluded rather than included. ("Extraneous" can refer either to *topical* or *conceptual relevance*, with the latter being more important.)

5. **Modality principle**: Students learn better from animation and narration than from animation and on-screen text. (This principle assumes use of a *concise narrated animation*, text that omits unneeded words.) (See p. 135.)

6. **Redundancy principle**: Students learn better from animation and narration than from animation, narration, and on-screen text. (This principle is based on *capacity-limitation hypothesis*, which holds that learners have limited capacity to process material visually and auditorily [p. 152]. Eliminating redundant material results in better learning performance than including it [p. 153]).

7. **Individual differences principle**: A particularly important finding is that design effects are stronger for low-knowledge learners than for high-knowledge learners, and for high-spatial learners than for low-spatial learners (p. 184).

The above are examples of design principles under which learning *may* be enhanced by the use of various display or delivery media. Principles such as these are particularly important, as they are research-based and tested (Mayer, 2001). Any design principles adopted should meet similarly stringent empirical tests.

Multimedia, Productivity and Performance

The previous discussion suggests that multimedia implementation, while potentially valuable to learning, requires strategic planning to exploit pedagogic possibilities and avoid the pitfalls of misapplication. The point has further been stressed that the existing literature on technology-based learning is applicable to multimedia planning, especially the known pedagogic and representational characteristics of individual media identified in actual learning situations. There are nonpedagogic considerations, too, related to organizational impacts and various costs from the use of multimedia.

A realistic decision to incorporate multimedia in ODL should recognize that multimedia, like most technologies, are unlikely initially, or perhaps ever, to save the organization time or money (Quinn & Bailey, 1994; Burge, 2000; Cassidy, 2000). In fact, multimedia may in the short-term increase operational complexity, create "organizational chaos" (Murgatroyd, 1992), and promote time-wasting behaviors by users throughout the organization (Laudon, Traver, & Laudon, 1996; Fernandez, 1997; Evans, 1998; Fahy, 2000; Dalal, 2001). The early effects of multimedia, like other technologies in complex organizations, may well include *lower* organizational productivity (Black & Lynch, 1996).

Another caveat is financial: the economics of technologies generally suggest that the total cost of ownership (TCO) of multimedia technologies will constantly rise (Oberlin, 1996), and that no genuine cost savings may ever actually be achieved by some users (Welsch, 2002). The rationale for adopting multimedia technologies, therefore, is more related to *performance* enhancements, such as greater flexibility, improved learning, and higher satisfaction and completion rates for users, than to cost savings (Oberlin, 1996; Daniel, 1996; Fahy, 1998).

This point is significant, because, historically, technology users have sometimes confused performance and productivity outcomes in technology implementations, underestimating the costs and long-term impacts of technology, while, to the detriment of realistic expectations, overestimating and overselling possible productivity benefits (Dietrich & Johnson, 1967; McIsaac, 1979; Mehlinger, 1996; Strauss, 1997; Lohr, 1997; Wysocki, 1998; Greenaway, 2002; Hartnett, 2002). For the future of multimedia, avoiding these kinds of mistakes is critical: unrealistic expectations produce disappointment, and may result in skepticism among instructors and managers about the value of educational innovation generally, and educational technologies in particular ("Nothing travels through an educational vacuum like a technological bandwagon.")

Organizational Issues in Multimedia Adoption

Realistic expectations of multimedia require compatibility with the adopting organization's culture, structure, and finances (Welsch, 2002).

The culture of any organization includes its various values, beliefs, myths, traditions, and norms, as well as its historic practices and typical ways of doing business (including how it adopts or rejects innovations). Organizational culture may present the most serious challenges to those responsible for the strategic planning (Rogers, 1983; Stringer & Uchenick, 1986), including the problem of distinguishing whether any resistance encountered is due to simple unwillingness or to real inability (Welsch, 2002). (In the latter case, resistance may be rationale and appropriate, a sign that conditions are not right for an innovation to succeed.) The problem is thought to be particularly acute in slow-to-change enterprises such as public education (Senge, 1990).

Another problem for adoption of complex innovations such as multimedia is the attitude in some organizations that training is an optional activity (Gordon, 1997). Ironically, it is technologically illiterate managers and administrators who most often resist training initiatives, both for themselves and their staff, to avoid embarrassment in an area in which they know their expertise is not as great as their subordinates'. The needs analysis stage of planning is the best place to assure that cultural issues like these are recognized and evaluated in advance.

Planning for multimedia implementation need not be timid. The needs assessment should carefully distinguish *climate* from culture and respond accordingly. Climate consists of the commonly held viewpoints and opinions in the organization, directly influenced by widely recognized measures of organizational health and success, such as enrollment or student achievement and performance relative to competitors. Climate is more "constructed" and temporary than culture, based upon elements such as student and staff perceptions of how well the organization is performing its fundamental tasks. By its nature, climate is more manageable than culture. Managers, by their reactions to external developments, can influence how staff members interpret the outside events that may shape climate. Climate is an area in which planning can have an impact, through the efforts of planners to influence the internal recognition and interpretation of outside events.

In addition to culture, structural factors within the organization may also affect multimedia innovations. The presence and adequacy of the required technological infrastructure, including software, hardware, communications, and networking systems, should be assessed. Personnel in the form of knowledgeable management, maintenance, training and support staff, key consultants, and cost-effective contract help are also critical structural elements. If not already provided for, the costs of system upgrades and ongoing maintenance (including initial and recurrent training for staff) should be assessed in a structural review, preceding the introduction of multimedia systems. Ongoing costs should be identified in budget projections.

Finances are a vital part of any multimedia adoption in ODL. Assessing organizational finances also introduces complexity into the planning process, as costs are inherently difficult to predict accurately, sometimes even to identify completely. While precise accuracy in cost analysis may be difficult, potential purchasers of technologies should be aware that, as noted above, the total cost of ownership of multimedia technology will likely be well above the purchase price, exceeding the purchase price by many times (Oberlin, 1996; Black & Lynch, 1996; Khan & Hirata, 2001; Welsch, 2002). Using a definition of productivity as the ratio of benefits to costs (Massy & Zemsky, 1999), the high cost of a technology may not be disqualifying if the payback is clear. Costs alone do not necessarily change the justification for a technology, but they could constitute a shock to an organization that has not adequately anticipated them.

Part of the rationale for investing in multimedia is the fact that technology provides flexibility: technologies are more scalable than human resources, *if* this aspect is exploited in the organizational vision. In general, scalability means that program growth may be more easily accommodated with technology than without it; costs do not escalate in line with growth as they do where enrollment increases are borne strictly by hiring more instructors and support staff. Multimedia resources may be augmented or trimmed without reference to collective agreements or other commitments. Another difference is that technologies such as multimedia tend to become more efficient the more use is made of them, lowering the break-even point and increasing their efficiency (Matkin, 1997; Harvard Computing Group, 1998; Watkins & Callahan, 1998).

The decision to acquire technology is fundamentally a strategic one, because technologies are means to various ends. Bates (1995) suggested that *accessibility* and *cost* are the two most important discriminators among technologies, and thus the most critical criteria in a technology acquisition process. A decision to "build" or develop a new multimedia technology option should bear in mind that there is now a rapidly increasing amount of available software (Gale, 2001). A careful analysis of needs and a search of available options should be performed, especially before a decision to develop is authorized, as even professional programming projects, in general, often end in failure (Girard, 2003), and instructors who lack special instructional design (ID) training are particularly apt to become bogged down in the development of ultimately mediocre materials (Grabe & Grabe, 1996).

Another factor in assessing the financial viability of various multimedia technologies is the potential target audience in relation to the expected costs of production. Perry (2000) cautioned that custom multimedia training courseware will likely not be cost-effective for fewer than 1,000 users. Bates (1995, 2000) also offered figures and usage considerations that help with the assessment of costs and benefits. Costs and time frames can be formidable: Szabo (1998) reported nearly a fourfold range (40 to 150 hours per hour of instruction) for development of very basic computer-assisted learning (CAL) in health education, and another study reported that a 6 hour module in weather forecasting, involving a production team of instructional designers, meteorologists, hydrologists, graphics artists, media specialists, computer scientists, and SMEs, consumed a year and cost $250,000 (Johnson, 2000).

Conclusions

Presented in this chapter was a discussion of factors (inherent, pedagogic, and organizational) that may impact planning for multimedia use. The suggestion here is that multimedia are more likely to affect pedagogical performance (how well the program or the organization does its work) than productivity (measured by profitability). In planning for multimedia implementation, it was suggested, performance outcomes should be the focus (improvements in quality of service, as measured by timeliness, accessibility, convenience, and responsiveness of program offerings and supports), rather than "bottom-line" outcomes.

Strategic planning in the form of ID promotes proper uses of multimedia technologies, especially (at the awareness and adoption stages). The best pedagogical arguments for use of multimedia technologies (providing more learner convenience, satisfaction and success) may be compelling enough, but problems in relation to existing organizational culture, structure and finances should not be overlooked. The adoption process includes distinguishing climate factors from culture (the former being more amenable to influence by effective leaders); considering the needs of affected groups in planning; acknowledging and respecting users' expectations; providing existing managers with training, so they can provide effective leadership; accurately assessing existing and needed technical resources; avoiding overselling potential benefits, thus keeping expectations realistic; and selecting, adapting, or (rarely) building products on the basis of demonstrable advantages, especially accessibility and costs.

Pedagogically, the principal contributions of multimedia technologies in teaching and training are likely to be increased flexibility, resulting in greater learner access and convenience, and more choices to users, including self-pacing, individualization, customization, and learner control. Positive impacts such as these on aspects of the teaching process can be anticipated, but problems should also be expected; media selection usually involves trade-offs, and the losses and gains in the choice of one delivery or presentation medium over another should be acknowledged.

For instructional designers, principles exist to guide development of multimedia. Among the most useful of these are the multimedia principles that address design issues such as contiguity, redundancy, coherence, and choices of delivery modes (Mayer, 2001). Adoption of these principles would, in general, likely result in "lean" multimedia design, with use of audio-textual and visual-pictorial elements based more directly upon empirical evidence about how these actually impact learning, rather than upon their technical features alone. Though perhaps less technologically elegant, such implementations promise to be more pedagogically effective and organizationally compatible.

References

Bates, A. W. (1995). *Technology, open learning and distance education.* New York: Routledge.

Bates, A. W. (2000). *Managing technological change.* San Francisco: Jossey-Bass Publishers.

Berge, Z. (1995). Facilitating computer conferencing: Recommendations from the field. *Educational Technology*, January–February, pp. 22–30.

Black, S., & Lynch, L. (1996). Human-capital investments and productivity. *American Economic Review, 86,* 263–267.

Bloom, B. S. (1984). The 2-sigma problem: The search for methods of group instruction as effective as one-to-one tutoring. *Educational Researcher*, June–July, pp. 4–16.

Bloom, B. S., Engelhart, M. D., Furst, E. J., Hill, W. H., & Krathwohl, D. R. (Eds.). (1956). *Taxonomy of educational objectives: The classification of educational goals. Handbook 1: Cognitive domain.* New York: David McKay Co., Inc.

Bruce, B. C., & Levin, J. (1997). Educational technology: Media for inquiry, communication, construction, and expression. Retrieved October 8, 1997 from the World Wide Web: http://www.ed.uiuc.edu/facstaff/chip/tax-onomy/latest.html

Burge, E. (2000). Using learning technologies: Ideas for keeping one's balance. *Open Praxis*, Vol. 1, pp. 17–20.

Campbell, M. (1999, November 11). Hey, what work? We're cruising the Internet. *The Edmonton Journal*, p. A-3.

Cassidy, J. (2000). The productivity mirage. *The New Yorker*, pp. 106–118.

Chen, Y., & Willits, F. (1998). A path analysis of the concepts in Moore's theory of transactional distance in a videoconferencing environment. *Journal of Distance Education, 13*(2), 51–65.

Chickering, A., & Gamson, Z. (1989). Seven principles for good practice in undergraduate education. *AAHE Bulletin,* March, pp. 3–7.

Clark, R.E. (1983). Reconsidering research on learning from media. *Review of Educational Research, 53*(4), pp. 445 - 459.

Clark, R.E. (1994). Media will never influence learning. *Educational Technology Research and Development, 42*(2), 21-30.

Crooks, B. & Kirkwood, A. (1988). Video-cassettes by design in Open University courses. *Open Learning*, November, pp. 13-17.

Daniel, J. (1996). Implications of the technology adoption life cycle for the use of new media in distance education. In J. Frankl & B. O'Reilly (Eds.), *1996 EDEN conference: Lifelong learning, open learning, distance learning* (pp. 138–141). Poitiers, France: European Distance Education Network.

Dalal, S. (2001, October 26). Futzers draining production budgets. *The Edmonton Journal,* pp. F-1, 8.

Dede, C. (1996). The evolution of distance education: Emerging technologies and distributed learning. *The American Journal of Distance Education, 10*(2), 4–36.

DeSanctis, G., & Gallupe, R. B. (1987). A foundation for the study of group decision support systems. *Management Science, 33*(5), 589–609.

Dietrich, J. E., & Johnson, F. C. (1967). A catalytic agent for change in higher education. *Educational Record*, Summer, pp. 206–213.

Evans, J. (1998). Convergances: All together now. *The Computer Paper.* February. Retrieved October 8, 1998 from the World Wide Web: http://www.tcp.ca/1998/9802/9802converge/together/together.html

Fahy, P. J. (1998). Reflections on the *productivity paradox* and distance education technology. *Journal of Distance Education, 13*(2), 66–73.

Fahy, P. J. (2000). Achieving quality with online teaching technologies. Paper presented at the *Quality Learning 2000* Inaugural International Symposium, Calgary, Canada. March. (Available from ERIC documents: ED 439 234.)

Fernandez, B. (1997, October 4). Productivity improvements not computing. *Edmonton Journal*, p. J16.

Fischer, B. (1997). Instructor-led vs. interactive: Not an either/or proposition. *Corporate University Review*, Jan/Feb., pp. 29–30.

Fletcher, J.D. (1992). Individualized systems of instruction. Institute for Defense Analyses.

Gagne, R. M. (1985). *The conditions of learning and theory of instruction* (4th ed.). New York: Holt, Rinehart and Winston.

Gale, S. F. (2001). Use it or lose it. *Online Learning, 5*(7), 34–36.

Garrison, D.R. (1989). *Understanding distance education: A framework for the future.* New York: Routledge.

Girard, K. (2003). Making the world safe for software. *Business 2.0, 4*(5), 64–66.

Gordon, E. E. (1997). Investing in human capital: The case for measuring training ROI. *Corporate University Review, 5*(1), 41–42.

Grabe, C., & Grabe, M. (1996). *Integrating technology for meaningful learning* (pp. 243–247). Toronto: Houghton Mifflin Co. Retrieved February 1999 from the World Wide Web: http://www.quasar.ualberta.ca/edmedia/ETCOMM/readings/Krefgra.html

Greenaway, N. (2002). Internet falling short of hype. *The Edmonton Journal*, June 12, p. A-13.

Grow, G. (1991). Teaching learners to be self-directed. *Adult Education Quarterly, 41*(3), 125–149.

Hartnett, J. (2002). Where have all the Legos gone? *Online Learning, 6*(2), 28–29.

Harvard computing group. (1998). Knowledge management-return on investment. Author. Retrieved March 14, 2000 from the World Wide Web: http://www.harvardcomputing.com

Heinich, R., Molenda, M., Russell, J. D., & Smaldino, S. E. (1996). *Instructional media and technologies for learning* (5th ed.). Englewood Cliffs, NJ: Merrill, an imprint of Prentice Hall.

Helm, P., & McClements, R. (1996). Multimedia business training: The big thing or the next best thing? In J. Frankl, & B. O'Reilly (Eds.). *1996 EDEN conference: Lifelong learning, open learning, distance learning* (pp. 134–137). Poitiers, France: European Distance Education Network.

Howard, B. (2001). 20 years of missed opportunities. *PC Magazine, 20*(15), 75.

Johnson, V. (2000). Using technology to train weather forecasters. *T.H.E. Journal Online*. June. Retrieved March 21, 2002 from the World Wide Web: http://www.thejournal.com/magazine/vault/articleprintversion.cfm?aid=2880

Joyce, B., & Weil, M. (1980). *Models of teaching* (2nd ed.). Englewood Cliffs, NJ: Prentice Hall.

Juler, P. (1990). Promoting interaction; maintaining independence: Swallowing the mixture. *Open Learning*, pp. 24–33.

Kemp, J. E. (1977). *Instructional design* (2nd ed.). Belmont, CA: Fearon-Pitman Publishing.

Khan, S., & Hirata, A. (2001). Lowering the TCO of video communications. Retrieved February 13, 2002 from the World Wide Web: http://www.tmcnet.com/tmcnet/articles/0501en.htm

Koumi, J. (1994). Media comparisons and deployment: a practitioner's view. *British Journal of Educational Technology, 25*(1), pp. 41-57.

Kozma, R. (1994). Will media influence learning? Reframing the debate. *Educational Technology Research and Development, 42*(2), pp. 7 - 19.

Laudon, K., Traver, C., & Laudon, J. (1996). *Information technology and society* (2nd ed.). Toronto: Course Technology Inc.

Levin, R. R., Anglin, G. J., & Carney, R. R. (1987). On empirically validating functions of pictures in prose. In D. M. Willows, & H. A. Houghton (Eds.), *The psychology of illustration: Volume 1, Basic research* (pp. 51–85). New York: Springer-Verlag.

Lohr, S. (1997, October 12). The future came faster in the good old days. *The Edmonton Journal*, p. B-1.

Maier, P., Barnett, L., Warren, A., & Brunner, D. (1996). *Using technology in teaching and learning*. London: Kogan Page.

Marchionini, G. (1988). Hypermedia and learning: Freedom and chaos. *Educational Technology*, pp. 8–12. Retrieved January 1999 from the World Wide Web: www.quasar.ualberta.ca/edmedia/ETCOMM/readings/Krefmar.html

Massy, W. F., & Zemsky, R. (1999). Using information technology to enhance academic productivity. Retrieved October 7, 1999 from the World Wide Web: http://www.educause.ed/nlii/keydocs/massy.html

Matkin, G. (1997). Using financial information in continuing education. Phoenix, AZ: American Council on Education.

Mayer, R. E. (2001). *Multimedia learning*. New York: Cambridge University Press.

McIsaac, D. (1979). Impact of personal computing on education. *Association for Educational Data Systems Journal, 13*(1), 7–15.

Mehlinger, H. (1996). School reform in the information age. *Phi Delta Kappan*, pp. 400–407.

Mezirow, J., & Irish, G. (1974). Priorities for experimentation and development in adult basic education. *Vol. 1, Planning for innovation in ABE*. New York: Columbia University, Center for Adult Education. (ERIC ED 094 163.)

Miller, M. J. (2002). Broadband optimism. *PC Magazine, 21*(3), 7–8.

Moore, M. (1993). Theory of transactional distance. In D. Keegan (Ed.), *Theoretical principles of distance education* (pp. 22–38). New York: Routledge.

Moore, M. G. (1989). Three types of interaction. *American Journal of Distance Education, 3*(2), pp. 1–6. Retrieved November 9, 2001 from the World Wide Web: http://www.ed.psu.edu/acsde/ajde/ed32.asp

Murgatroyd, S. (1992). Business, education, and business education. In M. G. Moore (Ed.), *Distance education for corporate and military training* (pp. 50–63). Readings in distance education, No. 3. University Park, PA: Penn State University, American Center for the Study of Distance Education.

Oberlin, J. L. (1996). The financial mythology of information technology: The new economics. *Cause/Effect*, pp. 21–29.

PC Magazine. (2003c). Broadband: Bringing it home. *PC Magazine, 22*(5), 25.

Perry, T. (2000). A history of interactive education and training. Retrieved February 4, 2002 from the World Wide Web: http://www.coastal.com/WhatsNew/online_history.html

Picard, J. (1999, June 10). *Creating virtual work teams using IP videoconferencing*. Presentation at the Distance Education Technology '99 Workshop, Edmonton, Alberta.

Quinn, J., & Baily, M. (1994). Information technology: The key to service performance. *Brookings Review, 12*, summer, pp. 36–41.

Rieber, L., & Boyce, M. (1990). The effects of computer animation on adult learning and retrieval tasks. *Journal of Computer-Based Instruction, 17*, pp. 46–52.

Roblyer, M. D., & Schwier, R. A. (2003). *Integrating educational technology into teaching, Canadian edition*. Toronto: Pearson Education Canada Inc.

Roblyer, M. D., Edwards, J., & Havriluk, M. A. (1997). *Integrating technology into teaching* (pp. 27–53). Columbus: Merrill.

Rogers, E. M. (1983). *Communication of innovations* (2nd ed.). New York: The Free Press.

Saettler, P. (1990). *The evolution of American educational technology.* Englewood, CO: Libraries Unlimited, Inc.

Senge, P. (1990). *Fifth discipline.* Toronto: Doubleday.

Stafford, D. (1999, December 15). Surfing from web-linked worksite a common practice, survey shows. *Edmonton Journal*, p. F-7.

Strauss, M. (1997, October 7). Web sites don't boost sales, survey of retailers says. *Globe and Mail*, p. B-8.

Stringer, R. A., & Uchenick, J. (1986). *Strategy traps.* Toronto: Lexington Books.

Szabo, M. (1998). *Survey of educational technology research.* The Educational Technology Professional Development Project (ETPDP) Series. Edmonton, Alberta: Grant MacEwan Community College and Northern Alberta Institute of Technology.

Thaler, J. (1999, May 15). Web in the workplace: Waste or help? *The Edmonton Journal*, p. I-1.

Walther, J. B. (1996). Computer-mediated communication: Impersonal, interpersonal and hyperpersonal interaction. *Communication Research, 20*(1), 3–43.

Watkins, K., & Callahan, M. (1998). Return on knowledge assets: Rethinking investments in educational technology. *Educational Technology, 38*(4), 33–40.

Welsch, E. (2002). Cautious steps ahead. *Online Learning, 6*(1), 20–24.

Where's the broadband boom? (2002). *PC Magazine, 21*(16), 23.

Wolfe, D. (1990). The management of innovation. In L. Salter, & D. Wolfe (Eds.), *Managing technology* (pp. 63–87). Toronto: Garamond Press.

Workers find online surfing too tempting. (2000, February 22). *The Edmonton Journal*, p. A-3.

Wysocki, B. (1998). Computer backlash hits boardrooms. *The Edmonton Journal*, May 1, p. D-3.

Zimmerman, H. (1972). Task reduction: A basis for curriculum planning and development for adult basic education. In W. M. Brooke (Ed.), *ABE: A resource book of readings* (pp. 334–348). Toronto: New Press.

Chapter II

Toward Effective Use of Multimedia Technologies in Education

Geraldine Torrisi-Steele, Griffith University, Australia

Abstract

While multimedia technologies are being used in educational contexts, the effective use of multimedia in these contexts remains problematic. In an attempt to contribute towards addressing this problem, this chapter presents a set of conceptual guidelines and a practical planning framework that is intended to inform the planning and design of more effective multimedia integration into educational contexts. A mixed-mode approach is advocated in this chapter. Multimedia technologies are viewed as part of a tool-set and tool selection should be appropriate to curriculum content and to the teaching and learning context.

Introduction

Whether or not multimedia technologies should be used in educational contexts seems to no longer be an issue. Multimedia technology is pervading almost all aspects of existence. The rationale for its use in educational contexts is grounded in social, economic, and pedagogical reasons. However, what does remain problematic is the effective use of multimedia technology in educational contexts. At the crux of addressing this problem is the notion that effective integration of multimedia in the curriculum depends not on the technology itself but rather on educators' knowledge, assumptions, and perceptions regarding the technology and its implementation in the specific learning context (Jackson & Anagnotopoulou, 2000; Bennet, Priest, & Macpherson, 1999). From a pedagogical perspective, it is generally accepted that multimedia technologies have the potential to reshape and add a new dimension to learning (Relan & Gillani, 1997; Lefoe, 1998). In reality, however, this potential has largely failed to be realized. The fundamental belief underlying this chapter is that this potential will only be realized by informed pedagogical decision making and the formulation of teaching strategies designed to exploit multimedia technologies for maximum effectiveness within a particular learning situation. From this perspective, educator development that focuses on pedagogical change is a pivotal aspect of the effective use of multimedia technologies in educational contexts.

The term "multimedia technologies" is being used in this chapter to mean the entirely digital delivery of content using any integrated combination of audio, video, images (two-dimensional, three-dimensional), and text. In its most primitive form, the term "multimedia" is sometimes defined as content presentation using a combination of media [i.e., sound, images (static, moving, animated, video), and text]. From this perspective, any presentation that involves the use of, for example, face-to-face teaching, video recorder, and a slide show could be considered multimedia.

The distinguishing feature of digital multimedia, as used in this chapter (as opposed to the primitive form defined above), is the capacity to support user interaction. Hence, the term "multimedia technologies," as used in this chapter, will always imply that there is an element of "interactivity" present. The concept of interaction is considered along two dimensions: the capacity of the system to allow an individual to control the pace of presentation and to make choices about which pathways are followed to move through the content, and the ability of the system to accept input from the user and provide appropriate feedback to that input. Multimedia technologies may be delivered on computer via CD-ROM, DVD, or via the Internet, or on other devices such as mobile phones and personal digital assistants capable of supporting interactive and integrated delivery of digital audio, video, image, and text data. Multimedia technologies as referred to in this chapter also encompass new communications technologies such as e-mail, chat, and videoconferencing. Virtual reality technologies are also included.

It will be argued later in this chapter that various multimedia technologies are seen as part of a tool set or possible modes of instruction. Other modes include face-to-face teaching, print materials, and video and audio devices. A "mixed-mode" approach will be advocated in this chapter based on the argument that tool selection should be appropriate to curriculum content and to the teaching and learning context.

The contents of this chapter have been based largely on the author's professional development experiences with tertiary educators implementing online learning. However, the ideas discussed in this chapter are based on principles of good practice that apply to a broad range of teaching and learning contexts, including primary, secondary, tertiary, and other training environments.

Against this background, this chapter aims to provide a set of conceptual guidelines and a practical foundation (in the form of a planning framework) that will be of interest to those involved in planning and designing appropriate professional development targeted at promoting effective multimedia integration, and to individual educators in primary, secondary, tertiary, and other training environments who wish to implement multimedia technologies more effectively into the curriculum.

Multimedia Technologies in Learning Environments

When computer-based interactive multimedia emerged in the 1990s, innovative educators began considering what implications this new media might have if it was applied to teaching and learning environments. Within a relatively short time frame, the emerging multimedia and associated communications technologies infiltrated almost every aspect of society. So, what was initially viewed as a technology "option" in educational contexts has for social, economic, and pedagogical reasons become a "necessity." Many educational institutions are investing considerable time, effort, and money into the use of technology.

Socially, computer literacy is an essential skill for full participation in society. The use of multimedia technologies in educational institutions is seen as necessary for keeping education relevant to the 21st century (Selwyn & Gordard, 2003).

Economically, the belief prevails that the large-scale use of new multimedia and associated communication technologies for teaching and learning may offer cheaper delivery than traditional face-to-face and distance education and will also help establish and maintain competitive advantages for institutions by allowing them to tap into overseas markets (Bennet, Priest, & Macpherson, 1999, p. 207).

The pedagogical basis for the use of educational multimedia technologies has perhaps been the greatest driving force for the massive investments made by educational institutions into multimedia technologies. Literature abounds with rhetoric about the potential impact of multimedia technologies on traditional teaching practices. The central theme is that the integration of multimedia technologies will lead to a transformation of pedagogy from traditional instructivist teacher-centered approaches to the more desirable constructivist learner approaches that are seen as embodying essential characteristics of more effective learning environments (Tearle, Dillon, & Davis, 1999; Relan & Gillani, 1997; Willis & Dickson, 1997; LeFoe, 1998; Richards & Nason, 1999). From the learner-centered perspective, the teacher's role changes from the traditional (instructivist approach) role of instructor and supplier of knowledge to a role more closely aligned with support and facilitation of the active construction of knowledge by the learner (Tearle, Dillon, & Davis, 1999). The learner-centered approach implies empowerment of the individual learner and the ability to provide the learner with self-directed, more meaningful, authentic learning experiences that lead to lifelong learning. This implication is at the crux of constructivist-based pedagogical arguments for the integration of multimedia technologies in educational contexts (Selwyn & Gorard, 2003; Gonzales et al., 2002).

However, despite the well-documented and generally accepted potential of multimedia technologies to reshape teaching practices, it has been identified in literature that the promised impact of multimedia technologies on learning and pedagogical practices have largely not eventuated. There are relatively few positive impacts on educational practices for major investments of time, effort, and money by educational institutions (Cuban, 1986; Hammond, 1994; Oliver, 1999; Nichol & Watson, 2003; Conlon & Simpson, 2003; Selwyn & Gorard, 2003).

The reason for this lack of impact is seen to lie not with the attributes of the technology itself, but rather with the ways in which the technology has been implemented in learning contexts. More specifically, it is the educators' knowledge, assumptions, and perceptions regarding the technology and its implementation in the specific learning context that will determine its implementation and, hence, its effectiveness (Jackson & Anagnotopoulou, 2000; Bennet, Priest, & Macpherson, 1999). As is often noted in literature, the potential of multimedia technologies to reshape learning contexts (Relan & Gillani, 1997; Lefoe, 1998) will only be realized by informed pedagogical decision making and the formulation of teaching strategies designed to exploit multimedia technologies within the curriculum context.

Although it may be recognized by educators that multimedia technologies have the potential to offer new and improved learning opportunities, many educators fail to realize this potential. A number of educators using multimedia technologies in their learning environments are largely limiting its use to a tool for data access, communication, and administration (Conlon & Simpson, 2003). This is an "add-on" approach to multimedia technology use rather than a truly integrated curriculum approach. This lack of true integration results in minimal (if any) change in both pedagogical strategies and learning environment (Tearle, Dillon, & Davis, 1999; Strommen, 1999).

Failure to implement effective technology integration is attributed to the fact that educators, even experienced educators, are generally unprepared for the changes demanded by and produced by "technology infusion" (Charp, 2000). While some of the pedagogical "know how" of more traditional learning environments possessed by educators may transfer to new interactive multimedia contexts, educators often lack the skills and technical and pedagogical knowledge to effectively implement those technologies in their learning environments. Rakes and Casey (2002, online) observed the following:

> ...many [educators], especially more experienced teachers, have been unable to find effective ways to use technology in their classrooms. One possible explanation for this lack of success is that the use of technology in the classroom has been viewed in terms of simple skill acquisition instead of as a change process that affects the behavior of individuals on a very profound level.

If there is a lesson to be learned from the last few decades of "educational technology" development, it is that technologies themselves offer very little to the learning process. Conlon & Simpson (2003, p. 149) warned that if educators are "hastened" into adopting multimedia technologies without any clear educational vision of change, then significant transformation of teaching practice is unlikely. The importance of focus on educator development and resources that will foster continuous pedagogical growth and "re-engineering" becomes self-evident and is well documented in literature (Gonzales et al., 2002; Burns, 2002; Pierson, 2001; Charp, 2000; Collis, 1996; Rakes & Casey, 2002).

Against this context, some of the key issues that need be addressed in educator development will be identified and discussed. Five key guidelines and a planning framework for facilitating more effective multimedia technologies integration will be presented.

Toward More Effective
Technology Integration

The preceding discussion has directed attention to the notion that while multimedia technologies have the potential to reshape practice, the potential is often unrealized due to the fact that educators are often ill-equipped to meet the challenges of change demanded by multimedia technologies and to exploit change made possible by them. This notion is supported by an earlier study (Torrisi & Davis, 2000) conducted by the author into the experiences of tertiary educators developing online multimedia materials.

The data from the study highlight some of the key issues that need to be addressed in educator development efforts. Educators in the study were asked to identify what they believed were key competencies that students should develop as a result of undertaking study in the subject. Each educator was also asked to clarify what they believed to be the role of online materials in their course. Table 1 juxtaposes individual educator's responses for key competencies against the educator's stated intended use of online materials. Upon examination of responses as shown in Table 1, a lack of congruency between what educators identified as key competencies for their students and the stated use of online materials was found. This lack of congruency between stated key competencies and intended use of online materials is indicative of multimedia technology that is not truly integrated with the curriculum goals, content, objectives, and context, rather use is limited to being add-on or supplemental.

Insight into reason for supplemental use of multimedia technologies was revealed in interviews with the tertiary educators, whose comments suggested they perceived the use of multimedia online technologies as an exercise in translating materials into another medium, mostly for access and alternative to face-to-face or printed content delivery. This perception of technology use does not foster pedagogical change. It leads to counterproductive strategies that replicate more traditional methods with the new medium. The result is no impact or even negative impact on the learning environment. Rather, what is required is conceptualization of multimedia technology use in educational contexts as a process of transformation that acknowledges, and strives for, change in practice. In addressing this problem, it is useful to consider the idea of progressive technology adoption found in the literature.

Sandholtz, Ringstaff, and Dwyer (1997) suggested that supplemental use of multimedia technologies as was observed in this study should be viewed as the first stage of a continuum of change that culminates in a third stage of full integration and transformation of practice. The idea of progressive technology adoption is supported by others. For example, Goddard (2002) recognized five

Table 1: Comparison of stated key competencies cited by teaching staff as important for students to acquire for their subject area to staff member's stated intended use of the online materials

Key competencies as stated by individual educators for students in their teaching/subject area	Intended use of the online materials as stated by individual educators
Educator A • Critical analysis • Ability to research • Standard academic writing skills	• *An adjunct to face-to-face teaching; students could access lectures if they could not come to lectures* • *It's the way things are going*
Educator B • Rhythmic perception • Rhythmic literacy • Programming skills	• *Wanted to have a more efficient way of doing things* • *Students access the materials (notes, exercises) before coming to lectures* • *To decrease degree of coordination because links are made obvious on the Web page* • *Access to materials off campus*
Educator C • Challenge their assumptions • Analyze the thinking, underlying practices • Connect theoretical material with their own life experiences • Think through how values can be incorporated into a real-life situation	• *A Web site that students could move around in rather than work linearly and that would get them thinking; to really engage them* • *Wanted to use class contact time for students to engage with each other on the basis of content they already encountered rather than using time for presenting content alone*
Educator D • Analytical skills • Mathematical skills • The case study approach is commonly used.	• *Resource that would be accessed in tutorials* • *To reduce but not replace lecture hours eventually*
Educator E • Develop problem-solving skills • Understand the material covered rather than just memorize it, and then apply what they have been taught to new situations • Become more creative in the tasks assigned	• *The key advantage to the students was greater accessibility and a more convenient way of delivering of course materials* • *Through supplementary activities such as reading, research, foresee what is going to be taught and contribute more to the class, rather than "being a clean slate" when material is presented*
Educator F • Analysis, synthesis, creativity • Develop an analytical way of thinking and problem analysis	• *Resource would have the same attributes as opening a book* • *Students have access to the content, but it really is only an add on*

Note: Examination of responses shows a general lack of congruency between key competencies required and staff member's stated intended use of online materials, indicative of poor curriculum integration.

Source: Adapted from Torrisi & Davis (2000, pp. 172–173).

stages of progression: knowledge (awareness of technology existence); persua-
sion (technology as support for traditional productivity rather than as curriculum
related); decision (acceptance or rejection of technology for curriculum use—
acceptance leading to supplemental uses); implementation (recognition that
technology can help achieve some curriculum goals); and confirmation (use of
technology leads to redefinition of the learning environment—true integration
leading to change).

It is proposed here that framing the educational use of multimedia technologies
in terms of progressive levels of use and integration is valuable in that it forces
conceptualization of effective technology integration as a process of "change"
inherently leading to practice transformation rather than as simple skill acquisition required for translation of materials into a new medium.

Adopting the view that technology integration is a process leading to transformation and innovation directs attention also to the need to include elements of
reflective practice in any educator development guidelines and frameworks. The
term "reflective practice" is being used here to encompass the idea that
educators consciously make judgments about their performances and success of
strategies. The notion of evaluation (both formal and informal) is inherent in the
idea of reflective practice. According to Ballantyne, Bain, and Packer (1999),
lack of reflection leads to lack of awareness of the "appropriateness of...methods
in bringing about high quality student learning" (p. 237), resulting in the
perpetuation of traditional or ineffective teaching methods. The need for
educators to reflect on their practices cannot be understated. Development of
new strategies that appropriately integrate multimedia technologies into the
curriculum will only take place, according to Tearle, Dillon, and Davis (1999),
when the educator has "re-examined his or her approach to teaching and
learning" (p. 10).

In the 2000 study conducted by Torrisi and Davis, another key finding was that
among the concerns about the production process by educators, the principal
concern was the lack of knowledge about the attributes and possibilities of the
media and feelings of inadequacy in terms of how to exploit the potential of the
media available. Consistent with other findings on professional development
(Ellis, O'Reilly, & Debreceny, 1998), it appears that educators are primarily
interested in learning the technical aspects of multimedia technologies only
insofar as this knowledge is useful in informing pedagogical decisions and
options. The implication of this observation is that teaching development efforts
aimed at effective integration of multimedia technologies in educational contexts
must teach educators how to use the technology within the context of "matching
the needs and abilities of learners to curriculum goals" (Gonzales et al., 2002,
p. 1).

The view upheld in this chapter is that using multimedia technologies within the curriculum context implies appropriate use of technologies. This view of appropriate technology use supports a mixed-mode approach to curriculum design. That is, the emphasis is on exploiting the attributes of various multimedia technologies and other strategy options in terms of their appropriateness to content requirements, context, learner needs, and curriculum goals. Some guidelines and a development framework that encapsulate these views are discussed below.

Guidelines and a Development Framework

In the discussion above, some key issues to be addressed in teacher development resources and approaches have been identified by drawing upon data from an earlier study (Torrisi & Davis, 2000). The author's perspective on addressing those issues was also alluded to. Drawing on issues identified in the preceding sections, this section presents the following:

1. A set of guidelines useful for guiding educator development activities
2. A planning framework that may be used to guide teacher development or by individual teachers in order to facilitate the effective integration of multimedia technologies in learning environments

A brief case study is also described in order to illustrate implementation of the notions presented.

Educator Development Activities—Five Key Guidelines

It has been established in the preceding sections that while multimedia technologies are seen as having the potential to reshape practice, the fact remains that implementation often results in little impact on the teaching space. The attributes of the multimedia technologies are not effectively exploited to maximize and create new learning opportunities. At the crux of this issue is the failure of educators to effectively integrate the multimedia technologies into the learning context. The following guidelines are suggested for guiding educator development toward the effective integration of multimedia technologies into learning environments.

- *Guideline 1:* **The goal of implementing multimedia technologies into learning spaces is to exploit the attributes of multimedia technologies in order to support deeper, more meaningful learner-centered learning. Realization of this goal necessarily transforms the teaching and learning space.** The knowledge-delivery view of multimedia technologies must be challenged, as it merely replicates teacher-centered models of knowledge transmission and has little value in reshaping practice. Constructivism is the guiding philosophy.

- *Guideline 2:* **Transformation is only achieved through integration of multimedia technologies into the learning space.** Integration implies that technology use is inextricably linked with the total curriculum as opposed to the superficial add-on approach that is the result of a view of translation.

- *Guideline 3:* **Integration and subsequent transformation is achieved via an ongoing evolutionary process through which educators' knowledge of multimedia technologies draws more closely toward inextricable linkages with curriculum goals and the educator's knowledge of pedagogy.**

- *Guideline 4:* **Equipping educators with knowledge about the potential of the multimedia technologies must occur within the context of the total curriculum needs** rather than in isolation of the academic's curriculum needs.

- *Guideline 5:* **Evolutionary process leading to transformation and integration of multimedia technologies is fueled by sustained reflection on practice.** Sustaining reflection on practice from the beginning of endeavors in online materials development through to completion stages, after which debriefing and further reflection feed back into a cycle of continuous evolution of thought and practice. Collaborative work and sharing of experiences and ideas with other educators is also of benefit here.

In addition to the above guidelines, two considerations as identified by Torrisi and Davis (2000) are important to recognize as contributing to effective professional development conducive to long-term transformation in practice.

First, it is important that professional development programs are not designed in isolation of the educators operating context. Traditional training workshops removed from the immediate teaching context of the educator fail to be effective. Programs must empathize with and address concerns that arise from educators' earlier attempts at innovation through technology. Ongoing support opportunities, both technical and pedagogical, must be inextricably linked with educators' everyday practice. If appropriate technology use is to be a reality, then professional development must do as Fatemi (1999) stated:

> ...more than simply show teachers where in a curriculum they can squeeze in some technology....Instead, it helps them learn how to select digital content based on the needs and learning styles of their students, and infuse it into the curriculum rather than making it an end in itself. (p. 1)

Professional development programs will be most effective, as Bennet et al. (1999) stated, if educators are able to "connect the use of new technology to their own teaching experiences" (p. 212). The planning framework described below focuses on these ideas.

Second, in order for educators to be willing to use multimedia technologies in the classroom, it is necessary that they feel confident in their use from a technical perspective. Hence, professional development programs need to provide opportunities for developing basic computer competencies necessary for developing confidence in using technology as a normal part of teaching activities. Again, it is stressed that learning technical aspects must occur not in isolation of educators' teaching contexts, but rather in parallel with and integrated with pedagogical development. In this way, acquisition of technical knowledge is appropriate to the needs of the educators and is thus more likely to be relevant.

A Planning Framework

The five key guidelines above, together with issues discussed in this paper, can be embodied in a framework that provides a more concrete approach to curriculum planning conducive to the integrated use of multimedia technologies. The framework may be used to guide educator development (as has been done by the author) or may be useful as a guide for individual educators as they plan for multimedia technology use. The framework aims to highlight the use of multimedia technologies as part of the set of tools that is available for educators in executing teaching and learning strategies.

The framework is thus directed toward appropriate and judicious use of multimedia technologies. It also encourages educators to consider the attributes of them and then consider how to exploit those technologies for producing more meaningful and varied learning experiences; in so doing, allowing technology use to be an integral part of "knowledge spaces" which "allow users to explore as they wish" (Brown, 1997).

Figure 1: Framework for appropriate integration of multimedia technologies into the learning environment. Environment attributes include human resources, financial resources, and other infrastructure and institutional limitations. Multimedia and other emerging multimedia technologies form part of the set of tool choices that the educator might choose on the basis that the attributes of the chosen tool(s) best fits with the learning context and desired outcomes.

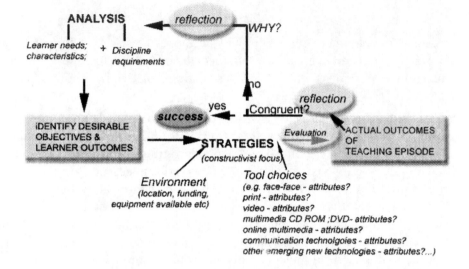

Source: Adapted from Torrisi-Steele (2001).

Consistent with learner-centered approaches, the process begins with an analysis of learner characteristics and of learner needs in relation to the content that is to be taught. In defining learner needs, the demands of the content must also be taken into account. As stated in Jamieson (1999), "The content of student learning (what is taught) logically precedes the method of teaching content…without content there is no teaching method" (p. 2). On the basis of this analysis, desired learner outcomes and objectives are identified.

In formulating teaching and learning strategies, the framework demands that the choice of tools be an informed choice based on integrated knowledge of strategy, learner needs, content requirements, environmental constraints (location, available equipment, funding, etc.), and tool attributes. Thus, the aim of technology integration more naturally precipitates from using the framework.

The fundamental view expressed by the model is that multimedia technologies and other emerging technologies are part of a tool set that, along with other available options (face-to-face teaching, print, etc.), are available choices for

Table 2: Some common tool choices for teaching and learning and their main advantages and disadvantages

Tool	Advantages	Disadvantages
Textbook and other print materials	Portable, inexpensive, simple, "low-tech," easy to use, preorganized quantities of information, accessible without special equipment, can be inexpensive, most educators familiar with this medium and have production expertise	Become outdated, cannot update easily, static information presentation, no interaction possibilities
Video	Motivational, sound and images to convey information, readily available, easy to use, inexpensive	Linear information presentation, multiple copies for student access at home can be problematic/expensive, video production can be expensive and time consuming, requires VCR access and display mechanism
Face-to-face teaching	Can respond to needs of students dynamically, can be used to promote discussion, collaborative learning, enables clarification and analysis of information	No flexibility for students in terms of attendance, access limited to on campus
Multimedia CD ROM	Can convey information using video, audio, sound and text; once produced, inexpensive to replicate for student access; option for nonlinear information presentation, so learners are able to explore at their own pace, forming their own pathways; high interactive learning potential	Costly both in terms of time and money to produce; production requires a high level of technical expertise; software and content become outdated—cannot update easily without undergoing another development and production run
World Wide Web—Web sites and related Internet technologies	Increasingly supporting multimodal presentation—text, images, sound, video, and higher levels of interactive possibilities; access to up-to-date information; potential for collaborative learning with learners in multiple locations (e.g., chat, videoconferencing); potential for anytime, anyplace; highly motivational; updating of information relatively easy Wealth of up-to-date information available along with nonlinear nature, interactivity and multimodal presentation can support discovery orientated strategies	Requires costly technical infrastructure (networks, workstations, video conferencing facilities) Development of own online materials: complex requiring expertise; can be costly and time-consuming; involves a high level of commitment Updating Web materials can be difficult/frustrating if not technically competent to some degree Sophistication of Web materials available to students is limited by access factors such as bandwidth, modem capabilities Not all educators are familiar with/comfortable with the new media technologies—steep learning curve both in technical understanding and implementation strategies; lack of awareness of these issues is one of the greatest pitfalls in adopting multimedia technologies; **as technology capabilities increase, so do complexity, commitment required, and the potential of "things not working"**

strategy implementation. Inherent in the presented framework is the philosophy that learning about multimedia technologies is an exercise in identifying the attributes of that technology and, at the same time, considering those attributes in terms of usefulness in the curriculum (Table 2). This approach addresses the problem of the "blanket approach" to multimedia technologies use that some-times arises when the hype surrounding a new technology emphasizes the technology itself rather than learning as the primary concern. The proposed framework does not exclude the use of more traditional approaches or tools such as print, etc., if they are deemed appropriate to the learning situation.

It is also worth noting that the framework encourages evaluation of strategy outcomes and reflection on existing as well as new strategies. Consideration of the use of multimedia technologies occurs with the goal of modifying or replacing existing strategies that, upon reflection, are considered ineffective. This is considered an important characteristic of the framework for two reasons:

1. It promotes the perspective that multimedia technologies are implemented with the primary goal of pedagogical change (thus helping to dispel the idea of a simple translation approach to technology adoption).

2. This encourages educators to draw on prior knowledge and experiences with prior teaching and make stronger connections between these experi-ences and the use of the technology (Bennet, Priest, & Macpherson, 1999). This is an important aspect of professional development efforts aimed at facilitating technology adoption for two reasons: perceptions of relevance are increased; and feelings of inadequacy that may be experienced by educators in dealing with new technology are minimized (Torrisi & Davis, 2000).

Reflective practice forms the cornerstone of the framework and is consistent with the notion of an evolutionary approach to technology integration. Execution of the strategy must be followed by a careful analysis of congruency of intended and actual outcomes. This analysis may involve formative and summative evaluation methods as well as personal reflection. The key question now becomes the following: Are the desired/anticipated outcomes congruent with actual outcomes? If they were, then the strategy is a success. Any discrepan-cies, however, need to be considered in the light of reflection of the process— Why did the discrepancies occur? In what ways might the strategy be changed or improved? Were the tool choices appropriate? The approach thus leads to a cycle of reflection followed by modified implementation followed again by reflection. Reflection on the process is not limited to assessment of whether outcomes were satisfactory, but rather encourages inspection of each stage of the planning process in order to identify shortcomings in either analysis or strategy. Aside from facilitating better technology integration into the curriculum, this approach may assist in overcoming some of the resistance to technology adoption, in that technology adoption becomes motivated by the need to improve practice.

The brief case study below illustrates an application of the framework and the beliefs expressed in this chapter.

A Case Study

The following case study is for a course in human services at tertiary level study. The case study summarized in Table 3 illustrates the key tenet of the framework described above that requires decision making regarding the tool choices for strategy implementation to be based on consideration of learner characteristics, desired learner outcomes, discipline requirements, and environmental consider-ations.

Table 3: Based on the planning framework described, this table illustrates how, for a tertiary-level human services course, decision making about tool choices for implementing strategies satisfies the constraints and demands of environment, learner characteristics, discipline requirements, and desired outcomes as well as addresses issues with previously used strategies. From the perspective of multimedia technology use, multimedia technologies are exploited in terms of attributes that will satisfy these demands and constraints. This facilitates appropriate and integrated technology use.

Tool choice (indicated by *) Issue/consideration	Multimedia-based Web site	Web communications technologies	Print	video	Face-to-face
Environment: Good technical infrastructure (computer laboratories and Internet access) allowing for on-campus access outside working hours; the majority of students have computer and Internet access at home; regular on-campus contact time is also scheduled	*	*		*	*

Table 3: continued

Tool choice (indicated by *) / Issue/consideration	Multimedia-based Web site	Web communications technologies	Print	video	Face-to-face
Learner characteristics Mostly mature (nonschool learners) learners, with a high proportion of learners in full-time employment, with a cross section of abilities, backgrounds, and experiences; on-campus attendance is sometimes problematic	*	*	*		
Desired learner outcomes • "Challenge their own assumptions"	*	*			*
• "Analyze the thinking underlying practice"		*			*
• "Connect theoretical material with their own life experiences"	*	*			*
• "Think through how values can be incorporated into a real-life situation"	*			*	*
Discipline requirements: Off-campus practicum sessions— need for easily portable materials and off-campus access as well as communication with peers off-campus; thinking through and changing beliefs is a core goal of the subject	*	*	*	*	*

Table 3: continued

Tool choice (indicated by *) — Issue/consideration	Multimedia-based Web site	Web communications technologies	Print	video	Face-to-face
Issues with previously used strategy relying on face-to-face contact with print materials: Students failing to engage with reading materials prior to class, so much of valuable face-to-face contact time is used for delivery of content rather than active discussion. Some students miss out on classes on occasion, because they are working or have other commitments	* *Web multimedia materials More interactive and stimulating— encourage more active involvement with content*	*			

Resulting Subject Form

Given the adequate technical infrastructure, a subject Web site is used as the principal organizing medium for the subject and also as the primary means of preparation before engaging in face-to-face contact time. The Web site outlines weekly schedules and presents appropriate simulations and interactive exercises to introduce learners to course content and begin the process of self-reflection on beliefs and practices. The potential of multimedia-based Web sites to be used for more dynamic and engaging presentation of content prior to class time is exploited. Interactive case scenarios are presented via the Web site where they encourage students to explore their existing knowledge. This will "free-up" face-to-face class time for more valuable, deeper discussions rather than pure content presentation and initial reflection. Participation in discussion is important in helping students to analyze their own assumptions and in exposing them to the feelings and thoughts of others. The sharing of experiences, particularly after practical placements, is an important mechanism in this subject. Face-to-face contact is seen as an important tool for achieving learner outcomes that focus on analysis of beliefs and practices.

The Web site also enables students to have around-the-clock access to class materials. Chat rooms are useful in enabling students to support each other and collaboratively solve problems, especially when away from campus on practicum. Support is also available from tutors at certain times of the week, during which students can log in while off campus. This is an important mechanism for helping students to connect theoretical knowledge with the experiences they are undergoing at the time. E-mail is also useful in encouraging and maintaining student–faculty contact during practical and other off-campus times.

Print materials will still be used but primarily as an easily portable reference source, especially while on practicum, rather than as a primary source of information prior to attendance at face-to-face class times.

Future Trends

The range and nature of multimedia technologies are constantly changing. In an educational context, the challenge is to develop approaches to planning that can be used to facilitate integration of existing and future technologies. By conceptualizing the role of technologies in the learning context as a component of a set of tools, it is intended that the framework and ideas presented in this chapter be one step in the direction of "generic" planning approaches that will provide guidance to educators and those involved in their professional development in both current and future technological environments. Planning approaches need to be contextually framed so that the key focus is to exploit the attributes with the aim of providing deeper, more meaningful learning experiences that will equip students with the lifelong learning skills demanded in the present and the future.

Evidently, with the dynamic nature of multimedia technologies, there will always remain a need for ongoing professional development that will present opportunities for educators to investigate the attributes of multimedia technologies as they emerge in terms of usefulness for their particular teaching contexts. From this perspective, ongoing research focusing on which technologies are being used in what contexts and what results are being obtained becomes important. Such research will highlight the attributes of the technology that are worth exploiting and for what purposes and could result in models of implementation so that educators could draw upon one another's experiences.

Conclusions

The framework and ideas presented in this chapter precipitated from concern about the ineffective and often inappropriate use of multimedia and associated technologies in learning contexts.

The fundamental belief expressed in this chapter is that effective use of multimedia and other technologies in teaching and learning environments occurs when multimedia technologies arc integrated fully and appropriately into the curriculum. The primary goal for integrating multimedia and associated technologies into the curriculum is to provide for a learning environment that espouses more meaningful and deeper learning.

It is advocated throughout this chapter that multimedia and associated technologies are considered as part of a tool set available for strategy implementation. If, how, and when to integrate technologies are decided by taking into account constraints and conditions imposed by the environment, learner characteristics, desired learning outcomes, and the nature of the content, and by reflecting on success or otherwise of previously used teaching practices. Also highlighted is the important role of reflective practice. Another key theme is the need to foster the view that technology integration is an evolutionary, transformative process rather than an exercise in translation of strategies to another medium. The five guidelines for multimedia technology use and the planning framework presented in this chapter incorporate these views.

The dynamic, rapidly evolving technological environment characteristic of the present and the future represents ongoing challenges for educators striving to make use of these new tools to the best advantage for a more effective learning environment and more meaningful learning outcomes. Despite the dynamic nature of technical environments, it is the author's belief that there is at least one constant premise upon which educator development aimed at multimedia technology integration efforts can develop—that is that change in practice is inextricably linked with successful integration of multimedia technologies in teaching and learning contexts. Nurturing the acceptance of this premise needs to be a matter of priority in current and future educator development efforts in the area of educational application of technologies.

References

Ballantyne, R., Bain, J. D., & Packer, J. (1999). Researching university teaching in Australia: Themes and issues in academics' reflections. *Studies in Higher Education, 24*(2), 237–257.

Bennet, S., Priest, A., & Macpherson, C. (1999). Learning about online learning: An approach to staff development for university teachers. *Australian Journal of Educational Technology, 15*(3), 207–221.

Brown, T. (1997). *Multimedia in education—Conclusions.* Retrieved September 27, 1999 from the World Wide Web: http://129.180.87.4/Units/CurricSt/CSIT513/573/573_12.html

Burns, M. (2002). From black and white to color: Technology, professional development and changing practice. *T.H.E. Journal, 29*(11), 36–42.

Charp, S. (2000). Technology integration. *T.H.E. Journal, 29*(11), 8–10.

Collis, B. (1996). *Pedagogy.* Retrieved September 10, 2002 from the World Wide Web: http://www2.openweb.net.au/TT96University/BC.html

Conlon, T., & Simpson, M. (2003). Silicon Valley versus Silicon Glen: The impact of computers upon teaching and learning: A comparative study. *British Journal of Educational Technology, 34*(2), 137–150.

Cuban, L. (1986). *Teachers and machines: The classroom use of technology since 1920.* New York: Teachers College Press.

Ellis, A., O'Reilly, M., & Debreceny, R. (1998). *Staff development responses to the demand for online teaching and learning.* Paper presented at ASCILITE '98 conference, Wollongong. Retrieved March 20, 2003 from the World Wide Web: http://www.ascilite.org.au/conferences/wollongong98/ascpapers98.html

Fatemi, E. (1999). *Building the digital curriculum. Education Week on the Web.* Retrieved July 16, 2001 from the World Wide Web: http://www.edweek.org/sreports/tc99/articles/summary.htm

Goddard, M. (2002). What do we do with these computers? Reflections on technology in the classroom. *Journal of Research on Technology in Education, 35*(1), 19–26.

Gonzales, C. L. P., Hupert, N., & Martin, W. (2002). The Regional Educational Technology Assistance Program: Its effects on teaching practices. *Journal of Research on Technology in Education, 35*(1), 1–18.

Hammond, M. (1994). Measuring the impact of IT on learning. *Journal of Computer Assisted Learning, 10*, 251–260.

Jackson, B., & Anagnostopoulou, K. (2000). *Making the right connections: Improving quality in online learning. Teaching and Learning Online: New pedagogies for new technologies. International Centre for Learner Managed Learning, Middlesex University.* Retrieved April 15, 2003 from the World Wide Web: http://webfeedback.mdx.ac.uk/_lmlseminar/_private/_abstract14/finland.htm

Jamieson, P. (1999). *Improving teaching by telecommunications media: Emphasising pedagogy rather than technology.* Paper presented at the Ed-Media 1999 World conference on Educational multimedia, hypermedia and telecommunications, Charlottesville.

Lefoe, G. (1998). *Creating Constructivist learning environments on the Web: The challenge of higher education.* Paper presented at ASCILITE '98 conference, Wollongong. Retrieved March 20, 2003 from the World Wide Web: http://www.ascilite.org.au/conferences/wollongong98/ascpapers98.html

Nichol, J., & Watson, K. (2003). Editorial: Rhetoric and reality—The present and future of ICT in education. *British Journal of Educational Technology, 34*(2), 131–136.

Oliver, R. (1999). *Teaching and learning with technology: Learning from experience. In On the Edge Leading the learning revolution.* Paper presented at the Proceedings of the Australian Curriculum Assessment and Certification Authorities Conference, Perth.

Pierson, M. E. (2001). Technology integration practice as a function of pedagogical expertise. *Journal of Research on Computing in Education, Summer,* 413–430.

Rakes, G. C., & Casey, H. B. (2002). *An analysis of teacher concerns toward instructional technology.* International Journal of Educational Technology. *3*(1). Retrieved March 30, 2003 from the World Wide Web: http://www.outreach.uiuc.edu/ijet/v3n1/rakes/index.html

Relan, A., & Gillani, B. (1997). Web-based instruction and the traditional classroom: Similarities and differences. In B. H. Khan (Ed.), *Web-based instruction.* New Jersey: Educational Technology Publications.

Richards, C., & Nason, R. (1999). *Prerequisite principles for integrating (not just tacking-on) multimedia technologies in the curricula of tertiary education large classes.* Paper presented at the ASCILITE '99 Conference. Brisbane. Retrieved March 30, 2003 from the World Wide Web: http://www.ascilite.org.au/conferences/brisbane99/papers/papers.htm

Sandholtz, J., Ringstaff, C., & Dwyer, D. (1997). *Teaching with technology.* New York: Teachers College Press.

Selwyn, N., & Gorard, S. (2003). Reality bytes: Examining the rhetoric of widening educational participation via ICT. *British Journal of Educational Technology, 34*(2), 169–181.

Strommen, D. (1999). *Constructivism, technology, and the future of classroom learning.* Retrieved April 15, 2003 from the World Wide Web: http://www.ilt.columbia.edu/ilt/papers/construct.html

Tearle, P., Dillon, P., & Davis, N. (1999). Use of information technology by English university teachers. Developments and trends at the time of the National Inquiry into Higher Education. *Journal of Further and Higher Education, 23*(1), 5–15.

Torrisi, G., & Davis, G. (2000). Online learning as a catalyst for reshaping practice—The experiences of some academics developing online materials. *International Journal of Academic Development, 5*(2), 166–176.

Torrisi-Steele, G. (2001). Appropriate use of multimedia technologies in tertiary learning environments. *Staff and Educational Development International, 5*(2), 167–176.

Chapter III

Interactive Multimedia for Learning and Performance

Ashok Banerji, Monisha Electronic Education Trust, India

Glenda Rose Scales, Virginia Tech, USA

Abstract

Developments in information and communication technologies (ICT) are rapidly transforming our work environments and methods. Amongst these changes, the advent of interactive multimedia technology has meant new approaches to instruction, information and performance support implementations. The available resources can be amalgamated in a suitable way to create an enabling environment for learning, training and performing. Concise descriptions of the salient aspects are presented along with basic design principles for communication and performance support. Guidelines for design and suggestions for implementation are provided for the benefit of the practitioners.

Introduction

Undoubtedly, the advent of computers and communication technology has forever changed our daily lives. Today, we have the fantasy amplifiers (computers), the intellectual tool kits (software and hardware), and the interactive electronic communities facilitated by the Internet that have the potential to change the way we think, learn, and communicate. However, these are only tools. The late Turing Award winner Edsger Dijkstra said, "In their capacity as a tool, computers will be but a ripple on the surface of our culture. In their capacity as intellectual challenge, they are without precedent in the cultural history of mankind" (Boyer et al., 2002). The onus is on us, our innovative ideas as to how we harness the technology for education, training, and business in order to lead or lag in the new social order. In this regard, we may remember that Charles Darwin said, "It's not the strongest of the species who survive, nor the most intelligent, but the ones most responsive to change."

In this chapter, we will review these current developments in teaching and learning from a broader performance support systems perspective. Then we will suggest a performance-centered design approach in support of developing teaching and learning solutions for the knowledge worker of today.

Lessons from the Past

There are many examples from the past indicating the rush to implement cutting-edge technologies (Marino, 2001). All of these began with a grand promise as a total solution to a long-standing problem. For example, in 1922 Thomas Edison predicted that "the motion picture is destined to revolutionize" the educational system and will largely supplement textbooks. Radio was hailed with the promise to "bring the world to the classroom." Similarly, educational television was touted as a way to create a "continental classroom" (Cuban, 1986). How much of these hopes have been met as of today?

On similar lines, recently, there has been much hype about interactive multimedia and the Internet as the remedies for all problems in training and education. However, as a knowledge resource, multimedia productions, the Internet, and a library have similar attributes. It is particularly wrong to assume that putting all the information on the Internet will make learning happen. The Internet is useful, but it does not guarantee learning any more than a good library ensures creating knowledgeable persons (Clark, 1983).

From a technocratic perspective, there is a tendency to assume that installing computers and networks will solve every conceivable problem. However, the value and benefits of technology will come only through leveraging it for dynamic and strategic purposes that place the focus first on learning and performing and second on the technology (Dede, 1998; Bare & Meek, 1998).

The key lessons from the past indicate that including performance-centered design techniques tends to improve the usability of the information or learning systems. As we move from the "Information Age" into the "Knowledge age," it is important to consider technological solutions to support teaching and learning (Reeves, 1998). In the transition from the "Old Economy" to the "New Economy," a key outcome of the transformation is a dramatic shift from investments in physical capital to investments in human or intellectual capital. A well-designed holistic approach toward training and development is therefore needed to support the learning needs of the knowledge worker (McArthur, 2000). In this regard, we need to consider the benefits of a user- and performance-centered approach from the standpoint of design. The remaining portion of this chapter will discuss how the electronic performance support systems approach can help in the challenges associated with the new paradigm.

Performance Support Systems

There are three primary impacts of information and communication technologies (ICT). These are the methods in which the following occur:

(a)   Information is distributed and retrieved.

(b)   Knowledge and expertise are stored and acquired.

(c)   Skills are learned and transferred.

These technologies have made important impacts in transforming education, training, and skill development approaches. In 1991, Gloria Gery introduced a framework for electronic support (Gery, 1991, 2002). While definitions vary, it is widely agreed that performance support systems do the following:

- Enable people to perform tasks quickly, because they provide integrated task structuring, data, knowledge, and tools at the time of need

- Do not tax the performer's memory or require performers to manipulate too many variables

- Enable task completion, with learning as a secondary consequence

Taking a broader view, we can say that an electronic performance support involves "a human activity system that is able to manipulate large amounts of task related information in order to provide both a problem solving capability as well as learning opportunities to augment human performance in a job task" (Banerji, 1999a). Such systems provide information and concepts in either a linear or a nonlinear way, as they are required by a user. The EPSS concept provides a holistic design framework encompassing a custom-built interactive guidance, learning, information, and knowledge support facility that is integrated into a normal working environment. Such systems are concerned with effective human–task interaction in which the computer provides an interface to various job tasks and becomes an aid in achieving efficient task performance.

Components and Types of EPSS

In most modern workplaces, computers are used for decision making, task performance, task sequencing, planning, and also learning, thereby replacing many manual methods. In such situations, the work is not done solely by people or solely by computers but by human-computer systems. The computers and communication technology thus act as a powerful tool by providing an interface to the basic job tasks that are involved. People and computers thus tend to work cooperatively and symbiotically, combining the advantages of the powers of each in order to achieve more effective job performance (Licklider, 1960).

Thus, human-task interaction within the human activity system (HAS) forms the foundation of EPSS. The HAS involves the following three subsystems, as shown in Figure 1:

(a)   The tool subsystem

(b)   The task subsystems

(c)   The people subsystem

The tool subsystem provides an interface to various job tasks and becomes an effective aid in achieving efficient task performance. It can also be a means for improving performance. However, the performance generally gets hindered in the absence of an appropriate "interface." These are the barriers of task performance that a support system should strive to minimize. The dimensions of these barriers include knowledge, skill, information, decision, processes, and procedures. The function of an EPSS would be to reduce the "permeability" of the interface through appropriate means. These include eLearning facility and Knowledge Management, among many others (Dickelman & Banerji, 1999).

There could be three principal ways in which the "tools system" interfaces the "task system," and, three broad classifications of EPSS can be made depending on how they render support in task performance:

Figure 1: Concept map of human activity system

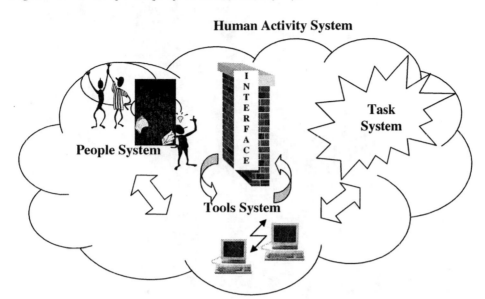

Type 1: In this type, tasks are performed with computer and software tools, such as word processors, spreadsheets, and so on. Support for this type of application is tied with the software tools and, therefore, can be called *software-integrated EPSS*. The simplest examples are cue cards, animated help in Microsoft applications (Figure 2), and wizards.

Type 2: In this type, computer-based tools mediate the organizational tasks and practices, such as banking systems, enterprise resource planning systems, air ticket booking, along with hotel and car booking systems, and so on. Supports are needed as an integrated part of this type of application so that the user can perform competently with minimal training. These types of applications can be called *job-integrated EPSS*.

Type 3: In this type, computer-based systems mediate and facilitate the various operations and job roles, such as knowledge-based tasks, repair and maintenance jobs, and so on. Support for this type of application can be called *operation-integrated EPSS*. The emerging technologies involving wearable computers and virtual reality applications supporting repair jobs fall in this class of applications.

Numerous examples of EPSS applications are available in the literature (Banerji, 2003; Dickelman, 2001; Gery, 1991; Hall, 2003). However, detailed discussion of specific EPSS tools is not possible within the confines of this chapter.

Figure 2: Animated help in Microsoft applications

Interactive Technologies for Communication

Let us now examine multimedia technology as a tool for communication and information transfer. Communication is central to the development of human society and is responsible for all the knowledge that we have accumulated so far. By the word "communication," we mean the process of transmission of data and information from one person to another, which ultimately may lead to knowledge after processing in the mind of the recipient.

The communication process for information transfer is usually bidirectional. The chain of events starts with a trigger in the mind of the sender (Person A), who, in turn, gives the idea a form by encoding it in a language or expression or picture. The encoded message (signal) is then transmitted to the receiver (Person B), who must have the appropriate decoder to understand the message conveyed by the signal. The receiver may appropriately respond by similarly returning a message to the sender after suitable encoding.

The process of communication, however, continues only if the receiver has the appropriate decoder/encoder. This model is shown in Figure 3. This model can also be easily modified for human–computer communication by replacing "Person B" in the model with a computer. The developments in multimedia and Internet technologies provided the necessary impetus for this evolving human–computer symbiosis utilizing the various communication modes and channels. Their possible applications are limitless, as the technology is under constant evolution.

Figure 3: Encoder-decoder and channel model of communication

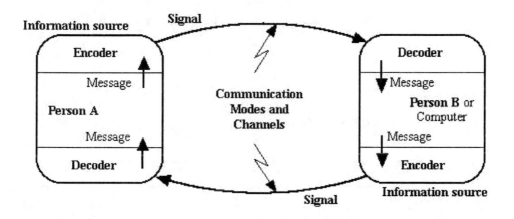

Information source: The process responsible for selecting or formulating the desired message.
Message: The material that the information source wishes to transmit.
Signal: The form in which the message is actually sent to the recipient.
Transmission channel: The medium through which the message is sent.
Source: Adapted from Wilbur Schramm's model (1954), as referred to in Tannenbaum (1998).

In the case of human-computer communication, interaction with the computer and the communicative dialogue takes place through some limited modes and channels. The modes are mainly visual, audio, and tactile. Within each mode, there can be various channels. Examples include text, graphics, animation, and video channels in visual mode; voice, sound, and music in audio mode; discrete and continuous tactile interaction modes using keyboard and mouse/joystick, etc. The effectiveness of this communication depends on how well the modes and the media components have been selected and combined. Various interactive technologies are available for this purpose. Detailed discussion on these will be beyond the scope of this chapter. However, the above model is important for conceptualizing and realizing the three types of EPSS discussed earlier.

Design Principles

The foregoing discussions on human–task interaction and interactive technologies for communication give us the necessary foundation for appropriate design of interactive multimedia for learning and, particularly, for performance support. Although the complexity of the application domain can vary considerably, we can design an appropriate performance support solution based on a set of 10 fundamental principles and guidelines. These are listed in Table 1. The 10 basic principles formulate the design strategies for EPSS, including its major supporting components—eLearning and knowledge management (Banerji, 1995).

Table 1: Basic principles of performance support

Num ber	Principle	Remarks
1.	**Specify and prioritize** the critical areas of underperformance within the application domain and then **identify appropriate strategies** to improve performance	Suggests a methodology for identification of critical areas of performance deficiency and a top-level approach for their remedy
2.	Attempt to **design mechanization aids and automation tools** to facilitate increases in personal and organizational performance with respect to task-oriented skills	
3.	Identify relevant **generic and application-oriented tools and processes** that will provide on-the-job support and improve task performance	Possible measures for prioritizing tasks could be based on cost, quality, error rate, and task performance time
4.	Attempt to identify and, if possible, eliminate all unnecessary **information blockages and constrictions** within an organization or a work environment	Suggests generic tool sets for information provision, information dissemination, intervention of JIT
5.	Identify an appropriate **combination of media, multimedia, hypermedia, and telecommunications** in order to optimize information flow and interpersonal communications	Training and learning facilities, including eLearning, within a performance support environment
6.	Where a user or employee has an identified skill deficiency, attempt to rectify the situation using **just-in-time (JIT) training and learning techniques**	
7.	Whenever feasible, a performance support system should accommodate **individual learning styles** and thus attempt to maximize its utility for as wide a range of users and task performance situations as is possible	Accommodates the importance of various types of users and their learning styles
8.	Identify appropriate groups of people who have the expertise needed to solve demanding problems and provide the infrastructure necessary to **facilitate group working**	Suggests computer-supported collaborative work (CSCW), the use of intelligent agents, and Knowledge Management
9.	Whenever feasible, attempt to use **intelligent agents** within an EPSS facility in order to (a) **identify the skills needed** for a given task, (b) **locate sources of organizational expertise** relevant to these tasks, and (c) **enhance software components**	
10.	Attempt to provide facilities to **create a corporate pool of knowledge and skill assets** that can be used to maintain and enhance performance levels	Permeate benefits of performance support right across an organization; create a corporate knowledge pool and skill asset (knowledge capital) that can be made available throughout an organization and is available when needed

Implementation Approach

Performance means to complete a task such as a piece of work or a duty according to a usual or established method. It also means mastering the task using the most efficient and effective techniques. One aspect of mastering a task using a performance support system is the reliance upon the cognitive partnership between the user and the performance support tool. The important functions and performance measures are as follows:

(1)   Reduction in task performance time

(2)   Reduction of operational error

(3)   Improvement of the quality of task performance

(4)   Reduction in cost

These can be achieved through appropriate design of EPSS (Barker & Banerji, 1995; Banerji, 1999a; Gery, 2002).

EPSS for Teaching and Learning

The four parameters, time, error, quality, and cost, form the justification for the use of the EPSS approach in any workplace design/redesign. For example, these are equally applicable in any academic institution or corporate university for supporting (a) the students in their learning tasks, (b) the faculty in their tasks of delivering knowledge, and (c) the employees in their management tasks and functions. Let us elaborate one approach.

Despite the advent of powerful, inexpensive, easy-to-use computer technology, the uptake of computer-assisted learning and computer-based training methods within most academic institutions had so far been slow. However, a new wave in the form of *Virtual Classroom, Virtual University, Web-Based Training* is currently sweeping across most institutions all over the globe. These are clubbed under the term eLearning (or e-learning), which provides opportunities for new modes of information exchange, information transfer, and knowledge acquisition.

It is conceivable that for some time to come, lectures will continue to be the mainstream mechanism for the bulk dissemination of information and knowledge to large groups of students. Given this situation, it is important to address the issue of how best to leverage technology to improve the quality of students' learning experiences and at the same time provide a more effective and efficient framework for the faculty to develop and present material. One way in which this could be done is to create an electronic performance environment that simultaneously fulfils the needs of both faculty and students. The model of required support for this purpose is shown in Figure 4.

The model shown in Figure 4 is based on the recognition of the currently accepted strategy. It suggests how we can incorporate the new strategy in making the shift (a) from teacher-centered instruction to student-centered learning, (b) from information delivery to information exchange, and (c) from passive learning to active/exploratory/inquiry-based learning.

The distinguishing characteristic of knowledge and skill is that it derives from and finds its meaning in activity. Knowledge is dynamic. Its meaning is constructed and reconstructed as the individual grapples with the use of knowledge through conceptualization, analysis, and manipulation. This naturally has important implications for curriculum development. The objectives of education in any discipline are conventionally attained through (a) classroom training (conceptual understanding), (b) tutorials (analysis), and (c) laboratory practice (practical skill or manipulation).

However, in view of the rapidly changing practices, revitalizing education and training, particularly technical education, has become a matter of concern. This

Figure 4: Concept map of support system for teaching and learning

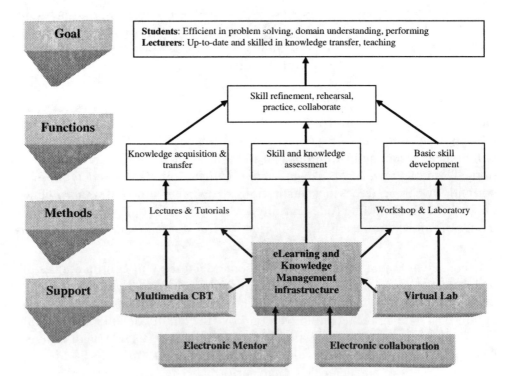

is because of two factors. First, setting up an appropriate up-to-date laboratory is costly and takes time. Second, accessibility of the laboratory is limited to fixed available hours. The existing practices therefore do not support open and flexible learning (Barker, 1996; Baker et al., 1995). Therefore, the central challenge lies in how to provide cost-effective learning opportunities for a larger and more diverse student population. Following on the human activity system model (Figure 1) and the basic principles of performance support system design (Table 1), Figure 4 suggests an approach for a support system for teaching and learning. This can be achieved by incorporating the virtual laboratory, multimedia computer-based training (CBT), including eLearning, knowledge management infra-structure, and the support components made available through the Internet and communication facilities, as shown in Figure 4.

Conclusions

This chapter described design approaches to assist the knowledge worker of today by leveraging technology to support learning and performance. The basic premise of the approach is incorporating new techniques to deliver just-in-time learning into an EPSS design. Design for this purpose needs sound judgment and decision about pedagogy, which is often the main cause of failure, not the technology. It should be realized that merely hosting Web pages with all the information about the subject is not what eLearning is about. Better learning will not occur if only a conversion of media is effected—from paper to digital.

With sound design, the potentials of interactive multimedia technologies for learning and performing are many. Technology is available now to make learning interesting and activity oriented. It is possible to create low-cost alternatives for learning with active experimentation through virtual laboratories, where learning occurs through practicing and visualizing the concepts. Most importantly, it is possible to make these benefits available in a consistent way to a wider cross-section of people covering a large geographical area.

Gary S. Becker, Nobel laureate and professor of economics and sociology at the University of Chicago, argues the following (Ruttenbur, Spickler, & Lurie, 2000):

The beginning of this century should be called "The Age of Human Capital." This is because the success of individuals and economies succeed will be determined mainly by how effective they are at investing in and commanding the growing stock of knowledge. In the new economy, human capital is the key advantage. (p. 12)

In the knowledge-based economy, organizations as well as individuals need to focus on protecting their biggest asset: their knowledge capital. Therefore, the leaders of companies competing in the knowledge economy have to recognize the importance of efficient knowledge management as well as the importance of developing and enhancing their intellectual capital leveraging technology.

The increasing economic importance of knowledge is blurring the boundaries for work arrangements and the links between education, work, and learning. In this regard, the electronic performance support approach provides a holistic framework for workplace design and redesign.

Of course, the human mind is not going to be replaced by a machine, at least not in the foreseeable future. There is little doubt that teachers cannot be replaced with technology. However, technology can be harnessed as a tool to support the new paradigm. We can derive much gain by adopting information and communication technologies appropriately, especially as we look for new solutions to provide the knowledge worker with immediate learning opportunities.

References

Banerji, A. (1995). Designing electronic performance support systems. *Proceedings of the International Conference on Computers in Education (ICCE95)* (pp. 54–60). Singapore, December 5–8.

Banerji, A. (1999a). Performance support in perspective. *Performance Improvement Quarterly*, *38*(7). Retrieved from the World Wide Web: http://www.pcd-innovations.com/piaug99/PSinPerspective.pdf

Banerji, A. (1999b). Multimedia and performance support initiatives in Singapore Polytechnic. *SP Journal of Teaching Practices*. Retrieved from the World Wide Web: http://www.vc.sp.edu.sg/journals/journals_intro.htm

Banerji, A. (Ed.) (2001). The world of electronic support systems. Retrieved February 6, 2004 from the World Wide Web: http://www.epssworld.com/

Bare, J., & Meek, A. (1998). *Internet access in public schools* (NCES 98-031). U.S. Department of Education. Washington, DC: National Center for Education Statistics.

Barker, P., & Banerji, A. (1995). Designing electronic performance support systems. *Innovations in Education and Training International*, *32*(1), 4–12.

Barker, P., Banerji, A., Richards, S., & Tan, C. M. (1995). A global performance support for students and staff. *Innovations in Education and Training International*, *32*(1), 35–44.

Boyer, R. S., Feijen, W., et al. (2002). In memoriam Edsger W. Dijkstra 1930–2002. *Communications of the ACM*, *45*(10), 21–22.

Clark, R. E. (Winter 1983). Reconsidering research on learning from media. *Review of Educational Research, 53*(4), 445–459.

Cuban, L. (1986). *Teachers and machines: The classroom use of technology since 1920.* New York: Teachers College Press.

Dede, C. (1998). *Six challenges for educational technology.* Retrieved from the World Wide Web: http://www.virtual.gmu.edu/SS_research/cdpapers/ascdpdf.htm

Dickelman, G., & Banerji, A. (1999). Performance support for the next millennium: A model for rapidly changing technologies in a global economy. HCI 99 Conference, Munich.

Dickelman, G. J. (Ed.) (2003). EPSS design contest awards. Retrieved February 6, 2004 from the World Wide Web: http://www.pcd-innovations.com/

Gery, G. (2002). *Performance support—Driving change* (pp. 24–37). The ASTD E-Learning Handbook, Ed. Allison Rossett. New York: McGraw Hill.

Gery, G. J. (1991). *Electronic performance support systems: How and why to remake the workplace through the strategic application of technology.* Boston, MA: Weingarten Publications.

Hall, B. (Ed.) (2003). Retrieved February 6, 2004 from the World Wide Web: http://www.brandonhall.com

Licklider, J. C. R. (1960). Man–computer symbiosis. *IRE Transaction of Human Factors in Electronics, HFE*-1(1), 4–11.

Marino, T. (2001, July/August). Lessons learned: Do you have to bleed at the cutting edge? *The Technology Source.* Retrieved from the World Wide Web: http://ts.mivu.org/default.asp?show=article&id=860#options

McArthur, K. E. (2000). *Teachers use of computers and the Internet in public schools* (NCES 2000090). U.S. Department of Education, Washington, DC: National Center for Education Statistics.

Reeves, C. T. (1998). *The impact of media and Technology in Schools.* A research report prepared for the Bertelsmann Foundation. Retrieved from the World Wide Web: http://www.athensacademy.org/instruct/media_tech/reeves0.html

Ruttenbur, B. W., Spickler, C. G., & Lurie, S. (2000). *eLearning the engine of the knowledge economy.* Retrieved from the World Wide Web: www.morgankeegan.com; http://www.masie.com/masie/researchreports/elearning0700nate2.pdf

Tannenbaum, R. S. (1998). *Theoretical foundations of multimedia* (Chapter 5). New York: W.H. Freeman & Co. Computer Science Press.

Chapter IV

Teaching, Learning and Multimedia

Loreen Marie Butcher-Powell,
Bloomsburg University of Pennsylvania, USA

Abstract

"We must not forget that almost all teaching is Multimedia" (Schramm, p.37). Today, the magnetism of multimedia is clearly oblivious via the use of streaming video, audio clips, and the Internet. Research has shown that the use of multimedia can aid in the comprehension and retention of student learning (Cronin & Myers, 1997; Large Behesti, Breulex & Renaud, 1996; Tennenbaum, 1998). As a result, more educators are utilizing Web-based multimedia materials to augment instruction online and in the classroom. This chapter provides a theoretical framework for transforming Student Centered Discussion (SCD), a traditional based pedagogy strategy, to a new multimedia pedagogy SCD strategy. The new multimedia SCD pedagogy represents a new way of teaching and learning. As a result, positive responses and feedback have been collected from students in their ability to interpret facts, compare and contract material, and make inferences based on recall of information previously presented or assigned in article readings.

Introduction

Research has shown that students can integrate information from various sensory modalities into a meaningful experience. For example, students often associate the sound of thunder with the visual image of lightning in the sky. When the cognitive impact of two given interaction modalities differ enough, different learning modes can be induced. Moreover, an interaction modality, which affects a learning mode, also has consequences for the learning performance (Guttormscn, 1996, 1997). Therefore, a teacher is faced with the need to integrate various combinations of sensory modalities, such as text, still images, motion, audio, animation, etc., to promote the learning experience.

Multimedia is multisensory; it engages the senses of the students. Multimedia can be defined in a variety of ways, but in this chapter, the term "multimedia" refers to a Web-based interactive computer-mediated application that includes various combinations of text, sound, still images, audio, video, and graphics. Multimedia is also interactive; it enables both the student and the teacher to control the content flow of information (Vaughan, 1998). A major part of using multimedia in instruction involves engaging students in sense-making activities, such as conversations and chats about external representations that use concepts, symbols, models, and relationships. As a result, multimedia has introduced important changes in the educational system and has impacted the way teachers communicate information to the student (Neo & Neo, 2000).

Learning

Learning is fundamentally built up through conversations between persons or among groups, involving the creation and interpretation of communication (Gay & Lentini, 1995; Schegloff & Sacks, 1973; Schegloff, 1991). More importantly, learning is established and negotiated through successive turns of action and conversations (Gay et al., 1995; Goodwin & Hertage, 1986; Schegloff, 1991). Thus, conversations are means by which people collaboratively construct beliefs and meanings as well as state their differences.

Brown, Collins, and Duguid (1989) argued that learning involves making sense of experience, thought, or phenomenon in context. They hypothesized that student representation or understanding of a concept is not abstract and self-sufficient, but rather it is constructed from the social and physical context in which the concept is found and used. Further, Brown et al. (1989) emphasized the importance of implicit knowledge in developing understanding rather than acquiring formal concepts. It is, therefore, essential to provide students with authentic experiences with the concept.

Students can engage in learning conversations in distributed multimedia environments. Multimedia technologies, such as graphics, simulations, video, sound, and text, allow instructors to use multiple modes and representations to construct new understanding and conceptual change of enhancing student knowledge. Brown et al. (1989) stated that learning involves making sense of thoughts, experiences, or phenomena in contexts. Multimedia allows for the accommodation of diverse learning styles. Different media provide different opportunities for communication and activities among students. For example, online conversations provide a common background or mutual knowledge about beliefs and assumptions during conversation.

The Distinct Ways of Learning

There are multiple ways of learning. Four of the most common and distinct ways to learn are independent learning, individual learning, cooperative group learning, and collaborative group learning (Kawachi, 2003). For the purpose of this chapter, it is important to understand the differences between cooperative and collaborative learning.

Traditionally in a cooperative learning environment, knowledge is learned by the student via the teacher or other students repeating, reiterating, recapitulating, paraphrasing, summarizing, reorganizing, or explaining the concepts. Meanwhile, in collaborative learning, knowledge is not learned by the student via the teacher, but rather knowledge is learned via an active dialogue among students who seek to understand and apply concepts. Using multimedia in collaborative environments allows students to participate in genuine learning activities by which they can reflect as well as modify their understanding of concepts (Brown et al., 1989; Gay, Sturgill, Martin, & Huttenlocher, 1999; Harasim, Hiltz, Teles, & Turoff, 1995; Wegerif, 1998; Murphy, Drabier, & Epps, 1997). The ability to read and respond to a message posted to an online forum creates opportunities for the creation of knowledge.

With the use of multimedia, students can utilize the information presented to them by the teacher, and represent it in a more meaningful way, using different media elements. Fortunately, there are many multimedia technologies that are available for teachers to use to create innovative and interactive courses. A review of literature on multimedia educational tools revealed some interesting innovative and rich multimedia-based learning tools. Jesshope, Heinrich, and Kinshuk (n.d.) researched the ProgramLive application. The ProgramLive application is a rich multimedia-based tutorial of the Java programming language. ProgramLive's interface represents a notebook, within a browser. There are tabs to the side of the notebook display that can be used for navigation of the material, as well as pop-up explanations of key concepts.

Millard (1999) developed an Interactive Learning Module for Electrical Engineering Education and Training titled the Interactive Learning Modules (ILM). ILM presents Web-based multimedia tutorials created with Macromedia Director. ILM provides a mechanism for the creation of supplementary material for lectures and collaborative problem solving and simulation environments. ILM is highly modular for the usage of various materials to be used in multiple courses. Similarly, the Multimedia Learning Environment (MLE) developed by Roccetti and Salomoni (2001) is a networked educational application that also provides course material in a student-based manner. MLE provides a virtual learning environment, through a client application, where the multimedia educational material is structured in Adaptive Hypermedia, from which sets of hypermedia pages are dynamically retrieved and presented to the student via tailoring the contents and presentation style to the students needs (Roccetti et al., 2001).

Further, Jesshope, Heinrich, and Kinshuk (n.d.) are currently developing an integrated system for Web-based education called the Teaching Integrated Learning Environment (TILE). This system uses Web-based delivery of course material, including interactive multimedia presentations, problem solving, and simulation environments in which students learn by doing. Like MLE, TILE provides students with an interactive multimedia environment and instructors with a multimedia environment for managing, authoring, monitoring, and evaluating student learning.

The multimedia educational tools, described above, have been traditionally used in two ways, either as a vehicle for students to learn theory and application beyond the subject matter or as a tool used by the teacher to support teaching. As a result of multimedia educational tools, teachers are faced with a significant need to provide a more multimedia-based approach to learning, and to create a new educational pedagogy that emphasizes collaborative learning via multimedia.

Numerous studies have been conducted in the attempt to determine how effective multimedia is in teaching (Blank, Pottenger, Kessler, Roy, Gevry, Heigel, Sahasrabudhe, & Wang, 2002), however, very few studies have been conducted to illustrate and determine the factors that may aid in a new multimedia pedagogy strategy for teaching. This chapter was designed to provide the theoretical framework for how teaching is enhanced using Web-based multimedia. The objective of the chapter will be to explain the latest pedagogical teaching strategies for utilizing interactive Web-based multimedia educational tools. As a result, this chapter will provide instructors with a positive and effective example for utilizing Web-based multimedia in teaching.

A New Global Environment
for Learning

A new multimedia pedagogical model for learning in a collaborative environment was incorporated in the Information Science and Technology (IST) undergraduate program at Pennsylvania State University (PSU), Hazleton, Pennsylvania (USA). The transformation from a traditional lecture-based model to an interactive Web-based multimedia application was accomplished using A New Global Environment for Learning (ANGEL). ANGEL is PSU's course management system (CMS) that is currently in use within the University's system (Pennsylvania State University, n.d.). ANGEL is an interactive Web-based multimedia application developed by CyberLearning Labs Incorporated, for constructive, collaborative, inquiry-based, and problem-solving Web-based learning. ANGEL allows for interaction, testing, presentations, audio, video, forums, file submissions, and many more multimedia features. Through ANGEL, instructors are able to use multimedia effectively in aiding in the students' learning and retention process (Pennsylvania State University, n.d.).

Pedagogical Strategy

Beginning with the philosophy that "learning is not a spectator sport" (Chickering & Gomson, n.d.), students are encouraged to get involved in their educational experience. The probability of students' learning improving by getting involved, talking and writing about what they have learned, relating it to past experiences, and most importantly applying it to their daily lives, is much greater than by students sitting in classes listening to teachers, memorizing prepackaged assignments, and spitting out answers. The goal of each course is to provide the students with a challenging, critical thinking, novel, technology-focused, and learner-centered educational experience, where they learn by pursuing knowledge, improving basic communication skills, and, most importantly, taking responsibility for their own learning (Brown et al., 1989).

To obtain such a goal, the following procedures were used. The classes were structured toward creating a problem-based learning (PBL) and a student-centered discussion (SCD) environment for students utilizing a multimedia course management system, ANGEL. PBL is traditionally used in courses that provide more student-centered learning experiences. The origins of PBL began in the medical education field (Barrows, 1986, 1999). PBL is a student-centered pedagogical approach in which learning is taught through suggested real-world problems. PBL establishes the importance of clearly formulated effective real-world problems. An effective problem has a realistic context and is couched in appropriate vocabulary. The problem should be complex and ill-structured, without clear-cut, easy answers or nuances and subtitles that are not immediately apparent. Moreover, the problem should support both discovery and self-directed learning while engaging the interest and the curiosity of the student (Desmarchais, 1999).

SCD is a delivery system for the application of educational goals in the classroom. This process is accomplished by integrating basic discussion skills in the classroom. The technique is one that models after all competency levels of Blooms Taxonomy in a limited structured time period. The discussion and team-building process that occurs in SCD promotes the active engagement of the students in their own educations. This technique requires the student to actively take responsibility for conducting a productive and meaningful discussion (Wright & Shout, n.d.). SCD has been proven to be an interactive model that encourages students to develop effective communication and interpersonal skills as well as strengthen critical-thinking skills (Butcher-Powell & Brazon, 2003). Moreover, Wright et al. (n.d.) stated that this model is effective regardless of discipline or knowledge base.

The addition of multimedia technology into a PBL and a SCD environment further enhances the students' learning experience. Figure 1 illustrates this focus.

Figure 1: The multimedia PBL–SCD curriculum model

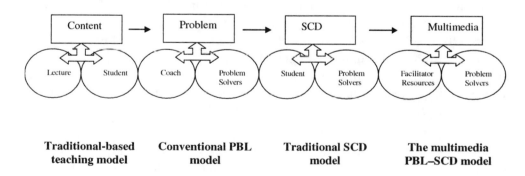

Traditional-based teaching model   **Conventional PBL model**   **Traditional SCD model**   **The multimedia PBL–SCD model**

Class Structure

The original version of the PBL and SCD was modified in order to incorporate multimedia into the class. The classes meet every Tuesday and Thursday for approximately one hour and 10 minutes for one 15-week and one 14-week semester. On every Tuesday, the PBL and SCD models were used in class. To accomplish a cohesive learning experience, the students are first divided into small groups consisting of four students. Each group has 30 minutes to discuss, ponder, debate, question, learn, and solve the problem from a video clip stored on ANGEL. Additional resources, such as articles, notes, and existing Web cases were made available to the students in a digital library on ANGEL. After the 30 minutes were over, the entire class was combined into one big circle, upon which students received another video clip that expanded upon the first video clip. The students were to engage in a larger PBL and SCD environment to create a solution to the problem identified in the video clips.

After the class session was over, students were required to log on to ANGEL and write a brief summary of what they learned from the video clips, and how that relates to their lives. In addition, the students were required to search the Web and find an article on the subject matter and post it to ANGEL for Thursday's class. On Thursday, an interactive PowerPoint lecture supporting Tuesday's video clip and the students' PBL and SCDs were presented to the class and remained available in ANGEL for later student usage. After the 30 minute lecture, the remaining 40 minutes were left for the students to find and discuss an article or Web site in the forum section of ANGEL. Moreover, each student was also required to read and elaborate upon at least one other student's summary of a related article or Web site.

After the material was taught utilizing the defined methods, the students were required to take an online interactive time test via ANGEL. Traditionally, the test consisted of random multiple-choice, true and false, matching, and short-answer questions. ANGEL allowed authenticated users, during a specified time frame, various combinations of questions, and timed the test. More importantly, ANGEL allowed the teacher to make prerecorded video available during the test in order to guide a student through each excursion of the test. And, finally, ANGEL allowed the teacher to pregrade the test so that the students had immediate access to their grades after their tests were submitted. However, the answers to the test were only available for review after all students completed the test.

As illustrated above, this new multimedia pedagogical strategy allowed for inquiry to be accomplished via text mining and visualization tools. As a result, students were able to explore the emerging problems, solutions, and trends in their fields of study. Moreover, collaborative learning was also achieved via live links and remote-controlled "video" sessions by reviewing multimedia recorded lecture sessions that encouraged students to interact with instructors and digital libraries.

Data Source and Collection Instrument

The data population consisted of undergraduate students (n = 32) in the Information Science and Technology major at PSU Hazleton, Pennsylvania, USA. The students ranged in age from 20 to 28 (M = 20.51, SD = 2.68). Academic classification was represented by juniors (n = 26) and seniors (n = 8). The teaching team consisted of one instructor utilizing two classes to explore student perceptions and experiences with the cohesive multimedia pedagogical strategy. Data were gathered in pre- and postquestionnaires and in student diaries. The pre- and postquestionnaires consisted of 11 questions to assess the students' interest in group project work and whether or not they were motivated in their project development. The questionnaire also tried to determine the students' levels of understanding and critical-thinking skills. The questionnaire was measured using a five-point Likert scale. The scale measurements were 1, strongly agree; 2, agree; 3, undecided; 4, disagree; and 5, strongly disagree. The scales and all questions in the questionnaire were developed after a review of literature guided by the theoretical base. An expert panel of faculty and doctoral-level graduate students evaluated the face and content validity of the question-naire.

Results and Discussion

The feedback at the time of writing indicates that the new multimedia pedagogy approach used in the classes is fully endorsed by students and leads to intense student engagement and an effective level of learning. Thus, over 80% (87.7%) of the students (n = 32) had a computer with Internet access at home and were able to fully take advantage of the new multimedia way of learning. At the beginning of the course, most (90.6%) of the students were excited and eager to be taught using the new multimedia pedagogy. Furthermore, almost all of the students (96.87%) at the end of the course felt they had learned a great deal of theory, content, and application with the new multimedia pedagogy. Consistently, students (96.87%) indicated that they would like to see this new multimedia pedagogy applied to all of their undergraduate classes. The perceived benefit of the new multimedia pedagogy to the student mean was 1.92 (SD = 0.63). This indicated that students agreed with the perceived benefits of the new multimedia pedagogy strategy.

Inferential t-tests were used to determine if significant differences ($p < 0.05$) existed in the perception of additional workload as a result of the adoption of the new multimedia strategy. The t-test revealed that no significant differences ($t = 1.59, p = 0.114$) existed in the additional workload mean between the students who liked and did not like the new multimedia way of learning. Furthermore, no significant differences existed in the additional workload mean between the students who earned a B or better and the students who earned a B- or less. More importantly, no significant differences existed between the students who earned a B or better or the students who earned a B- or lower, as they strongly agreed that this was a great way to learn.

Moreover, the students' experiences with this new multimedia pedagogical strategy were also demonstrated throughout the semester by the student's ability to interpret facts, compare and contrast material, and make inferences based on recall of the information previously presented or assigned information in the given article. Most importantly, the student's readiness for the class was instantly recognized.

Overall, the new multimedia pedagogical strategy represents a new way to develop and deliver classroom discussions and material. In traditional classroom discussions, the faculty member assumes the role of the discussion leader. He or she identifies the questions that will be discussed and maintains a teacher-centered structure. In contrast with traditional classroom discussions, the new multimedia pedagogical strategy online approach is much more student-centered through the usage of multimedia enhancements. As a result, the instructor assumes the role of discussion facilitator, instead of discussion leader. This shift from discussion leader to discussion facilitator forces students to become responsible for their behavior and interaction in the discussion.

Limitation

The integration of multimedia into the classroom and online is essential if multimedia is to become a truly effective educational resource. However, the integration and the change in pedagogy are difficult, time consuming, and resource-intensive tasks. Research has shown that teachers need time working with the technology before they will be at a level of comfort to change or modify their pedagogy (Redmann et al., 2003).

Conclusions

Despite a rapidly growing recognition of the potential impacts of such interactive multimedia developments, teachers have relatively little understanding of the extensive benefits surrounding the use of new multimedia resources in the classroom. The dearth of knowledge exists in a wide variety of domains, including but not limited to the design and development of new systems and tools to retrieve and manipulate documents, as well as the uses and impacts of such new tools on both learning and problem solving. Previous research documents the improvement in learning as a result of the use of multimedia (Blank et al., 2002), while other researchers have not found any significant differences in learning between multimedia-based and traditional-based pedagogical approaches (Moore & Kearley, 1996). As efforts to illustrate the impact of multimedia in instruction continue, one fact remains: Modern multimedia-based pedagogical approaches have roots of the oldest traditional human communication methods. However, in the future, multimedia pedagogical strategies will have a much more profound impact on how instructors approach and engage students in the process of education and communication.

As the complexity of using multimedia in the classroom continues, new teacher and student technologies will become robust, and ad hoc methodologies will give way to more interactive student competence for learning.

References

Barrows, H. (1999). The minimum essentials for problem-based learning. Retrieved March 2003 from the World Wide Web: http://www.pbli.org/pbl/pbl_essentials.htm

Barrows, H. S. (1986). A taxonomy of problem based learning methods. *Medical Education, 20*, 481–486.

Blank, G. D., Pottenger, W. M., Kessler, G. D., Roy, S., Gevry, D., Heigel, J., Sahasrabudhe, S., & Wang, Q. (June, 2002). Design and evaluation of multimedia to teach java and object oriented software engineering. *Proceedings of the American Society for Engineering Education*. Montreal, Canada.

Brown, J. S., Collins, A., & Dugid, P. (1989). Situated cognition and the Culture of Learning. *Educational Researcher, 18*, 32–42.

Butcher-Powell, L. M., & Brazon, B. (February, 2003). Workshop: Developing interactive competence: Student centered discussion. *Journal of Computing Science in Colleges, Proceedings of the 18th Annual CCSC Eastern Conference, Bloomsburg, PA, 18*(3), 235–240.

Chickering & Gomson. (n.d.). Seven principles of good practice in undergraduate education. Retrieved April 2003 from the World Wide Web: http://www.hcc.hawaii.edu/intranet/committees/FacDevCom/guidebk/teachtip/7princip.htm

Cronin, M. W., & Myers, S. L. (Spring 1997). Effects of visual versus no visuals on learning outcomes from interactive multimedia instructions. *Journal of Computing in Higher Education, 8*(2), 46–71.

Desmarchais, J. E. (1999). A Delphi technique to identify and evaluate criteria for construction of PBL problems. *Medical Education, 33*(7), 504–508.

Gay, G., & Lentini, M. (1995). Use of communication resources in a networked collaborative design environment. *Journal of Computer-Mediated Communication,1*(1). Retrieved April 2003 from the World Wide Web: http://www.ascusc.org/jcmc/vol1/issue1/IMG_JCMC/ResourceUse.html

Gay, G., Sturgill, A., Martin, W., & Huttenlocher, D. (1999). Document-centered peer collaborations: An exploration of the educational uses of networked communication technologies. *Journal of Computer-Mediated Communication, 4*(3). Retrieved January 13, 2004 from: http://www.ascusc.org/jcmc/vol4/issue3/gay.html

Goodwin, C., & Hertage, J. (1986). Conversation analysis. *Annual Review of Anthropology, 19,* 283–307.

Guttormsen Schar, S. G. (1996). The influence of the user-interface on solving well- and ill-defined problems. *International Journal of Human–Computer Studies, 44,* 1–18.

Guttormsen Schar, S. G. (1997). The history as a cognitive tool for navigation in a hypertext system. In M. J. Smith, G. Salvendy, & R. J. Koubek (Eds.), Vol. 21B, pp. 743–746.

Harasim, L., Hiltz, S. R., Teles, L., & Turoff, M. (1995). *Learning networks: A filed guide to teaching and learning online.* Cambridge, MA: MIT Press.

Jesshope, C., Heinrich, E., & Kinshuk. (n.d.). *Online education using technology Integrated Learning Environments.* Massey University, New Zealand. Retrieved February 2003 from the World Wide Web: http://www.tile.massey.ac.nz/publicns.html

Kawachi, P. (2003). Choosing the appropriate media to support the learning process. *Media and Technology for Human Resource Development, 14*(1&2), 1–18.

Large, A., Behesgti, J., Breuleux, A., & Renaud, A. (1996). Effect to animation in enhancing descriptive and procedural texts in a multimedia environment. *Journal of the American Society of Information Science, 47*(6), 437–448.

Millard, D. M. (1999). Learning modules for electrical engineering education and training. *Proceedings of the American Society for Engineering Education.*

Moore, M.G. & Kearsley, G. (1996). *Distance Education: A Systems View.* Wadsworth Publishing.

Murphy, K. L., Drabier, R., & Epps, M. L. (1997). Incorporating computer conferencing into university courses. *1997 Conference Proceedings: Fourth Annual National Distance Education Conference* (pp. 147–155). College Station, TX, USA: Texas A & M University. Retrieved January 2003 from the World Wide Web: http://disted.tamu.edu/~kmurphy/dec97paphtm

Neo, M., & Neo, T. K. (2000). Multimedia learning: Using multimedia as a platform for instruction and learning in higher education. *Paper presented at the Multimedia University International Symposium on Information and Communication.*

Pennsylvania State University. (n.d.). Overview and tools. Retrieved February 9, 2003 from the World Wide Web: http://cms.psu.edu

Redmann, H. D., Kotrlik, W. J., & Douglas, B. B. (2003). A comparison of business and marketing teachers on their adoption of technology for use in instruction: Barriers, training, and the availability of technology. *NABTE Review, 30,* 29–35.

Roccetti, M., & Salomoni, P. (2001). A Web-based synchronized multimedia system for distance education. *Proceedings of the 16th ACM Symposium on Applied Computing* (pp. 94–98).

Scardamalia, M., & Bereiter, C. (1993). Collaborative knowledge building. In E. DeCorte, M. C. Linn, H. Mandl, & L. Verschaffel (Eds.), *Computer-based learning environments and problem solving* (pp. 41–66). Berlin: Springer-Verlag.

Schegloff, E. A. (1991). Conversation analysis and socially shared cognition. In L. Resnick, J. Levine, & S. D. Bernard (Eds.), *Socially shared cognition* (pp. 150–172). Washington, DC: American Psychological Association.

Schegloff, E. A., & Sacks, H. (1973). Opening up closings. *Semiotica, 7,* 289–327.

Schramm, W. (1977). *Big media, little media.* Beverly Hills, CA: Sage Publications.

Tennenbaum, R. S. (1999). *Theoretical foundation of multimedia*. New York, NY: Computer Science Press.

Vaugh, T. (1998). *Multimedia: Making it work* (4th ed.). Berkeley, CA: Osborne/McGraw Hill.

Wegerif, R. (1998). The social dimension of asynchronous learning networks. *Journal of Asynchronous Learning Networks, 2*(1), 34–39.

Wright, D., & Shout, L. (n.d.). Developing interactive competence through student-centered discussion. Retrieved March 2003 from the World Wide Web: http://home.kiski.net/~dwright/scd/hme.html

Chapter V

Reaching Students of Many Languages and Cultures:
Strategies for Developing Computer-Based Learning Units

Rika Yoshii, California State University, San Marcos, USA

Alfred Bork, University of California, USA

Alastair Milne, California State University, San Marcos, USA

Fusa Katada, Waseda University, Japan

Felicia Zhang, University of Canberra, Australia

Abstract

To address the global problems of learning, we must make our development strategies ready to support the many different languages and cultures in the world. This chapter discusses how the Irvine-Geneva development strategy supports, and can be made to support further, development of global materials. We will first discuss essential characteristics of the kind of learning software that will successfully address global education. We will then discuss our design and translation strategies for current software with those characteristics, the tools we have developed for facilitating them, and our implementation strategies. We will end our discussion with linguistics issues related to globalization in general.

Introduction

As the education community begins to address the global problems of learning, we must make our development strategies ready to support the many different languages and cultures in the world. While more computer-based materials become available via the Internet, the majority is still written for English speakers, making the materials virtually inaccessible to many students, or forcing them to learn in English in styles inappropriate for many cultures (Yoshii, Katada, Alsadeqi, & Zhang, 2003).

This chapter discusses how the Irvine-Geneva development strategy supports, and can be made to support further, development of global materials. The Irvine–Geneva development strategy brings together a *philosophy of tutoring design* with a *system of learning software development* oriented toward embodying that philosophy in pedagogically strong designs. These designs are given to software development teams to implement them in well-engineered units, using software tools oriented to that philosophy.

We will first discuss what we submit are essential characteristics of the kind of learning software that will successfully address global education. We will then discuss our design and translation strategies for current software with those characteristics, the tools we have developed for facilitating them, and our implementation strategies. We hope the readers will expand on our strategies and use and even possibly enhance our tools in developing their materials. We will end our discussion with linguistics issues related to globalization in general.

Background: Learning Material for Global Education

What the characteristics will be of the learning software that will successfully address global education is clearly subject to much debate; however, we present the following characteristics as essential. We note that some of these characteristics require, or at least benefit by, distance learning.

1. ***Individualization***: The software must adapt automatically to each student as it progresses. Global education inherently implies a world of different types of students. Each student will have unique abilities and learning problems. The software must recognize these as it works with the student, treating each student as an individual, providing individualized pacing and appropriately chosen help sequences.

2. ***Collaborative Learning***: We recommend designing to allow collaborative learning, as well as individual learning. For collaborative learning, we recommend a group of two to three students sitting around a computer. One obvious group that would benefit is those students who are unfamiliar with computers.

3. ***Mastery***: The software should be designed to bring all students to understand everything the material has to give them, with no assumptions of human teachers taking over any part of the material. Where this involves the acquiring of skills, not just the learning of facts, the designers must take the additional demands into account, providing for, at least, practice, encouragement, and the student tiring from time to time.

4. ***Culture***: The material should match and respect the culture of each student group. From an ethical point of view, it is important to respect people's pride in their cultural identities and heritages. We will explore this in more detail later in the chapter.

5. ***Languages***: The material must be amenable to translation into many different languages with many different writing systems. This effort cannot simply use direct translations, as discussed later in this chapter, because each culture has its own views of the world and its own ways of expressing them.

6. ***Autonomy***: The software should not depend on, or even presume, any institutions of learning as their environments. Although they may well be used there, the units should still work autonomously with the student, depending on no additional aid.

7. ***Motivation***: The software must be intrinsically motivating. Many of the enticements and goads usual to classrooms, such as grades, assessments, or teacher instructions, may not be available; but where a classroom presentation can be made exciting and engaging, instilling excitement about the domain, a presentation in the software should be able to do at least as well. Again, however, what is motivating will likely depend on the student's culture.

8. ***Affordability***: The software must not be kept from its necessary audiences by its cost (see also the next item). In estimating necessary consumer cost, all significant expenses that are not otherwise defrayed must be included:

for instance, development, evaluation, delivery, later support and release of updated versions, and any commercial profit margins involved.

9.   ***Delivery***: Delivery mechanisms must be available for reaching everyone, even very poor students, including those in environments without schools (see above about autonomy). Note that designers must resolve potential conflicts between this and other items above: no amount of motivation and individualization will benefit students if doing so requires the software to use capacities the students' equipment does not have.

The development strategy developed at the University of California, Irvine (UCI), in cooperation with the University of Geneva, is capable of meeting all the requirements just stated (Bork et al., 1992).

Evolution of the Development Strategy

The evolution of what is now the Irvine–Geneva development strategy began over 30 years ago. It has had, roughly, the major phases discussed next (Bork, 1987).

Birth of the Methodology and Tools

In the first phase, the project at UCI developed the central methodology and programming tools to be used in producing highly interactive learning units. From the start, it was recognized that for any learning software project to achieve the nine major characteristics from page 75, a genuine software engineering approach was necessary. This meant bringing groups of expert teachers or tutors together with highly capable programmers. The two groups needed to communicate by a means both straightforward enough and detailed enough to give teachers a relatively low learning curve yet give programmers all the pedagogical details that the teachers wanted the software to realize with each student. Thus was born the *script*: a visual document providing a semiformal notation for teachers to design pedagogical flow.

In this early stage, there was no automation, to any degree, of the creation and editing of pedagogical designs. When the evaluation of the learning software showed (almost inevitably) necessary revisions in the pedagogical design, updating the paper scripts reliably was so nearly impossible that the revisions were usually made to the software alone; and a given script could thereby become inaccurate, or worse, obsolete. The delivery system was a specific mainframe with specialized graphics terminals; no personal computers or networking were available. This phase lasted years, comprising a long run of many different projects, and a wealth of learning material was produced (in physics, mathematics, and evolutionary biology). However, these materials were confined not only to UCI but also to the particular mainframe where they were developed.

Transportable and Translatable Software

In the second phase, the Centre Universitaire d'Informatique (CUI) of the University of Geneva began a long collaboration with UCI as individual micro-computers were starting to be available, the forerunners of today's personal workstations. An entire new set of tools for the programmers was developed (Franklin et al., 1985) in a programming language not only transportable among machines but also much more oriented to software engineering goals: software more correctly implemented, more reliable, and easily amenable to necessary changes. With the broadening of scope brought by several European colleagues, these tools also evolved to support translation needs among European languages, including attempts to make a given learning unit choose automatically the language it would use, from among those provided for it. The first projects were done in the wholesale translation of learning software originally scripted in English. Scripts remained on paper and resistant to updates, including translation. However, the need for creating and altering scripts in soft copy was becoming ever more pressing, and the first explorations were being made into achieving it.

Incorporating Multimedia

With the arrival of the digital videodisc, the programmers' tools evolved yet again, to incorporate live sound and video into the windowing already used by the existing text and graphic display. But no evolution of the scripts was required: they were already flexible enough that teachers needed only a few refinements of convention to specify multimedia content, both repurposed and original. These were applied in a prototypal project to develop student comprehension of spoken Japanese, with actual Japanese television footage, courtesy of Nippon Television (Yoshii, 1992).

Script Editing Online and the World Wide Web

By the final stage of this project, CUI Geneva, under our late colleague Bertrand Ibrahim, made it possible for the first time for teachers to create and edit scripts online with a UNIX-based interactive system, called at the time IDEAL (Bork et al., 1992) and more recently DIVA. This was used not only in the spoken Japanese project but also in at least two others of very different domains. IDEAL was also the first effort to generate automatically as much as possible of the program code to implement the script (Ibrahim, 1990). Currently, support tools for creating learning software in Java are being developed at California State University San Marcos (CSUSM) (Yoshii, 2002). One overriding goal is to develop learning software that is inherently deliverable over the World Wide Web.

It will be noted that project arrangements described above imply significant costs. While a full discussion of project financing issues is beyond the scope of this chapter, we maintain that larger projects are actually helpful here. They not only produce larger amounts of learning software that increasing numbers of students will need, they can also help distribute costs and reduce or eliminate repetition of overhead items, ultimately resulting in less expense per unit of learning software. This has been true of most of our projects, which have been funded by nonprofit organization grants, and by both grants from and contracts with large corporations.

Development Strategy in Relation to Global Education

There are four important aspects of the development process covered by the Irvine–Geneva development strategy—management, design (including translation), implementation, and evaluation. In the following sections, we will discuss the latter three in relation to global education.

Starting Point: Interaction and Individualization Go Hand in Hand

The strategy we use for pedagogical design aims to create learning software that is interactive, in the sense that a human tutor is interactive, when working with no more than a few students. Some current application of the term *interactive* uses it simply when multimedia or Internet connection is involved. This is emphatically not adequate for our meaning. To this end, we identify certain fundamental properties that we maintain that the pedagogical design must achieve:

Quality of interaction: The "quality" refers to the amount of information that the software can obtain from the student's answer (or other action), to assess the student's progress and choose as a result the action the software should take next. The notation in our scripts is well oriented to the display of conversational questions and the reading of free-form, conversational answers typed at the keyboard (or possibly spoken into a microphone). Our strategy usually considers multiple choice questions to be low-quality interactions—they are usually very limited in the number of alternatives and limit what the student will contribute to simply choosing among prepackaged answers.

Frequency of interaction: High-quality interactions will still have limited helpfulness if they only happen rarely in the script. Experience suggests that the script should let no more than 20 or 30 seconds pass between interactions. This not only contributes to the quality of information the software can gather about the student but also keeps them more involved and participating.

Individualization: This results when the material analyzes the information obtained from frequent, high-quality interactions to choose, for the student, the most appropriate among a variety of available actions. Providing the following actions in the design can enhance the degree of individualization:

- Having the design decide which material to present next, including whether it should be remedial, and if so, what kind.

- Having the design choose the path with a more appropriate pace for the student, if the student's history shows problems, or where possible, adjust the pace on the current path.

- Having the design choose an alternate technique or style intended to work better with the student. The further interactions along that path will let the software analyze whether the student is benefiting from that technique. When the learning material incorporates many learning strategies (for example, a variety of exercises for learning the same concept), individualization makes learning material suitable for students of many different cultures.

It falls to the pedagogical designers, discussed in the next section, to make sure these fundamental qualities are present in the design.

Design: Supporting Interaction, Individualization, Collaborative Learning, and Mastery

The pedagogical design is the major determinant of the software's tutoring quality. Hence, we emphasize the designers being experienced and accomplished teachers and/or tutors in their subject domains who are expert in addressing student learning problems. In a large project, there will be many design groups, each with three to five teachers. Because the script should be the product of consensus and mutual inspiration among experts, fewer than three in a group are not recommended.

A good and effective design requires that the designers specify in a script *all* details that affect student learning (Bork et al., 1992; Yoshii, 1992). The fundamental elements of a script are summarized below:

• The messages including everything the designers want to say to the student and are to be presented, either in voice or on the screen. The software will present the student with exactly the language the teachers put in the script.

• All the graphics and animation, which the designers must specify by prescribing what they decide are its necessary features. Specialists in graphics will fill in the designs needed there, from the designers' specifications.

• The script notation provides elements for natural-language *comments* or *directives*, where the designers include all necessary information, addressed to programmers, other designers, translators, or whomever else they need.

• All multimedia content, which the designers must specify as they do for the graphics.

• Details of each interaction with the student, including analysis of the student answer and resulting actions from the software.

• Arrows indicating the flow among all of the above.

See Figure 1 for an example of a scripted exercise. The script notation is well oriented toward interactions that support *individualization*, because, for each interaction, the following must be specified:

• *Answer Categories*: The designers must list for each interaction all categories into which all the reasonable possible answers can fall. For each category, the designers must list "answer patterns" that will be used to match against student input. More categories for a given input lead to greater interaction quality.

- ***How to proceed next from each category of answer***: Typically from a category matching satisfactory answers, the script would lead to confirmation and praise, and then to the next material. From categories matching predicted wrong answers, the script would lead to hints or help sequences specific to the problem represented by each category. Because the student may be asked to retry the same question a number of times, the number on an arrow coming out of each answer category indicates how many times the student's answers have matched the category.

By observing the number of answer categories and arrows coming out of each category, it is easy to assess roughly how responsive the material is to a variety of student answers.

The script notation also supports *individualization* through the use of student performance information as follows:

- As part of the actions resulting from any answer category, the designers may specify what information about the student answer(s) to record.

- As with student inputs, the designers can create categories to test the recorded information at any point they consider that the software needs it, to choose the most appropriate next action for this student's performance. For example, the past performance plus the current answer may suggest an appropriate hint to give, or a sequence of answers may suggest a different difficulty level for the student. And most importantly, a sequence of such tests may be used to determine the *mastery* of a given part of the material.

Further, to ensure quality of the software, teachers are instructed to do the following:

- Create frequent interactions throughout the software, as already described.

- Make the design adaptable to use by groups of two or three students, not just one student.

In our experience, teachers from a breadth of areas, nationalities, and academic backgrounds have been able to design with the scripting notation within an hour of being introduced to it.

Figure 1: Sample script

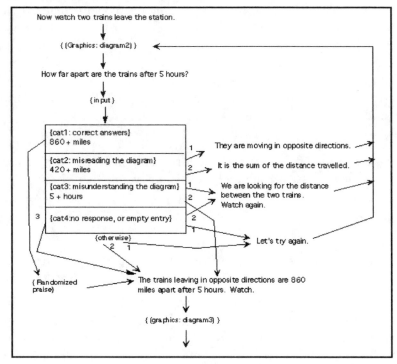

International Design Groups for Multicultural Designs

How do we create designs for multiple cultures and languages? Having each design group create a different version of a script for each different language would be time-consuming and costly, not to mention the number of designers we would need in each group. Therefore, we assume here that the design is created first for one language, while preparing for delivery in multiple languages for multiple cultures.

Often, there are differences in how a given subject is taught in different cultures. There are also differences in the ways students are praised or given help. There are visual aids to which certain cultures respond to better than others, or which some cultures find offensive or ridiculous. The learning software must supply a variety of techniques borrowed from many different cultures and must provide interactions comfortable to any one culture.

In listing answer categories in a script, the designers must cover a variety of answers given by the students of different cultures. For example, consider the question "How do you measure your body temperature?" It is common in

English-speaking countries that the student will put a thermometer in the mouth, but in some cultures, including Japanese, this is not appropriate—Japanese students will put a thermometer in their armpit.

Therefore, for a design to work with a variety of cultures, the design groups must have strong international composition. The designers must be careful not to equate the single language of their design with a single culture. For example, we must recognize the cultural differences among students of French-speaking countries. We recommend involving teachers who understand their local educational requirements and the need to be culturally sensitive. If delivery in multiple languages is anticipated, the design groups should involve bilingual teachers and linguists from the anticipated cultures so that they can foresee whether there will be possible difficulties in translating the material into their languages.

However, as the number of cultures in the world is not only very large but subject to change, unique reactions and responses from different cultures cannot always be anticipated, even by the most international group of designers. It is therefore important to incorporate a scripting mechanism that is fuzzy enough and flexible enough to be modified to include handling these cases. For example, in our scripts, the designers can insert comments to document how answer-matching patterns have been chosen and what is essential in translating them.

In the next section, we describe the process of "translating" a completed script.

Translation to New Languages and Making Cultural Adjustments

Why should we make the material available in many different languages when students of many countries are able to understand English or other commonly spoken languages? In what languages should the students learn? Nations (or indeed any regions of distinct culture and language) and their citizens "typically" demand education in their mother tongue to respect and sustain their national or regional identity and unity (Lo Bianco, 2002). The situation can become more complex for regions and countries in which a number of languages are spoken, for example, Canada, Switzerland, or India. Fortunately, some of them already have solutions in place that designers of learning software should follow. For example, faced with some 200 indigenous languages, India follows a three-language policy, whereby children learn Hindi and English as well as a local language at school (Comrie, Matthews, & Polinsky, 1996).

Assuming initial scripting was done as recommended above, those scripts must now be translated into one or more other languages. However, the same need for transcultural awareness (or greater) exists as in the original design sessions: merely translating the texts in the scripts, and audio in the multimedia content, would frequently result in what has been called cultural imperialism (Phillipson, 2002). Each translation effort must be guided by appropriate cultural (and political) expertise, in order to revise the script to adjust to appropriate practices in the culture of the target language. Our ultimate goal is that the resulting document be as authentic and natural in its culture as the original document.

There are at least three aspects to the translation of a script, and related cultural adjustments:

- Messages
- Multimedia, graphics, and simulations (and texts within them)
- Student responses

Messages

In the first aspect, the messages addressed to the student are translated. The translator must be familiar with the climate of the students using the software and with acceptable demeanor and approach from tutor to student in the target culture. Sufficient familiarity with students learning the subject matter is also needed in order to be able to choose the common phrases for that field, if any are available. And when it arises (as it will) that some target language does not provide those phrases, the translator must be able to fill in an appropriate glossing of concepts in the field.

Multimedia, Graphics, and Simulations

The second, and possibly most costly, aspect is the production of new multimedia to replace all language-dependent multimedia that was prescribed for the original design, translated, and, where necessary, recast in the target culture. Multicultural considerations already described above will, of course, also guide the design of the new multimedia. Close coordination of the new multimedia production with the project management and designers will be found to be essential. Related to this but still separate is the translation of occurrences of text in simulations and other graphics. The original production of these components should isolate and mark this text so that it is not overlooked in translation. It will also help if the containing graphic design can be made, from the start, as independent as possible of the screen positions of these text fragments, because translation will almost invariably change the space they occupy. However, this will not always be fully possible, so designers must be prepared to act on notification from translators that revised graphic or simulation design is needed for the new language's version.

Student Responses

Whereas translated multimedia is probably the most costly component, the most demanding component to translate is surely the sets of the keyword patterns by which the software analyzes student inputs. A simple direct translation of the keywords in the English patterns may produce a different effect—in fact, a serious error—in the translated version. Instead, the translator must be comfortable both with what was intended in the entry and with how students in the target culture would naturally express it. Consider a case of translating even a simple English interaction to Japanese. Given a yes/no question, American students may say "yes" to affirm and "no" to negate, whether the question was phrased as positive or negative, for example, "Do you know this song?" "Yes" [I do]. "Don't you know this song?" "Yes" [I do]. In Japanese, the typical translation of "yes" is *"hai"* and of "no" is *"iie."* However, when the question phrasing is negative, Japanese reverses the use of the words. The translator must therefore substitute patterns for *"hai"* and *"iie"* according to context and not by blanket replacement of "yes" and "no."

The following are further examples:

- There are languages that do not use an explicit word for either or both of "yes" or "no," for example, Finnish and the Scottish Gaelic. What Mandarin Chinese does is similar—because there is no single word for "yes" or "no," the positive of the verb is used to express the meaning of "yes" and the negative to express the meaning of "no."

- French and German each use a third word (French, *"si"*; German, *"doch"*) for an affirmative response to a negative question.

- Phrases involving prepositions, especially in casual conversational use, virtually defy straightforward translation. It is essential that the translator recreate the intention in the appropriate conversational idiom of the target language.

There may still be differences in answer categories due to the students' culture (as opposed to language) that the designers missed and the translator must catch during the translation process.

With all these requirements of translation and cultural adjustments, follow-up design sessions with a small group of teachers of the target culture may be necessary. With proper script-editing software, script modifications are easy.

Affordable Development: Script Editing Made Easier

We have stated that our scripts were initially on paper and therefore prohibitively difficult to update, and that any translation would become a new project. The design is now often entered directly into the computer where it can be updated easily. Interactive script editors, of which we now have two very different versions, make this possible. If the script is still done on paper, we can transcribe it into an editor later. The first script editor was written by Bertrand Ibrahim and his group at the CUI of the University of Geneva (Ibrahim, 1989). Another script editor is being developed in Java at California State University, San Marcos (Yoshii, 2002).

Geneva Script Editor (IDEAL)

The first working script editor, originally called IDEAL (Interactive Development Environment for Assisted Learning), and more recently DIVA, was produced at the University of Geneva. It was created for (mostly UNIX) graphical workstations, and it was oriented to generate implementations of the designers' scripts in a high-level programming language, as human programmers would do from paper scripts. For the first time, designers could work out scripts easily, revising and editing as they went. What had been a quickly learned notation now became almost trivial, mostly handled automatically by the editor itself.

IDEAL was intended from the first to support multilingualism in the scripts it edits. To this end, it was arranged in two levels: the script editor, to work directly on scripts; and a so-called "synchronous editor," that synchronized the flow diagrams with the files holding their textual content, so that each may be manipulated independently of the other.

Thus, when a designer creates a new element of the script and enters its textual content, the diagrammatic portions are placed in the script's own file, and the text is placed in a separate but associated file dedicated to text messages and all other language-dependent text in the script, one language for a given file. It is thereby relatively easy (for scripts where direct translation is appropriate for a given target culture) to produce an additional text file in the target language. In the easiest translation cases, it would only be necessary to make a copy of the previous message file and then proceed from message to message in the script editor, turning each message and each text comparison into its translated form.

Because the message files are all plain text, it is entirely possible to edit them with a plain text editor, and indeed, because IDEAL runs under UNIX, to apply any of the myriad of small but useful transformation programs that UNIX provides.

However, the sensitivity of an accurate translation to the context of the source message implies that doing them in IDEAL is the safest way. (For instance, it would be unwise blindly to translate Japanese "*hai*" to French "*oui*" without seeing whether it is displayed in a positive or negative context.)

Figure 2 shows how IDEAL renders the elements of the script in its window. It will be seen that it closely simulates the handwritten form. However, two refinements may be seen:

- The generalized script "comment" is now formalized into two types: either a "directive" to the programmer or a "documentation node" for the design. Designers should take advantage of the latter to provide guidance for translators when necessary information for them may not otherwise be clear from the script

- A so-called "subgraph" component is now provided, which lets a section of script be created to be self-contained and named, so that various other parts of the script can use it if they need it. Division into subgraphs may be used as an organizational tool, for example, for isolating culturally sensitive areas that may need replacement during translation.

Figure 2: IDEAL script components

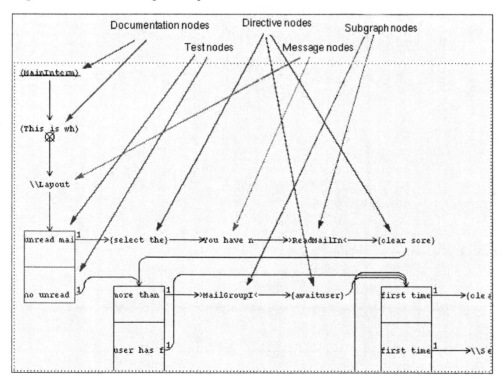

A sample of an IDEAL window with an actual section of script, taken from a UNIX workstation display, is shown in Figure 3. The bit of script in its editing pane demonstrates the following:

- Elements for analysis and decisions made both on student input, and on conditions of current student history. Translators will need to concentrate particularly on the former.

- The same limited size for every script component in the drawing. This both simplifies the drawing and maximizes the amount of script logic visible at one time. Display and editing of the component's whole text are easily obtained just by double-clicking the component, creating a separate window to edit just the text.

Figure 3: IDEAL Script Editor screen

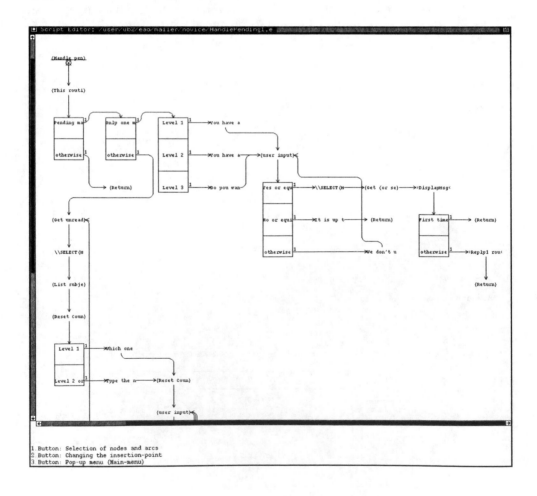

- The editor's placement of the arrows leading from element to element, and its automatic numbering of them. The designer (or translator) needs only to select the two elements that need a joining arrow: The editor takes care of positioning it appropriately for the current positions of all script components in the window.

- Panes for prompting and information (particular to the kind of workstation in use) below the pane displaying the script.

- Pop-up menus (not visible in the examples), which make it easier to get quick access to commands with minimal mouse movement.

San Marcos Script Editor

The San Marcos script editor was developed and is being enhanced with the goal of interpreting the entered script to cause the actions of the tutoring system. The designers first create an overall design by creating tracks and listing the names of their exercises for each track. With the exercise creation screen, the designers first specify the initial text-display speed, and then using tabs, the designers can go to various screens for specifying components of an exercise—instructional material, questions, student-answer categories with patterns, hints, and graphics. The designers specify connections between these components using "sequence signals."

Figure 4 shows an example screen for specifying all questions of an exercise. The signal ##SG101## following each question indicates that after displaying the question, the system should display the graphics sequence numbered 101. Signals allow such actions as go to the next exercise, go to the specified exercise, and go to the specified component (e.g., question or hint) with or without clearing that window, and do them based on student performance. Any learning software created with the editor will automatically store student performance records, holding such things as how many times the student answered in a given way during the current session and in previous sessions.

In specifying the answer categories and patterns for an exercise, the designers may enter lists of synonyms and name them. For each answer category, the designers write patterns using actual words, numbers, synonym names, and predefined symbols such as "*" to mean "any" and "~" to mean "not."

The script editor also allows creation of simple graphics sequences. See Figure 5 for the graphics editor screen. By clicking buttons, the designers can draw, move, or delete objects such as circles, rectangles, lines, and arrows. By using the Show button, the specified graphics sequence can be displayed for the designers.

Figure 4: Entering questions

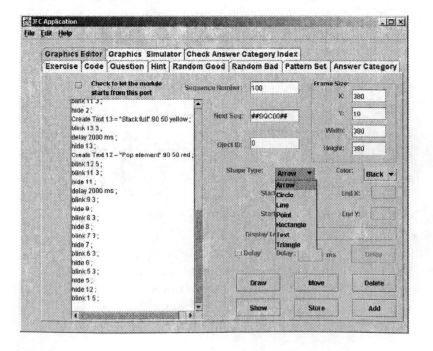

Figure 5: Graphics Editor

Script Editors Helping the Translation Process

To aid the translation effort, the messages can appear in one window in the initial language, and in another window, the translator can create the translated material. Or, in IDEAL, for translations of larger scope, entire separate script files can be edited side by side.

Currently, these editors use the Roman alphabet. Even for Japanese, which prefers non-Roman characters, transliteration into *Roomaji* can be used for scripting purposes. The San Marcos editor, written in Java, has double-byte encodings available for character representation supporting Java input tools (Campione et al., 1998), making it easier to support Chinese and Japanese characters.

Representing textual characters with double-byte codes is a major enhancement for letting the scripted program inherently support virtually any alphabet or script system in the world to which translation may be needed. Double-byte encodings replace the previous single-byte encodings, of which ASCII and its extensions are typical. Single-byte encodings can represent at most 2^8 or 256 characters; standard (nonextended) ASCII represents at most 127. In contrast, a double-byte encoding can represent up to 2^{16} or 65,566. Not only is this enough for virtually any script system in the world, it is enough to represent several of the major ones simultaneously.

Java is designed to be represented in Unicode, one of the major double-byte systems standardized by the International Standards Organization (ISO). This is very important, because strings of text in which each character contains 2 bytes instead of one break many long-standing assumptions on which text-handling algorithms are based. By relying on text-handling tools and properties provided in Java, the San Marcos Script Editor/Interpreter can make sure no such breaks occur.

Beyond this, at least three major areas present themselves for translating scripts to go anywhere in the world:

- *Display*: Origin and direction of text display will change with certain script systems, for instance, various Semitic scripts are written right to left. Chinese and Japanese can be written either left to right then top to bottom, or top to bottom then right to left. Also, both the revised phrasing in the translation and the space required to spell it will significantly affect the placement on the screen and hence its design.

- *Student textual input*: How to input text that differs significantly from keyboard contents tends to become a subproject in its own right. Increasingly, operating systems like Windows or MacOS make some solutions available, but they are not guaranteed consistency with each other or consistency in the internal text representations they create.

- **Text analysis**: Because analysis algorithms depend heavily on exactly how text is represented in computer memory, it is essential that means of student input result in the same storage as that used by internal answer-matching, and that it supports all variations of the answer-matching algorithm that the scripts require.

Fortunately, the tools provided in the Java language give us means to address all these issues, whether through direct support or by providing a general platform on which such support can be built for the editor and interpreter.

Affordable Implementation: Minimizing the Need for Programmers

At this stage, except in the case of the San Marcos system, development moves from design to a running program. This will require at least one programmer, and possibly more. All graphics, multimedia, or both that the script requires must be created in a way that the program can control. However, the programmer will need no special knowledge of an authoring system, but will simply work with a high-level programming language. Ideally, the running program should undergo beta testing to discover and eliminate as many program errors as possible.

The IDEAL script editor can produce much of the program code from the stored script. Exactly how much will vary for any given project, because it depends on how much the designers have used the script's directives to specify additional features, components, or behaviors. The code uses the tools described starting on page 76, which were intended to provide consistent support of common necessities, all oriented toward the student with little sophistication in computer usage. Construction then follows the course typical of any software project. A programmer (or programming team if the design's needs go that far) "builds" the whole project—generating executable binary versions from all the source code, and organizing the results into the deliverable packaging, along with all other material that they must use while running. If the scripts' directives specify further behavior or features, the programmer(s) will also create and integrate the source code for them, as a subproject of the whole unit.

In contrast, the San Marcos script editor comes with a script interpreter, which executes the stored script itself. Both are written in Java. No programmer is necessary. During the design session, alteration between the editor and the

Figure 6: Script interpreted

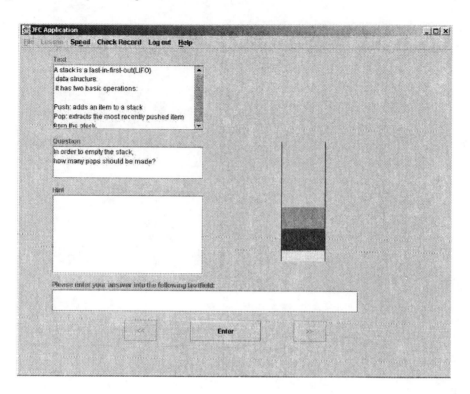

interpreter can be used to test partial designs. The learning material is limited to the features allowed by the script interpreter. However, a consequence of using the Java language is that we expect to be able to provide a "hook" and an API to let programmers, if available, implement features not already available to the interpreter. Object technology already provides for such a capability; and the Java language allows for the runtime reading and executing of additional Java components. Note that the inclusion of this ability would still permit the creation of scripts without additional features, in the cases where Java programmers were not available.

See Figures 6 and 7 for example screens of a system interpreted by the script interpreter.

Figure 7: Script interpreted

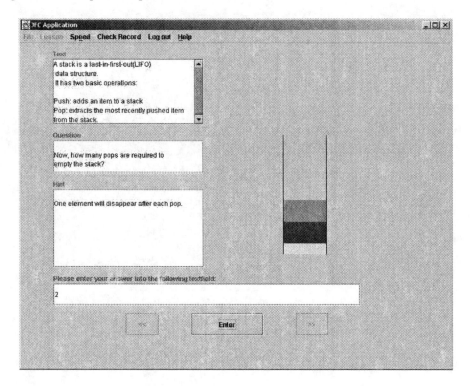

Full Evaluation in Each Language

No matter how skilled the designers and translators are, several rounds of formal evaluation are important. We normally do this for the language of the original design, but in a multiple-language project, it must be done with each new language. Sizable numbers of students in each of the languages must run their versions of the program, and it must save various data observed during their progress to determine where the design is, in whatever way, leaving the students with problems. Students in each culture must learn effectively. After each round of evaluation, results are analyzed and corrections or refinements are made in the program. With the script editors, many or most program changes can be made directly in the stored script, and new code is generated and rebuilt (for IDEAL) or interpreted quickly (for CSUSM).

Note that the concentration here is on the effectiveness of (and any problems in) the design. Ideally, the majority of program bugs (at least serious ones) will have been eliminated by the time evaluation is done.

Translators and designers should also remain aware that graphics, simulations, and multimedia that are part of the material are also subject to design improvements from evaluation.

Maintenance in Many Languages

Even after delivery, changes are possible, even likely. Even the most sophisticated commercial software typically still has bugs after five years or more of release. If the units are available in several languages, and we need to make a change, that change will initially be made in one language. Then we need to identify what changes are necessary in the remaining languages. As pointed out above, IDEAL synchronizes different language versions of a script. Because the editor knows where to find each piece of text in different language versions, the editor facilitates keeping all versions current.

Affordable Delivery

An important factor leading to low costs for a student-learning hour is an affordable delivery system. Initially, we expect a variety of delivery methods, including Internet and CD-ROM. It has been projected that two-way satellite connections will become an inexpensive delivery method for large numbers. We also can use, particularly for poor parts of the world, a less expensive learning appliance than current personal computers, to provide just learning. A much simpler operating system will be sufficient.

Linguistic Views on Global Education

What follows now is a different perspective. Independent of the Irvine-Geneva development strategy discussed so far, we present the views of linguists on global education.

A Linguistic View on Learning Environments for Languages

So far, examples from science and mathematics have been used to illustrate the different aspects of the Irvine–Geneva development strategy. However, when it comes to dealing with the creation of learning units for languages, the political and ideological dimension of language use comes into play. Governmental agencies, program designers, education experts, local teachers, learner input, and other stakeholders such as international organizations will need to be consulted. As the use of language units will have an enormous impact on a country's identity and economy, it is vital for us to respect the wishes of different governmental agencies about the choice of language (both the language being taught and the language used to present the material) for the language units. However, in some cases where international organizations play a crucial role in the development of a country, the stakeholders might not share the same ideology with regards to investments in education (Lo Bianco, 1999).

To avoid being locked in an ideological debate about how investments in education should be made and run the risk of paralyzing the project, in our opinion, what is at stake is not the choice of language(s) but what flexibility we can build into our learning environment. A well-planned and strategically thought out learning environment not only can be sensitive to the issue of language use in different cultures, but it can also accommodate the goals of different ideologies. An example of such a language learning environment could consist of a number of different multilingual learning objects, such as interactive learning units, put forward in this chapter; a video database (Davis, 2003); an audio–video browser; and a speech analysis program for providing positive feedback (Zhang & Newman, 2003), Web sites, helpful learning tools, and so on. These materials would enable each student to make up his/her own "learner's database" as he/she goes along. Of course, having a flexible learning environment will also be beneficial for other subject areas.

In a language learning environment like this, if it is necessary to have investments in literacy skills quantified in terms of some proxy measure of wider educational outcomes, it can be incorporated in the program. The accessibility and ease in using the range of programs also means the rights and development of both developing and developed nations to education can also be bolstered.

Linguistic Divide to be Overcome

As we see in the foregoing discussion, reaching students of many languages and cultures is, or soon will be, a technological reality. We expect it to be a vehicle to advance social benefits and equality on a global scale. However, it is also true that the opposite has been effected against less affluent social groups that have less access to the information networks. The now familiar expression, "digital divide," identifies the effect of information technologies on the social class structure. The problem raised here is not new: similar issues applying to computer technologies in education have been discussed since the pioneering stage of the field (Hertz, 1987). Today, however, the rapidly spreading availability of the Internet and computers has given birth to a new expression, "the ubiquitous society," which makes us feel that the digital divide is to be overcome and should not deter us from advancing information technologies.

More fundamental, persistent problems lie in a purely linguistic sense. This is because information technologies and language are inseparable, and because the situation surrounding world languages is complex. The problem here is described in terms of a chain of three "D"s of linguistics: linguistic diversity, linguistic disparity, and linguistic divide (Katada, 2002, 2003). Linguistic diversity characterizes the fact that more than 6,000 languages are spoken around the world (Comrie, Matthews, & Polinsky, 1996). Under linguistic diversity, linguistic disparity is an unavoidable reality. Currently, no one can deny that English as a global lingua franca has gained ascendancy in nearly all areas of human activities (Crystal, 1997; McArthur, 2002). The linguistic disparity is then mainly against the non-English world, which effectively creates a divide between social classes, between those who have access to English and those who have not; hence, the linguistic divide. Language is our humanity and so is linguistic diversity. As long as linguistic diversity exists in one way or another, the chain of three "D"s of linguistics will not disappear from any issues of globalization, including education.

Earlier we discussed various translation requirements and the necessity of cultural adjustments, a main purpose of which is to avoid the linguistic divide. We note here that a technological solution may be forthcoming that would make the linguistic divide largely disappear (Katada, 2002, 2003). For example, among notable technologies advancing day by day, the Universal Networking Language developed by the UNL project at the United Nations University is a global lingua franca of computers that mediates between any language pairs. It is expected that by 2006, the UNL will be able to handle any language pairs from about 180 countries and areas of the world, according to the *Nikkei* in Japan (1997). Similar and competitive projects are well underway. It should no longer be a dream that papers written in French are directly read in Swahili on the Internet. Perhaps it is not unreasonable to expect that, some day, such technologies can be used to develop computer-based learning units in many languages. After all, the linguistic divide is to be overcome and not deter us from advancing in the field.

Conclusion

We discussed a strategy for developing learning materials for many languages and cultures:

- Design sessions and design scripting tools that support interaction, individualization, collaborative learning, and mastery
- International groups of designers for multicultural designs
- Support software tools capable of supporting multiple languages and of facilitating changes during translation and cultural adjustments
- Script editors and interpreters minimizing the need for programmers
- Evaluation and maintenance for multiple languages and cultures

The existence of extensive materials in several languages, with different cultures, allows for extensive research with large numbers of students on the issues of cultural differences. For example, how do students in different cultures differ in the way they learn arithmetic? What are the differences in learning styles in different cultures (e.g., what were the effects of collaborative learning; what sequence of exercises did they need; what common errors were made; what help sequences helped them, etc.)? Much of the student performance records can be kept on the computer and can be analyzed later for these purposes. These ideas are expanded further in Bork and Gunnarsdottir (2001) and in papers at www.ics.uci.edu/~bork.

We can overcome the digital divide and the linguistic divide through careful selection of development and delivery strategies sensitive to cultural and language issues.

Acknowledgment

We wish to acknowledge the many contributions of the late Prof. Bertrand Ibrahim of the University of Geneva, who passed away most unexpectedly in July 2001. He was instrumental in first expanding our attention to the many problems, both subtle and important, of making the production system support multilingual learning units. He contributed much additional design and software to its management. The relatively short description given here of the IDEAL (later DIVA) visual development environment belies the size and complexity of the development effort it required, including maintaining it for us remotely from over 10,000 miles away. Bertrand headed all of that with competence, grace, and humor. His contributions and his friendship will be sorely missed.

We also thank Ervin Sarok, Hong Vo, Tsu-Shu Tseng, Xiaoqing Wu and Yibin Miao for their work on the Script Editor and Interpreter.

This paper is based on an earlier paper entitled Computer-Based Learning Units for Many Languages and Cultures *by Alfred Bork and Rika Yoshii, which appeared in the Proceedings of the International Conference on Computers in Education, December 2002, pp. 924–928, published by IEEE. Copyright 2002 IEEE.*

References

Bork, A. (1987). *Interaction: Lessons from computer-based learning. Interactive media: Working methods and practical applications,* D. Laurillard (Ed.). Chichester, England: Ellis Horwood Limited.

Bork, A. et al. (1992). The Irvine-Geneva course development system. *Proceedings of IFIP* (pp. 253–261), Madrid, Spain, September.

Bork, A., & Gunnarsdottir, S. (2001). *Tutorial distance learning—Rebuilding our educational system.* New York: Kluwer Academic.

Campione, M., & Walrath, K. (1998). *The Java tutorial* (2nd ed.). Reading, MA: Addison Wesley Longman.

Comrie, B., Matthews, S., & Polinsky, M. (1996). *The atlas of languages: The origin and development of languages throughout the world.* New York: Facts on File.

Crystal, D. (1997). *English as a global language.* Cambridge: Cambridge University Press.

Davis, J. (2003). *Media ON Demand: MonD player.* Sydney: Classroom Video.

Franklin, S. et al. (1985). *StringAnalysis Unit reference guide, Ports Unit reference guide, Keyed Files reference guide.* Educational Technology Center, University of California, Irvine.

The Geneva Script Editor images were obtained from http://cui.unige.ch/eao/ideal/SyncEd/doc/script.gif and big.gif

Hertz, R. (1987). *Computers in the language classroom.* Reading, MA: Addison-Wesley.

Ibrahim, B. (1989). Software engineering techniques for CAL. *Education & Computing, 5*, 215–222.

Ibrahim, B. (1990). Courseware CAD. *Proceedings of the IFIP fifth World Conference on Computers in Education* (pp. 383–389). Sydney, Australia, 9–13 July, North-Holland.

Katada, F. (2002). The linguistic divide, autolinguals, and the notion of education-for-all. *Proceedings of the International Conference on Computers in Education 2002* (pp. 1522–1523). IEEE Computer Society.

Katada, F. (2003). A new aspect of language education in the ubiquitous age. *Proceedings of the EDMEDIA Conference*, AACE.

Lo Bianco, J. (1999). *Globalisation: Frame word for education and training, human capital and human development/rights.* Melbourne: Language Australia Ltd.

Lo Bianco, J. (Ed.). (2002). *Voices from Phnom Penh, Development & language: Global influences & local effects.* Melbourne: Language Australia Ltd.

McArthur, T. (2002). *The Oxford Guide to World Englishes.* Oxford: Oxford University Press.

Phillipson, R. (2002). Global English and local language policies. *Englishes in Asia: Communication, identity, power and education.* A. Kirkpatrick (Ed.). Melbourne: Language Australian Ltd.

Yoshii, R. (2002). The CSUSM script editor-interpreter pair: Tools for creating conversational tutoring systems, *Proceedings of the 8th ALN-Sloan Conference.*

Yoshii, R. et al. (1992). Strategies for interaction: Programs with video for learning languages. *Journal of Interactive Instruction Development, 5*(2), 3–9.

Yoshii, R., Katada, F., Alsadeqi, F., & Zhang, F. (2003). Reaching students of many languages and cultures. *Proceedings of the EDMEDIA Conference*, AACE.

Zhang, F., & Newman, D. (2003). Speech tool, Canberra, Australia, University of Canberra, Australia.

Chapter VI

Designing for Learning in Narrative Multimedia Environments

Lisa Gjedde, Danish University of Education, Denmark

Abstract

Narrative is fundamental for learning and the construction of meaning. In the design of interactive learning programs, the need for narrative is often neglected, and the emphasis is on information design rather than the design of experiential learning environments. This chapter presents research related to the development of two prototypes of narrative interactive multimedia learning environments, from an experiential and situated learning perspective and proposes a model for a narrative learning process, related to a situated and experiential learning perspective.

Background

Narrative is fundamental for the construction of meaning on a personal as well as on a community level. The narrative format has been a traditional way of teaching in many cultures, and teachers may develop a competence as storytellers, drawing on narrative for motivation, and for experiential and contextual learning by using stories or having the learner's develop stories themselves (Gudmundsdottir, 1991). The concept of narrative encompasses both the narrative expression in the form of story-making and narrative as a cognitive tool for the construction of knowledge, which includes the construction of culturally embedded knowledge as well as being an important part of knowledge sharing (Bruner, 1990; Schank, 1995). It also plays an important part in collaborative and experiential learning. The concept of situated and collaborative learning has been put forth by Brown, Collins, and Duguid, (1989) in their seminal article on Situated Cognition and the Culture of Learning: "Learning, both outside and inside school, advances through collaborative social interaction and the social construction of knowledge." The role of narrative in this learning process is important for distributed and embedded knowledge.

Narrative and Multimedia

Research into interactive multimedia as a resource for instruction and learning has previously pointed to problems in the organization and presentation of the material in relation to the cognitive processes of the students. Researchers from the MENO-project (Multimedia in Education and Narrative Organisation), located at the Open University and University of Sussex, have been investigating the role of narrative in relation to comprehension and learning in interactive multimedia, based on findings that the degree of narrative structure would affect the learners' level of comprehension. They found (Laurillard et al., 1998) that "learners working on interactive media with no clear narrative structure display learning behaviour that is generally unfocused and inconclusive." Based on a hypothesis of narrative as fundamental for learning, they designed an experimental study with three versions of material on a CD-ROM, with different degrees of narrative structure, and tested the different versions in classroom settings. The CD-ROM offered video sequences and a notepad for collecting material as well as questions to guide the exploration. Their conclusions point to the importance of designing interactive multimedia environments (Plowman et al., 1999), "so learners are able to both find narrative coherence and generate it for themselves." Groundbreaking cognitive psychologist and AI-researcher Roger Schank (1995), has likewise found narrative reasoning and construction to be fundamental for cognitive processes. At a theoretical level, Schank (with Abelsson) has contributed seminally through his cognitive models of goals, scripts, and plans. At the level of development and research, he has developed several prototypes and multimedia training programs that draw on narrative elements like case stories. He has advocated different learning architectures, which offers the possibility for sharing knowledge and natural learning and that stories can be used as a fundamental mode of communication and learning not only in case-based learning architectures but also in exploratory and incidental learning. Schank's prototypes of learning architectures with their call for life-like learning situations can be seen as exponents for experiential learning (Schank & Cleary, 1995).

The above-mentioned projects focused on their exploration of narrative in relation to educational and cognitive processes. They, however, do not provide prototypes that afford an exploration of the potentials of learning in an open environment, where the learner's own production of multimedia narratives is supported by offering multimedia tools.

Experiential learning is most often characterized by learning from primary experience. In relation to the research projects presented here, it is suggested that a fictional and imagination-based experience may offer a context for experiential learning that may provide material for expression and reflection. An influential model for experiential learning, which has been developed by David A. Kolb, draws on the work of John Dewey and Jean Piaget. However, in relation to the development of principles for the design of narrative interactive learning environments, it is important to include a focus on the situated and social aspects of the learning process.

There are potential learning advantages to be gained by constructing multimedia learning environments, not primarily as way of presenting encyclopedia-style factual material, but rather through offering the learners an experiential pathway into the material. It is further suggested that this may be enhanced by providing a narrative experience through a narrative framework, through narrative visual elements, as well as offering multimedia tools for narrative construction.

This chapter raises some questions related to the development of such prototypes of narrative interactive multimedia learning environments from an experiential and situated learning perspective and suggests a model for a narrative learning process, related to a situated and experiential learning perspective.

Design of Narrative Interactive
Learning Environments

Designers of educational interactive multimedia programs are facing a challenge as to how to design learning environments that may enhance the collaborative learning that is situated as well as cognitive, through the use of narrative in the design and content. They are also facing the challenge of how to engage the learner in interactive experiences that are meaningful at the level of participation and expression of the learner. The participation may be in an immersive experience that allows the learner to actively engage in the action or to identify with the protagonist of the story. It may also be an experience with elements of role-playing, where the learner takes the action forward by using imagination as well as factual knowledge, and thus interacts by moving the story line forward. Engaging the learner in an imaginative productive way, where the learner is guided to participate in the development of the narrative plot and contribute to the development of the story, may be a way of engaging the learner at multiple levels of involvement.

Often, the use of story in education presents the teacher in a role as storyteller and the students as listeners that follow the unfolding of the narrative. The use of narrative in educational media calls for ways to engage the learner in a process of narrative that is meaningful and fully draws on the possibilities of the media for creation of media expression by the user, and thus for engaging the learner at different levels.

By placing the learner in the role as a storyteller, the learning context becomes one that may enhance the level of involvement as well as the inclusiveness of the situation, as the learner may approach the task from a different point of view and use different modalities of expression: images, sound, movement, etc.

Another issue to be explored in the development of narrative multimedia learning environments concerns the creation of content that is meaningful, that may be engaging for the learner and takes into consideration possible differences in gender-specific interests and social and cultural backgrounds.

Some of these issues related to the development of an architecture and design for narrative based on principles for experiential and situated learning, with the creation of authentic tasks, have been explored in two research projects funded by the Danish Ministry of Education, as part of a program to further the development and research of the use of ICT in schools.

Participatory Content Design

The Narrative Universes of Children

This project is on the creation of content and the design of interactive multimedia narratives by children within the Danish Language and Art curriculum. The project involved students of Grades 4 to 6 in a study drawing on principles of participatory design. Four classes at four different schools, numbering about 100 students and six teachers, participated in this project, which aimed at exploring children's narrative universes and their narrative construction and collaboration in multimedia productions and the creation of content design supporting that.

The research design included two separate phases. The first phase was an investigation of the narrative universes, which the children in this age group produced, when prompted to produce stories and develop imagery to illustrate them. The children produced stories and drawings, working in groups, for a period of weeks. They were allowed to use different modes of expression, ranging from making giant storybooks to be used for the kindergarten pupils, to the use of tape recorders and puppet theatre. The main purpose with this first phase was to prompt the creation of narrative material in order to inform the design process for the animation program. In this way, the learners would help create relevant content material, which subsequently could be used in relation to the animation program they were to use in the second phase.

The second phase focused on the learner's construction of interactive narratives using a simple animation program that allowed for production of interactive multimedia narratives by the learners. Based on the analysis of the stories and narrative universes created by the children during the first phase, a series of narrative universes was developed by the researchers based on the content created by the children. These universes were then produced into graphic material, by professional artists, in order to be used by the learners in the animation program.

The animation program allowed the learner to use these images and also to construct and modify the images and animations and the use of text and sound. This led to the creation of a rich material of interactive stories provided by the learners as well as classroom observation of their collaborative processes in their construction of the interactive narratives. This process in which most of the students where highly motivated, led to other processes of informal collaborative learning leading to mastery of the program and production of the story in which they were involved.

The collaborative learning was expressed in the creation of shared environments, with narrative elements, e.g., characters, settings, and themes. The program aimed at creating a context that would support the development of the learners' narrative competences and their construction of interactive narratives that were relevant to them, and it would also support their sharing of experiences. A further analysis of this rich material may reveal more of the learner's strategies for developing interactive media literacy and expressive nonlinear narrative competencies, and how this type of learning environment may support situated and collaborative learning and knowledge construction.

Narrative Framework – Narrative Expression

Another project related to the development and research of narrative multimedia learning environments is the project "Narrative in interactive Web-based learning environments." This project explores the interplay between the narrative context that includes a narrative setting, with access to resources including stills, audio, and text, and the learner's collaborative production of narratives using these resources. The prototypes are produced and explored as action research using a qualitative methodology. It is an iterative design process involving an educational setting with three secondary schools with students in Grades 8 and 9.

In order to facilitate this process of collaborative learning, it is important that the context be motivating and appealing and that it offer familiar and interesting figures, settings, and issues that may be the frame for further exploration and narrative development relating to that theme (Gjedde, 2002). Part of the development of the script for the frame narrative included the showing of documentary film material from the historical period that this multimedia learning program addressed. This film was shown to the target group of Grade 8 students, and they were asked to fill out a questionnaire, subsequently, that focused on the different content areas of the film about the German occupation of Denmark during the Second World War, rating it for interest. The questionnaire and discussion of the film showed gender-specific preferences for the subjects. These were addressed in the development of the script for the frame narrative in order to provide content material, which would be interesting and motivating for the different students in relation to their preferences.

The illustrations that are used in this Web-based interactive multimedia program were made by an award-winning Danish artist. By applying a certain aesthetic expression on purpose, they are meant to address the target group and help create an immersive experience.

Figure 1: Multimedia narrative interface

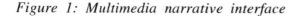

Figure 1 shows part of the room, which is the main interface in the program. It is navigable at 360 degrees, allowing the learner to explore the room and the artifacts, which are related to the narrative learning process.

Most of the artifacts are interactive and will open up to the activities that are available in this learning environment. The activation of the picture over the desk, which is indicated on the figure, will take the learner into the frame narrative. The frame narrative will guide the learner through some fictional but historically correct episodes, and lead the learner to some questions to continue the storytelling, either from the point of view of the male or female protagonist. The book on the table will provide access to a specially designed Web builder. Through this production tool, material from the databases holding sound and image files can be integrated in the Web-based multimedia stories produced by the learners. All the relevant source materials and production tools can be accessed as artifacts in the room, being held, for instance, in the cupboard, the book on the table, and the phone. This coherence between the graphic interface and the narrative environment is done in order to provide for a *pervasive narrative experience*, in which all actions and all materials are embedded in the context of the frame narrative. This is done in order to support the use of a narrative logic and narrative reasoning involved in the narrative experience, which provides for a shared learning environment that may facilitate the building of stories involving shared knowledge and experience in a community of practice.

Toward a Narrative Learning Process

Storytelling and the use of narrative in interactive multimedia programs can offer ways of engaging with the material at different levels. The narrative elements and the way they are embedded in an interactive learning environment can serve as cognitive artifacts, which support the construction of meaning through structure, content, and culturally implicated values. The narratives offer immersive experiences, which allow the user to engage at an emotional level and involve the user with different emotional states.

Developing and producing stories stimulates narrative thinking and a sense of causal relationships and analogy. It brings about possibilities for identification with the characters and situations, and in this way, it allows for multiple perspectives on situations and different points of view that are essential social skills. The development of this level of understanding and the competence to interpret and construct meaning are important skills and values in terms of the personal development and sense of cultural identity and personal values of the learner.

The stories offer materials for interpretation and reflection, and a shared cultural environment for doing so. In the interactive learning environment, the reflective process is distributed by the use of interactive log books and online conferences that allows for reflection on the process and productions.

The narrative learning process is framed by stories that are contextual, that make up the shared conceptual learning environment, which is characterized by its setting, characters, actions, and themes. The learner's development of the stories may lead to a process of research into the elements and factual material that are necessary for the unfolding of the story. The process of the articulation of the narratives in an interactive multimedia production may lead to the sharing of knowledge in a way that is socially and cognitively inclusive.

Through the narrative expression and articulation in digital media, a process that is experiential as well as situated in communities of practice, may be initiated. This model on a narrative learning process is presented in Figure 2.

The model for the narrative learning process in the interactive multimedia learning environment described above, involves five distinct learning approaches and activities that are interrelated and mutually supportive. This model suggests a process of dynamic learning in which the elements are synergically related:

Figure 2: Narrative learning process

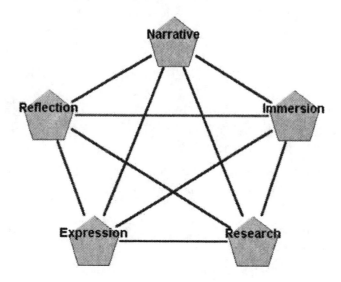

1.   *Narrative*. The top point of the pentad refers to the concept of narrative that is based on the premise that narrative is an important experiential and contextual frame and approach to learning. It relates to the narrative content as well as to the organizing narrative structure.

2.   *Immersion*. The concept of immersion is related to the experience of narrative content and structure. It is through the story and the related imaginative story elements that the learner experiences the immersion. It may be experienced further in the learning process as immersion in the subject matter and a research activity that is then expressed in the learner's own narrative articulation.

3.   *Research*. The activity of research is a learner-directed activity delving into information and themes related to the narrative and the curricular areas it is exploring. It is focused by the narrative and supported by the sense of immersion into the subject.

4.   *Expression*. The activity of expression is based on the research activity and is held in line by the narrative, which is the context it relates to and it further elaborates on or uses as a base for the construct of new narratives. It is also supported by the sense of immersion into the narrative context and characters.

5.   *Reflection*. This activity can be a reflection by the learners on the material presented in narrative or nonfiction form, as well as on the narrative expression produced by the fellow learners. It is thus offering the teacher an avenue for reflecting on the learners' concepts as they are expressed in narrative form. It can encompass a hermeneutic as well as an aesthetic, imaginative, and expressive process.

These above-mentioned points are relevant parameters to include in the evaluation of the learning potentials of narrative interactive learning environments. Key questions to be asked in such an evaluation include the following:

- To what extent does the narrative interactive learning environment offer a narrative experience with a content that is relevant, engaging, and pervasive?

- Does it provide tools for the learner to participate in a process of articulation?

- Is it to be used with a learning scenario that includes a process of reflection?

- What roles does it offer the learner and the teacher?

Conclusion

Experiential and narrative learning processes move the focus from the instructor toward the learner. It moves it from the transfer of information, toward the hermeneutic process of interpretation and construction of meaning. By building architectures for learning in interactive multimedia environments that take into account the hermeneutic narrative process and the expressive narrative process, reflection on the learner's own expression is included.

Principles for the development of narrative multimedia learning environments must ideally be based on educational and psychological principles as well as on including production theory, in order to offer the potentials for a satisfactory learning experience.

Using the approach of narrative learning may further the knowledge of how to design and make available an interactive multimedia learning environment that can support the learner toward the understanding of the events and the meaning they hold and not just aim at achieving knowledge of factual events. Having this as the overarching learning paradigm supporting the design, it may allow for the learners to enter into levels of learning in which they may be more likely to be involved at personal levels. Thus, the boundaries between formal and nonformal learning environments may be blurred and allow for the learners to be part of communities of practice that are situated in experiential settings and cater to their needs to express their own goals and learning.

Acknowledgments

The projects "The Narrative Universes of Children" and "Narrative in interactive Web-based learning environments" are funded by the Danish Ministry of Education, "ITMF-programme."

The project "The Narrative Universes of Children" has been carried out in collaboration with Leif Gredsted, Associate Professor, DPU.

References

Bruner, J. (1990). *Acts of meaning.* Cambridge, MA: Harvard University Press.

Dewey, J. (1939). *Education and experience.* New York: Collier Books.

Gjedde, L. (2002). Context, cognition and narrative experience in Sophies World. In B. H. Sørensen, & O. Danielsen (Eds.), *Learning and narrativity in digital media.* Samfundslitteratur: København.

Gudmundsdottir, S. (1991). Story-maker, story-teller; narrative structures in curriculum. *Journal of Curriculum Studies, 23*(3), 207–218.

Kolb, D. (1984). *Experiential learning: Experience as the source of learning and development.* Englewood Cliffs, NJ: Prentice Hall.

Laurillard, D., Stratfold, M., Luckin, R., Plowman, L., & Taylor, J. (1998). Multimedia and the learner's experience of narrative. *Computers and Education, 31,* 229–242.

Mandler, J. (1984). *Stories, scripts, and scenes: Aspects of Schema Theory.* Hillsdale, NJ: Erlbaum.

Plowman, L., Luckin, R., Laurillard, D., Stratfold, M., & Taylor, J. (1999). Designing multimedia for learning: Narrative guidance and narrative construction. *Proceedings CHI'99:ACM Conference on Human Factors in Computing Systems* (pp. 310–317). Pittsburgh, PA, USA,15–20 May.

Schank, R. C., & Abelson, R. P. (1995). *Knowledge and memory: The real story.* J. R. S. Wyer. Hilldale, NJ: LEA.

Schank, R. C., & Cleary, C. (1995). *Engines for education.* Hilldale, NJ: LEA.

Part II

Pedagogical Issues

Chapter VII

Principles of Educational Software Design

Vassilios Dagdilelis, University of Macedonia, Greece

Abstract

Despite the generalized use of Information and Communication Technologies (ICT) in teaching, their educational applications have not yet been standardized: a general consensus does not exist on how ICT can be applied to teaching nor on how educational software must be constructed. In this chapter, it is argued in favor of educational software construction being guided by a didactic problematique. In this framework we consider as a promising software category mindtools and, in particular, the so-called open microworlds. Their design must be guided by a number of principles: the tool logique, the multiple interface and the multiple representations principles. In this chapter, a detailed critique of these principles is also presented.

Introduction

From the time computers were invented until today, this latest decade has been intensely characterized, more than any of the previous ones, by the infiltration of the so-called new technologies in everyday life. Information and Communication Technologies (ICT) are also being integrated into education at all levels. In fact, this integration is a two-way process, as it has consequences for the educational system in which ICT are integrated. The influence of ICT on the way lessons are planned and conducted, on the administration of teaching institutions (schools, universities, and others), on existing teaching methodologies, on evaluation, and finally on the educational system in general, is so deep rooted, that ICT is likely to be the cause of a complete restructuring of the entire educational system.

Despite their use in teaching, which is constantly expanding, as well as the important influence they have on transforming current curricula, the educational applications of ICT have not yet been standardized, meaning that a general consensus does not exist on how ICT can be applied to teaching and a consensus does not exist that can be used as a general guideline for the development of educational software.

More specifically, concerning those points where a consensus of opinion does not exist, the following could be stated:

- **The characteristics of educational software:** There are many categories of educational software, which correspond to the different characteristics of that educational software as well as what its most appropriate use might be. The general characteristics of the software and its use are based on, explicitly or implicitly, learning theories, and pedagogic and didactic assumptions; therefore, these different points of view may be incompatible.

- **The usefulness of computers and educational software:** In certain situations, the effects of ICT on the educational system are obvious. For example, ICT have enabled long-distance learning to be reorganized based on new foundations due to the creation of computing networks and communication mechanisms among users at multiple levels (synchronous or asynchronous, with images, sound, video).

  In the majority of cases, even though the use of ICT is considered imperative, because, theoretically at least, ICT improve the lesson, this improvement, however, has not been amply documented. In other words, even though a basic reason for the use of ICT in education is the hypothesis that they improve both teaching and learning, the conditions that render teaching more effective are not actually known, and often, related research does not highlight any significant difference in the quality of the lessons based on ICT (http://teleeducation.nb.ca/nosignificantdifference/). Opinions have also been expressed which indirectly question the overall usefulness of ICT as a means of teaching support (Cuban, 2001; Stoll, 2000).

- **The validity and theoretical support of experimental data:** All over the world, experimental teaching methods and research studies are being carried out in order to discern the particular uses that will be most effective from a teaching perspective. One part of the research, as well as one section of the international literature related to the pedagogic uses of ICT, is geared at describing the characteristics of successful educational software. Unfortunately, research on teaching in the last few years, even though numerous, is not usually accompanied by a satisfactory theoretical background and thus has not managed to come up with substantial data to enable the design of adequate educational software and organize effective didactic situations.

- **The absence of a method for the construction of educational software:** Nowadays, two major categories appear to exist in the way educational software is constructed, each of which comprises several subcategories. In the first, the focus is on technology, meaning the technical features of the software and its construction method. In the second, the starting point is the teaching/learning process the software will support.

In this chapter, it is argued in favor of educational software construction being guided by a *didactic problématique*. Further, educational software must be created according to the most up-to-date learning theories and, more specifically, constructivism.

In this framework, the most promising software category is *mindtools* and, in particular, the so-called *open microworlds*.

The research to date, in conjunction with the large number of available educational software and, in general, digitalized educational material, have contributed to the relative progress that has taken place, but only in certain fields. Thus, concerning these mindtools, we have at our disposal a know-how that allows us to design, but only in certain situations, educational software and more general educational environments with notable functional features. This know-how can be summarized in the form of general design principles on which an educational environment can be based (or at least some sections of it).

These principles are the following:

- The principle of *tool logic*: Computers and ICT in general, should be used as tools in order to make learning easier.

- The principle of multiple interface: The interface should offer the users the ability to express themselves not only by direct manipulation of objects but also with an active formulation of commands and instructions.

- The principle of multiple representations: Knowledge within the context of educational environments should be expressed in many ways, through multiple frameworks that are interconnected and equivalent from a functional point of view.

In the following paragraphs, a detailed critique of these principles is also presented.

Educational Software Development Methods

Educational software was an area in which a medium level of production existed 20 years ago, however, in the last decade, in which time the graphical user interface (GUI) was established, production has become intense. Educational software originated mainly from two different sources, which in many cases cooperated: one source was software-producing companies and the other was the academic institutions, such as university laboratories or research centers and institutes (Harvey, 1995; van der Mast, 1995). This dual source essentially corresponds to the fact that in the last decade there has been significant progress, both in the level of technological know-how as well as in teaching theory, because current teaching know-how, despite the serious drawbacks pointed out in the introduction, has greatly improved in comparison to 20 years ago.

As was natural, the large amount of production gradually led to the development of various models of educational software, which can be used as guidelines in the creation of new educational software; a creation which, very likely may, in turn, lead to the improvement or even to a radical revision of existing models. Needless to say, this cycle can continue for a long period of time.

In the international literature, numerous models on the construction of educational software have been proposed, such as that described by Lage et al. (2002). This representative model proposes the use of "an incremental prototype life cycle" of 11 stages along general lines that must be followed for the construction of educational software. It is obvious that this model has been influenced by the general methodology of software engineering and attempts to adapt its general characteristics to educational software.

This type of methodology, as well as others like it, even though they might be considered effective from the point of view of developing software, is independent of both its *content* and its *didactic use*. This model, which is structured according to the principles of software engineering, does not actually focus on the most important aspect of educational software, namely, its teaching characteristics. Therefore, the models in this category are useful in describing the process for the development of educational software but have little value as tools for analyzing how useful particular educational software is for teaching purposes.

Another method used generally in the design of educational means and environments (Instructional Design) can also be used, such as the model ADDIE (Analysis, Design, Development, Implementation, Evaluation). This category is usually referred to as *tutorial* software.

One final category we often come across is that which proposes lists of practical advice or checklists covering certain aspects of educational software (Beale & Sharples, 2002), with the drawback that it does not present a comprehensive set of principles on which this type of environment can be constructed.

The development of models or methods for the construction and use of educational software is, as a rule, either oriented toward the rationale of software engineering, or, consequently lacking in teaching parity, refers to the teaching characteristics of the software and is thus often fragmentary.

It is obvious that the construction of educational software should be based on some method, otherwise it is in danger of failing, of costing too much, or of being greatly delayed. This method, however, should be subject to the didactic rationale and not the other way round (Reusser, 1994). The basic characteristic of educational software should be its didactic efficiency rather than its technological supremacy, even though this, of course, is also desired.

Knowledge Theories and Didactic Problématique

Behaviorism and Constructivism

The many types of contemporary educational environments are certainly well-known: from the simplest drill-and-practice-type software to the more complex educational microworlds, a gamut of educational applications exists with a wide range of technical features, the interface, the audience they are geared to, and the goals aimed at. The wealth of environments is enormous, and their categorizations can be based on numerous criteria. It is generally accepted that the design of educational environments, whether digital or not, is guided, even at a subconscious level, by the pedagogic theories of the manufacturers. The choice of a theory is so important that most times it determines, directly or indirectly, the characteristics of the educational environment or even its type. Therefore, a large section of the educational applications with essential aims to convey knowledge and skills, many e-books for instance, belong to the behaviorist school (Collins, 1996).

Behaviorism and constructivism are two widely spread learning theories that are fundamentally different in their outlooks.

Behaviorism, which appears at an international level to be waning, assumes that learning is the result of a stimulus–response process. Learning is seen largely to be a passive procedure, where the subject attempts to adapt to the environment.

The constructivist approach, at polar ends with the behaviorist, is based on the hypothesis that subjects construct their own, personal knowledge through interaction with the environment; while learning essentially consists of a teaching methodology based on assimilating new information and then adapting the subject's mental structures in such a way as to be compatible with the new data. In the constructivist learning model, the subject, in attempting to explain or to examine questions, formulates hypotheses; searches for ways to verify or disprove these hypotheses; interacts with his or her environment (both material and human); redirects the results of experiences; and constantly reconstructs intellectual structures, the mental shapes, in such a way as to integrate them with the new data. Therefore, the educational environments of the constructivist paradigm differ greatly from those based on the behaviorism, because they favor active learning, cooperation between learners, investigation, formulation of hypotheses, as well as their verification or disproof. In other words, they promote actions and activities similar to scientific work, even though in reality, scientists' work is fundamentally different than that of students' work.

The Constructivist Approach

To a large extent, the various categories of educational software correspond to those of learning theories, which they are based on. For this reason, there is no general consensus on educational software. On the contrary, these various categories coexist. As is natural within the framework of the various schools of thought, extended argumentation has been put forward from all sides.

The main argument for the preference of the constructivist approach and, subsequently, for cognitive tools, can be expressed by borrowing the character-istic metaphor of Resnick et al. (1996), who, arguing in favor of the "constructivist" environments, claim that all parents would prefer their children to learn to play the piano rather than learn to use a stereo. Even though it is much easier to use a stereo, the experience offered in learning to play a musical instrument as well as the likelihood of composing musical scores is incomparably richer than merely using even the most advanced electronic device.

Of course, the counterargument to this is that if someone wants to listen to high-quality music, 99 times out of 100, they will use a stereophonic system rather than attempt the arduous task of learning to play the piano. Moreover, it is almost certain that even those people who know how to play the piano own some kind of stereophonic system.

Nevertheless, a basic part of the authors' reasoning remains indisputable: the richest experiences are not gained by the simplest means, perhaps the opposite occurs—experiences are usually analogous to *the power of expression* the means offers the user. In this way, learning the piano decisively contributes to the creation and development of a relationship between the person and music that is rich in feelings. It must be admitted, however, that sometimes this relationship requires the use of devices that reproduce rather than produce sound, that is, the stereo, not the piano.

What then, if any, is the conclusion? We could say that the choice of the *means* is determined by the type of *use* one requires. This is also the case for educational software—its characteristics depend on the use for which it was made.

Mindtools

Throughout human history, technology has obviously contributed to the development of the human intellect and especially to that of learning. Pea (1985) defined *cognitive technology* as "any medium that helps transcend the limits of the mind, such as memory, in activities of thinking, learning and problem solving." Within this more general framework, certain computing environments, more precisely the environments and their didactic use, are usually characterized as *cognitive tools* (Collins, 2000) or even as *mindtools* (Jonassen, 2000), i.e., "computer-based tools and learning environments that have been adapted or developed a function as intellectual partners with the learner in order to engage and facilitate critical thinking and higher order learning" (p. 9). This category of educational environments presents certain significant didactic features.

There are numerous definitions and a relatively adequate amount of literature on cognitive tools or mindtools. According to Jonassen, Peck, and Wilson (1999), an educational environment should support knowledge construction, explorations, learning by doing, learning by conversing, intellectual partners that support learning by reflecting. On the basis of this analysis, therefore, it is possible to evaluate the various sections and functions of educational software, or more precisely, of an educational environment. Those sections and functions that serve or support the above-mentioned uses are thus more desirable. For example, the existence of a system of written communication between learners is a desirable characteristic if it is a prerequisite for the creation of communication and subsequently a type of social interaction between learners; this, however, is a characteristic of particular significance in the development of knowledge on the subject according to current didactic theories (Laborde, 1983). It should be emphasized that this criterion is too broad and, as a consequence, has only limited usability.

The choice of a specific group of software and the knowledge theory supporting it, unavoidably creates a generalization of design principles or, more precisely, a generalized criterion: if the end result is the creation of an educational software, of an educational environment intended to function as a cognitive tool, then its various sections and their functions must also be in accordance with this same rationale.

Open Environments and Open Microworlds

Cognitive tools are not defined in any one way, and there are many types of software that fall into this category. The principles of their design have a general character, and although they cannot be applied to all types of educational environments, they are nevertheless useful as guides in the design of many such environments.

Cognitive tools, by their nature, are *open environments*. Those environments that do not have predetermined lessons or activities that the learner must follow but allow for the free development of activities within the framework of an area of knowledge can be considered as open environments.

There are many types of such environments, from Logo to the current ones such as the environments of so-called Dynamic Geometry (Bellemain, 1992) and others that are based on the synthesis of preexisting components (Rochelle et al., 1999). They have a number of characteristics in common that characterize them as mindtools and that have been "well-established" and, up to a point, have a theoretical basis.

Despite the fact that in recent years, open environments have been recognized as valuable learning environments, certain reservations have also been stated.

Collins (2000) asked whether the environment should encourage guided learning or exploratory learning, and highlighted the fact that open environments actually allow the learner to "play around" with the software. He, himself, however, argued in favor of environments which in the beginning are rather guided until the learners gain a certain level of skill in order to be able to use them on their own and who gradually will be liberated. In reality, however, all educational software functions within the particular context of a *teaching situation*. As a rule, learners are required to solve a problem or to explore the various angles of a problem. So, it is unlikely that they "play around" (Hoyles & Noss, 1993).

A special category of software with a large teaching potential includes the so-called *open microworlds*, that is, the environments in which predetermined activities and lessons do not exist, but where learners can define new objects (programs, geometric shapes, functions, natural laws) as well as the relationships between them, in order to experiment (Hoyles & Noss, 1993; Bellemain, 1992; Tinker, 1993).

The developments of open environments, which favor experimental learning and problem solving, have proliferated in recent years. In these environments, a specified teaching scenario or route does not exist; the teaching material that accompanies these environments simply indicates the type of didactic situation.

The potential of these environments is of particular importance to teaching: the ability to choose to decrease the teaching noise (that is, undesirable side effects such as extremely long calculations that can totally overshadow the real objective of the lesson), the intelligent help (in conjunction with intelligent messages), and the programming by demonstration (Bellemain, 1992; Cypher, 1994).

Furthermore, these environments allow learners to express their ideas, even if erroneous, and apply them until they come to a dead-end or to an obviously wrong conclusion (Dagdilelis et al., 2003). If we accept the basic principles of constructivism (Balacheff, 1986; translation from French), these are necessary conditions in order "to provoke a knowledge confrontation and thus develop learners' perceptions." Resnick et al. (1996) considered data that make the environment familiar to also be important. This familiarity does not aim at giving the learner motives but rather is necessary in order for the learner to be able to use a representational model in order to find the solution to the proposed problem. Such tools enable learners to represent their thought processes in external models for examination and reflection, and may further help them to improve these processes (Emrah, 1995).

The general principles described below are related to open environments designed with the rationale characteristic of the bulk of mindtools.

The Principle of *Tool Logic*

By nature, cognitive tools consist of environments in which the learner can explore phenomena from various angles and, by experimenting with these, reach certain conclusions. They are connected, either directly or indirectly, with possibly more than one field of knowledge (for example, working with Excel on a certain kind of problem requires a combination of programming and mathematics). They often provide the learner with the representation of a microworld, either natural or intellectual, and at the same time a series of tools needed for its exploration. For example, the so-called Dynamic Geometry environments [such as Cabri-Geometer (Bellemain, 1992) or Geometer Sketchpad (Roschelle & Jackiw, 2000)] consist of a simulation of Euclidian space (a totally mental construction that does not exist in reality), whereas the environments for the study of natural phenomena (such as Interactive Physics, 2003) represent natural space in which Newton's laws hold.

An important issue that arises is one concerning the dichotomy between an environment of "physical and epistemological faithfulness" (Collins, 2000). A true natural representation means that the educational environment depicts the actual situation, whereas an epistemological one means that in the educational environment, the same laws (mathematical, natural, etc.) apply, which also exist in nature. The most appropriate choice for either one or the other situation, or to be more precise, the necessity for natural faithfulness, because the other option is regarded as imperative, depends on the use the software is geared for. For example, the study of space from a geometric perspective might demand its simulation in order for the learner to be able to relate to and solve geometric problems under "real" conditions, such as measuring the distances of two points, which between them are not visible, or measuring the area of a golf course, which has an odd shape with a small lake in the middle. On the other hand, where the object of study might be the so-called theoretical (Euclidian) geometry, in which case the environment must "simulate" Euclidian space that, as stated above, does not actually exist because it is simply an intellectual construction, scientific faithfulness is adequate and sufficient.

The existence of natural faithfulness is a significant factor in the learning of concepts and relationships on account that it contains elements familiar to the learner. Furthermore, the existence of natural faithfulness makes it easier to apply the principle of *authenticity*, in other words, the teaching requirement for contextualized learning in an environment that is as close as possible to reality (Collins, 2000). Even though this principle has validity, the main object of research in a cognitive tool is not so much natural faithfulness as epistemological faithfulness, that is, the agreement of the environment and the reactions with the simulated system (Resnick et al., 1996).

Epistemological or physical faithfulness is not, however, a sufficient condition to justify the use of ICT. For example, an environment in which simply the construction of geometric shapes is possible does not make it a cognitive tool. The criterion is the principle of tool logic and its *didactic economy*. An educational environment contains a particular tool that supports a teaching method or the learning of certain concepts, and it should be designed as such. In addition, however, the potential of the teaching environment should be higher than that of usual environments. For example, software for physics should offer greater possibilities than that available in an actual laboratory. In other words, the design of an educational environment should be based on specific teaching needs, which are revealed by research on teaching or from the experience of teachers, rather than the other way around. This, of course, does not mean that the educational environment cannot break into new possibilities, but rather that in some way, the educational software should comprise the best possible means for the teaching of a concept or a technique.

Tool logic can, of course, vary as to its exact content from one area of knowledge to another and from one software program to another. Nevertheless, certain characteristics of educational environments, considered as cognitive tools for the learner, seem to play important roles in the learning process:

1. The environment should combine conviviality and usability. This means that the educational software should be simple and easy-to-use. An environment that requires complex procedures often forces the learner to focus on technical details instead of concentrate on the problem at hand. Novice programmers, for instance, often focus on dealing with the syntactic errors instead of with the construction of the algorithm—this is precisely the kind of *teaching noise* mentioned above. This fact has led to the creation of simpler languages in order to introduce learners to programming. A practical measure of usability is the effort and time needed to accomplish a task. More generally, the key criterion of a system's usability is the extent to which it enables people who use it to understand it, to learn and to make changes (Nielsen & Mack, 1994).

2. The possibility of avoiding *teaching noise* focuses on the essence (Tall, 1993). Teaching noise does not only come from a nonoptimal interface, as was the case in the above paragraph, but also from the use of methods and procedures that are inappropriate for the user. An essential function of educational environments is that in solving a problem, the user does not get caught up in any time-consuming processes that are counterproductive to learning. For example, a software such as Excel executes complex calculations with high precision and thus avoids teaching noise. This means that any in-between procedures that might take a lot of time and do not benefit learning are done away with. Usually, teaching noise can initially be

an *object of learning*, which evolves into a means; and teaching economy often imposes its marginalization in the process of problem solving (Douady, 1993). For instance, basic calculations are an object of learning in the first years of schooling, which however, become the means to solving complex problems in physics and mathematics in the 11th or 12th year of school. Now, if a software allows the problems to be completed quickly, then this releases the learner from a tedious process that has no learning benefit (only the execution of many basic calculations). For this reason, in many software programs, the available information or representations can be increased or reduced, depending on the needs of the lesson (Bellemain, 1992; Dagdilelis et al., 2003).

3. The environment's large potential for expression is revealed in stages through the possibility of creating composite structures, with more specific and stronger tools. The procedures in Logo, the macroconstructions in the environments of dynamic geometry, and the formulae in Excel and the other spreadsheets, are examples of this type, because they offer the user the possibility to compose new objects of the corresponding space (construction processes, geometric shapes, and algebraic relationships, respectively) based on the software's relatively simple primitives.

4. The possibilities to adapt to the user's needs and provide teaching help are given. This is perhaps the most difficult prerequisite from a technical point of view, because adapting to the needs of the user is materialized at multiple levels. For example, a module of the system can offer intelligent guidance in the use of the software. But, adaptation can be extended to more interesting teaching fields. For instance, in a contemporary educational environment, recordability, that is, the ability to continuously record the user's actions, is now a common option that presents interesting possibilities (Bellemain, 1992). Besides the obvious use of these records by the teacher, who, at times, with the help of the software itself, can analyze the learners' actions and gain valuable insights and results, the system can diagnose certain characteristics of the learners and offer them the necessary help by showing them the weaknesses in their solutions or even help them solve the problem in a variety of ways. In certain environments (such as Cabri-Geometer; Bellemain, 1992) of this type, the software can decide on, for the accuracy or not of a question the learner is formulating (e.g., are these points on the same straight line?), whether to point out the possible weaknesses of a program or to propose improvements or even correct solutions reached by the learner.

5. The possibility of communication is provided. Contemporary constructivist theories believe that humans do not learn in isolation but construct their knowledge through interacting with their environment, which consists of

other people, including co-learners and teachers. The progress of network technology in the last decade has created the preconditions for the development of communication systems, even between learners and teachers who are geographically separated. However, it must be emphasized that, despite all its progress, technology is not yet adequately functional, and despite the theories that support the value of communication, we have but a few satisfactory examples of use that surpass the level of being commonplace.

Within tool logic, teaching economy imposes the integration into the environment of those elements that have a meaning from a teaching point of view. Therefore, the parts that characterize the environment, such as the multimedia elements, should serve some teaching goal and should not exist merely for effect.

The most important consequence of the principle of tool logic, however, is the need for educational software to be incorporated *into teaching*. This fact means that it is essential for educational software to be accompanied by a description of the corresponding didactic situations, within the framework in which the application will be used. This is necessary because even the best software is meaningless if it does not function within the context of a didactic situation (Brousseau, 1986a, 1986b). On the other hand, software exists that, although not educational, can be used as a cognitive tool within teaching, such as Excel and spreadsheets generally, as well as mathematics software such as Mathematica and the like.

The opposite phenomenon can, of course, be assumed, of the use of extremely rich software in an elementary way, especially in the situation where a corresponding didactic problématique does not exist.

Role of the Interface and the Principle of Multiple Interface

The interface of contemporary educational environments plays an incredibly significant role in the process of learning, because it essentially determines the way in which learners will formulate their ideas. In this way, the interface indirectly determines an environment's expressive power (Climaco et al., 1993). The expressive power of an environment indicates how quickly and simply the tools enable a description of situations the users can immediately perceive in terms of existing goals and needs. It stands to reason that the environment should support a means of expression that will be simple but at the same time have the ability to formulate complex concepts. These two requirements can, however, be antithetical. In reality, there are at least two different systems that serve them.

Modern interface is characterized by the existence of graphics (GUI). In these new graphic environments the specific elements are the "*image-action*" and the *objectification* metaphor: actions are substituted by the duo *icons* and *actions with the mouse* (for example, clicking on the icon of a diskette has the result of saving the active file). This progress of the interface, in turn, leads to the development of a very interesting ability, that of direct manipulation (Bellemain & Dagdilelis, 1993). With direct manipulation, the user can "handle" objects (their representations) on the monitor, using a mouse directly on the image of the "object." An obvious characteristic of direct manipulation is, of course, that it does not require any kind of formulation on the part of the user. In order to destroy a file, all that is needed is to "throw it away" and to "empty" the "recycling bin." This, however, does not necessarily mean that the nonexplicitly expressed commands in every environment are direct use: in the *e-examples* of NCTM (National Council of Teachers of Mathematics), for instance, there is also a tiny programming environment for primary school children that does not require any written formulation—they use an iconic language—while in the past, there were other software with similar characteristics. In modern graphic environments, concepts and their relationships acquire a pseudomaterial basis, they appear to be—and behave as though they are—materials; for example, in the environments of Dynamic Geometry, the straight-line sections act as though they were elastic (they can elongate or shrink simply by dragging and dropping their ends), and in certain environments of Dynamic Algebra, the graphic representations function as though they are wire (they too permit modifications such as parallel transformation or flexure simply by drag and drop; Function Probe, 1999).

Direct manipulation, in this way, acquires particular importance as a teaching possibility, because it allows the user to express, in a direct way, relationships and choices that, in everyday terms, are unclear, because usually the user can *act* on them but not *express* them. In this way, direct manipulation gives the ability to choose a shade of color from a palette, the free-hand design of a shape, or the construction of a digital object, activities that are possibly familiar to the user but cannot easily be described (Eisenberg, 1996). Moreover, the conflict between "I do" and "I explain how to do" (Duchateau, 1992), is well-known as one of the common difficulties of novice programmers. For example, novice programmers can easily understand the design rule of a recursive shape, such as embedded squares or Koch's snowflakes, but they come up against great difficulty when they attempt to construct a recursive procedure that designs them (Carlisle, 2000; Dalit, 2001).

The advantage that direct manipulation has on teaching is particularly obvious in the cases where it is an essential *teaching variable*, that is, a factor that can greatly affect the teaching and learning processes by being present or absent. Early educational software for geometry, for instance, which were mainly based on the explicit formulation of commands (such as GEOMLAND; Sendov & Sendova, 1995), turned out to be more difficult to use by young learners. In certain cases, the use of the "objects" or at least certain elements of the system is carried out through intermediate iconic mechanisms, such as sliders, of which Microworlds Pro and Avakeeo are well-known examples (Microworlds Pro, 1999; Koutlis & Hatzilacos, 1999). Nowadays, technology even allows for commands to be given indirectly to computers by demonstration (Bellemain, 1992; Cypher, 1994).

Direct manipulation comprises one end of the scale, while on the other end are the explicit formulation environments (such as Logo). Nevertheless, the inexplicit manipulation of objects is not the only solution and can coexist with the explicit expression of commands. International research shows (di Sessa et al., 1995; Hoyles, 1995; Sendov & Sendova, 1995; Laborde & Laborde, 1995) that direct manipulation is neither the only means nor the most appropriate solution for all situations. If direct manipulation offers ease in expression, explicit formulation offers the possibility to express composite concepts and relationships. Written formulation offers a large expression potential to the user, who can describe sophisticated relationships such as recursion or patterns with much greater ease than with either direct or indirect manipulation. In reality, the formulation of definitions, properties, and relationships is a component of the concepts themselves; it requires specialized knowledge that should be cultivated in the learner (Laborde, 1983).

The majority of typical languages, which enables a high degree of structure, are usually programming languages of some sort. Programming languages, of course, have their own teaching value but are, in some way, incredibly decontextualized, which means that they function in abstract and, thus, are often difficult to learn. On the contrary, in recent years, a generation of specific languages has appeared that has been adapted to the particularity of the environments in which they function. Thus, languages are being developed that allow the formulation of geometric or other causal dependencies (Sketchpad, 2003). In fact, the existence of these languages can make the software much more functional, because up to now, the tendency has been for software development to constantly add new features and tools, resulting in the creation of environments with scores of abilities but with problematic in-depth use (Eisenberg, 1996). It is worth noting that this problem as well as its suggested solution were highlighted 30 years ago in the area of programming. Dijkstra (1972) characterized certain languages as "baroque monstrosities" and argued in favor of languages with a small repertory of commands but that had a high possibility of composing new ones.

Particular teaching problems, such as the choice of functional syntax and the appropriate formalism arise due to the existence of specific descriptive languages. However, with the use of various techniques, these problems can nowadays be dealt with to a satisfactory degree.

So, as current research shows, each of the methods of expression (manipulation or formulation) has its advantages and disadvantages; therefore, the best construction strategy for educational environments is to incorporate both methods that have the capacity to be used for contemporary needs. Perhaps the best examples are computers and their operating systems. The two most popular systems (Windows and Unix in various forms) coexist, serving different groups of users and converging to become a "double" nature, as it were—Windows has written commands, while for the Unix-like systems, X-Windows have now become an important component.

Multiple Representations

The progress of technology (high-analysis monitors, fast processors and graphic cards, effective algorithms, etc.) has enabled, to a great extent, the development of technical illustrations with animated or unanimated images or video. Current educational environments are using these new means all the more extensively: animated images that are also interactive. The particularly significant role of images has often been emphasized in the international literature (Tall, 1993; Kaylan, 1993).

The progress of technology has also increased the potential of another section of educational environments, namely, that of *multiple representations*. A representation, in this case, is a system that symbolizes certain knowledge. For example, a mathematical function can be represented as a formula or as a graph; an algorithm can be represented in the form of diagrams or in a textual programming language.

Support multiple representational forms enable the learner to represent concepts and meaningful relationships between concepts both verbally and pictorially (Kozma, 1992) and allow the learner access to the different representations simultaneously, so that interrelationships are directly available (Emrah, 1995).

Multiple representations are not necessarily totally based on pictures. According to Beale et al. (2002), they include interactive systems of "external representations. External representations are observable, and often manipulatable, structures, such as graphs, tables, diagrams or sketches that can aid problem solving or learning" (p. 18). Here, external representations are regarded in the broad sense of the term, including in them *textual representations*, in other words, subordinate texts. The importance of external representations is that each one can comprise a significant teaching aid for the learner, because it contains important information. For example, these types of representations can make obvious the relationship between data-producing sets with common characteristics, tendencies, or properties. Of course, these representations have the disadvantage that, although they make certain properties of the concepts under study obvious, they leave out certain others. Often, one type of external representation is particularly useful in order to solve a certain category of problems but is inappropriate for all the others. This drawback is overcome by the existence of multiple external representations.

Of particular interest are those external representations that are dynamic and interconnected and in fact bidirectional. In other words, they present *symmetrical possibility*. In educational environments, one form of expressing a concept or relationship is often preferred over another, due to the particular *didactic contract* (Brousseau, 1986) that commonly exists in school environments or simply due to technical reasons. Thus, a graphic representation of a function can often result from its analytical expression, and the change to the analytical expression causes a modification of the curve but not the opposite. This modification has been previously pointed out (Bellemain & Dagdilelis, 1993; Schwarz, 1993) and integrated into earlier pilot software or more recently, into well-known software (such as Function Probe, 1999). However, this possibility is limited, as it can be used only for certain categories of functions that are known beforehand. At school, most explored functions are known beforehand, so this is not a concern.

Recent research studies on teaching in various scientific fields have shown (Douady, 1993; Tall, 1993) that *multiple representations* clearly have teaching value. For example, the representation of a mathematical function in an analytical, graphical, and numerical way with the ability of direct interaction between the various frameworks of expression allows the learner to produce more complete images of the concept being examined and to develop significant notions on it, even when lacking basic knowledge (Tall, 1993). Environments should offer the option of choice between one or multiple representations, depending on the teaching needs at the time. In this way, for instance, multiple representations for computing programs executed simultaneously on DELYS (Dagdilelis et al., 2003)—a software developed by the University of Macedonia (Thessaloniki, Greece) for the teaching of programming—the user can decide which functions will be visible and which will not.

Synthesis

In the above paragraphs, three basic principles for the design of modern educational environments were presented: the principle of tool logic, the principle of multiple interfaces, and the principle of multiple representations. Although the number of such principles has not been exhausted, as the research data show, they contribute significantly to the development of educational environments with high didactic specifications.

The rationale behind the examination of these design principles was focused on their teaching functions rather than on the logic of software engineering. This is the reason why general principles related to those categories of educational software that appear to be the most promising, that is, cognitive tools, were chosen. The main conclusion from the study of these educational environments is that a basic factor for their effective use in teaching is the *didactic situation in which they are applied*. The value of cognitive tools lies precisely in their ability to support situations with a rich teaching potential. With few exceptions, research on teaching does not seem to have progressed at the same rate as that on the technology of educational software. This fact explains the general impression, which exists internationally, that educational software has not yet succeeded in achieving its goal to improve teaching to the level expected. This is a direction that should be followed in order to succeed in the design and construction of even better quality educational environments and also simultaneously to make better use of existing software.

References

Balacheff, N. (1986). Une étude des processus de preuve en mathématique chez les élèves de collèg, Thèse de Doctorat d'Etat en Didactique des mathématiques, Grenoble, France.

Beale, R., & Sharples, M. (2002). *Design guides for developers of educational software*. British Educational, Communication and Technology Agency.

Bellemain, F. (1992). Conception, realisation et experimentation d'un logiciel d'aide à l'enseignement lors de l'utilisation de l'ordinateur. *Educational Studies in Mathematics*, 23, 59–97.

Bellemain, F., & Dagdilelis, V. (1993). *La manipulation directe comme invariant des micromondes educatifs*. Fourth European Logo Conference, Athens, Greece.

Brousseau, G. (1986a). Fondement et methodes de la didactiques de mathématiques. *Recherches en Didactique des Mathématiques, 7*(2).

Brousseau, G. (1986b). *Theorisation des phénomènes d'enseignement des mathématiques.* Thèse d'etat, Univesité de Bordeaux I, 1986.

Carlisle, E. G. (2000). Experiences with novices: The importance of graphical representations in supporting mental models. In A. F. Blackwell, & E. Bilotta (Eds.), *Proc. PPIG* 12 (pp. 33–44).

Climac, J. N., Antunes, C. H., and Costa, J. P. (1993). Teaching operations research using "home made" software. In D. L. Ferguson (Ed.), *Advanced educational technologies for mathematics and science*, NATO ASI Series, F: Computer and System Sciences, Vol. 146 (pp. 305–338). Springer Verlag.

Collins, A. (1996). *Design issues for learning environments, international perspectives on the design of technology-supported learning environments.* S. Vosniadou, E. De Korte, R. Glaser, & H. Mandl (Eds.). Mahweh, NJ: Lawrence Erlbaum Publishers.

Cuban, L. (2001). *Oversold and underused: Computers in classrooms.* Harvard, MA: Harvard University Press.

Cypher, A. (Ed.). (1994). *Watch what I do—Programming by demonstration.* Cambridge, MA: The MIT Press.

Dagdilelis, V., Evangelidis, G., Satratzemi, M., Efopoulos, V., & Zagouras, C. (2003). DELYS: A novel microworld-based educational software for teaching Computer Science subjects. *Computers and Education, 40*(4).

Dalit, L. (2001). Insights and conflcts in discussing recursion: A case study. *Computer Science Education, 11*(4), 305–322.

di Sessa, A., Hoyles, C., Noss, R., & Edwards, L. (1995). Computers and exploratory learning, setting the scene. In di Sessa et al. (Eds.). *Computers and exploratory learning,* NATO ASI Series, F: Computer and System Sciences, Vol. 146 (pp. 1–12). Springer Verlag.

Dijkstra, E. W. (1972). The humble programmer. *Communications of the ACM, 15*(15), October, 859–866.

Douady, R. (1993). L'ingenierie didactique, un moyen pour l'enseignant d'organiser les rapports entre l'ensegnement et l'apprentissage. *Cahier de DIDIREM, 7*(19).

Duchateau, C. (1992). From DOING IT…to HAVING IT DONE BY… The Heart of Programming. Some Didactical Thoughts, NATO Advanced Research Workshop *Cognitive Models and Intelligent Environments for Learning Programming*, S. Margherita, Italy.

Eisenberg, M. (1995). Creating software applications for children: Some thoughts about design. In A. A. diSessa, C. Hoyles, & E. Noss (Eds.), *Computers and exploratory learning,* NATO ASI Series, F: Computer and System Sciences, Vol. 146. Springer Verlag.

Emrah, O. (1995). Design of computer-based cognitive tools. In A. A. diSessa, C. Hoyles, & E. Noss (Eds.), *Computers and exploratory learning*, NATO ASI Series, F: Computer and System Sciences, Vol. 146. Springer Verlag.

Function Probe. (1999). Retrieved from the World Wide Web: http://questmsm.home.texas.net/

Harvey, J. (1995). *The market for educational software, Critical Technologies Institut- RAND*, prepared for Office of Educational Technology, U.S. Department of Education. DRU-1 04 –CTI.

Hoyles, C. (1995). Thematic chapter: Exploratory software, Exploratory cultures? In di Sessa et al. (Eds.), *Computers and exploratory learning*, NATO ASI Series, F: Computer and System Sciences, Vol. 146 (pp. 19–219). Springer Verlag.

Hoyles, C., & Noss, R. (1993). Deconstructing microworlds. In D. L. Ferguson (Ed.), *Advanced educational technologies for mathematics and science*, NATO ASI Series, F: Computer and System Sciences, Vol. 146 (pp. 385–413). Springer Verlag.

Interactive Physics. (2003). Retrieved from the World Wide Web: http://www.interactivephysics.com/description.html

Jonassen, D. H. (2000). *Computers as mindtools for schools: Engaging critical thinking*. New Jersey: Merrill/Prentice Hall.

Jonassen, D. H., Peck, K. C., & Wilson, B. G. (1999). *Learning with technology: A constructivist perspective*. New Jersey: Merrill/Prentice Hall.

Kaylan, A. R. (1993). Productivity tools as an integrated modeling and problem solving environment. In D. L. Ferguson (Ed.), *Advanced educational technologies for mathematics and science*, NATO ASI Series, F: Computer and System Sciences, Vol. 146 (pp. 439–468). Springer Verlag.

Koutlis, M., & Hatzilacos. (1999). "Avakeeo": The construction kit of computerised microworlds for teaching and learning Geography. Retrieved from the World Wide Web:= http://www.ncgia.ucsb.edu/conf/gishe96/program/koutlis.html

Kozma, R. B. (1992). Constructing knowledge with learning tools. In P. A. M. Kommers et al. (Eds.), *Cognitive tools for learning*, NATO ASI Series, F: Computer and System Sciences, Vol. 81 (pp. 305–319). Springer Verlag.

Laborde, C. (1983). Langue naturelle et écriture symbolique, deux codes en interaction dans l'enseignement mathématique. Didactique des mathématiques.

Laborde, C., & Laborde, J. M. (1995). What about a learning environment where Euclidean concepts are manipulated with a mouse? In di Sessa et al. (Eds.), *Computers and exploratory learning*, NATO ASI Series, F: Computer and System Sciences, Vol. 146 (pp. 241–262). Springer Verlag.

Lage, F. J., Zubenko, Y., & Cataldi, Z. (2001). An extended methodology for educational software design: Some critical points. *31th ASEE/IEEE Frontiers in Education Conference, T2G-13, 2001*, Reno, Nevada, USA.

MicroWorlds Pro. (1999). *Logo Update On Line*, Vol. 7, Number 2.

Nielsen, J., & Mack, R. (1994). *Usability inspection methods*. New York: John Wiley & Sons.

Pea, R. D. (1985). Beyond amplification: Using the computer to reorganize mental functioning. *Educational Psychologist, 20*(4), 167–182.

Resnick, M., Bruckman, A., & Martin, F. (1996). Pianos not stereos: Creating computational construction kits. *Instructions, 3*(6).

Reusser, K. (1994). Tutoring mathematical text problems: From cognitive task analysis to didactic tools. In S. Vosniadou, E. De Corte, & H. Mandl (Eds.), *Technology-based learning environments*, NATO ASI Series, F: Computer and System Sciences, Vol. 137 (pp. 174–182). Springer Verlag.

Roschelle, J., & Jackiw, N. (2000). Technology design as educational research: Interweaving imagination, inquiry & impact. In A. Kelly, & R. Lesh (Eds.), *Research design in mathematics & science education* (pp. 777–797), Mahwah, NJ: Lawrence Erlbaum Associates.

Roschelle, J., DiGiano, C., Koutlis, M., Repenning, A., Jackiw, N., & Suthers, D. (1999). Developing educational software components. *IEEE Computer, 32*(9).

Schwarz, J. L. (1993). Software to think with: The case of algebra. In D. L. Ferguson (Ed.), *Advanced educational technologies for mathematics and science*, NATO ASI Series, F: Computer and System Sciences, Vol. 146 (pp. 469–496). Springer Verlag.

Sendov, B., & Sendova, E. (1995). East or West—GEOMLAND is best, or Does the answer depend on the angle? In di Sessa et al. (Eds.), *Computers and exploratory learning*, NATO ASI Series, F: Computer and System Sciences, Vol. 146 (pp. 59–78). Springer Verlag.

Sketchpad. (2003). Retrieved from the World Wide Web: http://www.keypress.com/sketchpad/

Stoll, C. (2000). *High tech heretic: Reflections of a computer contrarian.* Anchor Books.

Tall, D. (1993). Interrelationships between mind and computer: Processes, images, symbols. In D. L. Ferguson (Ed.), *Advanced educational technologies for mathematics and science,* NATO ASI Series, F: Computer and System Sciences, Vol. 146 (pp. 385–413). Springer Verlag.

Tinker, R. F. (1993). Modelling and theory building: Technology in support of student theorizing. In D. L. Ferguson (Ed.), *Advanced educational technologies for mathematics and science*, NATO ASI Series, F: Computer and System Sciences, Vol. 146 (pp. 91–114). Springer Verlag.

Van der Mast, C. (1995). Developing educational software: Integrating disciplines and media (pp. 1–96). Ph.D. thesis, Technische Universiteit Delft.

Chapter VIII

Multiple Representations in Multimedia Materials:
An Issue of Literacy

Michael Sankey, University of Southern Queensland, Australia

Abstract

The movement toward utilising multimedia learning environments in teaching has increased dramatically in recent years. This chapter reports on current research trends relevant to the development of these environments. Specifically analysing issues related to designing for an ever increasing multiliterate clientele. It highlights the use of multiple representations and investigates some cognitive constraints present when displaying this information. Lastly, when learners are given a level of choice in accessing materials they may be further empowered in their knowledge acquisition. An understanding of these basic concepts will play an important role in our approach to Instructional Design. Therefore a set of recommendations is made for the design of these materials.

Introduction

The trend toward using multimedia learning environments as the preferred basis for teaching (particularly teaching at a distance) has increased dramatically, particularly over the last five years. This chapter reports on current research trends investigating the development of multimedia course materials. Specifically, it analyzes relevant instructional design (ID) issues and reflects on the concepts involved in catering to a multiliterate clientele and how the use of multiple representations may enhance the learning opportunities of students, primarily postsecondary learners. First, it will investigate the role that learning styles play in the learning process and what should be considered when preparing instructional material, looking closely at the importance of visualization in the representation of concepts and the current understandings of what it means to be literate in a culture saturated with visual elements. It will be seen that our understanding of these basic concepts will play an important role in our ID approach to teaching and learning, particularly when using visual and multiple representations in the multimedia learning environment. Second, it will investigate the cognitive constraints experienced by learners when information is displayed in multiple ways in such an environment, and whether it will be beneficial to learner cognition to provide users with a level of interactive choice. Finally, a set of recommendations will be made as to an appropriate format and potential way forward for the design and delivery of multimedia instructional materials.

Different Learning Styles

In developing instructional materials, contemporary educators are required to be keenly conscious that many learners, for many reasons, have vastly different learning styles. Although most researchers agree that different learning styles exist, and freely acknowledge the significant effect that learning styles have on the learning process, they are unable to form a consensus regarding the establishment of a single set of accepted principles (Vincent & Ross, 2001). For instance (see Figure 1), a recent study conducted by Liu and Ginther (1999) found that approximately 20–30% of American students were auditory learners; about 40% were visual; while the remaining 30–40% were tactual/kinesthetic, visual/tactual, or some combinations of the above (Study 1). Another study (Study 2) found that approximately 50% were auditory, followed by 33% visual, and 17% kinesthetic (Vincent & Ross, 2001). Although these figures vary, it is clear that people learn in different ways. In a similar vein, it is now known that

Figure 1: Two studies showing different results in learning styles

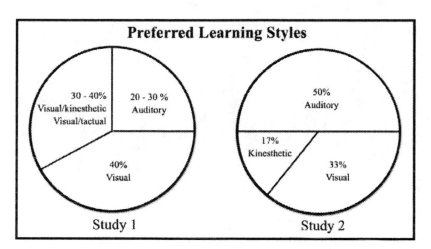

because individuals have different sensory preferences or cognitive styles, learning is more effective when multiple sensory channels are involved (Kearnsley, 2000). This being the case, it is imperative (Stokes, 2002) that "instructional materials, as well as teaching styles, should be matched with cognitive styles for greatest learner benefits" (p. 12), and this imperative becomes a matter of priority given the cultural shift that has occurred in a media-saturated environment.

In traditional learning environments, it is seen that many instructional events only target one genetic cognitive style. This situation, for today's learner, is highly unsatisfactory. This is particularly so for those with learning styles inappropriately matched with the learning task at hand (McKay, 1999). It has been highlighted in several studies in recent times that there are distinct learning advantages to matching the presentation of learning materials to a user's cognitive style, particularly for the young and the less able of all ages (Atkinson, 2001; Moreno, 2002). On the other hand, however, it is also seen (McKay, 1999) that "when there is a mismatch between cognitive style and the mode of presentation, it is argued that performance is deemed to be reduced" (p. 324). Fortunately, there seems to be a growing awareness, among some instructional designers (IDs) at least, of the important role that individual differences play in determining a learner's cognitive style (McKay, 1999). The challenge then for all educators is to present material in multiple ways, so as to encourage sufficient retention of information and to facilitate satisfactory learning in a culture that over recent decades has changed so considerably. One understandable problem with this (DePorter, 1992) is that "many people don't even realise they are favouring one way or the other, because nothing external tells them they're any

Many students today struggle with text based learning materials

different from anyone else" (p. 114). Consequently, many students struggle with the text-based learning materials provided in a variety of traditional learning environments.

Instructional designers, therefore, must address the complex interrelationships that exist between learning tasks, a learner's cognitive processes, and media attributes (Gunawardena, 1992). Figure 2 shows a representation of the different learning styles, indicating that many learners use a combination of styles. This will require teaching to utilize a variety of presentation techniques that will help students interact with materials and to satisfy their different learning needs (Lih-Juan, 1997). To illustrate this, in both school and university environments, academic work has become increasingly verbal (teacher/lecturer talking at the front of the classroom) in an effort to make teaching appear more personal. There are unfortunate consequences, however, for those pupils whose cognitive style is for processing information using images rather than verbal means (Atkinson, 2001). In other words, some learners may have great difficulty interpreting and understanding verbal instructions, especially when lengthy and complex, and would respond better to what they see. On the other hand, there are those learners who have difficulty reading but are careful listeners and remember well what they have been told (Flattley, 2002). Anderson (2001) goes as far as to say, "Optimal learning occurs when the instruction is exactly matched to the aptitudes of the learner" (p. 45). Interestingly, there is substantial research to suggest that computer-aided learning (multimedia) has the potential to improve much of this dichotomy, as materials can be presented in a variety of forms and thus be more sensitive to style differences (Atkinson, 2001; Mayer, 2001). Before we investigate this claim more closely, it is necessary to look at the role visualization plays in the representation of information, particularly as images play such an important role in the multimedia environment, not to mention society.

Figure 2: A representation of the different learning styles

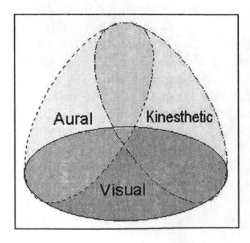

Visualization in Representation

Aristotle once stated that, "without image, thinking is impossible" (McKeon, 1941). Interestingly, Stokes (2002) noted that much of the research reported in educational literature today would support this, asserting that using visual strategies in teaching results in a greater degree of learning. This is because people find it easier to learn and remember knowledge visually (Andrewartha & Wilmot, 2001). Unfortunately, in most university classes, very little visual information is presented. Students mainly listen to lectures and read material written on whiteboards, in textbooks, or on handouts. In the case of distance education students, students interact with study books or computer screens that contain very few visual references. Felder and Soloman (2001) contended that most people are visual learners, and that if sufficient visual content were included in learning materials, students would retain more information. This is primarily because learners today (particularly those entering university straight from high school) have grown up surrounded by constant visual stimuli and have become highly sophisticated in their abilities to assimilate and process visual data. These students now expect that a high percentage of their learning should be transmitted visually (Evans, 2002). Fortunately, many educational researchers are now calling for increased attention to the use of graphical inscriptions in education (Roth, 2002). The question is, how far are their voices carrying?

Although visual images are an integral part of human cognition, they tend to be marginalized and undervalued in the education system (McLoughlin & Krakowski, 2001). Kress and van Leeuwen (1996) suggested that this is fundamentally due to a basic lack of understanding, that there are many elite academics who are horrified by these thoughts, seeing any addition of pictures to learning materials as "dumbing down" academic content. On the contrary, images are an essential component of education, having always been used (to some degree) to support learning and teaching in a variety of ways. Images provide access to complex visual information and experiences that cannot be replicated in purely textual terms. This is because, as stated in Evans (2002), "pictures interact with text to produce levels of comprehension and memory that can exceed what is produced by text alone" (p. 1). Further, visual forms of representation are important, not just as heuristic and pedagogical tools, but as legitimate aspects of reasoning and learning. Linking this with the multiple modes of representation that technologies can now offer, the visual experiences learners encounter can result in a higher level of cognition being attained (McLoughlin & Krakowski, 2001). It is hoped, therefore, that as more visual elements are incorporated into learning materials, with a view to achieving an optimal balance between verbal and visual cues, interdependence between these two modes of thought will be fostered.

Ultimately, due to advances in technology, the ability to transmit and display both realistic images and graphical representations of information should (it is hoped) provide an impetus for educators to come to a deeper understanding of the role of visualization in learning. Theorists have emphasized that visual thinking is a fundamental and unique part of the perceptual process, and that visualization is the indispensable partner to the verbal and symbolic ways of expressing ideas and thoughts (McLoughlin & Krakowski, 2001). The imperative is for instructional designers and educators alike to stay abreast of changes, both in cultural and technological areas. Increasingly all forms of communication are being transferred via the grammar of the visual, resulting in learners becoming more sophisticated in their abilities to recognize and interpret visual meaning as well as to utilize visual information to enhance social, cultural, or learning activities (Evans & Shabajee, 2002). Instructional designers must take into account the range of symbolic and visual forms that enable the construction, analysis, and refinement of ideas (McLoughlin & Krakowski, 2001). For it is increasingly being found that utilizing symbolic, visual, and verbal (in the case of multimedia) representations facilitates and strengthens the learning process by providing several mutually referring sources of information (Moreno, 2002). As will be seen below, educators need to foster a variety of new types of literacies to make education relevant to the demands of this new millennium.

These demands will necessitate that those involved in designing and writing of teaching materials, both traditional and multimedia-based, be aware of the processes involved in the production of images. As Muffoletto (2001) believed, understanding the process by which images become images, images that will, in turn, represent or refer to the creation of meaning, may be deemed as useless "if teachers do not incorporate the notion of multiple perspectives into their daily pedagogy" (p. 7). This is not a new thought, as DePorter (1992) stated, "when you're aware of how you and others perceive and process information, you can make learning and communication easier" (p. 110). This suggests that an effective instructional format would facilitate a combination of cognitive styles, thereby necessitating the introduction of visual-texts [images] (McKay, 1999). This would then become almost mandatory if, as is being suggested, visual communication is capable of disseminating knowledge more effectively than almost any other vehicle of communication (Flattley, 2002). There is, therefore, a real need to know how to communicate using images, which includes being alert to different forms of visual messages and being critically aware of how to read and view images as a language.

This argument is not limited simply to visual literacy. In considering what it means to be literate in contemporary culture, it is seen that literacy is on the verge of reinventing itself—it now not only includes visual literacy but also technological, computer, critical, media, and other literacies. Being literate in the future implies having the ability to decode information from all types of media (Grisham, 2001). Therefore, educators are required to personally cultivate a philosophy of multiple literacies, then foster and train learners in the full variety of literacies available to them. Ultimately, it is the educator who will empower their students and make education relevant to the demands of the future. For in a very real sense, our technology rich, postmodern condition requires us to be increasingly multiliterate.

Multiple Literacy

Kellner (2000) believed that literacies are socially constructed by educational and cultural practices and that they evolve and shift in response to social and cultural change, he wrote:

> ...one could argue that in an era of technological revolution and new technologies we need to develop new forms of media literacy, computer literacy, and multimedia literacies that I and others call by the covering concept of "multiliteracies" or "multiple literacies." New technologies and cultural forms require new skills and competencies and if education is to be relevant to the problems and challenges of contemporary life it must expand the concept of literacy and develop new curricula and pedagogies. (p. 249)

This being the case, multiple literacies are required if we are to meet the challenges of today's society. These literacies, according to Stokes (2002), include "...print literacy, visual literacy, aural literacy, media literacy, computer literacy, cultural literacy, social literacy, and eco literacy" (p. 11). If maximum benefit is to be extracted from information presented by modern communication technologies, both in terms of engagement and learning, a future-oriented approach must be adopted. Such an approach will prepare students to function in an increasingly technology-based society and give them the ability to "read" the world and communicate through multiple modes of communication.

Initially, this will require the reconceptualization of the notion of literacy, so that verbal texts, graphs, drawings, photos, and other communicative devices will all be seen as texts to be read. This understanding will then need to be applied to the development of new, inclusive, curriculum. If Web sites, CD-ROMs, and multimedia presentations are to be the medium of education in the future, there is need to theorize the literacies necessary to interact with these new multimedia environments and to gain the necessary skills to enable individuals to learn, work, and create in these emergent cultural spaces and domains (Kellner, 2000). Being multiliterate in a society that recognizes a full range of multiple learning styles will therefore require the development of theories and strategies for the multiple representations of concepts for instruction, if for no other reason than to be totally democratic (see Figure 3). If students are to be prepared to operate in a multiliterate manner (O'Rourke, 2002), then "we must provide them with opportunities to both express themselves and make sense of the world through multiple modes of communication (linguistic/textual, visual/graphical, musical/audio, spatial, gestural) sometimes all operating simultaneously" (p. 57). It would seem that the way forward in this regard is to conceptualize and demonstrate the use of multiple representations, utilizing the latest multimedia technologies and techniques.

Figure 3: Multimedia will allow us to more fully cater to the multiliterate learner

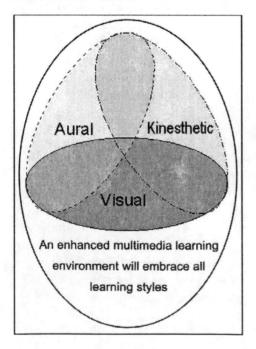

Utilizing traditional teaching media, such as textbook and printed study material, makes the consideration of individual learning styles, when designing instruction, very difficult. Instead, educators and IDs have relied upon the notion of a "generic" or "model" user to help them conceptualize (or possibly simplify) the learning process. Inevitably, this model user would be a read/write learner, who is equipped with a set of common or average cognitive characteristics. This is where interactive multimedia can play such an important facilitating role. It is in the use of multiple representations in this environment that the preferred modality of the user, over that of an arbitrary generic construct, can aid in the construction of meaning. This is because multimedia programs have been found to better cater to today's increasingly less homogeneous student cohort (Andrewartha & Wilmot, 2001). In a

CD based and CD supported teaching materials

practical sense, this is further evidenced by many of the major textbook publishers, who, anticipating this cultural shift, have moved vigorously into the multimedia marketplace, producing and promoting CD-ROMs and Web sites that support their texts. Clearly, multimedia does not hold all the answers, but it does offer certain previously nonexistent opportunities for the educator.

Multiple Representation and Multimedia

The use of multiple representations, particularly in computer-based learning environments, offers a wonderful variety of possibilities to the ID/educator. For instance, Bodemer and Ploetzner (2002) informed us that, "multiple representations can complement each other, resulting in a more complete representation of an application domain than a single source of information does" (p. 2). It has also been found that users both prefer and respond more positively to materials that contain visual elements. This is primarily because recall and memory are improved when information is presented visually or is supplemented by the use of images (Evans, 2002). Further, Ainsworth and Van Labeke (2002) stated that, "Learning with multiple representations has been recognized as a potentially powerful way of facilitating understanding for many years." They also stated the following:

> ...early research concentrated on the ways that presenting pictures alongside text could improve readers' memory and comprehension of text. In the last two decades, the debate has widened to include an extensive variety of representational formats including animations, sound, video and dynamic simulations. (p. 1)

When an illustration is placed alongside or just above text, or an image contains an annotated caption, student recall and comprehension of that information are improved. This is consistent with the constructivist theory on learning that involves the construction of connections between visual and verbal representa-

Figure 4: The words "atomic blast" by themselves may mean very little, but the inclusion of an image dramatically increases meaning

"When the atomic bomb explodes a huge mushroom cloud is formed that stretches way up into the sky."

Source: http://www.rockingham.k12.va.us/EMS/WWII/WWII.html

tions of a given system (McLoughlin & Krakowski, 2001). To illustrate this point, a simple example is offered.

This written explanation by itself may mean very little to a person who has never seen a huge mushroom cloud or atomic blast. However, if an image of an atomic blast were placed with or near this text (see Figure 4), the reader would have an instant reference point. Simply put (Doolittle, 2002), "students learn better from words and pictures than from words alone" (p. 1). It can be seen in this simple example that both language and image are important means of symbolic representation, so when the written message fails to communicate a concept fully, visual communication can be relied upon.

Learning, therefore, can be seen to be more effective when more than one sense modality is utilized. For instance, this is seen in verbal and visual processing when connections are clearly made between the information contained in each modality. This is further supported by research into multiple representations conducted by Ainsworth (1999), which obtained results indicating that single representational strategies do not differ significantly in their degrees of effectiveness. However, "where the learner employed more than one strategy, their performance was significantly more effective than that of problem solvers who used only a single strategy" (p. 137). When learners are given the opportunity to use multiple representations, they may be able to compensate for any weakness associated with one particular strategy of representation by switching to another (Ainsworth, 1999, p. 137). Further, Ainsworth (1999) stated that, "it can be seen that there may be considerable advantages for learning with complementary processes because, by exploiting combinations of representations, learners are less likely to be limited by the strengths and weaknesses of any single one" (p. 137).

For computer-based multimedia, the notion of visual literacy therefore takes on increased importance. Computer screens are clearly more graphic (visual) and interactive than traditional media, leading the user to scan visual fields, perceive and interact with icons and graphics, and use devices, such as a mouse, to interact with desired material and fields (Kellner, 2000). Animation (with the combination of sound and image), which falls within both the visual and auditory fields, plays a pivotal role in this new medium, as computer-generated animation. This strategy potentially aids the learner to build mental representations for comprehension by utilizing multiple sensory channels, resulting in more recall than visual-only or auditory-only presentations (Anderson, 2001). Therefore, verbal explanations when presented with animated graphical representations will lead to a greater understanding than representation utilizing a single modality. Animated pictures, it would appear, have an enabling function that allows the user to perform a higher degree of cognitive processing than with static pictures (Schnotz, 2002). This is primarily due to the fact that (Lai, 2001), "animated pictures can present different states of a subject matter, and provide more information to a learner." Quite simply, when material is made more interesting, students select more information for active processing.

One of the most obvious benefits of utilizing interactive multimedia is that of providing a virtually limitless array of resources that can be incorporated into a lesson plan, providing learning experiences that would otherwise be unavailable to students. However, this important feature, if not handled correctly, may in fact prove detrimental to the learning process. This is essentially due to the fact that processing multiple representations on the screen may place additional, and quite often unnecessary, cognitive demands on the learner. Individual differences within users also play a role in this scenario, for students may learn at a deeper level using multimedia interactive environments, but only when the advantages of multiple representations are not outweighed by individual differences in cognitive load (Moreno, 2002). For example, learners may have to direct attention simultaneously to different representations, especially if multiple representations are combined with other dynamic components, such as complicated sound, animated movement, and interactive text. This requires the learner to process large amounts of information at the same time. Very often these demands overburden student cognitive capabilities, resulting in the user learning very little (Bodemer & Ploetzner, 2002). The best combinations of the above must be considered and be tested for optimum usability.

Cognitive Constraints and Benefits

Two specific theories should be taken into account when designing instructional multimedia events (there are many other cognitive theories that could be considered, but not in this context). These two theories are Dual Coding Theory and Cognitive Load Theory. Both theories focus, to different degrees, on the use of short-term or working memory, in which text, either auditory or written, and images are processed simultaneously. These theories seem at first to give contradictory predictions about the influence of instruction on learning when text and pictures are combined (Gellevij et al., 2002). However, common ground can be found when considering these theories (see Figure 5). The author believes this ground, when applied, can be very effective in the design of multimedia learning environments.

Figure 5: Common ground may be found between Cognitive Load and Dual Coding theories

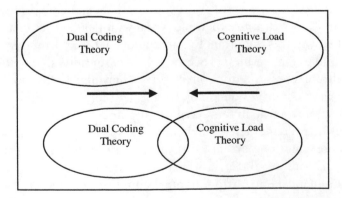

Cognitive Load Theory

Cognitive Load theory suggests that when large amounts of information are presented at one time, the learner can experience cognitive overload in working memory, as working memory only has a limited capacity. What happens in effect is that the learner becomes overwhelmed with what is being presented, resulting in a loss of direction and focus. This is based on the assumption that a learner has limited processing capacity and only finite cognitive resources. If a learner is required to devote mental resources to activities not directly related to schema construction, learning may be inhibited (Kalyuga et al., 2001). It has also been *unrelated* shown that students learn more effectively when extraneous words, pictures, and sounds are excluded from materials (Sweller, 1999). It is therefore essential that multimedia presentations focus on clear and concise presentations, rather than on all the "bells and whistles" or unnecessary information that will potentially impede student learning (Doolittle, 2002). In other words, if one form of instruction is intelligible and adequate (for example, a simple animation), providing the same information in a different form will impose extraneous cognitive load on the learner (Sweller, 2002). In a multimedia context, the main factors influencing cognitive load seem to be screen design displaying text, graphics, and animation.

The overuse of visuals in a presentation may steer learners to the exciting or entertaining aspects of a learning environment, but usually this is at the expense of encouraging thoughtful analysis of underlying meaning. Therefore, it may interfere with the intent of the lesson (Stokes, 2002). Too many elements at one time may overburden working memory, decreasing the effectiveness of processing. This is particularly the case when students with little prior knowledge of an environment are faced with excessive interactions or more controls than are necessary (Lai, 2001). On the one hand, it has been found that experienced individual learners who are able to establish their needs earlier in the learning episode and are uniquely qualified to act on their prior knowledge experience less overload (Lai, 2001). This is primarily due to the fact that an unlimited number of elements can be held in long-term memory in the form of hierarchically organized schemas, and these schemas can be brought into working memory and treated as a single element (Kalyuga et al., 2001). Consequently, it is often seen that poor instructional choices are made when students are faced with complex instructional content or when they do not have sufficient prior knowledge of an environment. For multimedia learning to be effective, it is important to design material in a way that minimizes the amount of cognitive load (Moreno, 2002). Interestingly, and not to discount the previous argument, some cognitive psychologists working with Cognitive Load theory now acknowledge that more effective working memory capacity is available if learners work in multiple modes, as long as reasonable constraints are provided.

Dual Coding Theory

Dual Coding theory, on the other hand, suggests that working memory consists of two distinct systems or substorage areas: verbal and nonverbal. This theory differs from Cognitive Load theory that builds on the idea that there is only one working memory with only a limited capacity (Gellevij et al., 2002). The verbal system processes narrative (spoken) information, while visual information, both image and text, is processed by the nonverbal system. Cognitive psychologists believe that one way to stretch the capacity of working memory is to utilize both of these storage areas (Clark, 2002; Mayer, 2001; Tabbers, 2002). This means that narrative and pictures may be processed at the same time but in two distinctly different areas of working memory. Consequently, presenting information in two sensory modalities (visual and auditory) increases the amount of working memory available and, comparatively speaking, decreases the cognitive load caused by the instructional format.

Combining verbal information with graphical elements should maximize memory resources, allowing processing to be distributed over multiple systems; thereby, making the learning episode more effective. The key concept involved in the visualization of information is to make use of the visual system to efficiently process information that otherwise may require more cognitive effort (Ainsworth, 2003). By utilizing the human visual system in this way, to process information in parallel with verbal information, we can bypass or reduce the bottleneck effect that can occur within working memory. Further, utilizing illustrations or simple (rather than complex) images can further reduce the load on working memory, for they are spatial, and in a sense, nontemporal. Text, by contrast, is read in temporal sequence and requires extra memory to keep all the parts in one place (Kirsh, 2002), therefore, requiring more cognitive processing. With text presented as audio, the learner can listen to a narration and at the same time look at a picture. Similarly, if a picture is too complex, the learner has to search the image at the same time as he or she is listening to the text. That means that the text and corresponding parts of the picture are not perceived simultaneously, causing a split-attention effect (Tabbers et al., 2000) or overload.

Sweller (2002) informed us of the following:

> ...under split-attention conditions, rather than presenting a diagram and written text that should be physically integrated, it may be possible to present a diagram and spoken text. Because the diagram uses a visual modality while speech uses the auditory modality, total available working memory capacity should be increased resulting in enhanced learning. (p. 1506)

Change clock text — use animations + audio speech — w button 2 repeat

This means that students may better understand an explanation when corresponding spoken text and pictures are presented at the same time, rather than separated in time (Mayer & Moreno, 1999). Mayer and his fellow researchers from the University of California have repeatedly shown in their testing that users benefit significantly from this multimodal approach to instructional design, with the most common form being a mixture of spoken text and pictures (Gellevij et al., 2002). Simply put, students learn better from animation and narrative rather than from animation, narration, and on-screen text.

A Learner-Centered Approach

The next step is tying together the concepts investigated above of an individual learning style, the multiple representation of information, and the creative use of multimedia environments. It has been seen as difficult, if not impossible, to design learning environments to cater to the "generic" learner, who does not actually exist. The beauty of the multimedia environment, however, is that it may be customized by the developer, and in some cases the user, to suit a particular learning style or combination of learning styles. This being the case, it can allow the learner to adapt a presentation to his/her individual cognitive needs, by actively deciding about the "what" and the "how" of a given presentation (Schwan, 2002). This suggests that if the learner is presented with a choice of representation, the one that best suits their needs can be selected. Evidence in recent research by Ainsworth and Van Labeke (2002) suggested that this strategy will significantly improve learning.

Learner choice is the foundational paradigm shift that needs to occur in the delivery of education today. One that moves us from a model where a learner is given virtually no choice, to one in which a learner can be a co-driver in his or her learning. If students perceive that they have a level of control over their learning experiences, they are more likely to use information-processing approaches that focus on the content as a whole and see connections between the parts, thereby actively thinking about the structure of the information presented (Anderson, 2001). Therefore, adult learners should be primarily guided in their learning by the multimedia program but be given a certain level of freedom to make conceptual connections between component parts. However, as we saw above, allowing too much freedom can generate a level of insecurity, particularly with the inexperienced learner (Andrewartha & Wilmot, 2001).

When a presentation can be broken down into learner-controlled, stepwise segments (see Figure 6), rather than one continuous presentation, learners can better understand a larger number of different concepts (Schnotz, 2002). In

Figure 6: This presentation is broken down into learner-controlled segments (stepwise segments), rather than presented in a continuous presentation. Users are given the choice to view the text if they want.

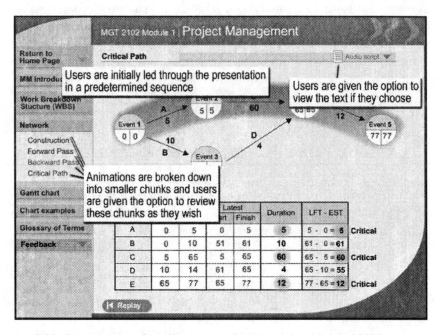

Note: Available for viewing at: http://www.usq.edu.au/users/sankey/mgt2102/

Figure 6, we see a screen capture from a Project Management Course offered at the University of Southern Queensland in which students are taken through four animated sequences that demonstrate how to construct a network flow diagram. Students are initially led through the presentation in a predetermined sequence and are then allowed to experiment with the environment, to the effects of changing certain perimeters. At any time, the student can view the text that is being narrated by clicking on an icon at the top right of the screen. This is for students who would prefer to read, instead of listen to, the presentation. Students can replay the sequence if they like or jump to the next sequence if they feel they already know the concept being discussed.

It should be noted that a multimedia presentation that has too many embedded controls, as discussed above, might limit the effectiveness and efficiency of the learning event, actively retarding assimilation (Lai, 2001). Therefore, using continuous simulation pictures and too many controls is likely to cause cognitive overload, whereas stepwise simulation pictures (breaking the animation down into shorter segments) will avoid cognitive overload by scaffolding the learning and by giving more control of the presentation to the learner.

As the ability to exert control over actions within the multimedia environment is ultimately a pleasing experience for the learner, allowing too much control of the process may have the opposite effect and direct learner attention toward the operation of the program, rather than toward the content. Due to the limited capacity of working memory, students cannot simultaneously focus on the content area and control the learning process at the same time (Lai, 2001). It is therefore recommended that only limited program control be allowed, giving learners the opportunity to concentrate on the task at hand. The practical challenge for IDs therefore, is to use the power of computer graphics in empirically justifiable ways.

Recommendations for Future Designs

Many universities have begun to embrace the translation of courses onto the World Wide Web. Unfortunately, instead of utilizing the unique interactive opportunities of the computer, most online courses simply replicate the Transmission of Information Model that is common practice in the classroom or in traditional distance education. Jona (2000) believed that most online courses are simply fancy "page turners," purely being digital presentations of lecture notes, facts, and concepts that the learner progresses through sequentially. Learning management systems are seen as simply being repositories for these documents but with the added advantage of having some neat communication tools to help teachers and students interact with each other. However, if the philosophy of the construction of learning does not change with the new technology, really, the student has gained very little. The key is not to disregard this new learning environment and return to the old, but to enhance it with other available techniques and technologies, to provide a more complete package. This includes multimedia environments that incorporate a combination of learning strategies and techniques, to cater for a broad multiliterate learner community. To do this, we must strategize a number of learning principles, based on current research that provides a comprehensive set of recommendations. Based on the above and previous research conducted in this field, a set of 12 strategies or design principles, though not exhaustive, are outlined below:

- "Less is more." Lean text that gets the point across is better than lengthy elaborated text. Use inclusive language and precise text to minimize the amount of reading from the screen.

- Socially engage the learner, where appropriate, with conversational language.

- Prevent the need for visual search. Make it obvious where to find certain elements. Place all related information together, so the learner does not have to hunt for it.

- Do not use images for the sake of it. There must be pedagogical benefit for their inclusion. Use simple graphics initially where possible, then add to complexity as you progress. Scaffold visual learning where appropriate. Incorporate, where possible, images that tell a story providing a reference point or anchor for the information being transmitted.

- Avoid including additional music or sounds, unless an essential component.

- Provide ample opportunity for learners to make decisions as they learn, providing a rich set of resources (as an option) to help them make decisions. Give the learner some control over the learning environment, ensuring that the instructional strategy is made clear.

- When creating animation, use image and spoken text, allowing the two sources of information to be processed concurrently in working memory.

- In utilizing animation, allow access to a text-based version of the material for those learners who prefer to read instruction rather than listen. This is useful for learners with high prior knowledge.

- Build knowledge gradually, with stepwise segments of information (sequentially), not one long presentation. A useful e-learning environment will present information in small chunks to hold interest.

- Ensure that the background image or color does not interfere with the clarity of information presented in the foreground. Use variations in color or intensity to highlight important information.

- If pictures and text are presented together on a page or screen, present them simultaneously, rather than separately. The two representations can then be processed in working memory at the same time. Use captioned images or incorporate the text into the image, if appropriate.

- Avoid referring to an image or diagram that appears on another page or screen. If need be, repeat the image.

Conclusion

The new technologies and cultural spaces discussed require a rethink of education in its entirety, ranging from the role of the teacher; teacher–student relations; classroom instruction; distance and online education; grading and testing; the value and limitations of books, multimedia, and other teaching materials; and the goals of education (Kellner, 2000). It should be emphasized that use of visual and other alternate forms of literacy are not being promoted here to supplant the need for linguistic literacy, rather to support and enhance it. As stated by Flattley (2002), "As educators we must literally get back to the drawing board—or the computer or television screen—to develop visual materials for instruction." McKay (1999) believed that if we are able to move beyond individual instruction to individualized instruction, we may start to design instruction that caters for a range of cognitive/learning styles. It is a time, as Kellner (2000) informed us to do as follows:

> ...put existing pedagogies, practices, and educational philosophies in question and to construct new ones. It is a time for new pedagogical experiments to see what works and what doesn't work in the new millennium. It is a time to reflect on our goals and to discern what we want to achieve with education and how we can achieve it. (p. 259)

This chapter has attempted to outline the foundational pedagogical constructs and assumptions utilized in the development of multimedia learning environments. It has been shown that educators and IDs, in designing instructional environments, must take into consideration different learning styles and the possibilities offered in and by the multiple representation of concepts. Visualization in representation and the use of multimedia must play an important role when catering for today's multiliterate clientele. Certain cognitive constraints and benefits have been considered, principally relating to establishing effective learning strategies. These areas are particularly important when catering to students who have learning modalities that may differ from the "traditional" style. Finally, allowing the user a certain amount of choice or control in their learning episode is both a highly desirable and appropriate option, one that has the potential to further empower a student's learning experience. The learning of a variety of concepts, using a diversity of instructional formats, shows how this instructional designer has responded to an investigation of current research in this field as contained in the set of recommendations above.

References

Ainsworth, S. (1999). The functions of multiple representations. *Computers and Education*, *33*(2–3), 131–152.

Ainsworth, S., & Loizou, A. (2003). The effects of self-explaining when learning with text or diagrams. *Cognitive Science (In Press)*.

Ainsworth, S., & Van Labeke, N. (2002). Using a multi-representational design framework to develop and evaluate a dynamic simulation environment. In R. Ploetzner (Ed.), *International workshop on dynamic visualizations and learning*. Tubingen, Germany: Knowledge Media Research Center.

Anderson, M. D. (2001). Individual characteristics and Web-based courses. In C. R. Wolfe (Ed.), *Learning and teaching on the World Wide Web* (pp. 45–72). San Diego: Academic Press.

Andrewartha, G., & Wilmot, S. (2001). Can multimedia meet tertiary education needs better than the conventional lecture? A case study. *Australian Journal of Educational Technology, 17*(1), 1–20.

Atkinson, S. (2001). Cognitive styles and computer-aided learning (CAL): Exploring designer and user perspectives. Paper presented at the *PATT-11 conference: New media in education,* Eidenhoven, The Netherlands.

Bodemer, D., & Ploetzner, R. (2002). Encouraging the active integration of information during learning with multiple and interactive representations. In R. Ploetzner (Ed.), *International workshop on dynamic visualizations and learning*. Tubingen, Germany: Knowledge Media Research Center.

Clark, R. (2002). Six principles of effective e-learning: What works and why. *The eLearning Developers' Journal*. Retrieved September 10, 2002 from the World Wide Web: http://www.elearningguild.com/pdf/2/091002DES-H.pdf

DePorter, B. (1992). *Quantum learning: Unleashing the genius in you*. New York: Dell Publishing.

Doolittle, P. E. (2002). Multimedia learning: Empirical results and practical applications. *Irish educational technology users' conference*, Carlow, Ireland.

Evans, J. (2002). The FILTER generic image dataset: A model for the creation of image-based learning & teaching resources. *ASCILITE 2002, Winds of change in the sea of learning: Charting the course of digital education, 19th annual conference of the Australasian Society for Computers in Learning in Tertiary Education*, Auckland, NZ.

Evans, J., & Shabajee, P. (2002). Preliminary results from the FILTER Image Categorisation and Description Exercise. *The international conference on Dublin core and metadata for e-communities*. Florence, Italy: Firenze University Press.

Felder, R. M., & Soloman, B. A. (n.d.). *Learning styles and strategies*. Retrieved March 14, 2001 from the World Wide Web: http://www2.ncsu.edu/unity/f/felder/public/ILSdir/styles.htm

Flattley, R. (2002). *Visual literacy.* Department of Psychology, Pima College. Retrieved April 9, 2003 from the World Wide Web: http://dtc.pima.edu/psychology/Visual_Literacy.html

Gellevij, M., van der Meij, H., de Jong, T., & Pieters, J. (2002). Visuals in instruction: Functions of screen captures in software manuals. In R. Ploetzner (Ed.), *International workshop on dynamic visualizations and learning.* Tubingen, Germany: Knowledge Media Research Center.

Grisham, D. L. (2001). Technology and media literacy: What do teachers need to know? *Reading Online.* Retrieved July 1, 2002 from the World Wide Web:http://www.readingonline.org/editorial/edit_index.asp?HREF=april 2001/index.html

Gunawardena, C. N. (1992). Changing faculty roles and audiographics and online teaching. *The American Journal of Distance Education,* 6(3), 58–71.

Jona, K. (2000). Rethinking the design of online courses. *ASCILITE 2000, Learning to choose, choosing to learn. 17th annual conference of the Australasian Society for Computers in Learning in Tertiary Education,* Southern Cross University, Coffs Harbour, Australia.

Kalyuga, S., Chandler, P., & Sweller, J. (2001). Learner experience and efficiency of instructional guidance. *Educational Psychology, 21*(1), 5–23.

Kearnsley, G. (2000). *Online education: Learning and teaching in cyber space.* Belmont, CA: Wadsworth/Thomson Learning.

Kellner, D. (2000). New technologies/new literacies: Reconstructing education for the new millennium. *Teaching Education, 11*(3), 245–265.

Kirsh, D. (2002). Why illustrations aid understanding. In R. Ploetzner (Ed.), *International workshop on dynamic visualizations and learning.* Tubingen, Germany: Knowledge Media Research Center.

Kress, G., & van Leeuwen, T. (1996). *Reading images: The grammar of visual design.* London: Routledge.

Lai, S.-L. (2001). Controlling the display of animation for better understanding. *Journal of Research on Technology in Education, 33*(5), Summer.

Lih-Juan, C. (1997). The effects of verbal elaboration and visual elaboration on student learning. *International Journal of Instructional Media, 24*(4), 333–340.

Liu, Y., & Ginther, D. (1999). Cognitive styles and distance education. *Online Journal of Distance Learning Administration, 2*(3), Fall. Available from the World Wide Web: http://www.westga.edu/~distance/liu23.html

Mayer, R. E. (2001). *Multimedia learning*. Cambridge: Cambridge University Press.

Mayer, R. E., & Moreno, R. (1999). Instructional technology. In F. Durso (Ed.), *Handbook of applied cognition*. New York: Wiley.

McKay, E. (1999). An investigation of text-based instructional materials enhanced with graphics. *Educational Psychology*, *19*(3), September, 323–335.

McKeon, W. R. (Trans.) (1941). *Aristotle. "On memory and reminiscence." The basic works of Aristotle* (pp. 607–617). New York: Random House.

McLoughlin, C., & Krakowski, K. (2001). Technological tools for visual thinking: What does the research tell us? *Apple University Consortium Academic and Developers Conference*, James Cook University, Townsville, Australia: Australian National University.

Moreno, R. (2002). Who learns best with multiple representations? Cognitive theory implications for individual differences in multimedia learning. *Proceedings of ED-MEDIA 2002, The world conference on educational multimedia and hypermedia and telecommunications*. Denver, Colorado, USA.

Muffoletto, R. (2001). An inquiry into the nature of Uncle Joe's representation and meaning. *Reading Online*. Retrieved July 1, 2002 from the World Wide Web: http://www.readingonline.org/newliteracies/lit_index.asp?HREF=/newliteracies/muffoletto/index.html

O'Rourke, M. (2002). Engaging students through ICTs: A multiliteracies approach. *TechKnowLogia,* (April–June), 57–59. Retrieved November 2, 2002 from the World Wide Web: http://www.TechKnowLogia.org

Roth, W. M. (2002). Reading graphs: Contributions to an integrative concept of literacy. *Journal of Curriculum Studies, 34*(1), 1–24.

Schnotz, W. (2002). Enabling, facilitating, and inhibiting effects in learning from animated pictures. In R. Ploetzner (Ed.), *International workshop on dynamic visualizations and learning*. Tubingen, Germany: Knowledge Media Research Center.

Schwan, S. (2002). Do it yourself? Interactive visualizations as cognitive tools. In R. Ploetzner (Ed.), *International workshop on dynamic visualizations and learning*. Tubingen, Germany: Knowledge Media Research Center.

Stokes, S. (2002). Visual literacy in teaching and learning: A literature perspective. *Electronic Journal for the Integration of Technology in Education, 1*(1, Spring), 10–19. Retrieved April 9, 2003 from the World Wide Web: http://ejite.isu.edu/Archive.html

Sweller, J. (1999). *Instructional design in technical areas*. Melbourne: ACER Press.

Sweller, J. (2002). Visualisation and instructional design. In R. Ploetzner (Ed.), *International workshop on dynamic visualizations and learning*. Tubingen, Germany: Knowledge Media Research Center.

Tabbers, H. K. (2002). *The modality of text in multimedia instructions: Refining the design guidelines*. Heerlen, The Netherlands: Open University of the Netherlands.

Tabbers, H. K., Martins, R., & van Merrienboer, J. J. D. (2000). Multimedia instructions and cognitive load theory: Split-attention and modality effects. *Association for Educational Communications and Technology national conference,* Long Beach, California.

Vincent, A., & Ross, D. (2001). Learning style awareness: A basis for developing teaching and learning strategies. *Journal of Research on Technology in Education, 33*(5), Summer.

Chapter IX

Empirical Validation of a Multimedia Construct for Learning

Paul Kawachi, Kurume Shin-Ai Women's College, Japan

Abstract

A multimedia construct for learning based on the Theory of Transactional Distance has been developed consisting of four stages of decreasing transactional distance. This model has been applied in various teaching and learning contexts, on- and off-line, and its validation was investigated. Results confirmed in practice the four distinct sequential stages. Difficulties were discovered in navigating through the collaborative second and third stages, consistent with findings from related studies on acquiring critical thinking skills. Specific areas for attention were identified to promote learning using multimedia.

Introduction

Previous Models of Learning

Two significant models have been proposed to identify the essential steps of learning critical-thinking skills: one by Dewey (1933) and another by Brookfield (1987). Dewey proposed five phases of reflective or critical thinking:

1.   Suggestions, in which the mind leaps forward to a possible solution

2.   An intellectualization of the difficulty or perplexity that has been felt (directly experienced) into a problem to be solved, a question for which the answer must be sought

3.   The use of one suggestion after another as a leading idea, or hypothesis, to initiate and guide observation and other operations in collection of factual material

4.   The mental elaboration of the idea or supposition (reasoning, in the sense in which reasoning is a part, not the whole, of inference)

5.   Testing the hypothesis by overt or imaginative action

Brookfield also proposed five phases to develop critical thinking:

1.   A triggering event

2.   An appraisal of the situation

3.   An exploration to explain anomalies or discrepancies

4.   Developing alternative perspectives

5.   Integration of alternatives in ways of thinking or living

However, the steps given in the above models do not correlate with each other. The steps are not clearly distinguishable, and the actual process need not be sequenced linearly. So these models are not sufficiently clear to constitute the basis of a syllabus. A new clear and practical model is proposed based on the distinct ways of learning. And this new model will constitute the basis for an intelligent syllabus for acquiring critical-thinking skills using multimedia.

The Distinct Ways of Learning

There are four distinct ways of learning (Kawachi, 2003a): learning alone independently, alone individually, in a group cooperatively, and in a group collaboratively. Here it is important to distinguish cooperative learning from collaborative learning, in order to deploy these in the new model detailed below.

Cooperative learning essentially involves at least one member of the group who "knows" the content soon to be learned by the other(s). Learning takes place through the "knower" repeating, reiterating, recapitulating, paraphrasing, summarizing, reorganizing, or translating the point to be learned.

Collaborative learning follows a scientific process of testing out hypotheses. A participant publicly articulates his (or her) own opinion as a hypothesis, and being open to the value of conflict allows this to be negated if possible by others, in which case the original participant or another offers up a modified or alternative hypothesis for public scrutiny. In collaborative learning, disagreement and intellectual conflict are desirable interactions. All participants share in coconstructing the new knowledge together, and this learning occurs inside the group as a type of consensus achieved through analysis and argument. In collaborative learning, there was no "knower" prior to the learning process taking place (in contrast to the situation of cooperative learning).

Need for a New Model of Learning

Largely as a result of the rapid expansion of open and distance education, learning theory has undergone a revolution to a social constructivist paradigm based on cognitive concepts of how we learn. Previous models of learning have been too vague for applying to current learning practices through computer-mediated communications. Hence, there is a need for a new practical model.

New Multimedia Learning Model

A new model for learning critical thinking using multimedia has been proposed by Kawachi (2003b). Design is a key characteristic generally lacking in the current applications to date of computer-mediated communications adopted in conventional face-to-face or distance education courses. The presented Design for Multimedia in Learning (DML) model translates conventional theoretical models of learning into an efficient practical design for use in the multimedia educational environment. While the two leading previous models have variously postulated five phases to critical thinking for learning, this new model has four distinct stages, and is directly underpinned by Moore's (1993) Theory of Transactional Distance. This theory, which involves educative-dialogue (D), prescribed structure (S), and student autonomy (A), tries to measure the psychological distance between the student and the information to be learned, and has been widely accepted as an effective theory underlying and informing open and distance education. The original theory only deals with one student, learning content with the interactions of a tutor. So it is adapted here to bring into account the important interactions among the student and other students (for a discussion here, see Kawachi, 2003b).

The four stages of the new DML model are as follows:

- In **Stage 1**, learning occurs in a group cooperatively, gathering and sharing information and fostering a learning community. Here synchronous-mode computer-mediated communications are best, such as chat and conferencing. However, it should not be forgotten that bridging telephony can simultaneously link 50 students synchronously with the tutor(s). Videorecording the interactions here could provide material for reflection in Stage 2, or as is often the case, the tutor as observer could take written notes for later distribution as a summary or transcription to the participants. This stage can be characterized by self-introductions (as a prelude to being a source of content material to other students), brainstorming (limited at Stage 1 to only accumulating new ideas, yet to be argued in Stage 2), involving divergent thinking to gather various different perceptions in order to explore and to frame each student's context, and helping each other as equals with obtaining content, especially in sharing personal experiences and past literature that has been read, which constitute old foundational knowledge. (Brainstorming is initiated by providing an ill-defined scenario or case study to elicit multiple perspectives.) The transactional distance initially is at a maximum (D- S-) with no teaching-dialogue and with no pre-set structure.

- In **Stage 2**, lateral-thinking (creative thinking around the problem) is used to generate and develop metaphors (an idea or conception that is basically dissimilar but formed from noting similarities between the initial information and the new concept) or new ideas, and these supported by argument. Students discuss, for example, their own problems that they have found which have brought them to participate in the current course, and then argue to identify possible solutions to each other's problems. Creative thinking here may derive from combining seemingly disparate parts, especially ideas contributed from others in different contexts into a new synergic whole. The teacher is still keeping academically at a distance away from the content under discussion, while the students are making their efforts to achieve some pre-set goals (to present own problem and reasons for engaging the current course, for example), which gives structure to their discussions (D- S+). Some time is needed for reflection here, and asynchronous modes such as e-mail and a bulletin board are effective because of the time interval incurrent between receiving the stimulus and the student's response. Moreover, these modes of interaction through written text also provide a written record to the student that enables recapitulation, retrieval of a theme, and recovery of someone's perspective, and so foster reflection.

- In **Stage 3**, the tutor engages the students with guiding comments in what Holmberg (1983) has described as a Guided Didactic Conversation, helping the students achieve the course structural requirements of understanding the general concepts to be learned (D+ S+). The tutor poses questions, and students defend their formulations. This stage is characterized by hypotheses testing and logical straightforward thinking (termed "vertical" thinking in contrast to "lateral" thinking) associated with problem solving and is collaborative. Problem-based learning can involve holding multiple alternative hypotheses at the same time, and evidence gathered can be assigned to examine simultaneously the various hypotheses. Asynchronous mode is ideal here, to allow sufficient time for cognitive connections and co-construction of new nonfoundational knowledge.

- In **Stage 4**, the final stage, the course requirements have largely been already achieved and there is no structure left, except to disseminate the achieved mental ideas and test them out in real life. This stage is characterized by experiential learning and is cooperative, and at minimum transactional distance (D+ S-), in synchronous mode, and with teaching dialogue to assist the students to reflect on their studies.

Student Autonomy in Learning

Definitions of "autonomy" in learning have in common an emphasis on the capacity to think rationally, reflect, analyze evidence, and make judgments; to know oneself and be free to form and express one's own opinions; and finally, to be able to act in the world (Tennant & Pogson, 1995). These qualities characterize the collaborative thought processes of Stage 3, and also the experiential aspect of Stage 4. Stage 1 has maximal transactional distance, and for a student to succeed here in independent learning, Moore (1993) pointed out that the student would need maximum autonomy (p. 27). Autonomy is thus seen as a highly powerful and desirable quality for independent learners. Not all students bring this high level of autonomy with them initially into their studies, and so the tutor must bring the student around to acquire this autonomy. The DML model illustrates a cyclical process—even an iterative process—through Stages 1 to 4 to equip and bring the student to go onto independent learning in a further new cycle starting at Stage 1 in a new learning venture.

Autonomy has also been related to recognizing one's interdependence on others (Boud, 1988). Interdependence relates to understanding the need to learn together with others, either in cooperative mode or at other times in collaborative. Interdependence is a maturity characterizing an adult student and is acquired through awareness and prior experience of the critical-thinking process. Toward the end of Stage 4, the student can have acquired this sense of interdependence. So in entering a new Stage 1 interaction, the student may be interdependent (post-Stage 4) and once more newly independent (starting a fresh Stage 1). These attributes of independence and interdependence have already been found to be separate, orthogonal, and coexisting in mature students at the end of their course (Chen & Willits, 1999).

While autonomy is defined as an attribute of the student, different distance education programs and the different stages in the DML model relate to different levels of autonomy for the student to be a successful learner. In a program at Stage 2, the deployed structure means that the student is charged with thinking rationally, but horizontally rather than vertically, and is analyzing already-given evidence, rather than finding new evidence, so the quality of autonomy is somewhat measured to fit the limited freedom given to the student. At Stage 3, different qualities of autonomy for hypotheses testing are needed for success— including a mature openness to new ideas that might be in conflict with one's previous and present conceived view of the world. The student needs to exercise the freedom to formulate or reformulate one's own conceptions. While in Stage 4, the quality of autonomy should include the willingness and ability to act to test out these newly constructed ideas to see experientially how they operate in practice.

It is difficult, therefore, and moreover unhelpful to assign an integrated level of autonomy to each stage in the DML model. The student should utilize measured amounts of the various qualities that constitute autonomy during each stage to support learning. Can the tutor and institution influence the level and qualities of autonomy used by the student? Yes. And explicit clear advice from the tutor may be all that is required. The student, however, might not yet possess the skills for exercising the full range of qualities constituting autonomy (in other words, is unequipped for full autonomy). The novice and nonexpert will likely need scaffolding help at different stages to cope.

Scaffolding for Learning

Scaffolding is the intervention of a tutor in a process that enables the student to solve a problem, carry out a task, or achieve a goal that would be beyond the student's unassisted efforts (Wood et al., 1976, p. 190). In providing individualized scaffolding, the tutor knows the intended knowledge to be learned and has a fair grasp of the prospective development for the student. The distance between the unassisted level of capability and the potential level that can be achieved through scaffolding is Vygotsky's (1978) "zone of proximal development" (p.86). Vygotsky included the opportunity that such scaffolding could be from "more capable" other students, indicating a cooperative assistance (as opposed to a collaborative process). Wood et al. (1976) made this very clear: tutoring is "the means whereby an adult or 'expert' helps somebody who is less adult or less expert. …a situation in which one member 'knows the answer' and the other does not" (p. 89). Accordingly, we might be advised to reserve the term "tutor" for the cooperative Stages 1 and 4 only, and use a term "facilitator" for the collaborative processes of Stages 2 and 3.

In Stage 1, tutor intervention providing scaffolding includes making the outcomes of studying explicit to the student and ensuring that the student can comprehend the aims and objectives. If not, then tutor feedback and error correction become merely vehicles of information for imitation and copying, and vaporize these opportunities to acquire mastery. The tutor need not exercise full control over the discovery process. It is recognized that students also acquire learning through unexpected accidental discovery of knowledge.

Both Stage 2 (D- S+) and Stage 3 (D+ S+) are characterized by added structure.

In Stage 3, scaffolding should add a safe structure for the interactions involved in the analytic argumentation of hypotheses testing, which have led to some students feeling wounded, by so-called flaming. Zimmer (1995) proposed an effective framework involving three functional turn-taking steps ABA between two persons A and B, which when repeated as BAB give both participants the opportunities to give opinions and receive counteropinions empathetically, as follows:

A)   (Hello) Affirm + Elicitation

B)   Opinion + Request understanding

A)   Confirm + Counteropinion

B)   Affirm + Elicitation

A)   Opinion + Request understanding

B)   Confirm + Counteropinion

I should also like to propose another framework drawn from some ideas of Probst (1987) for collaborative learning in literature and art, in which transactions are not aimed at hypotheses-testing characterized by counteropinion but rather a new insight built on critical reflection that while shared may be personalized in each individual. In literature, learning is not cooperative: there is no "knower"; the tutor does not guide the student to some pre-set conclusion of the meaning of the text. In literature, the tutor or any student (A) elicits opinion to initiate the three functional turn-taking steps BAB (followed by ABA), as follows:

A)   (Hello) Affirm + Elicitation

B)   Opinion/Analysis + Request understanding

A)   Affirm + Elicitation of evidence

B)   Reflect + Elicit other opinions/Analyses

A)   Opinion/Analysis + Request understanding

B)   Affirm + Elicitation of evidence

A)   Reflect + Elicit other opinions/Analyses

This framework—basically of reflective analysis followed by articulation, bring in ideas from their own reading or those elicited from other students, then repeat reflective analysis with accommodation to construct a new insight—involves the same cognitive processes that occur in individual learning. In the group, content comes from texts and other students, while in individual learning, content comes only from texts. In both cases, it is the transactions between the student and the content that creates the new knowledge in the student.

Courses based on experiential learning that focus on Stage 4 in synchronous mode can also benefit from explicit scaffolding. In non-face-to-face (nonvideo, nonaudio) synchronous "chat" text-based conferencing, students should be directed to articulate their feelings explicitly. Neubauer (2003a) found that once students had become skilled in explicitly stating their feelings (such as "I am confused…"), then their learning improved by better sharing experiences, and they then more highly valued their text-based content—more than if they had used visual face-to-face cues. So, scaffolding can also assist in Stage 4 synchronous chat experiential learning.

On the Number of Participants

In both the above frameworks, I suggest that any participant(s) may be behind either voice, so the framework could be effective for more than two persons at the same time. Bork (2001) has suggested that the optimal number may be four in collaborative transactions, in an optimal online class size of 20 students, while six has been reported by Laurillard (2002), and about 10 by others. Wang (2002) has asserted that engaging as many participants as possible would maximize diversity and optimize collaborative learning. Zimmer (1995) has found that provided participants are aware of the framework, then collaborative learning succeeded in practice for a group of 12 students.

The optimum number of active participants in synchronous cooperative learning is different from that for asynchronous collaborative learning. An online survey of those on the DEOS-L listserv, who have had relevant experience in conducting synchronous chat (Neubauer, 2003b), found the optimum number was from 10 to 20 students: if students were new to the synchronous media, then five to seven students was optimum; in groups of 10 to 15 mixed-experience students, then 10 was optimum; while if students were experienced and the moderator (tutor) also was experienced, then 15 was optimum. And the upper limit of 20 students was suggested to keep the discussion at a sufficiently fast rate to maintain high interest levels. There seemed to be a marked difference between respondents who found that five to seven was optimum and those who found that 20 was optimum, and this difference might be related to the task at hand. Five to seven new students would imply that they were at Stage 1, forming a learning community with personal introductions and so on, while 20 students were likely at Stage 4, sharing course experiences. A note should be added here to the effect that non-native-speakers of English might be slower and more apprehensive (than native speakers) about their actively participating in synchronous discussions (see, for example, Briguglio, 2000; Kawachi, 2000). That these synchronous discussions are cooperative and not collaborative, however, should mean that their state anxiety should be lower and performance higher than if collaborative discussion were conducted synchronously.

Using a Framework

These two frameworks illustrate and scaffold the interactions, either synchronous or asynchronous, for learning collaboratively in a group. The framework indicates what content should optimally be included in an utterance, and specifies in what serial order to progress towards achieving discovery and coconstruction of new understanding and new knowledge. It should also be noted that the use of a framework also implies some timeliness in replies. The system would not function if turn-taking were violated or not forthcoming. Participants need to take responsibility for the group succeeding by actively providing what is required and when it is required. In this way, some pacing is inevitable if the group is to move towards achieving its goal.

To some large extent, nonresponse in an asynchronous environment can be overcome by others offering up the required content in time. This is often the case in synchronous free discussions. However, group cohesiveness depends on the active participation of all members of the group. If a student does not participate, the group is fragmented and not functioning as a whole. Prior to the task, coping strategies should be acquired, agreed upon, and then used when required, such as prearranging the time frame allowed within which a student should contribute, pairing up students to provide backup in case one is at a loss, or having the moderator provide behind-the-scenes coaxing and elicitation.

Methodology for Validation of the Model

Research into preferred learning styles has suggested that while some students may be field-dependent, others are field-independent. Lyons et al. (1999) described how some are so-called right-brain dominant. These students tend to be intuitive and prefer informal unstructured learning environments and group discussions in empathetic elicitation, sharing, and valuing each other's experiences and views (who would prefer cooperative learning in a group). Others are so-called left-brain dominant and are analytic, rational, and objective (who would prefer collaborative learning in a group).

In order to validate the model empirically, hypertext linkages were added purposively into a Web-based course. The Internet is a nonnarrative media in which no predetermined pathway through it is provided to the student newly logging on. Hypertext linkages on corporate business Web sites have been categorized by Harrison (2002), but there has been no categorization to date of hypertext usage in educational Web sites. Here, some links were colored red to indicate that examples could be reached by clicking on the highlighted linkage, while other links were colored blue to indicate to the student specifically that reasons could be reached. The courseware was reduced in content by removing all preexisting or customary references to examples and reasons except for the colored hypertext links.

It was then postulated that during traveling through the courseware, some students preferred to see examples, while others preferred to see reasons, with both groups achieving learning of the general concepts with no significant difference in achieved quality of learning.

The students examined in this study were all Japanese, and Japanese students are known to prefer cooperative learning in a group and avoid critical evaluation of others, preferring instead to preserve group harmony through empathetic sharing (Kawachi, 2000).

By coloring each hypertext or telling the students directly what color it would be or which content could be reached through which link, it was then planned that students would not open a link simply from curiosity but would pass across any link they decided was not wanted and move onto opening a link that might be helpful in their accomplishing the task at hand. Students were monitored in their selection. Students were also required to keep journals as a written "think-aloud" record for formative and summative evaluation. Students were also interviewed during and after their online studies. E-mail messages were also kept. Students were continually encouraged to interact with each other. This was to keep the group on task cohesively, providing peer support and pacing to some degree, as well as for the designed cooperative or collaborative interactions.

Results

The above method for empirical validation of the DML model in Japan using specially designed hypertext courseware to investigate cooperative and collaborative pathways during learning was not entirely successful. The study found that students at the undergraduate level could successfully move through the first two stages but could not engage the third stage due to lack in sufficient foundational knowledge and experiential maturity. Interviews were conducted on the students, but these also failed to identify any cause for the breakdown in the learning cycle. Validation at the graduate and continuing adult education level is ongoing.

Course and Student Assessment

Summative records of achieved learning from each student indicated the particular stage reached by the student, and to a fair degree of accuracy, where within a stage was reached by the student. In each stage, indeed at any time throughout the course, interactions were recorded for formative and summative evaluations, of both the course itself and of the student's individual participation, contribution, learning process (including choices made), and quality of learning outcomes. In Stage 1, handwritten notes, audiorecording, or audio-video recording can serve these purposes. Only written reports, interviews, and tutor observations were used in the present study. In Stage 2 and Stage 3, the asynchronous modes are performed through written contributions, such as by mail, teletext, fax, or e-mail, so that records can be easily stored and retrieved.

Nonacademic and academic exchanges between the student and others can usually be recorded (though recording telephone conversations needs informed consent). At the present time (June 2003), it remains technologically difficult, if not impossible, to record the hypertext-enabled learning narratives of each student. Some adaptive hypermedia can restrict the available hypertext choices, but at present, think-aloud, recall, and separate audio-video recording are the only means with which to track the pathways and learning processes of the students who were using interactive hypermedia. In the present study, the student journals, triangulated with interviews and observations, were used. Stage 4 is characterized by social constructivist experiential learning, which usually entails some form of public articulation of the student's tentative or summative perspective achieved from the previous stages. For example, a written thesis is the most common instrument of evaluation here. Oral presentation at a conference and publication of a report in an academic journal are also common instruments. In the present study, the final demonstration was different depending on the course. In all courses, there was a written summative report from each student. In one course, there was project work including a poster presentation and group journal thesis published. This thesis included individual reports of pathways and a group collective report.

In the empirical validation of the DML model in this study, the students were not paced, but the course was of predetermined duration. The aim at the outset was to bring all the students through all four stages to present some new personal meaning they had each achieved through the four-stage process. Observations and written records gathered during the course were revealing that many students were slower than expected—this was even after the course was tailored to be at a comprehensible level fitting to each particular class. Within-class individual cognitive and affective differences were greater than expected. It thus transpired that the summative reports from the students, rather than confirming all had successfully completed the four stages, instead revealed the location within the model that they had each reached.

The small seminar class of six second-year undergraduates completed the four stages during the one year and adequately demonstrated their new socially constructed knowledge in an exhibition presentation, in a published journal, and in reflective reports of their experience and how the course had changed their thinking. The teaching aim was to scaffold and promote a desire in each of them for lifelong learning. Two of the six went on to engage in higher learning at another university.

Adult Motivations to Learn

In this validation study, student motivation to learn in a preferred way had a potential influence on the performance in certain stages. Therefore, to investigate any influence, students were surveyed by questionnaire on their preferred approaches to learning and their motivations. The questionnaires and self-reports were followed up by interviews. How to initiate each and all the various intrinsic motivations to learn has been previously reported by Kawachi (2002c). However, that study was based on the taxonomy of Gibbs et al. (1984), which used data from about 1960 which pre-date multimedia learning technologies. Briefly, there are the four intrinsic motivations: vocational, academic, personal, and social. These were discovered in the present study simultaneously in varying levels depending on the task and with individual differences. However, beyond these, there was suggested some motivation to lifelong learning that was difficult to accommodate within the nearest category of intrinsic personal challenge. This motivation was suggested by only the older postgraduate students. It is tentatively labeled the "aesthetic" motivation to learn. The discovery and illuminatory methodology used here was informed by various interview open responses leading into focused discussions, and it followed a grounded-theory approach. Two orthogonal dimensions were found and labeled as positive and negative incidences of *jouissance* occurring accidentally during the learning process. These incidences only occurred when the student was markedly actively learning—struggling to construct meaning to discover suddenly how things fit together in a shot of joy (positive *jouissance*) or how things had been mistaken and misunderstood (negative *jouissance*). This aesthetic motivation was concluded to be acting along the process of the interaction between the student and the content-to-be-learned (actually *to* the student *from* the content-to-be-learned, a unidirectional motivation). Aesthetic motivation derives *from* the process. There was a similar motivation acting in the opposite direction —*to* the process—of expressive motivation, in which the student is driven to proceed, by the joy of doing (as might occur for example in writing poetry, or fine-art painting). As an illustration, aesthetic motivation drives a hobby fisherman; positive *jouissance* occurs when the fisherman catches a surprisingly large fish, and alternatively, negative *jouissance* occurs when a fish escapes suddenly. Both these types occur only in the adult or mature person with an already fully formed self or culture, and they occur as a bursting of this bubble, momentarily and transiently. The fisherman's experience is increased by the *jouissance*, and he is more driven to continue fishing. Aesthetic motivation is the motivation to lifelong learning. The tutor needs to understand the limits of the student's context or worldview and guide the student to approach the limits of his or her world, hopefully to experience *jouissance* and initiate aesthetic motivation to learn.

Summary of Results

Repeated empirical studies found that only small classes with close tutor moderating, and preferably of students with sufficient background knowledge, could successfully engage the collaborative learning tasks and complete all four stages in this model. Most undergraduate students, especially in larger classes or even in small groups but with reduced tutor monitoring, could not engage the collaborative Stage 3. A similar finding was also reported by Perry (1970), in the United States, who concluded that college students were maybe not yet sufficiently mature to acquire the skills of critical thinking. It is well known (Kawachi, 2003c) that collaborative learning characterizes the construction of nonfoundational (graduate-level) knowledge rather than the acquisition of foundational knowledge (at the undergraduate level).

Discussion

Scaffold Efficacy

The DML model was designed and intended to act as scaffolding to guide the teacher (in the present study, the author), inform the process, and assist student learning. It was not completely successful. This was due to the limited duration of the course and the levels of maturity in the students. The limited duration of the shorter (6-month) courses meant that the self-pacing or unpaced nature would not allow for the students to complete the full learning cycle. The low levels of maturity in the undergraduate younger students meant that they found much difficulty in navigating Stage 3.

Four separate modes of learning were serially linked in this DML model. Stage 1 employed synchronous media for cooperative brainstorming; Stage 2 employed asynchronous media for collaborative lateral thinking; Stage 3 employed asynchronous media for collaborative vertical thinking and problem-based learning; and Stage 4 employed synchronous media for experiential learning. This model indicates the need to change the type of media employed during the learning process, for example, from synchronous to asynchronous to move from Stage 1 to Stage 2. While Stage 3 proved difficult for some students, the largest hurdle was found in moving from asynchronous collaborative Stage 2 to asynchronous collaborative Stage 3. This needs to be discussed. The task activities of Stage 3 require the students to raise doubts about others, to question the teacher and the text, and to search for one's own opinion, even though this might be against the established opinions of others in authority. One reason for the students not moving into Stage 3 was that the activities of Stage 3 were inconsistent and incongruous with their own lives or cultural views of the world (for example, see Briguglio, 2000, p. 3, for a discussion of Jones, 1999, unpublished report).

These questioning skills may be characteristic of a mature adult. In support of this DML model to master these questioning skills of Stage 3, Halpern (1984) reported that all adults should learn to question input prior to acquisition, in what he described as a "content" effect: "When we reason we do not automatically accept the given premises as true. We use our knowledge about the topic (content) to judge the veracity of the premises and to supply additional information that influences which conclusion we will accept as valid" (p. 359). Adults generally have more experience than adolescents from which to draw additional information, so they can be expected to be more questioning during learning from a teacher or other resource. Younger or immature adults can be expected to not yet hold adequate foundational knowledge with which to engage the Stage 3 questioning and answering.

Moreover, a gender difference might be operating here. Raising doubts about others, and having others raise doubts about you, may be an undesirable activity for some students—not only for women but also for those who may be disadvantaged by physical or mental dysfunctions and those who may not be adequately literate. There are many kinds of literacy involved here—linguistic literacy in a first language, linguistic literacy in the language as medium of the education (notably in English as a foreign language), information literacy (the capability to find information efficiently), cyber-literacy (the capability to handle virtual systems and manage oneself within these), and technological literacy (the capabilities to manage and interact through the human–computer interface). In such cases, the need for conservation of self may rise higher than the internal drive or need for progression through further education.

Women who try distance education may be more likely to bring with them higher levels of self-doubt and anxieties that can add a more cautious approach to their questioning of authorities. Also, traditionally, higher education has not been part of their world and self-concept, so they are operating in a somewhat alien world, and one that is not congruous with their present conception of the world. This may also be true for men, because adults generally have already established their social world and self, and where this does not include higher education—as in those who engage in higher education for the first time as a "second chance"— then the students might understandably be reluctant to argue with others in academia. Adults who are returning to higher education or are at the postgraduate level may find no incongruity.

Belenky et al. (1997) reported that the aim for participating in education is different between women and men. They write that women want to be at the center and not be far out from others, and they value the comfort that being in the group brings to their learning and self-development. They write that men, on the other hand, want to excel and be out ahead of the group, and they may feel threatened by another person being too close or approaching. Asynchronous media may provide women the time needed to move the group forward as a whole, without one moving alone, too far from the center. However, this might require unusually good communication skills and literacies.

On Pacing

There was no pacing imposed during this empirical validation of the model. Four courses were each of one 6-month academic semester, consisting of about 15 lessons, each 90 minutes, plus out-of-class interactions equivalent to at least a further 200 hours and, in many cases, much more. In another two courses, the duration was double that and continued for 1 year. No pacing was used, because through previous experience, it was found that pacing induced students to adopt a performance orientation (for discussion, see Abrami & Bures, 1996, p. 38), rather than adopt a deep approach to their learning. This was an ethical decision, which negatively confounded the findings. However, literature studies later indicated that in paced (Gunawardena et al., 1997, 2001) and unpaced (McKinnon, 1976; Piaget, 1977; Renner, 1976a, 1976b) learning, students similarly reached to various levels, not completing the four stages, and mostly reaching to somewhere between the middle of Stage 2 and the middle of Stage 3, as in the present study.

In the two courses of one-year duration, findings showed that the students generally had reached the end of Stage 4. One course was a small seminar class of six second-year undergraduate students, and the other was of eight postgraduate adult students. Both were closely guided by the tutor. A similar class of adult students was unpaced and closely guided but over only six months, and they reached only to the middle of Stage 3.

All the courses were compulsory, so no student was allowed to drop out without having to repeat the course. This fact influenced the decision to have no pacing and to focus on the students' deep learning achievements.

Other Studies Measuring Transactional Distance

The present study, through close monitoring, followed each student through the learning-cycle process from an initial maximum transactional distance to less and less transactional distance. Hypertext navigation paths and serial written reports were used, together with interviews. These were very effective as measures of the progress of each student and were fairly effective as a measure of the transactional distance. The transactional distance varied during the course, becoming more reduced. Thus, the present study was a longitudinal study of measuring transactional distance.

A cross-sectional study measuring transactional distance was recently reported by Chen and Willits (1999).

Chen and Willits (1999) designed, piloted, and applied a questionnaire to measure the transactional distance in a videoconferencing course. They applied factor analysis to determine the loadings on dialogue, structure, and autonomy. They surveyed 202 students participating in 12 different courses (suggesting that their questionnaire had up to 70 items, if the 202 were treated as one cohort together for factor analysis). The items in each factor indicated that each concept of D, S, and A was complex and not simple. Their study was limited by the fact that they could not use factor analysis to discover structure, dialogue, and autonomy as three factors initially and used simply three separate questionnaires pasted together as one, and three separate analyses – one for each of them. This was likely because dialogue, structure, and autonomy are interrelated by a simplex structure, not a hierarchical structure. Factor analysis is inappropriate for simplex structures (Bynner & Romney, 1986). Dialogue and structure are related horizontally in that the amount of structure influences the amount of dialogue, so a simplex structure exists, and factor analysis should not be used. Structural path analysis would reveal this, but Chen and Willits did not report doing any path analysis. Nevertheless, they found that lower transactional distance was correlated with a higher level of learning outcome.

Their results support the use of the DML model to reduce systematically the transactional distance during a course to increase the quality and level of learning.

Implications and Future Studies

Implications and Problems Arising

The problems arising can be clearly seen: while the DML model serves as a comprehensive model for using multimedia and advanced learning technologies to achieve critical learning and develop lifelong learners, few students actually proceed beyond Stage 2 or 3—both the collaborative stages. The results falling from this are that so-called educationalists have their students afloat without winds in the doldrums. Students are using computers to chat and find (old foundational) knowledge, relating personal whims in Stage 1, and sharing interesting anecdotes in Stage 2, and not engaging academic knowledge-creation in Stage 3. While such depressing results were not seen in the present study, the obtained results were mixed. Some students could succeed to complete a full learning cycle of the model, and a couple went on to lifelong learning. But most undergraduate students found navigating the collaborative process of Stage 3 too difficult, despite the availability of scaffolding giving much additional structure to facilitate the required dialogue (from D- S+ Stage 2, to D+ S+ Stage 3).

It was also apparent that students found it difficult to move from Stage 3 to Stage 4. They reported that they could discover knowledge, views, and perspectives from other students and the World Wide Web and could make their own opinions from weighing these critically. However, they reported difficulty in relating the theoretical perspective of Stage 3 to their own practical context in Stage 4 experientially. (A solution is given here next, rather than in the following section, for clarity.) Dialogue is very important in Stage 3, and a lot is needed. So, guided conversation is used. After largely achieving coconstruction of new understanding and knowledge, they need to move into Stage 4. To help them manage this, the tutor should increase dialogue even more by introducing synchronous conferencing. In the present study, personal presentations were made publicly to other students concerning the impact of the new knowledge on their lives and how they would try out new ideas in their lives. According to Moore (1993) the institution here should "take measures to reduce transactional distance by increasing the dialogue through use of teleconferencing" (p. 27). Students will lose some autonomy (A-) in going to synchronous mode, because they must become more empathic with others, but they will gain in dialogue (D+) and also in responsiveness to their own wants and needs and own context (with S- decrease in institutional structure).

Concerning the use of the World Wide Web and multimedia to promote students' learning, Herrington and Oliver (1999) reported that the higher-order thinking (of Stage 3 and Stage 4 here) was supported by using a situated-learning framework for relating the discussion to the student's own context. When using multimedia in situated learning, there was much less lower-order discussion and less social chat (Herrington & Oliver, 1999), indicating that multimedia could be applied to move students from Stage 1 to Stages 2 and 3. The implication here is that increasing the use of multimedia might have helped younger students cope better with the collaborative Stage 3.

Suggested Solutions

The various interactions between the student and tutor, student and other students, and student to content, and the quality, quantity, and frequencies of these constitute the academic dialogue in the educative process. The amount of dialogue needs to be carefully measured to suit each student's learning preferences and the task at hand. It is not true that simply increasing the amount of dialogue will solve all these interaction problems.

Adults generally need their prior experience and knowledge to be valued. Stage 3 entails collaborative argument. This needs an openness and receptiveness to have one's ideas be contradicted. Taking in new conflicting perspectives or information means, first, deconstruction of the existing cognitive knowledge network, where such deconstruction can be painful, especially when the prior understanding (like an old and trusted friend) has served the adult well to date. Concerning the uptake of learning technologies in their own courses, teachers, for example, have expressed a willingness to accept the innovation only insofar as it can be taken in small safe steps, permitting the teacher the safety-net option of recoursing to their proven methodology. The tutor should closely guide adults to moderate the amount of new conflicting information to prevent loss in their self-esteem. This is especially important during the Stage 3 collaborative argument and is not unimportant in the cooperative stages. Adults with a preference to field dependence (defined by Walter, 1998, as "those who gradually build towards generalisations about patterns from repeated exposure") will want to receive much information and likely enjoy cooperative learning in a group, while adults with a preference to field independence (defined by Walter, 1998, as "those who tend to see patterns and general principles in a flash of insight") are likely to want very much less input and may prefer the reflective process of collaborative learning in a group. The tutor is going to have a difficult time trying to moderate the amount of information proffered in student-to-student interactions.

To manage the quantity of new information, and the quality and frequency, the tutor could direct cooperative massive exchanges away from Stage 2 and Stage 3 to a virtual "coffee-shop" set up expressly for this purpose, to keep the collaborative forum uncluttered. Then, the tutor will need to direct field-dependent learners to this virtual coffee-shop to assist their learning in their preferred way. This will also keep the online main forum clearer for the field-independent learners, during cooperative learning when field-dependent learners may be up-loading voluminous perspectives.

In Stage 3, there is a benefit to everyone to have diversity as wide as possible in different perspectives through which to test multiple hypotheses. Overloading to field-independent learners ought to be avoided, so careful use of hypertext is suggested here. For example, hypertext could be used in Stage 3 to give available links to reasons, keeping the main forum relatively uncluttered. It is necessary for the tutor to preascertain the field-dependence/independence of the participants and then closely guide each type separately, or to utilize some technique such as adaptive hypertext to accommodate these differences, equitably. The DML model indicates when, how, and why such adaptive hypertext will be useful. Using adaptive hypertext, the institution can provide extra interactivity to field-dependent students in the asynchronous collaborative stages, when there may be online silence among the field-independent learners. In the absence of adaptive hypermedia, the tutor should carefully tailor the amount of tutor-to-student messages to each type of learner.

Future Studies

Future studies are required to explore further why students find Stage 3 difficult to navigate through. In law and in health care and medicine, the collaborative critical-thinking skills in Stage 3 are especially important. Several institutions base their curricula now on trying to impart these skills using problem-based learning, though not all students prefer or choose this way of learning (for example, see Mangan, 1997, for law, and see Barrows, 1998, for medicine). Using this DML model, the current attention to problem-based learning processes can therefore be understood, and problem-based learning can be seen clearly in relation to the other ways of learning.

Since the present preliminary results were confounded by gender differences as well as by the use of English as a foreign language, further extended studies are underway. To investigate the correlation, if any, between the use of English as a foreign language and any potential overload (suggested by reduced reading and writing speeds by non-native-English users by Kawachi, 2002a, 2002b), identical courseware in various languages has been identified (namely Pocock & Richards, 1999), and students studying in their native language will be followed and comparatively measured.

Student motivations to learning online remain an area for further studies. How to initiate each and all the various intrinsic motivations to learn has been reported by Kawachi (2002c). However, further studies are warranted, because current taxonomies of adult motivations to learn pre-date multimedia learning technologies.

Conclusion

The DML model has been tested out in Japan, in large and small classes. Larger classes were divided into small groups of five or six students each. However, only in the small classes did students move successfully through the whole learning cycle. It was concluded that learning critical thinking using multimedia was better suited to graduate-level students or to small groups of tutor-guided undergraduate students. It was also concluded that tutor (the author) guidance was an important element and was too thinly spread while trying to manage five or six small groups simultaneously. In the larger classes, students did not achieve mastery of the collaborative learning, despite trying to use the frameworks provided.

The deployment of learning technologies does not result simply in the status quo plus technology, but instead results in a new complex educational environment. The DML model tested out here provides a clear guide to technology users. However, the relative amount of time to be spent in each stage of this model is not prescribed and must be varied according to the students' own pace and according to the topic under study. Quality in learning outcomes can be defined as learning that has been achieved efficiently in terms of resources, is long lasting, and has personal meaning in the relevant desired context. To assure quality, the available learning technologies need to be utilized strategically. Different students naturally bring various learning preferences with them, and a single mode of teaching will be inappropriate. The advantage of multimedia is that multimedia can be designed to appeal to these various preferences simultaneously. The model of learning critical-thinking skills investigated here provides a scaffold to all the agents involved in education, including the administrators, teachers, nonacademic support, and students. This model as a scaffold serves as a cue and support to all these agents. Some students (or some teachers) might be uncomfortable in a particular stage of this model, where learning proceeds through a nonpreferred way. For example, field-dependent learners may prefer the synchronous cooperative stages, while field-independent learners may prefer the asynchronous collaborative stages. Nevertheless, critical thinking is a universally avowed desirable goal in adult education, and adults need to acquire these skills and should be strategically flexible in their approaches to study. The model dictates when switching to another approach is required, to proceed optimally and learn efficiently the full repertoire of skills that interlink for critical thinking. There is no argument that some courses may utilize only one way of teaching and learning. This model shows how such courseware might be improved for all-round human resource development.

Computer-mediated communications are being utilized for an increasing number of students in both conventional classrooms and at a distance, in synchronous mode and in asynchronous mode. This could suggest that more research and design resources might be forthcoming. Yet there is little research to date on why and when to utilize these technologies. In some studies, synchronous videoconferencing technologies have been bought and can technically connect the various agents for the learning process, but the tutors and institutions aim for collaborative learning, for which the synchronous technology is inappropriate and unsuccessful. Remarkable efforts are being made by many institutions worldwide to apply these new technologies for learning, yet the instructional design and the technology selected continue to be important factors causing the failures to achieve higher-order thinking skills (Abrami & Bures, 1996, p. 37). The present DML model is the only practical model proposed to date for selecting and ordering the utilization of learning technologies for acquiring critical-thinking skills. As such, the DML model constitutes an intelligent syllabus to be tested out further.

References

Abrami, P. C., & Bures, E. M. (1996). Computer-supported collaborative learning and distance education. *American Journal of Distance Education, 10*, 37–42.

Barrows, H. (1998). *Problem based learning.* Southern Illinois University School of Medicine. Retrieved January 10, 1999 from the World Wide Web: http://edaff.siumed/dept/index.htm

Belenky, M. F., Clinchy, B. M., Goldberger, N. R., & Tarule, J. M. (1997). *Women's ways of knowing: The development of self, voice and mind* (10th anniversary ed.). New York: Basic Books.

Bork, A. (2001). What is needed for effective learning on the Internet. Special issue on curriculum, instruction, learning and the Internet. *Educational Technology and Society*, (in press). Retrieved June 10, 2002 from the World Wide Web: http://www.ics.uci.edu/~bork/effectivelearning.htm

Boud, D. (1988). Moving toward student autonomy. In D. Boud (Ed.), *Developing student autonomy in learning* (2nd ed.) (pp. 17–39). London: Kogan Page.

Briguglio, C. (2000). Self directed learning is fine—If you know the destination! In A. Herrmann, & M. M. Kulski (Eds.), *Flexible futures in tertiary teaching—Proceedings of the 9th Annual Teaching Learning forum*, February 2–4, 2000, Curtin University of Technology, Perth, Australia. Retrieved May 14, 2003 from the World Wide Web: http://cea.curtin.edu.au/tlf/tlf2000/briguglio.html

Brookfield, S. D. (1987). *Developing critical thinkers: Challenging adults to explore alternative ways of thinking and acting*. San Francisco, CA: Jossey-Bass.

Bynner, J. M., & Romney, D. M. (1986). Intelligence, fact or artefact: Alternative structures for cognitive abilities. *British Journal of Educational Psychology*, 56, 13–23.

Chen, Y. -J., & Willits, F. K. (1999). Dimensions of educational transactions in a videoconferencing learning environment. *American Journal of Distance Education*, 13(1), 45–59.

Dewey, J. (1933). *How we think: A restatement of the relation of reflective thinking to the educative process*. Lexington, MA: D.C. Heath and Company.

Gibbs, G., Morgan, A., & Taylor, E. (1984). The world of the learner. In F. Marton, D. Hounsell, & N. J. Entwistle (Eds.), *The experience of learning* (pp. 165–188). Edinburgh: Scottish Academic Press.

Gunawardena, C., Plass, J., & Salisbury, M. (2001). Do we really need an online discussion group? In D. Murphy, R. Walker, & G. Webb (Eds.), *Online learning and teaching with technology: Case studies, experience and practice* (pp. 36–43). London: Kogan Page.

Gunawardena, C. N., Lowe, C. A., & Anderson, T. (1997). Analysis of global online debate and the development of an interaction analysis model for examining social construction of knowledge in computer conferencing. *Journal of Educational Computing Research*, 17(4), 397–431.

Halpern, D. F. (1984). *Thought and knowledge: An introduction to critical thinking*. Hillsdale, NJ: Lawrence Erlbaum Associates.

Harrison, C. (2002). Hypertext links: Whither thou goest, and why. *First Monday*, 7(10). Retrieved October 10, 2002 from the World Wide Web: http://firstmonday.org/issues/issue7_10/

Herrington, J., & Oliver, R. (1999). Using situated learning and multimedia to investigate higher-order thinking. *Journal of Educational Multimedia and Hypermedia*, 8(4), 401–422. Retrieved May 6, 2003 from the World Wide Web: http://dl.aace.org/9172

Holmberg, B. (1983). Guided didactic conversation in distance education. In D. Sewart, D. Keegan, & B. Holmberg (Eds.), *Distance education: International perspectives* (pp. 114–122). London: Croom Helm.

Kaplan, H. (1997). Interactive multimedia & the World Wide Web. *Educom Review*, 32(1). Retrieved May 21, 2003 from the World Wide Web: http://www.educom.edu/web/pubs/review/reviewArticles/32148.html

Kawachi, P. (2000). *Why the sun doesn't rise: The impact of language on the participation of Japanese students in global online education.* Unpublished MA ODE Thesis, Open University, Milton Keynes, UK. Available from the author by e-mail: kawachi@kurume-shinai.ac.jp

Kawachi, P. (2002a). Poverty and access: The impact of language on online collaborative learning for Japanese learners. In H. P. Dikshit, S. Garg, S. Panda, & Vijayshri (Eds.), *Access & equity: Challenges for open and distance learning* (pp. 159–170). New Delhi: Kogan Page.

Kawachi, P. (2002b). On-line and off-line reading English rates: Differences according to native-language L1, gender, and age. *Proceedings of the 16th annual conference of the Asian Association of Open Universities,* Seoul, Korea, November 5–7. Retrieved January 10, 2003 from the World Wide Web: http://www.aaou.or.kr

Kawachi, P. (2002c). How to initiate intrinsic motivation in the on-line student in theory and practice. In V. Phillips et al. (Eds.), *Motivating and retaining adult learners online* (pp. 46–61). Essex Junction, VT: Virtual University Gazette. Retrieved August 25, 2002 from the World Wide Web: http://www.geteducated.com/vug/aug02/Journal/MotivateRetain02.PDF

Kawachi, P. (2003a). Vicarious interaction and the achieved quality of learning. *International Journal on E-Learning, 2*(4), 39-45. Retrieved January 16, 2004 from the World Wide Web: http://dl.aace.org/14193

Kawachi, P. (2003b). Choosing the appropriate media to support the learning process. *Journal of Educational Technology, 14*(1&2), 1–18.

Kawachi, P. (2003c). Initiating intrinsic motivation in online education: Review of the current state of the art. *Interactive Learning Environments, 11*(1), 59-81.

Laurillard, D. (2002). *Rethinking university teaching* (2nd ed.)*: A conversational framework for the effective use of learning technologies.* London: RoutledgeFalmer.

Lyons, R. E., Kysilka, M. L., & Pawlas, G. E. (1999). *The adjunct professor's guide to success: Surviving and thriving in the college classroom.* Needham Heights, MA: Allyn & Bacon.

Mangan, K. S. (1997). Lani Guinier starts campaign to curb use of the Socratic method. *Chronicle of Higher Education,* (11 April), A12–14.

McKinnon, J. W. (1976). The college student and formal operations. In J. W. Renner, D. G. Stafford, A. E. Lawson, J. W. McKinnon, F. E. Friot, & D. H. Kellogg (Eds.), *Research, teaching, and learning with the Piaget model* (pp. 110–129). Norman, OK: Oklahoma University Press.

McLoughlin, C., & Marshall, L. (2000). *Scaffolding: A model for learner support in an online teaching environment*. Retrieved May 14, 2003 from the World Wide Web: http://cea.curtin.edu.au/tlf/tlf2000/mcloughlin2.html

Moore, M. (1993). Theory of transactional distance. In D. Keegan (Ed.), *Theoretical principles of distance education* (pp. 22–38). London: Routledge.

Neubauer, M. (2003a). *Asynchronous, synchronous, and F2F interaction*. Online posting May 23 to the Distance Education Online Symposium. Retrieved May 23, 2003 from the World Wide Web: http://lists.psu.edu/archives/deos-l.html

Neubauer, M. (2003b). *Number of online participants*. Online posting January 22nd to the Distance Education Online Symposium. Retrieved January 22, 2003 from the World Wide Web: http://lists.psu.edu/archives/deos-l.html

Palincsar, A. S. (1986). The role of dialogue in providing scaffolding instruction. *Educational Psychologist, 21*, 73–98.

Perry, W. G. (1970). *Forms of intellectual and ethical development in the college years: A scheme*. New York: Holt, Rinehart and Winston.

Piaget, J. (1977). Intellectual evolution from adolescence to adulthood. In P. N. Johnson-Laird, & P. C. Wason (Eds.), *Thinking: Readings in cognitive science*. Cambridge, UK: Cambridge University Press.

Pocock, G., & Richards, C. D. (1999). *Human physiology: The basis of medicine*. Oxford : Oxford University Press (and same courseware in Japanese, in French, and in Spanish).

Probst, R. E. (1987). Transactional theory in the teaching of literature. *ERIC Digest* ED 284 274. Retrieved April 24, 2002 from the World Wide Web: http://www.ed.gov/databases/ERIC_Digests/ed284274.html

Renner, J. S. (1976a). Formal operational thought and its identification. In J. W. Renner, D. G. Stafford, A. E. Lawson, J. W. McKinnon, F. E. Friot, & D. H. Kellogg (Eds.), *Research, teaching, and learning with the Piaget model* (pp. 64–78). Norman, OK: Oklahoma University Press.

Renner, J. S. (1976b). What this research says to schools. In J. W. Renner, D. G. Stafford, A. E. Lawson, J. W. McKinnon, F. E. Friot, & D. H. Kellogg (Eds.), *Research, teaching, and learning with the Piaget model* (pp. 174–191). Norman, OK: Oklahoma University Press.

Reynolds, B. (2003). Synchronous instruction in D/E. Online posting May 27 to the Distance Education Online Symposium. Retrieved May 27, 2003 from the World Wide Web: http://lists.psu.edu/archives/deos-l.html

Rosenshine, B., & Meister, C. (1992). The use of scaffolds for teaching higher-level cognitive strategies. *Educational Leadership, 49*(7), 26–33.

Tennant, M.C., & Pogson, P. (1995). *Learning and change in the adult years: A developmental perspective*. San Francisco, CA: Jossey-Bass.

Vygotsky, L. S. (1978). *Mind in society: The development of higher psychological processes*. Cambridge, MA: Harvard University Press.

Walter, C. (1998). Learner independence: Why, what, where, how, who? *Independence*: Newsletter of the IATEFL Learner Independence Special Interest Group, *21*, 11–16.

Wang, H. (2002). The use of WebBoard in asynchronous learning. *Learning Technology Newsletter, 4*(2), 2–3. Retrieved June 10, 2002 from the World Wide Web: http://lttf.ieee.org/learn_tech/

Wood, D., Bruner, J. S., & Ross, G. (1976). The role of tutoring in problem solving. *Journal of Child Psychology and Psychiatry, 17*, 89–100.

Zimmer, B. (1995). The empathy templates: A way to support collaborative learning. In F. Lockwood (Ed.), *Open and distance learning today* (pp. 139–150). London: Routledge.

Chapter X

Multimedia, Cognitive Load and Pedagogy

Peter E. Doolittle, Virginia Polytechnic Institute & State University, USA

Andrea L. McNeill, Virginia Polytechnic Institute & State University, USA

Krista P. Terry, Radford University, USA

Stephanie B. Scheer, University of Virginia, USA

Abstract

The current emphasis, in education and training, on the use of instructional technology has fostered a shift in focus and renewed interest in integrating human learning and pedagogical research. This shift has involved the technological and pedagogical integration between learner cognition, instructional design, and instructional technology, with much of this integration focusing on the role of working memory and cognitive load in the development of comprehension and performance. Specifically, working memory, dual coding theory, and cognitive load are examined in order to provide the underpinnings of Mayer's (2001) Cognitive Theory of Multimedia Learning. The bulk of the chapter then addresses various principles based on Mayer's work and provides well documented web-based examples.

Introduction

Improving the efficiency and effectiveness of instruction has consistently been a primary goal of education and training. In pursuit of this goal, cognitive psychology has provided considerable insight regarding the processes that underlie efficient and effective instruction. The past 50 years are replete with empirical studies addressing the characteristics inherent in human learning and the influence of these characteristics on instruction. Unfortunately (Anderson, Reder, & Simon, 1998), this "science of human learning has never had a large influence upon the *practice* of education [or training]" (p. 227; italics added). This gap between research and practice is lamentable and serves to deny learners and teachers access to powerful forms of teaching, training, and learning.

Fortunately, the current emphasis on the use of instructional technology has fostered renewed interest in integrating human learning and pedagogical research (see Abbey, 2000; Rouet, Levonen, & Biardeau 2001). As Doolittle (2001) has stated, "it is time to stop professing technological and pedagogical integration and to start integrating with purpose and forethought" (p. 502). One area within instructional technology that has begun this integration is multimedia. The domain of multimedia has matured beyond technology-driven applications into the realm of cognition and instruction. As stated in Rouet, Levonen, and Biardeau (2001), "There is a subtle shift of attention from what *can* be done with the technology to what *should* be done in order to design meaningful instructional applications" (p. 1). This shift has involved the technological and pedagogical integration between learner cognition, instructional design, and instructional technology, with much of this integration focusing on the role of working memory in the development of comprehension and performance.

Specifically, a focus has developed addressing the limited resource nature of working memory and cognitive load. Cognitive load simply refers to the working memory demands implicitly and explicitly created by instruction and how these demands affect the learning process. Those learning tasks that are poorly designed or involve the complex integration of multiple ideas, skills, or attributes result in increased cognitive load and decreased learning. This relationship between cognitive load, working memory, and instruction/training has proved to be especially significant when the instruction is in the form of multimedia. According to Mayer (2001), "the central work of multimedia learning takes place in working memory" (p. 44).

This chapter focuses on multimedia and the mitigating effects of cognitive load on teaching, training, and learning. A central organizing theme throughout the chapter is the development of theoretically sound pedagogy (see Figure 1). Theoretically sound pedagogy involves instruction that is based on empirical research and sound theory designed to illuminate the nature of human learning and behavior. Such theoretically sound pedagogy may then be molded to fit specific learning environments, learning goals and objectives, and learners.

Working Memory, Dual Coding and Cognitive Load

When pursuing theoretically sound pedagogy, it is essential to ground one's conclusions in the human memory literature. Unfortunately, while there is a plethora of research findings exemplifying the structure and function of human memory, a singular model of memory to which one can refer has yet to emerge. Currently, the three most prevalent models are Atkinson and Shiffrin's (1968) dual-store model, Baddeley's (Baddeley, 1986; Baddeley & Hitch, 1974) working memory model, and Anderson's (1983, 1990, 1993) functional ACT-R model. Each of these models has roots in the early information-processing work of Broadbent (1958) and Peterson and Peterson (1959).

Figure 1: The development of theoretically sound pedagogy

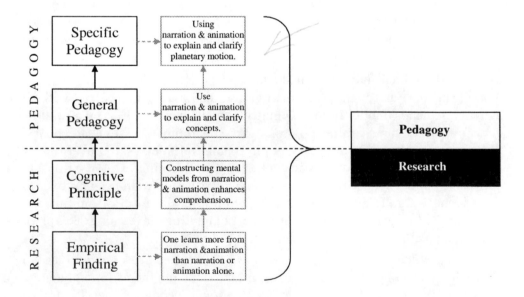

Memory Models and Working Memory

Atkinson and Shiffrin (1968) emphasized the structural nature of memory, delineating three essential structures, *sensory memory*, *short-term memory*, and *long-term memory*. Atkinson and Shiffrin asserted that individuals experience the world through their senses, momentarily storing these senses in raw sensory formats at their sensory sites. These sensations, if attended, may then be encoded into a mind-friendly format and consciously held in short-term memory, where if the individual rehearses this encoded experience, the experience may be transferred to long-term memory. The *dual-store* of Atkinson and Shiffrin's model refers to the short-term memory store, where a small amount of information or experience may be held temporarily, and the long-term memory store, where an unlimited amount of information or experience may held indefinitely. This idea that there were two storage components, each with different processing capabilities, was developed from Broadbent in the 1950s through Atkinson and Shiffrin in the 1960s and was well accepted in the early 1970s. Unfortunately, in the 1970s, testing of the dual-store model revealed inconsistencies in the need for two storage components. By the 1980s, the dual-store model, with its two storage components, was being replaced by a unified working and long-term memory model.

Two separate memory stores were eliminated, and what remained was a single memory store, long-term memory, and a constellation of related processes, termed working memory, responsible for the regulation of reasoning, problem solving, decision making, and language processing (Miyake & Shah, 1999). Working memory is often confused with, or made synonymous with, short-term memory, as working memory has retained certain short-term memory characteristics. For example, a central characteristic of short-term memory was a limited capacity due to a hypothesized small storage space. This limited capacity is also a characteristic of working memory, but the rationale has changed from a limitation based on structure (i.e., space) to a limitation based on function (i.e., processing). Working memory limitations are currently seen as a function of ongoing processing and the nature of the information being processed (see Miyake & Shah, 1999). While working memory and short-term memory share certain similar characteristics, although for differing reasons, they are also significantly different.

Perhaps the most obvious difference between short-term memory and working memory is that short-term memory was construed as a storage location or "box," while working memory is defined as a set of cognitive processes responsible for the support of complex cognition. A second, and related, difference involves purpose. Typically, short-term memory is described as subservient to long-term memory, where long-term memory is responsible for the cognitive processing and short-term memory is merely a workspace for memorization (Baddeley, 1999). Working memory, however, is interpreted as working synergistically with long-term memory, playing a primary role in control and regulation functions (Cowan, 1999). This emphasis on synergy underlies the third difference, which is related to the influence of long-term memory on short-term and working memory. The traditional relationship between short-term memory and long-term memory is one of *independence*, where short-term and long-term memory communicate, as two individuals talking on the telephone, sharing ideas but each operating in only distantly related realms. The relationship between working memory and long-term memory, however, is one of *interdependence* (Baddeley & Logie, 1999; Ericsson & Kintsch, 1995). The interplay between working memory and long-term memory is integrated to such an extent that any discussion of human cognitive performance in the absence of either working or long-term memory would be incomplete.

Thus, an exploration of human cognitive performance in a multimedia environment would need to address this working and long-term memory interdependence. This interdependence is evident in two theories that are currently guiding the development of multimedia instructional technology—dual-coding theory and cognitive load theory.

Dual-Coding Theory

Building on working and long-term memory interdependence, Paivio (1971, 1990) created a theory of cognition that emphasizes the mind's processing of two types or codes of information, verbal and nonverbal. Specifically, Paivio (1990) stated that memory and cognition are represented within two functionally independent, but interconnected, processing systems (see Figure 2). One system, the *verbal system*, is specialized for the representation and processing of verbal information (e.g., words, sentences, stories), while the other system, the *nonverbal system*, is specialized for the representation and processing of nonverbal information (e.g., pictures, sounds, smells, tastes). Each system holds and processes representations that are modality-specific (i.e., visual, auditory, tactile, gustatory, olfactory), that is, the representations retain certain properties of the concrete sensorimotor events on which they are based (Clark & Paivio, 1991). It is important to note that these representations are not exact copies of one's experiences, but rather they represent imprecise facsimiles (Paivio, 1990).

The interaction between the verbal/nonverbal processing and modality-specific perceptions can be somewhat confusing. A central point is that regardless of modality, verbal experiences are processed by the verbal system, and nonverbal experiences are processed by the nonverbal system (see Table 1). An everyday

Figure 2: A schematic representation of Paivio's (1990) dual-coding model, including both verbal/nonverbal channels and representational, associative, and referential processing

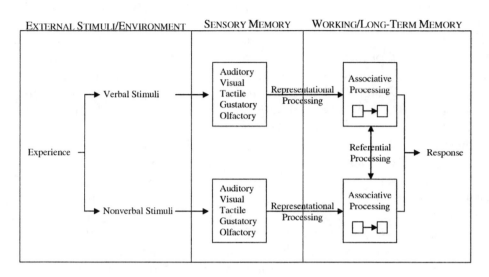

Table 1: Examples of verbal/nonverbal cognitive processing based on specific modality experiences

| | Cognitive Processing | |
Modality	Nonverbal	Verbal
Visual	Looking at pictures, animations, or clouds	Reading a book, a billboard, or the label on clothing
Auditory	Listening to music, airplanes taking off, or nature sounds	Listening to a speech, a song, or a conversation
Haptic	Touching silk, another's hair, or the texture of wood	Reading Braille, finger spelling, or sign language
Gustatory	Tasting food, licking an envelope, or eating snow	NA
Olfactory	Smelling food, a rainstorm, or noxious gases	NA

example of dual coding would include an individual looking at a weather map on the computer while listening to a weather report (e.g., http://www.weather.com/activities/verticalvideo/vdaily/weeklyplanner.html). The words encountered listening to the weather report would be processed by the verbal system, while the visual images encountered looking at the weather map would be processed by the nonverbal system.

Paivio (1990), upon delineating this relationship between verbal/nonverbal processing and modality-specific perceptions, focused primarily on the verbal/

nonverbal processing aspects of the dual-coding theory. According to Paivio (1990), three levels of processing enable verbal and nonverbal representations to be accessed and activated during cognitive tasks (see Figure 2). *Representational processing* is characterized by direct activation; that is, a verbal or linguistic sense experience directly activates a verbal representation and a nonverbal or nonlinguistic sense experience directly activates a nonverbal representation. For instance, reading on-screen text (verbal) directly activates the verbal system, while seeing an on-screen image (nonverbal) directly activates the nonverbal system. *Referential processing* refers to the indirect activation of the verbal system through experience with nonverbal information and the indirect activation of the nonverbal system through experience with verbal information. For example, reading on-screen text (verbal) may indirectly activate a mental image (nonverbal) based on the on-screen text; similarly, viewing an on-screen image (nonverbal) may indirectly activate a concept label (verbal) for that image. Consequently, referential processing is indirect in nature, because it requires crossover activity from one symbolic system to another. Finally, *associative processing* refers to the activation of representations within either system by other representations within that same system. For example, for a student with an aversion to technology, the word "computer" (verbal) might elicit verbal associations such as "hate" or "stupid" (verbal); conversely, the sight of a computer (nonverbal) might elicit images or visceral responses (nonverbal) reminiscent of unpleasant experiences using the computer.

Studies examining verbal/nonverbal processing have revealed two central findings (Mayer, Heiser, & Lonn, 2001; Sadoski & Paivio, 2001). First, processing experiences verbally and visually lead to greater learning, retention, and transfer than do processing experiences only verbally (Clark & Paivio, 1991; Paivio, 1975). For instance, in studying the process of osmosis, viewing an animation with a text description of the process (see http://edpsychserver.ed.vt.edu/5114web/modules/slideshows/slideshows.cfm?module=4) results in better learning, retention, and transfer than simply reading a text description. Second, both verbal and visual channels of information processing are subject to memory limitations such that each channel may be overloaded, reducing processing capacity and speed, and learning, retention, and transfer. For example, a multimedia slide show that includes auditory narration (verbal), subtitles of the auditory narration (verbal), and text within the slides themselves (verbal) is certain to overload an individual's verbal channel (http://edpsychserver.ed.vt.edu/5114web/modules/memory5_apps1/slideshow1.cfm). These two findings play a central role in multimedia pedagogy (see Mayer & Anderson, 1991; Schnotz, 2001) and are further explored in the next section, which addresses cognitive load theory. The construct of cognitive load is a means for assessing the memory limitations mentioned previously and for understanding the beneficial effects of adding visual information to verbal information.

Cognitive Load Theory

Cognitive load is a multidimensional construct that refers to the memory load that performing a task imposes on the learner (Paas & van Merrienboer, 1994; Sweller, van Merrienboer, & Paas, 1998). Inextricably linked with cognitive load theory is the notion that working memory is a limited resource; therefore, a careful distribution of the cognitive load within working memory is needed to successfully perform a given task (Chandler & Sweller, 1991, 1992). Further, cognitive load theory is based on several assumptions concerning human cognitive architecture (Mousavi, Low, & Sweller, 1995), including the following:

1.   People have limited working memory and processing capabilities.

2.   Long-term memory is virtually unlimited in size.

3.   Automation of cognitive processes decreases working memory load.

Ultimately, the central premise of cognitive load theory is that working memory is limited and, if overloaded, learning, retention, and transfer will be negatively affected.

Cognitive load theory posits that instructional materials impose upon the learner three independent sources of cognitive load—intrinsic cognitive load, extraneous cognitive load, and germane cognitive load (Gerjets & Scheiter, 2003; Paas, Renkl, & Sweller, 2003). Together, intrinsic, extraneous, and germane cognitive load comprise the total working memory load imposed on the learner during instruction (Tindall-Ford, Chandler, & Sweller, 1997) (see Figure 3).

Figure 3: Scenarios of the relationship between working memory capacity and the three components of cognitive load (i.e., intrinsic, extraneous, and germane cognitive load)

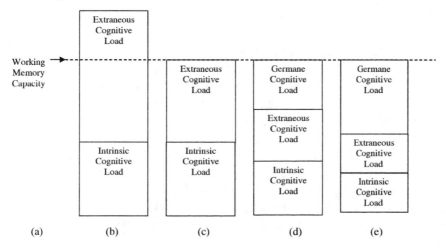

Intrinsic cognitive load represents the inherent working memory load required to complete a task. As an inherent component of a given task, intrinsic cognitive load is beyond the direct control of the instructional designer. Sweller (1994) suggested that the amount of interaction between learning elements, element interactivity, is a critical factor influencing intrinsic cognitive load. Element interactivity (Tindall-Ford et al., 1997) occurs when the "elements of a task interact in a manner that prevents each element from being understood and from being learned in isolation and, instead, requires all elements to be assimilated simultaneously" (p. 260). For example, learning the syntax of a computer language imposes a heavy intrinsic cognitive load, because to learn word and rule orders, all the words and rules must be held in working memory simultaneously.

What constitutes an element does not depend solely on the nature of the material, but it also depends on the expertise of the learner (Gerjets & Scheiter, 2003; Tindall-Ford et al., 1997). High element interactivity may not result in high cognitive load if expertise has been attained, thus allowing the learner to incorporate multiple elements into a single element, or "chunk," through schema acquisition or automaticity. This may be evidenced in the use of online simulations. For example, the Neurodegenerative Disease Simulation Model, a Java applet, can be daunting and create significant cognitive load for the novice due to the multiple options available, the complexity of the graphs, and the lack of automated skills related to the operation of the simulation (http://www.math.ubc.ca/~ais/website/guest00.html). For the experienced Neurodegenerative Disease Simulation Model user, however, the cognitive load is significantly reduced as the options are incorporated into schemas that act as an independent element, and the actual operation of the simulation is automated. Thus, using the simulation may result in extremely high intrinsic cognitive load for novices while imposing very little cognitive load on experts.

In addition to intrinsic cognitive load, the manner in which information is presented to learners and the activities required of learners can impose additional cognitive load (Paas, Renkl, & Sweller, 2003). While intrinsic cognitive load is determined by the nature of the material, *extraneous cognitive load* reflects the effort required to process instructional materials that do not contribute to learning the material or completing the task. In this sense, extraneous cognitive load can be seen as "error" in the overall instructional process. Fortunately, extraneous cognitive load is, to a large extent, under the control of instructional designers (Sweller et al., 1998). For example, when animation and text are combined, extraneous cognitive load is increased if the animation and text are not presented simultaneously (Moreno & Mayer, 1999). Specifically, imagine a simulation in which the directions are presented first, followed by the simulation (see http://webphysics.ph.msstate.edu/jc/library/2-6/index.html). In this case, the learner must read the directions, maintain the relevant directions in working memory, and then attempt to use the simulation. The simulation has an innate level of cognitive load, intrinsic cognitive load, to which is being added an additional cognitive load, extraneous cognitive load, as the result of having to maintain the directions in working memory. A simple solution to this extraneous cognitive load would be to provide the directions on the same page as the simulation.

The third type of cognitive load is *germane cognitive load*. Germane cognitive load is the cognitive load appropriated when an individual engages in processing that is not designed to complete a given task, but rather, is designed to improve the overall learning process (e.g., elaborating, inferencing, or automating). Engaging in processes that generate germane cognitive load is only possible when the sum of intrinsic and extraneous cognitive load is less than the limits of an individual's working memory. In addition, like extraneous cognitive load, germane cognitive load is influenced by the instructional designer. The manner in which information is presented to learners and the learning activities are factors relevant to the level of germane cognitive load. However, while extraneous cognitive load interferes with learning, germane cognitive load enhances learning by devoting resources to such tasks as schema acquisition and automation (Paas et al., 2003). For example, a student may engage in solving an historical murder mystery (http://web.uvic.ca/history-robinson/), resulting in both intrinsic and extraneous cognitive load. If sufficient working memory capacity remains, the student may also engage in practicing a metacognitive strategy for assessing the primary sources that serve as data for solving the murder mystery. Using a metacognitive strategy is not essential to engaging the murder mystery, however, this use will lead to greater automaticity of the strategy, elaboration on the primary sources, and ultimately, enhanced learning.

Overall, total cognitive load is comprised of the sum of intrinsic, extraneous, and germane cognitive load. This summative nature leads to several interesting scenarios (see Figure 3), all limited or constrained by an individual's working memory capacity (see Figure 3a). These differing scenarios will all be examined using a common example, a Social Justice Resource Center database site (see http://edpsychserver.ed.vt.edu/diversity/).

In the first scenario, if the sum of the intrinsic and extraneous cognitive loads exceeds one's working memory capacity, then learning and performance of the given task will be adversely affected (see Figure 3b). In the case of the Social Justice site, the Advanced Search page could easily overwhelm the working memory capacity of a database/search novice (Figure 4). The Advanced Search page contains complex functions for Boolean searches, data restriction, and layout control, all possibly contributing to excessive extraneous cognitive load.

If, however, the sum of intrinsic and extrinsic cognitive load is equal to one's working memory capacity, then one should be able to complete the given task successfully (see Figure 3c). Continuing the Social Justice example, the extraneous cognitive load may be reduced by instructing a student to focus only on understanding and using the Boolean operator search fields and ignoring the data restriction and layout options. Providing or focusing on fewer options is likely to reduce extraneous cognitive load.

While this situation is acceptable, it does not provide any cognitive resources for engaging in additional and beneficial processing beyond the mere completion of the task. If cognitive load is reduced further, such that the sum of intrinsic and extraneous cognitive load is less than one's working memory capacity, then one may engage in additional synergistic processing, yielding germane cognitive load, resulting in increased overall performance (see Figure 3d). For a database/ search novice, no use of the Social Justice Advanced Search page is likely to result in germane cognitive load. To facilitate germane cognitive load, a new Web page may need to be developed that simplifies the task at hand, such as a Basic Search page (Figure 5). The Basic Search page has only one field to complete

Figure 4: The Advanced Search page of the Social Justice Resources Center that when used by novices to search for social justice resources results in high intrinsic and extraneous cognitive load

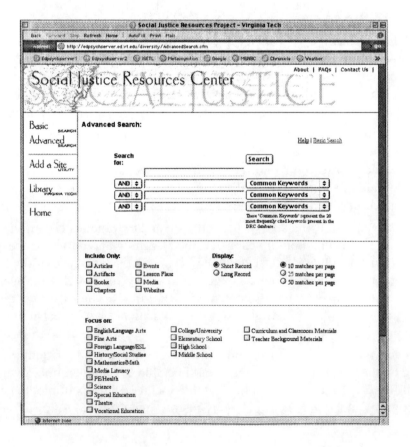

with very simple directions. The use of the Basic Search page would allow the user to engage in secondary processes, generating germane cognitive load, such as generating a schema of database use, elaborating on potential keywords, and combining keywords into more precise search phrases.

Thus, the ultimate goals of instruction are to (a) create tasks that have inherently low to moderate intrinsic cognitive load, (b) develop instructional designs that reduce extraneous cognitive load, and (c) foster engagement in active processing that facilitates germane cognitive load (see Figure 3e). An example that satisfies all three of these criteria would include searching the Social Justice Resources Database using the Basic Search page that combines a manageable task with an efficient environment to produce effective learning and performing.

This effective and efficient learning and performing is shaped by careful attention to the constraints and guidelines provided by dual-coding theory and cognitive load theory. And, just as dual-coding theory informs cognitive load theory, cognitive load theory informs the cognitive theory of multimedia (see Mayer, 2001). By considering factors that may place an undue burden on the learner while engaged in multimedia cognition, designers can develop multimedia environments that promote effective and efficient learning.

Figure 5: The Basic Search page of the Social Justice Resources Center that when used to search for social justice resources results in low intrinsic and extraneous cognitive load

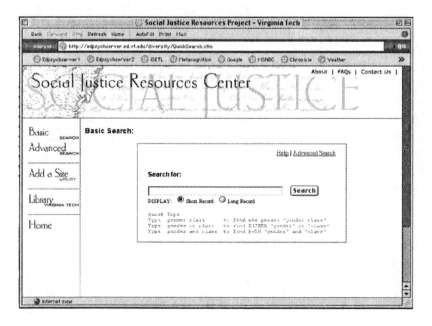

A Cognitive Theory of Multimedia

Creating multimedia that balances the constraints of human memory (e.g., dual coding and cognitive load) with the goals of education and training (e.g., meaningful learning, retention, and transfer) requires a theory of multimedia instruction grounded in the science of human learning. Until recently, multimedia meant multiple media *devices* used in a coordinated fashion (e.g., cassette tape player and a slide show) (Moore, Burton, & Myers, 1996). However, advances in technology have combined these media so that information previously delivered by several devices is now integrated into one device (e.g., computer, kiosk) (Kozma, 1994). Thus, multimedia is now typically defined as the integration of more than one medium into a common computer-based communication framework; specifically (von Wodtke, 1993), "multimedia refers to the integration of media such as text, sound, graphics, animation, video, imaging, and spatial modeling into a computer system" (p. 3).

This common computer-based communication framework for multimedia instruction resulted in early research on multimedia focusing on capturing the capabilities of this new framework to deliver instruction (Moore, Burton, & Myers, 1996). However, the current focus of multimedia instruction has shifted away from this technology-centered approach to a more learner-centered approach, where the emphasis is on how to design multimedia frameworks to aid human cognition (see Abbey, 2001).

This learner-centered approach to multimedia instruction focuses on the cognitive processing of multimedia messages and the influence of this processing on learning, retention, and transfer. This processing of multimedia messages within a computer-based instructional environment is typically reduced to two channels of presentation/sensation—auditory and visual. Within this limited two-channel environment, *words* and *pictures* comprise the two main formats available for engaging in multimedia instruction. Words, or verbal information, include primarily auditory speech or printed text, whereas pictures, or visual information, include primarily static graphics (e.g., illustrations and photos) and dynamic graphics (e.g., animation and video).   Fortunately, advances in computer technology have resulted in the emergence of numerous ways of presenting these words and pictures. These advances allow designers to combine words and pictures in ways that were not previously possible. As a result, new research has emerged concerning the effectiveness of presenting instruction using both words and pictures.

Research focusing on exploiting the benefits and limitations of the mind's verbal and visual-processing channels in multimedia instructional environments has been championed by Richard Mayer and his colleagues (see Mayer, 2001). Mayer (2001), in pursuing this dual-channel multimedia research, specifically defines multimedia as "the presentation of material using both words and pictures....I have opted to limit the definition to just two forms—verbal and pictorial—because the research base in cognitive psychology is most relevant to this distinction" (pp. 2–3). This research base to which Mayer refers is centered on Baddeley's *working memory model* (Baddeley, 1986, 1999), Paivio's *dual-coding theory* (Clark & Paivio, 1991; Paivio, 1990), and Sweller's *cognitive load theory* (Chandler & Sweller, 1991; Sweller, 1994). As mentioned previously, these three theories are not independent but rather overlap, creating theoretical interdependencies. This interdependency is evident in Mayer's construction of the *cognitive theory of multimedia learning* (Mayer, 2001).

Mayer's (2001) *cognitive theory of multimedia learning* is premised on the following three assumptions: (a) learners process visual and auditory information in different cognitive channels—the dual-channel assumption; (b) each cognitive channel has a limited processing capability—the limited-capacity assumption; and (c) learners actively process this visual and auditory information—the active-learning assumption.

The *dual-channel assumption* holds that individuals have separate cognitive channels for processing auditory and visual information. For example, if a learner is watching a video clip with auditory narration, then the visual channel will process the video images, while the auditory channel will process the narration. This dual-channel assumption is consistent with Baddeley's (1986) working memory model and Paivio's dual-coding theory (Paivio, 1990).

The *limited-capacity assumption* builds on the premise that humans are limited in the amount of information that can be processed in either channel at one time. For instance, if a learner is watching a video clip with subtitled text, the visual channel could easily become overloaded attempting to process both the video images and the subtitled text, because the images and the text are processed visually. This limited-capacity assumption is consistent with Baddeley's (1986) working memory model and Sweller's (1994) cognitive load theory.

The *active-processing assumption* posits that learners actively engage in processing multimedia environments by (a) *selecting* relevant information from the environment, (b) *organizing* the information into coherent representations, and (c) *connecting* both visual and verbal representations (Mayer, 1997). For example, if a learner is watching a video clip with auditory narration, the learner will select relevant pictures from the video and relevant words from the narration, organize the pictures and words into coherent representations, and then combine these coherent representations into an overall conceptual model of the video clip. The active-learning assumption is consistent with Paivio's (1986) dual-coding theory and Baddeley's (1986) working memory model.

These three assumptions combine to create a model of multimedia processing based on a dual-channel, limited-capacity, active-processing learner. It is important to think of these three assumptions as an integrated whole, not as isolated factors, as each affects the other and in turn affects learning within multimedia instructional environments. For example, if too much visual information is presented (e.g., animation and on-screen text; http:// basepair.library.umc.edu/movies/mitosis1.mov), then the visual channel's capacity will be exceeded, leading to insufficient processing of that visual information (i.e., either the animation or on-screen text will not be attended to in their entirety). This situation could be corrected, however, by either eliminating some of the visual information (e.g., removing the on-screen text) or switching some of the visual information to an auditory channel (e.g., using audio narration instead of on-screen text (http://basepair.library.umc.edu/movies/mitosis.mov).

Within these three assumptions, Mayer (2001) posited five cognitive processes necessary for the generation of meaningful learning, retention, and transfer. These five processes are evident in the cognitive theory of multimedia and include the following: (a) selecting relevant words from the multimedia environment, (b) selecting relevant images from the multimedia environment, (c) organizing the selected words into a coherent representation, (d) organizing the selected images into a coherent representation, and (e) integrating the word and image representations with prior knowledge into a coherent mental model (Mayer, 2001). A learner watching a narrated slide show demonstrates these five processes (see http://edpsychserver.ed.vt.edu/5114web/modules/classical/ slideshow1.cfm). The learner selects relevant words from the narration and relevant images from the slide show. The learner then generates meaningful representations of the words and images. Finally, the learner integrates the words, pictures, and relevant prior knowledge into a coherent mental model of the narrated slide show.

These three assumptions and five processes, based on working memory, dual-coding theory, and cognitive load theories, serve as the framework for much of Mayer's work in multimedia learning. Mayer's work addressing multimedia learning has resulted in several principles of multimedia learning. It is important to note that Mayer's research focuses on the derivation of cognitive principles from empirical research, where the principles may then be used to create general pedagogy (see Figure 1). This clarification is important, as Mayer uses short tutorials within his research. However, the principles that are derived are not limited to tutorial-based instructional environments. The benefit of focusing on the derivation of cognitive principles is that these principles have generalizability beyond the contexts in which they are originally demonstrated. In the following section, several cognitive principles of multimedia are delineated and examples are provided that extend these principles into nontutorial instructional environments.

Multimedia, Principles and Pedagogy

The development of cognitive principles of multimedia is essential in the quest for theoretically sound pedagogy for multimedia instructional environments (see Figure 1). These cognitive principles serve as the bridge between empirical findings and general pedagogical principles. Over the past 15 years, Richard Mayer, Roxana Moreno, and their colleagues have continued in their efforts to generate empirical findings relative to multimedia learning. These empirical findings have coalesced into a series of cognitive and pedagogical principles relevant to learning and instruction within multimedia environments. The following section will introduce seven cognitive principles of multimedia that have emerged from their work. These seven principles include the multimedia principle, the modality principle, the redundancy principle, the coherence principle, the contiguity principle, the segmentation principle, and the signaling principle (see Table 2).

Multimedia Principle

The multimedia principle simply states that individuals learn, retain, and transfer information better when the instructional environment involves words and pictures, rather than words or pictures alone. Specifically, individuals who experienced a short tutorial explaining how bicycle tire pumps worked, where the instruction was in the form of words and pictures or narration and animation, learned, retained, and transferred the knowledge within the tutorial significantly better than individuals who experienced a tutorial where the instruction was in the form of narration or animation only (Mayer & Anderson, 1991, 1992). Thus, when constructing multimedia instructional environments, learning, retention, and transfer are facilitated by the use of both words and pictures, or narration and animation.

Theoretically, these results and the multimedia principle may be explained based on Paivio's (1990) dual-coding theory. When an individual experiences instruction both verbally and visually, the individual constructs verbal and visual representations of the explanations and subsequently integrates the two representations into a coherent model. This dual-channel integration has been demonstrated to provide for increased learning when compared to learning based on a single-channel representation (Clark & Paivio, 1991; Paivio, 1991). Further, these results and the multimedia principle are consistent with Mayer's (2001) cognitive theory of multimedia. Mayer posits that verbal and visual representations are informationally distinct, such that the informational sum of the integration of verbal and visual representations always exceeds the information present

Table 2: Brief Definitions of the Cognitive Principles of Multimedia

Principle	Definition
Multimedia principle	Individuals learn, retain, and transfer information better when the instructional environment involves words and pictures, rather than word or pictures alone.
Modality principle	Individuals learn, retain, and transfer information better when the instructional environment involves auditory narration and animation, rather than on-screen text and animation.
Redundancy principle	Individuals learn, retain, and transfer information better when the instructional environment involves narration and animation, rather than on-screen text, narration, and animation.
Coherence principle	Individuals learn, retain, and transfer information better when the instructional environment is free of extraneous words, pictures, or sounds.
Signaling principle	Individuals learn and transfer information better when the instructional environment involves cues that guide an individual's attention and processing during a multimedia presentation.
Contiguity principle	Individuals learn, retain, and transfer information better in an instructional environment where words or narration and pictures or animation are presented simultaneously in time and space.
Segmentation principle	Individuals learn and transfer information better in an instructional environment where individuals experience concurrent narration and animation in short, user-controlled segments, rather than as a longer continuous presentation.

in the verbal or visual representations alone. This integration of distinct verbal and visual representations, in turn, leads to greater learning, retention, and transfer. As Mayer (2001) stated, "In short, our results support the thesis that a deeper kind of learning occurs when learners are able to integrate pictorial and verbal representations of the same message" (p. 79).

This integration has ramifications for pedagogy, specifically, that multimedia instructional environments should utilize words or narration and pictures or animation. Combining words or narration and pictures or animation can be as simple as using static images to clarify on-screen text. For example, ACKY.NET provides a wealth of information regarding Web design, including several effective tutorials that consist primarily of static images and text (http://www.acky.net/tutorials/flash/bouncing_ball/). Another basic method of combining words or narration and pictures or animation is the use of streaming video for disseminating lectures (http://sinapse.arc2.ucla.edu/streaming/cnsi/seminars/spring2003/mceuen-rm8-mbr.ram). The video lecture scenario may be made more complete through the use of streaming video, with a concurrent slide show and hyperlinks (http://ra.okstate.edu:8080/ramgen/zayed/leadership_skills_a/trainer.smi). The key in these instances is that words or narration and pictures or animation are being combined for the purpose of enhancing instruction.

Modality Principle

The modality principle, which further clarifies the multimedia principle, states that individuals learn, retain, and transfer information better when the instructional environment involves auditory narration and animation, rather than on-screen text and animation. Specifically, individuals who experienced a short tutorial explaining the creation of lightning, where the instruction was in the form of auditory narration and animation, learned, retained, and transferred the knowledge within the tutorial significantly better than individuals who experienced a tutorial where the instruction was in the form of on-screen text and animation (Mayer & Moreno, 1998; Moreno & Mayer, 1999). Thus, when constructing multimedia instructional environments, learning, retention, and transfer are facilitated by the use of auditory narration and animation.

Theoretically, these results and the modality principle may be explained based on Baddeley's (1986) working memory model and Sweller's (1991) cognitive load theory. When on-screen text and animation are presented simultaneously, an individual is confronted with the task of attending to and creating two visual representations, which can easily overload the visual channel. When the visual on-screen text is transformed into auditory narration, the cognitive load of the visual channel is reduced, and the overall cognitive load of the instructional environment is better balanced between the auditory and visual channels. Further, these results and the modality principle are consistent with Mayer's (2001) cognitive theory of multimedia. Mayer supports the limited-capacity, dual-channel structure of memory responsible for the cognitive overload created by the presentation of two visual stimuli: on-screen text and animation. According to Moreno and Mayer (1999), "When learners can concurrently hold words in auditory working memory and pictures in visual working memory, they are better able to devote attentional resources to building connections between them" (p. 366).

Pedagogically, using both channels to foster connections implies that multimedia instructional environments should utilize narration and animation, as opposed to on-screen text and animation, whenever possible. Integrating audio and video in multimedia environments is reasonably common these days. Stanford University's Center for Professional Development provides a series of *Online Seminars* that consist of simple streamed lectures, which combine narration and video, on a variety of topics (http://stanford-online.stanford.edu/murl/cs547/). Another example that demonstrates the blending of narration and animation is the International Association of Intercultural Education's *The Big Myth* that provides lessons on creation myths and cultural pantheons from around the world (http://www.mythicjourneys.org/bigmyth/1_webmap.swf). In each of these instances, the multimedia instructional environment is enhanced through the use of concurrent auditory narration and animation.

Redundancy Principle

The redundancy principle, which provides an extension of the multimedia and modality principles, states that individuals learn, retain, and transfer information better when the instructional environment involves narration and animation, rather than on-screen text, narration, and animation. Specifically, individuals who experience a short tutorial explaining the creation of lightning, where the instruction was in the form of auditory narration and animation, learned, retained, and transferred the knowledge within the tutorial significantly better than individuals who experienced a tutorial where the instruction was in the form of on-screen text, auditory narration, and animation (Mayer, Heiser, & Lonn, 2001; Moreno & Mayer, 2002). Thus, when constructing multimedia instructional environments, learning, retention, and transfer are facilitated by the use of auditory narration and animation, without on-screen text.

Theoretically, these results and the modality principle may be explained based on Baddeley's (1986) working memory model and Sweller's (Chandler & Sweller, 1991) cognitive load theory. When on-screen text, auditory narration, and animation are presented simultaneously, an individual is confronted with the task of attending to and creating two visual representations based on the on-screen text and the animation, and attending to and creating an auditory representation based on the auditory narration. The task of attending to and creating two visual representations can easily overload the visual channel and impair the individual's ability to attend adequately to the auditory channel. When the visual on-screen text is eliminated, the cognitive load of the visual channel is reduced, and the overall cognitive load of the instructional environment is better balanced between the auditory and visual channels. Further, these results and the modality principle are consistent with Mayer's (2001) cognitive theory of multimedia. Mayer supports the limited-capacity, dual-channel structure of memory responsible for the cognitive overload created by the presentation of two visual stimuli: on-screen text and animation. According to Mayer et al. (2001), "in this case, learners are less likely to be able to carry out the active cognitive processes needed for meaningful learning" (p. 195) (e.g., elaboration, organization, reflection).

While the redundancy principle has significant ramifications for pedagogy, these ramifications will be combined with the recommendations from following principle, the coherence principle, and will be discussed at the end of the next section.

Coherence Principle

The coherence principle, which refines the redundancy principle, states that individuals learn, retain, and transfer information better when the instructional environment is free of extraneous words, pictures, or sounds. Specifically, individuals who experienced a short tutorial explaining either the creation of lightning or the workings of a hydraulic break, where the instruction was in the form of narration and animation, learned, retained, and transferred the knowledge within the tutorial significantly better than individuals who experienced a tutorial where the instruction was in the form of narration, animation, and interesting, but irrelevant, words, pictures, or sounds (Mayer, Heiser, & Lonn, 2001; Moreno & Mayer, 2000). Thus, when constructing multimedia instructional environments, learning, retention, and transfer are impeded by the inclusion of extraneous, irrelevant materials; therefore, multimedia should be kept simple and include only those attributes necessary for the instruction.

Theoretically, these results and the coherence principle may be explained based on Baddeley's (1986) working memory model and Sweller's (Chandler & Sweller, 1991) cognitive load theory. When extraneous materials are introduced into the multimedia instructional environment, these extraneous materials compete with the instructional materials for the limited resources of the individual's working memory. If these extraneous materials are significant, then cognitive overload can occur, and learning and performance will be negatively affected. According to Moreno and Mayer (2000), "these findings suggest that auditory overload can be created by adding auditory material that does not contribute to making the lesson intelligible" (p. 121).

The redundancy and coherence principles each have a common message for the building of pedagogy, specifically, that multimedia instructional environments should be clear and concise, avoiding the duplication of information and the inclusion of extraneous, noninformative elements. While the tendency in creating multimedia instructional environments is often to add "bells and whistles" (multiple representations of the same content, interesting sounds, or moving text), simple designs that are focused on the learner's attention and process are more effective. A simple, yet effective multimedia instructional environment is the *Who Killed William Robinson?* Web site at the University of Vancouver, British Columbia Web address (http://web.uvic.ca/history-robinson/). This site is composed of primarily static text and pictures, yet the design and implementation of the project is simple and straightforward. There is no redundant or extraneous material. Another that is simple, yet effective is the Advanced Education Psychology site at the Virginia Tech Web address (http://edpsychserver.ed.vt.edu/5114web/modules/classical/). These particular sites are prime examples of effective multimedia instructional environments that are not "tech heavy," that is, sites that do not rely on advanced technology but rather on effective multimedia design.

Signaling Principle

The signaling principle, which is related to the coherence principle, states that individuals learn and transfer information better when the instructional environment involves cues, or signals, that guide an individual's attention and processing during a multimedia presentation. Signaling (Meyer, 1975) "serves as guides…by giving emphasis to certain aspects of the semantic content or pointing out aspects of the structure of content so that the [individual] can see the relationships stated in the passage more clearly" (p. 1). Specifically, individuals who experienced a short tutorial explaining the creation of lift in aeronautics, where the instruction was in the form of narration and animation, and included auditory signals (e.g., intonation changes, pausing) and visual signals (e.g., arrows, color emphasis, summary icons), learned and transferred the knowledge within the tutorial significantly better than individuals who experienced a tutorial where the instruction was in the form of narration and animation but did not include signals (Mautone & Mayer, 2001). Thus, when constructing multimedia instructional environments, learning and transfer are facilitated by the use of auditory and visual cues and signals.

Theoretically, these results and the signaling principle may be explained based on Baddeley's (1986) working memory model and Sweller's (1991) cognitive load theory. When signals or cues are provided that focus an individual's attention on relevant, rather than irrelevant, information, the individual's expenditure of cognitive resources is more efficient, thus reducing cognitive load. In addition, this reduction in cognitive load, when coupled with cues and signals designed to make explicit relational links within the presentation information, results in the increased generation of connections between auditory and visual representations. According to Mautone and Mayer (2001), "signals encourage learners to engage in productive cognitive processing during learning, including selecting relevant steps in the explanation, organizing them into a coherent mental structure, and integrating them with existing knowledge" (p. 387).

Pedagogically, the signaling principle posits that multimedia instructional environments should include cues to assist in focusing learner's attention and fostering appropriate learner processing of the relevant information. Students often find Web pages and online instruction overwhelming, with too much to see and do. Using cues to guide a learner's attention and processing provides the learner with instructional scaffolding and learner support. As part of the online experience in the Department of Entomology, students have the option of participating in an online "course" called *The Whole Student*. This course combines streaming audio with static slides and provides cues for students through the use of effective navigation and by placing on the static slides the main points discussed in the audio (http://www.ento.vt.edu/ihs/distance/lectures/whole_student/). Another site that provides effective cues is Biology in Motion's *Evolution Lab*. This site provides cues through section headers, color, and graphics (http://biologyinmotion.com/evol/). The Whole Student and Evolution Lab sites both provide effective cues through strategic use of text and text attributes (e.g., boldface, color).

Contiguity Principle

The contiguity principle states that individuals learn, retain, and transfer information better in an instructional environment where words or narration and pictures or animation are presented simultaneously in time and space. Specifically, individuals who experienced a short tutorial explaining the creation of lightning, where the instruction was in the form of integrated on-screen text and animation (i.e., the text was presented spatially within the animation), learned, retained, and transferred the knowledge within the tutorial significantly better than individuals who experienced a tutorial where the instruction was in the form of separated on-screen text and animation (i.e., the text was presented spatially separated from the animation) (spatial contiguity effect; Moreno & Mayer, 1999). In addition, individuals who experienced a short tutorial explaining the creation of lightning, where the instruction was in the form of simultaneous narration and animation, learned, retained, and transferred the knowledge within the tutorial significantly better than individuals who experienced a tutorial where the instruction was in the form of narration *followed by* animation (temporal contiguity effect; Moreno & Mayer, 1999). The contiguity principle, as stated here, combines what Mayer and Moreno referred to as the spatial contiguity principle and the temporal contiguity principle (Mayer & Anderson, 1991; Moreno & Mayer, 1999). Thus, when constructing multimedia instructional environments, learning, retention, and transfer are facilitated when text or narration and pictures or animation are concurrent and are not separated in either time or space.

Theoretically, these results and the contiguity principle may be explained based on Baddeley's (1986) working memory model and Sweller's (Chandler & Sweller, 1991) cognitive load theory. When on-screen text is presented spatially separate from animation, the individual is forced to split attention between the two sources of information (Mayer & Moreno, 1998). This attention split requires extra working memory and processing resources and is more likely to result in cognitive overload than when the on-screen text and animation are integrated. Similarly, when narration is provided *prior to* viewing an animation, the individual must maintain the narration in working memory while viewing the animation if any connections between the narration and animation are to be created. This narration maintenance is cognitive resource intensive and is likely to result in cognitive overload at the onset of the animation. Mayer's (2001) cognitive theory of multimedia is consistent with these findings and rationales: "If we want students to build cognitive connections between corresponding words and pictures it is helpful to present them contiguously in time and space—that is, to present them at the same time or next to each other on the page or screen" (p. 112).

Applying the contiguity principle implies that multimedia instructional environments should be constructed such that words and pictures or narration and animation are displayed simultaneously and close together. Prime examples of this synchronization of time and place include the fusion of audio and video. For example, Brainware.tv's *Boardband Business Videos* (http://www.brainware.tv/previews/p1harn2.asx) and the Electronic Scholar's *Study of Teaching Videos* (http://www.electronicscholar.com/videos.html). Another example of synchronization includes the synthesizing of text and animation, where the text is integrated into the animation. An example of this type of synchronicity includes the *Projectile Motion* Java applet (http://galileoandeinstein.physics.virginia.edu/more_stuff/Applets/ProjectileMotion/jarapplet.html). This applet plots the path of a simulated projectile, given specific parameters (i.e., velocity, angle, mass), and provides integrated feedback on the projectile's maximum distance, maximum height, end velocity, and time aloft. The previous video examples represent temporal contiguity, where multimedia are experienced simultaneously, while the applet example represents spatial contiguity, where multimedia are experienced close together in space. It is important that multimedia instructional environments be both temporally and spatially contiguous.

Segmentation Principle

The segmentation principle states that individuals learn and transfer information better in an instructional environment, where individuals experience concurrent narration and animation in short, user-controlled segments, rather than as a longer continuous presentation. Specifically, individuals who experienced a short tutorial explaining the creation of lightning, where the instruction was in the form of 16 short, user-controlled segments of concurrent narration and animation, learned and transferred the knowledge within the tutorial significantly better than individuals who experienced the tutorial as a single, continuous narration and animation presentation (Mayer & Chandler, 2001; see also Mayer & Moreno, 2003). Thus, when constructing multimedia instructional environments, learning and transfer are facilitated by the user being able to control the rate of information presentation.

Theoretically, these results and the segmentation principle may be explained based on Baddeley's (1986) working memory model and Sweller's (Chandler & Sweller, 1991) cognitive load theory. When an individual has control over the rate of information presentation, the individual may pace the presentation such that time and cognitive resources are allotted for making connections between verbal and visual representations. Alternatively, during an automatically paced presentation, the individual may lack sufficient time and cognitive resources to make representational connections, resulting in cognitive overload. Mayer and Moreno (2003), in discussing the segmentation principle in light of the cognitive theory of multimedia, stated that "the learner is able to select words and select images from the segment; the learner also has time and capacity to organize and integrate the selected words and images" (p. 47).

The segmentation principle, pedagogically, supports the position that multimedia instructional environments should be created to allow the user control over the pacing of the environment, if the environment is likely to foster cognitive overload. A well-constructed example of allowing user control includes Virginia Tech's *Critical Media Literacy in Times of War* site (http://www.tandl.vt.edu/ Foundations/mediaproject/). This site integrates text, graphics, animation, and audio, while providing the learner with step-by-step navigational control. Similarly, the Joliet Junior College tutorial *Using a Secant Line to Approximate a Tangent Line* provides the learner with the ability to experience the tutorial in small steps (http://home.attbi.com/~waterhand/tangent.html). In each of these cases, the user is provided with the ability to slow his or her interaction with the multimedia instructional environment and thus provide added time and resources for active cognitive processing.

Summary

The explanations and examples of pedagogy based on the cognitive principles of multimedia provide an initial framework for creating multimedia instructional environments that are empirically and theoretically well grounded. This grounding is essential, as it has been demonstrated repeatedly that media itself, even multimedia, has little effect on learning unless the pedagogy that drives the media is focused on student learning (see Clark, 1983, 1994).

Collectively, these seven cognitive principles of multimedia provide a grounded framework within which to begin to build this learner-centered pedagogy. The multimedia and modality principles clearly delineate the benefits of using concurrent narration and animation in multimedia instructional environments.

Furthermore, the redundancy principle extends the multimedia and modality principles by demonstrating that providing redundant information in both auditory and visual-processing channels is detrimental when the visual channel also needs to process images. Further, the coherence principle refines the redundancy principle by demonstrating that irrelevant stimuli, as well as redundant stimuli, are detrimental to learning, retention, and transfer. However, the signaling principle may provide a potential solution to the overload caused by irrelevant or redundant stimuli by providing cues that may focus the learner's attention and processing and thus ameliorate the cognitive overload. While signaling may ameliorate the presence of extraneous stimuli, the coherence principle demonstrates, more generally, that proximity in time and space of narration and animation is beneficial to learning, retention, and transfer. Finally, the segmentation principle demonstrates that when a narration and animation sequence is likely to proceed too quickly for the learner to process information adequately, then allowing the user to control the progress of the narration and animation sequence pace is beneficial.

Conclusion

Improving instruction has been a primary goal of education and training. To foster this goal, educators have employed cognitive principles to highlight effective instructional practices. Unfortunately, a disconnect continues to exist between this science of human learning and daily educational practice. This gap denies learners and teachers access to powerful forms of teaching, training, and learning.

Fortunately, the field of instructional technology, generally, and the domain of multimedia learning, specifically, is providing an avenue for bridging this educational gap. Current research into pedagogical and technological integration within multimedia instructional environments is yielding significant and meaningful findings related to the improvement of learning, retention, and transfer. As discussed previously, the cognitive principles of multimedia, derived from Mayer's (2001) cognitive theory of multimedia, provide a solid foundation upon which to build a theoretically sound pedagogy. This process, however, of creating pedagogy from theory is fraught with difficulty and thus must be undertaken with care and forethought. According to William James (1899-1958):

> I say moreover that you make a great, a very great mistake, if you think that psychology, being the science of the mind's laws, is something from which you can deduce definite programmes and schemes and methods

of instruction for immediate schoolroom use. Psychology is a science, and teaching is an art; and sciences never generate arts directly out of themselves. An intermediary inventive mind must make the application, by using its originality. (p. 23)

Thus, pedagogy of any type is at least once removed from its theoretical underpinnings. With this caution in mind, it is necessary that we not only apply the pedagogy arising from the cognitive principles of multimedia with due diligence, but that we also continue to further investigate and refine the pedagogy of multimedia.

References

Abbey, B. (Ed.). (2000). *Instructional and cognitive impacts of web-based education.* Hershey, PA: Idea Group.

Anderson, J. R. (1983). *The architecture of cognition.* Cambridge, MA: Harvard University.

Anderson, J. R. (1990). *The adaptive character of thought.* Hillsdale, NJ: Erlbaum.

Anderson, J. R. (1993). *Rules of the mind.* Hillsdale, NJ: Erlbaum.

Anderson, J. R., Reder, L. M., & Simon, H. A. (1998). Radical constructivism and cognitive psychology. In D. Ravitch (Ed.), *Brookings papers on educational policy: 1998* (pp. 227–255). Washington, DC: Brookings Institute.

Atkinson, R. C., & Shiffrin, R. M. (1968). Human memory: A proposal system and its control processes. In K. W. Spence, & J. T. Spence (Eds.), *The psychology of learning and motivation: Advances in research and theory* (pp. 89–195). New York: Academic Press.

Baddeley, A. D. (1986). *Working memory.* Oxford: Oxford University Press.

Baddeley, A. D. (1999). *Essentials of human memory.* East Sussex, UK: Taylor and Francis.

Baddeley, A. D., & Hitch, G. J. (1974). Working memory. In G. H. Bower (Ed.), *Recent advances in learning and motivation.* New York: Academic Press.

Baddeley, A. D., & Logie, R. H. (1999). Working memory: The multiple-component model. In A. Miyake, & P. Shah (Eds.), *Models of working memory: Mechanisms of active maintenance and executive control* (pp. 28–61). Cambridge, UK: Cambridge University Press.

Broadbent, D. E. (1958). *Perception and communication*. London: Pergamon.

Chandler, P., & Sweller, J. (1991). Cognitive load theory and the format of instruction. *Cognition and Instruction, 8*(4), 293–332.

Chandler, P., & Sweller, J. (1992). The split-attention effect as a factor in the design of instruction. *British Journal of Educational Psychology, 62*(2), 233–246.

Clark, R. E. (1983). Reconsidering research on learning from media. *Review of Educational Research, 53*(4), 445–459.

Clark, J. M., & Paivio, A. (1991). Dual coding theory and education. *Educational Psychology Review, 3*(3), 149–210.

Clark, R. E. (1994). Media will never influence learning. *Educational Technology Research and Development, 42*(2), 21–29.

Cowan, A. (1999). An embedded-process model of working memory. In A. Miyake, & P. Shah (Eds.), *Models of working memory: Mechanisms of active maintenance and executive control* (pp. 62–101). Cambridge, UK: Cambridge University Press.

Doolittle, P. E. (2001). The need to leverage theory in the development of guidelines for using technology in social studies teacher education. *Contemporary Issues in Technology and Teacher Education, 4*(1), 501–516.

Ericsson, K. A., & Kintsch, W. (1995). Long-term working memory. *Psychological Review, 102*, 211–245.

Gerjets, P., & Scheiter, K. (2003). Goal configurations and processing strategies as moderators between instructional design and cognitive load: Evidences from hypertext-based instruction. *Education Psychologist, 38*(1), 33–42.

James, W. (1958). *Talks with teachers*. New York: Norton. (Originally published in 1899.)

Kozma, R. (1994). Will media influence learning: Reframing the debate. *Educational Technology Research and Development, 42*(2), 7–19.

Mautone, P. D., & Mayer, R. E. (2001). Signaling as a cognitive guide in multimedia learning. *Journal of Educational Psychology, 93*(2), 377–389.

Mayer, R. E. (1997). Multimedia learning: Are we asking the right questions? *Educational Psychologist, 32*(1), 1–19.

Mayer, R. E. (2001). *Multimedia learning*. Cambridge, UK: Cambridge University Press.

Mayer, R. E., & Anderson, R. B. (1991). Animations need narrations: An experimental test of a dual-coding hypothesis. *Journal of Educational Psychology, 83*(4), 484–490.

Mayer, R. E., & Anderson, R. B. (1992). The instructive animation: Helping students build connections between words and pictures in multimedia learning. *Journal of Educational Psychology, 84*(4), 444–452.

Mayer, R. E., & Chandler, P. (2001). When learning is just a click away: Does simple user interaction foster deeper understanding of multimedia messages? *Journal of Educational Psychology, 93*(2), 390–397.

Mayer, R. E., & Moreno, R. (1998). A split-attention effect in multimedia learning: Evidence for dual processing systems in working memory. *Journal of Educational Psychology, 90*(2), 312–320.

Mayer, R. E., & Moreno, R. (1998). Nine ways to reduce cognitive load in multimedia learning. *Educational Psychologist, 38*(1), 43–52.

Mayer, R. E., Heiser, J., & Lonn, S. (2001). Cognitive constraints on multimedia learning: When presenting more material results in less understanding. *Journal of Educational Psychology, 93*(1), 187–198.

Meyer, G. J. F. (1975). *The organization of prose and its effects on memory.* New York: Elsevier.

Miyake, A., & Shah, P. (Eds.). (1999). *Models of working memory: Mechanisms of active maintenance and executive control.* Cambridge, UK: Cambridge University Press.

Moore, D. M., Burton, J. K., & Myers, R. J. (1996). Multiple-channel communication: The theoretical and research foundations of multimedia. In D. H. Jonassen (Ed.), *Handbook of research for educational communications and technology* (pp. 851–875). Mahwah, NJ: Lawrence Erlbaum Associates.

Moreno, R., & Mayer, R. E. (1999). Cognitive principles of multimedia learning: The role of modality and contiguity. *Journal of Educational Psychology, 91*(2), 358–368.

Moreno, R., & Mayer, R. E. (2000). A coherence effect in multimedia learning: The case for minimizing irrelevant sounds in the design of multimedia instructional messages. *Journal of Educational Psychology, 92*(1), 117–125.

Moreno, R., & Mayer, R. E. (2002). Verbal redundancy in multimedia learning: When reading helps listening. *Journal of Educational Psychology, 94*(1), 156–163.

Mousavi, S. Y., Low, R., & Sweller, J. (1995). Reducing cognitive load by mixing auditory and visual presentation modes. *Journal of Educational Psychology, 87*(2), 319–334.

Paas, F., & van Merrienboer, J. J. G. (1994). Instructional control of cognitive load in the training of complex cognitive tasks. *Educational Psychology Review, 6*(4), 351–371.

Paas, F., Renkl, A., & Sweller, J. (2003). Cognitive load theory and instructional design: Recent developments. *Educational Psychology, 38*(1), 1–4.

Paivio, A. (1971). *Imagery and verbal processes.* New York: Holt, Rinehart, and Winston.

Paivio, A. (1975). Coding distinctions and repetition effects in memory. In G. H. Bower (Ed.), *The psychology of learning and motivation* (Vol. 9, pp. 179–214). New York: Academic Press.

Paivio, A. (1990). *Mental representations: A dual coding approach.* New York, NY: Oxford University Press.

Peterson, L. R., & Peterson, M. J. (1959). Short-term retention of individual verbal items. *Journal of Experimental Psychology, 58*, 193–198.

Rouet, J., Levonen, J., & Biardeau, A. (Eds.). (2001). *Multimedia learning: Cognitive and instructional issues.* London: Pergamon.

Sadoski, M., & Paivio, A. (2001). Imagery and text: A dual coding theory of reading and writing. Mahwah, NJ: Erlbaum.

Schnotz, W. (2001). Sign systems, technologies, and the acquisition of knowledge. In J. Rouet, J. JU. Levonen, and A. Biardeau (Eds.), *Multimedia learning: Cognitive and instructional issues* (pp. 9–30). New York: Pergamon.

Sweller, J. (1994). Cognitive load theory, learning difficulty, and instructional design. *Learning and Instruction, 4*, 295–312.

Sweller, J., van Merrienboer, J. J. G., & Paas, F. G. W. C. (1998). Cognitive architecture and instructional design. *Educational Psychology Review, 10*(3), 251–296.

Tindall-Ford, S., Chandler, P., & Sweller, J. (1997). When two sensory modes are better than one. *Journal of Experimental Psychology: Applied, 3*(4), 257–287.

von Wodtke, M. (1993). *Mind over media: Creative thinking skills for electronic media.* New York: McGraw-Hill.

Chapter XI

Cognitive Skill Capabilities in Web-Based Educational Systems

Elspeth McKay, RMIT University, Australia

Abstract

This chapter represents a discussion on the interactivity of how people think and react to instructional materials in general, in the light of how this interaction may be affected by multimedia. Grounded in instructional design, where first principles take a fine grained approach to identify the learning/instructional context; this chapter provides an explanation of the differing terminology used by people when referring to multimedia instruction. A Meta-Knowledge Processing Model is proposed as a courseware designing tool. Several controversial issues that surround learning with multimedia are exposed. More work is needed to unlock the mysteries that surround multimodal instructional strategy development.

Introduction

Can Web-based educational systems (WBESs) really facilitate cognitive skill development? It would appear from the common rhetoric that learning occurs as a somewhat automatic process through interactive multimedia. Moreover, it is taken for granted that a collaborative approach to lifelong learning and knowledge transfer is a guaranteed WBES outcome. An examination of current multimedia courseware reveals that the opposite is true. This is where effective learning management systems (LMS) can make all the difference. To this end, there have been a number of developments toward identifying the management of collaborative instructional environments (Bhattacharya, 2000). However, if we want to sustain the momentum toward achieving positive outcomes from interactive multimedia in a shared knowledge/experiential learning network (Sims, 2000), we must first understand more about how to manage an individual's capacity to access information through human-computer interaction (HCI) (Preece, 1994). Once we understand more about the HCI phenomenon and learn how to manage the so-called *e-learning* environment successfully, we may be in a position to claim that interactive-context-mediated learning has arrived (von Wodtke, 1993).

This chapter discusses the interactivity of how people think and react to instructional materials in general, and how this interaction may be affected by multimedia. Written from the perspective of instructional design, where first principles take a fine-grained approach to identify the learning/instructional context, this chapter first provides a brief explanation of the terminology used by people when referring to multimedia instruction. To assist with this, a Meta-Knowledge Processing Model (see Figure 1) is proposed as a courseware design tool that identifies each complex variable involved in an interactive multimedia learning environment. Because multimodal instructional materials tap into an individual's spatial ability, several controversial issues, relating to cognitive skill acquisition within a WBES, will be exposed. In closing, this chapter will show how current progress points toward the future, revealing that much more work is needed to unlock the mysteries that surround multimodal instructional strategy development.

Dealing with the Terminology

What exactly is meant by HCI? The global leaders in this field at the Open University, in the United Kingdom, have defined HCI as comprising elements of computer science, cognitive psychology, social and organization psychology, ergonomics, human factors, artificial intelligence, linguistics, philosophy, sociol-ogy, anthropology, engineering, and design (Preece, 1994). The reader may perhaps appreciate that each one of these professions will have its own cultural semiotics or ways of viewing its domain and expressing itself. For instance, consider how the terms "information," "data," and "knowledge" are often treated completely differently by computer scientists and sociologists. In com-puter science, the first two terms are often treated as having different charac-teristics, while there will be difficulty expressing just what knowledge is. In sociology, there will be a different understanding of the same terms, for instance, information and data may have exactly the same meaning, while knowledge will be explained in many variations of complexity (Nonaka, 1994). Therefore, it may come as no surprise that understanding the terminology is a major issue in dealing with the complexity of interactive multimedia in education and training. Conse-quently, ontology (a branch of metaphysics that deals with the nature of being) (Angus, 1986) is gaining popularity among educational technology researchers in defining the complex nature of their learning environments.

This chapter examines the ontological/contextual issues involved in an interactivity of *instructional media* and the *cognitive style construct* as a metaknowledge acquisition process (McKay, 2000). Cognitive-style construct describes the interactive variables of an individual's information processing (cognitive) style (Riding & Rayner, 1998). Moreover, the term "metaknowledge" is used in this chapter to convey a model for describing knowledge about knowledge (Scandura & Dolores, 1990), that provides an ontological framework applicable in a WBES (McKay, Garner, & Okamoto, 2003). It is necessary to make this distinction to differentiate between the more common usage of the term, whereby knowledge is generated by an individual presented with various pieces of information. Gaining an insight into what happens when people interact with computers presents a fascinating challenge. Further work is currently underway to substan-tiate the speculated mechanisms surrounding the relationship between specific learning domains and notational transfer (to be proposed here as an internal/external exchange process) in an online learning context (McKay, 2002a, 2002b).

The purpose of approaching instructional design issues and cognitive skill capabilities in an interactive multimedia context in this manner is to further the discourse on cognitive skill acquisition per se in a WBES environment and to focus on the interactive effect of differences in cognitive construct (*how we represent information during thinking and the mode of processing that information*) (Riding & Cheema, 1991) and instructional format (*verbal(text)/image(pictures)*) (McKay, 2000a), with the examination of the interactivity of relatively new research variables (audio, color, and movement), to further complicate matters. Initial research has identified that it is the interaction of the integrated cognitive-style construct with instructional format that affects performance the most. The questions arising from the interactive effects of cognitive-style construct and multimedia upon cognitive performance may provide significantly different outcomes. Consequently, the following discussion examines the ontological framework (McKay, Garner, & Okamoto, 2002) involved in understanding the interactivity of Web-initiated instructional conditions and cognitive style as a metaknowledge acquisition process.

Instructional Design for WBES

For some, interactive multimedia in education and training may sit as a very comfortable concept. Nevertheless, there are many important instructional design matters relating to the issues of student learning through multimedia that researchers need to work on. Due to the multiple disciplines that constitute HCI, it is necessary to understand the linguistics in play. Therefore, by explaining to a more ubiquitous audience how these HCI-specific terms are represented by this author, new insights may be provided to some readers. Starting with the basics of instructional design, there are three major components of a theory of instruction: methods, conditions, and outcomes (Reigeluth, 1983).

Method of Delivery

Methods are the different ways to achieve different learning outcomes under different conditions. For instance, methods can take the form of an instructional agent (maybe a teacher or some other instructional medium) that directs its actions at a learner (Landa, 1983). In a WBES, this context-mediated modeling tool can include an instructional conditions agent that responds to the user's characteristics to ensure that optimal instructional conditions are brought into play to achieve the expected instructional outcomes.

Instructional Characteristics/Conditions

These *conditions* are the factors that influence the effects of the instructional methods employed and, as such, are important for prescribing instructional strategies. Instructional conditions have a twofold impact (Reigeluth, 1983). First, courseware designers may be able to manipulate them, as some conditions interact with the method to influence their relative effectiveness, such as instructional format. Second, there are instructional conditions that cannot be manipulated and, therefore, are beyond the control of the designer, such as learner characteristics. In fact, instructional theories and models specify the conditions under which each set of method variables should or should not be used.

Assessment practices in diverse cultures and learning domains may be studied using the model depicted in the Instructional Conditions component in Figure 2. Note that the term **conditions-of-the-learner** (Reigeluth, 1983) combines the interactive effects of the internal states of an individual and external events of the instructional delivery format on learning (McKay, 2000a); providing a computer-mediated context for e-learning environments. Investigation of this context-mediated process will help researchers reconstruct the ways that individuals deal with structure and how they subsequently remember prior experiences (Hoffman, 1998).

Outcomes are the various effects that provide a measure of value of alternative methods (delivery technologies) under different conditions (instructional format—audio/text/graphics/animation), as they focus on instruction rather than on the learner (Reigeluth, 1983). For instance, consider various instructional delivery alternatives that need to be included in a WBES to facilitate the expected cognitive performance for palm-held or desktop computers and mobile phone technologies.

These three components can be combined into a model for designing any instructional event, thereby facilitating development of an e-learning ontology—providing exact parameters required for robust research methodologies or experimental designs (Gay, 1992).

The Metaknowledge Processing Model, shown in Figure 1, articulates the complexity of the e-learning delivery environment. The *Method of Delivery Transfer Agent* (learning facilitator) directs the *Instructional Conditions* (learner characteristics and instructional format) according to the results of the *Learner Characteristics* (cognitive style) and *Event Conditions* (complexity of processing the learning material), and the *Measurable Instructional Outcomes* (cognitive performance). Directions for choice of *Instructional Format* are given by the *Method of Delivery Transfer Agent* (McKay & Martin, 2002). Consequently, the Metaknowledge Processing Model serves as a framework in which to continue the discussion on mechanisms for knowledge acquisition, and cognitive strategies for specific learning domains. In light of understanding how this chapter relates to interactive multimedia in an educational context, it is necessary to clarify what is meant by the term "knowledge acquisition" (Gonzalvo, 1994). However, the type of knowledge under examination will depend upon how one interprets the instructional goal or expected learning outcome (Lukose, 1992). Furthermore, the overall context in which the model exists will reflect different relationships among the various component parts. For instance, consider where there may be important differences between the

Figure 1: Metaknowledge Processing Model (McKay, 2000)

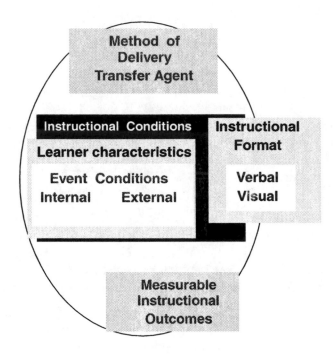

education and training sectors. In the education sector, there may not be very many alternatives for the method of delivery due to funding restrictions. The choices are often cost driven to squeeze out the very last drop from the equipment funds (Laurillard, 1993), often leaving less than desirable methods of engaging the learner with the instructional media, as opposed to decisions that should be made to optimize the educational outcomes. In the corporate sector, there is more concentration on providing delivery media that promotes knowledge sharing (Hedberg, Brown, Larkin, & Agostinho, 2001). This of course is not the only contextual environment that may exert dramatic effects upon the Metaknowledge Processing Model. The following environmental contexts are provided as mere examples to demonstrate how the model can be used as an effective instructional designing tool to enhance multimedia in education and training sectors.

Context Variation

Web site accessibility is gaining momentum. WBES designers are working toward providing enhanced multimedia platform functionality for a wide range of differences in individual's educational/training needs (Loiacono, 2003). Interactive context-mediated learning environments are also under scrutiny (McKay, Nishihori, & Garner, 2003) to fully exploit the visual nature of the multimedia environment (Brogan, 2002). The collaborative approach to learning is another example of a context-mediated environment that impacts on the Metaknowledge Processing Model. Once again, the notions of collaboration can vary (Dillenbourg, 1999). To this end, there are moves to establish some industry standards (Okamoto, Kayama, & Cristea, 2001). For instance, the Metaknowledge Processing Model is especially useful in determining where the relationships lie between the instructional media and expected outcomes from desktop video-conferencing sessions (Sharpe, Hu, Crawford, Gopinathan, Moo, & Wong, 2001). Moreover, learning networks are a seemingly natural extension of collaborative research (Bourne, 2000); where multimedia per se plays no part in the HCI (Miller, 2000). E-learning has become the buzzword for the 21st century. While there are many ways in which this term is applied, for instance, it can be applied easily to Web-based training as it can be to knowledge management (Rosenberg, 2001). Moreover, the term *metaknowledge acquisition process* is used in this chapter to mean the ontological framework represented in a hierarchy to identify each component, relationship, and interaction (Raban & Garner, 2001). The situations in which the Metaknowledge Processing Model may be embedded are endless.

Therefore, when dealing with the ontological complexities of interactive multimedia, in a collaborative online learning context, it may now be apparent how important it is to drill into each variable to locate the parameters and scope of the relationships that are involved in any interaction between the method and expected instructional outcomes (Figure 2). It should come as no surprise that in any given population of learners, there will be an enormous variation in the ways people think about the learning content, and moreover, there will be a wide variation of how those people will process that information. It has been said that imagers or *pictorial thinkers* are believed to experience difficulty with predominantly text-based learning material. They may have to translate text into a graphical form before they can absorb and assimilate the received information. This process may be tiring and even stressful for the learner (Douglas & Riding, 1993). Verbal-thinking learners may be similarly stressed, by trying to learn from pictorial-based material. They may miss out on the overall picture of the learning material, whereas their pictorial-thinking counterparts, who take a broader sweep of the same material, may ignore the fine detail involved (Laeng, Peters, & McCabe, 1998).

Figure 2: Context-mediated learning dynamics

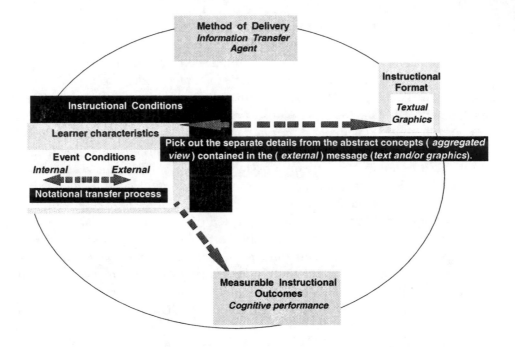

In a collaborative learning environment, the visual and verbal learners can share their understanding, thereby enriching the learning experience for both cognitive styles. Promoting and monitoring this interaction is the key to developing successful Web-based instructional materials (McKay, 2003). Research must further investigate the dynamics of this collaborative interaction and the complex nature of experiential learning tasks. Web-based experiential learning also raises questions, not only of the metaknowledge requirements for improved group interaction, but also, of the ontological requirements (such as how to deal with a diverse range of prior domain knowledge and skill) for modeling context-mediated group interaction in diverse cultures.

It is proposed that the ontology that deals with instructional conditions is the instructional component that is least understood in a general sense. More particularly, little is known of the likely effects of interactive multimedia in education and training. Much more research is needed in this area. It has been suggested that work should commence on investigating the interactivity of the cognitive-style construct and instructional format on performance outcomes (McKay, 2000a, 2000b). Moreover, in a WBES, educational researchers need to understand how people translate information that comes to them from multimedia (color, sound, movement) in a progression of environments (paper-based (text/pictures), computerized (text/pictures/sound/movement)). This activity has been described as *notational transfer* (McKay, 2002b), involving an internal/external exchange process.

In this chapter, the term *knowledge transfer* simply means the instances of understanding that occur as a result of experiential interaction with multimedia in general, and more specifically, in relation to accessing Web-mediated information. Moreover, due to the multisensory nature of multimedia, research is also needed to identify an individual's propensity toward spatial ability (Clements, 1983; Thompson, 1990).

Expected/Measurable Performance Outcomes

In any instructional event, it is important to identify the learning domain (the instructional content) that specifies the learning tasks for developing necessary skills and knowledge to achieve the measurable cognitive performance outcomes (the instructional goals). To this end, the term *cognitive skill acquisition* is referred to in this discussion as the set of cognitive skills associated with declarative (the *that*) and procedural knowledge (the *how*) (Merrill, 1980). In other words, this type of cognitive skill acquisition can be described in five discrete categories: *verbal information* (knowing basic terms), *intellectual skill development* (basic rules, discriminating and understanding concepts and principles), *intellectual skill* (higher-order rules, problem solving, the ability to apply concepts and principles in new situations), and two types of *cognitive strategies* [(identify subtasks, recognize unstated assumptions) and (knowing the how, recall of simple prerequisite rules and concepts, integrating learning from different areas into a plan for solving a problem)].

The following mechanisms may explain how individuals deal with the instructional format in terms of information processing, and the speculated internal/external exchange process.

Background on Information Processing

An explanation for how the cognitive-style construct (Riding & Rayner, 1998) interacts with a particular abstract or conceptual task that involves procedural programming knowledge may lie within the relationship of the instructional conditions' components, as shown in Figure 1 (McKay, 2000a, 2000b). It should be no surprise that individuals' performances vary on the strength of their cognitive-style construct and the task at hand. It has been demonstrated that there is an interactive effect of graphical instructional metaphors on logical reasoning and spatial relations (McKay, 2000a, 2000b). Consequently, a number of questions arise: can an explanation for this be found using between-item and within-item elaborations (McKay, 2002b)? Furthermore, can visual metaphors, used as an internal/external exchange agent, have the same interactive effect (for some novice learners) in environments other than the computer programming domain? Questioning this leads to the bigger question: how will a WBES impact on an individual's capacity to learn?

Spatial Ability and Notational Transfer

In the past, verbal (or analytic) ability was taken to be a measure of crystallized intelligence, or the ability to apply cognitive strategies to new problems and manage a large volume of information in working memory (Hunt, 1997), while the nonverbal (or imagery) ability was expressed as fluid intelligence (Kline, 1991). However, as electronic courseware lends itself to integrating verbal (textual) with nonverbal (graphical representations and sound), instructional conditions that generate novel (or fluid) intellectual problems, research into the effects of WBES on knowledge acquisition must be carried out to provide instructional designers with prescriptive models that predict measurable instructional outcomes for a broader range of cognitive abilities.

An empirical experimental research methodology for cognitive performance measurement was used to facilitate the prediction of whether the method of delivery will affect highly verbal/low-spatial learners, because they need a direct notational transfer agent (Figure 3), or whether the instructional conditions will disadvantage high-spatial/low-verbal learners, because they will be less able to pick out the unstated assumptions (McKay, 2002b).

Picking out these important instructional variables for some types of instructional outcomes provides appropriate instructional environments for a broader range of novice learners by means of an information-transfer agent, thereby controlling the choice of instructional format and instructional event conditions. Figure 3 shows how isolating the key components of the instructional conditions will provide the means to manipulate the method of delivery, which in turn may bring about a choice of information-transfer agent.

It is proposed that the external representation of the instructional material may require a direct notational transfer of the symbol system used for the instructional strategy (from the external representation of the instructional material to an internalized form in an individual's memory) (Goodman, 1968). For instance, the

Figure 3: Notation transfer process

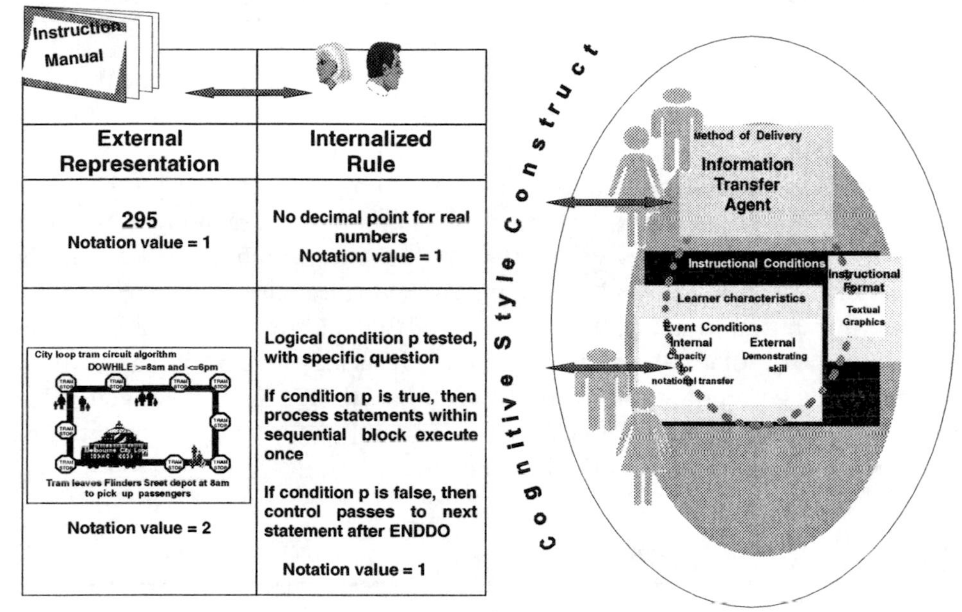

graphical details in a road map directly relate to the physical environment (in a 1:1 direct notation ratio, like the explicit representation of basic data-type rules in computer programming). In a programming environment, another example would be that a real number must not contain a decimal point (Figure 3). On the other hand, the embedded details in an abstract metaphor are said to require a non-notational transfer process. For instance, the programming loop shown as a graphical metaphor in Figure 3 requires a 2:1 transfer for the non-notational characteristics of the external representation to a single internal notational representation. While some learners may be adept at using this type of transfer to trigger prior experiential knowledge, others may not.

Taking this type of fine-grained approach to locating the complexity of the ontological requirements will provide Web designers with special insight. However, courseware authoring that offers WBESs without involving a customizable platform to individualize instructional strategies is much like implementing the closed systems of days gone by, and given the passing of time, this type of closed WBES will eventually fail (Preece, 1994). This leads us to our next topic of discussion: what are the key issues limiting the development and global dissemination of effective WBESs?

Issues Relating to Cognitive Skill Capabilities in WBES Environments

When considering the merits of interactive multimedia in education and training, a number of complex issues arise that involve a synthesis of disparate HCI paradigms. To begin with, not enough is known about the interactive effects of cognitive style and multimedia learning programs on expected performance outcomes. While it has been shown that not all people will respond to pictorial learning materials (McKay, 2000a, 2000b), further research is needed into the Web-mediated instructional environment to unravel the contextual complications that arise through multimedia. It is just assumed that multimedia means increased accessibility. For some parts of the community, this may well be the case. Notice the change of terminology here from "Web-based" to "Web-mediated". The term "Web mediation" infers that there is some type of interactive negotiation embedded in the Web-based instructional strategies.

The Issue of Method of Delivery

Has the approach to online learning undergone some kind of mystical transformation with the advent of multimedia in education and training? It may appear that in some quarters, unless learning materials are online, they are discarded. However, the voice from novice learners talking about their experiences with Web-mediated learning products may tell a different story. There appears to be a considerable gap in their expectations for how they feel about the capabilities of technology and the realities of online offerings. The task ahead for courseware designers is to fill this gap (Bush, 2002). Appropriate leadership is required to realize the rich potential that techno-educational materials can provide (Maddux, 2002).

It would seem that a common fault with much of the discourse on e-learning to date is that it remains limited to the mechanistic aspects of HCI. Unfortunately, this tendency leaves out one of the most important issues relating to courseware development—sound instructional design principles. It is therefore essential to look beyond software/hardware management and deal with the difficulties relating to maintaining the integrity of the learning activities per se. A common fault with current courseware designers is that they are not learning from past mistakes (Salomon, 2002).

In describing the gap in a novice-learner's expectations of interactive multimedia learning platforms: people become dissatisfied because they cannot manipulate and directly interact with the materials. Another pressing issue has to do with the accountability of the instructional design process. Credibility checks of the courseware designer's experience and qualifications should be clearly displayed in online learning sites. Moreover, learning content certification processes need to be identified to reassure that the materials have undergone sufficient quality testing. One such Web site providing training for this type of certification testing can be found at http://www.brainbench.com. Unfortunately, these programs do not extend to online or computer-based educational materials.

Web-based educational programs can, however, ignite a learner's imagination. Research has shown that, in some cases, students who have participated in online learning at higher levels than in their more traditional classroom sessions actually record the highest levels of perceived learning (Fredericksen, Pickett, Shea, Peiz, & Swan, 2000). While not directly related to an interactive multimedia delivery platform, this experimental research also reveals that in the absence of a structured classroom environment, courseware developers need to be aware of the expectation that learners will take a more active role in their own learning. As a consequence, the instructional strategies adopted for online education must be made crystal clear to the learner and facilitator alike. Web-based courseware designers must assume nothing. All types of questions from learners should be anticipated and answered by the facilitator in a friendly, nonjudgmental manner.

While on the surface, technological access to learning facilitation appears to offer increased benefits, there is an assumption that in Web-based courseware the students and instructors are somehow brought together (Quigley, 2002). However, in order to cope with techno-instruction, higher-order skill sets are required on the part of the learner, including knowing how to update personal skills when required by the instructional media, having the ability to use a range of thinking skills, knowing how to transfer collaborative learning in the real-world into the classroom environment, and being willing to engage in agile and flexible learning models (Cadena Smith & Shelley, 2002).

It would appear that most often the Web-based instructional material is text-based, with a tendency to emphasize asynchronous discussion forums, where questions and answers are posted online for all participants to view and become involved. While this type of learning experience may have its place in techno-pedagogy, it can become extremely frustrating for a novice learner wishing more immediate feedback.

It would appear that multimedia may tempt learners with the possibility to engage in a more visual instructional environment than commonly offered by the traditional approach to classroom experiences. Moreover, the online learning community is currently demanding more from technology than can be delivered (Quigley, 2002). For instance, beckoning on the techno-horizon are things like the teleportation of the instructional facilitator, providing a life-sized representation complete with the ability to eyeball participants, with lifelike body language responses. Sadly, this type of learning context will not be available for the majority of learners. Costs are immense. ISDN and broadband networks are needed for successful implementation. Clearly, enhanced techno-learning environments such as this will remain beyond the reach of most individuals for some time to come.

Herein lies the dilemma for those either taking up the development of e-learning content for a new project or embarking on a venture to convert existing instructional materials to a Web-mediated learning program that involves interactive multimedia. Courseware designers need to have their feet planted firmly on the ground. While dealing with the temptation of installing these new technologies, they also need to keep abreast of the emerging strategies from the instructional science paradigm. One advantage of the push towards increasing the uptake of e-learning is the growing awareness for sound instructional design principles (Gibbons & Fairweather, 1998).

Design Aspects with Method of Delivery

Problems that arise for interactive courseware design can be traced back to the lack of knowledge about the principles of instruction (Merrill, 2002). It is proposed that the ripple effect of bypassing fundamental rules will be magnified by an instructional strategy that involves multimedia. This is because not nearly enough attention is given by instructional designers to offer alternative strategies to achieve different learning outcomes, under different conditions. For instance, it has been shown that an expert will only require minimal access to a manual for basic rules, when a novice expects to be given a clear step-by-step procedure (Dreyfus & Dreyfus, 1986; Tennyson & Bagley, 1991).

The Issue of Instructional Conditions (Learner Characteristics/Instructional Format)

Drawing on the **Metaknowledge Processing Model** (see Figure 1) to articulate the *instructional conditions* in relation to interactive multimedia in education and training environments, it is useful at this point to explain the likely interactive effects of learner characteristics and instructional format (the multimedia delivery mechanism employed) on cognitive performance outcomes. There are at least two variables that will need to be examined: the *learner characteristics* and *instructional event conditions* (complexity of processing the learning material). In the first instance, learner characteristics, there are a number of ways to describe individual characteristics (cognitive style construct, skill capability). The cognitive-style construct has already been defined to describe *how we represent information during thinking (verbal/imagery)* and *the mode of processing that information (holistic/analytic)* (Riding & Cheema, 1991). While in the second instance, instructional event conditions, there is little hard evidence that explains how individuals will respond to the intellectual complexities of processing the interactive multimedia.

Long before the advent of technology and certainly before the emergent interest in bringing multimedia into classrooms, it was shown in a series of aptitude tests that there are two distinct creative types, based on two unlike reactions toward the world of experience. It was shown that the inability to notice visual objects was not always inhibitory of creative activities. The very fact of not paying attention to visual impressions may be due to the haptic aptitude (a need for a sense of physical contact or touch). Interestingly, one factor that was noticed in visual observations was the ability to see the whole object without awareness of detail. An individual may then analyze an object into detailed or partial impressions (Lowenfeld, 1945). These segmented details are then rebuilt into a new synthesis of the original whole. It is perhaps interesting to note that extreme haptical individuals have normal sight and use their eyes only when compelled (Lowenfeld, 1945). These individuals react as would a blind person who is entirely dependent upon touch and kinesthesis (http://pi-flora.com/cannect/haptic.htm, accessed September 2003).

Design Aspects with Instructional Conditions

Developing multimedia courseware has become a specialist's domain. Although software development tools make the production of the instructional content seem relatively easy, the real problem lies in the lack of expertise that can adopt a synergistic approach. The seemingly eclectic nature of HCI masks the requirement for a sound instructional design framework. There are two camps of expertise: on the one hand, some are the technocrats that cannot see there is too much attention given to the mechanics of the multimedia, while others view the pedagogical detail in a unilateral sense, not realizing the power of the multisensoral instructional environment.

The Issue of Measurable Instructional Outcomes

There is a direct relationship between the method of instructional delivery (media) and the measurable instructional outcomes in the **Metaknowledge Processing Model** described earlier in this chapter. There is an important distinction to make here. The method of delivery will be chosen to move a learner through the instructional strategies to achieve each particular instructional goal. As such, the measurable outcomes must focus on instruction rather than on the learner (Reigeluth, 1983). Therefore, a thorough task analysis is necessary to identify the expected learning outcomes in terms of human performance.

An individual's capabilities can be described as falling within the following categories: *intellectual skills*, *cognitive strategies*, *verbal information*, *motor skills*, and *attitudes* (Gagne, 1985). Although this taxonomy was derived prior to multimedia entering into educational/training settings, it is still a useful model upon which to describe the varieties of learning that people undergo throughout a lifetime. Unfortunately, many Web-based learning materials do not take into account this range of capabilities or the learners' skills at applying them.

Design Aspects with Measurable Instructional Outcomes

Failing to conduct a thorough task analysis for each set of instructional outcomes will result in weak and ineffective testing methodologies. It is a simple naivety to believe that the testing process should involve nothing but a set of questions and answers. When, in fact, test design is a complex process. First, there must be an understanding of the expected cognitive performance outcomes (achievable goals). Second, the types of skills and knowledge acquisition must be clearly identified. Third is the absolute requirement that the testing instrumentation be calibrated to ensure validity of each testing item. Fourth, there should be several ways of testing for the same type of skills and knowledge. Failure on any one of these processes means that the assessment cannot be guaranteed to reveal the true nature of cognitive performance.

Argument about Intellectual Skills

Currently, interactive multimedia appears to offer a generic approach towards intellectual context. An individual learns to interact with the environment using symbols, otherwise described as *knowing* (or procedural knowledge). This includes being able to translate simple instructions like finding a bus stop or dealing with a more complex procedure to distinguish hierarchical relationships necessary for problem solving and organization, like knowing which bus to catch home in rush hour. If the courseware does not include instructions or explanations relating to the visual effects of the information presented, there can be no guarantee that the intended message will be obvious to many people.

Argument on Cognitive Strategies

Go to any Web site and see the variety of attractive screen displays that involve multimedia. How many of these Web sites invite you to stop and reflect on the information presented. Instead, there is more often a range of colorful objects designed into the screen display, urging a quick click of the mouse to dive into cyberspace. It is proposed that this type of instant information grab bag will weaken the particular ways people choose to make decisions—*knowing what about a process*. This includes how people remember and think about past learning events. Moreover, the stigma of a bad experience can be long lasting; therefore, matching learner/facilitator cognitive understanding is preferable (Sonnier, 1989). Therefore, there is great risk in developing the quick-click approach to designing interactive multimedia for education and training.

Argument with Verbal Information

Web-mediated material that presents textual descriptions of concepts in a short precise manner may well have a place within multimedia courseware. However, even the term "interactive multimedia" provides an invitation for instructional designers to rush away from taking a finer-grained approach to presenting simple rules uncluttered by the technology. There are specific times when a learned capability for *knowing that* (otherwise described as declarative knowledge), requires the most basic statements about the underlying rules. This includes knowing how to read words without fully understanding what they mean.

Argument with Motor Skills

Research needs to be conducted to determine the extent of damage that occurs to humans when they sit for hours, looking into a computer screen, moving only their fingers, and perhaps elbows. This is perhaps the most profound change in the way individuals spend their waking hours. By spending long hours in one position, it is proposed that we will lose our capacity to execute particular movements that involve eye-hand coordination. Quite apart from the concentration needed to carry out a particular task, these types of movements involve multiple muscle responsiveness. For instance, take the small muscle coordination, like holding a pair of scissors or typing, or larger muscle control for folding paper or cutting pictures out of a magazine and pasting them into a book.

Argument Surrounding Attitudes

There can be no doubt that vital to any learning experience is mindset. People who show an aversion to computer systems, for instance, will need to have alternative instructional resources available to balance the intensity of interactive multimedia. There is great risk that such a person will just shut off and not wish to engage with the technology. Consequently, the mental beliefs an individual has acquired will be affected for things such as choosing particular personal actions that include his or her ability to decide which topic to study next or having enough motivation to try new things.

Unfortunately, while modern communications technology may appear to offer enhanced accessibility to information and the subsequent potential for acquisition of new knowledge, it does not really follow that there is any increase in accessibility for large sections of society. Indeed, there is an emerging international trend for researchers to focus on corporate training and workforce accessibility (Section508, 2001).

The Issue of Accessibility and Exclusivity

While some fine research is being conducted, unfortunately, this work mostly involves physical impairment. While there are many types of human functional disability—some of which are the result of the aging process (Vanderheiden, 1990)—the focus is mainly towards catering to the more definable functional limitations of computer users, with only limited research specifically designed to assist those recovering from a severe medical condition that hinders concentration and motivation (Fuller, 1998). Australia is following the movement brought about by the Disability Discrimination Act 1992, with some work currently underway towards improving general accessibility to information. Current initiatives include the draft Schools Online Curriculum Content Initiative (SOCCI) accessibility standard, and a review by the W3C to develop enhanced technologies that include specifications, guidelines, software, and tools. The Web Access Initiative (WAI), in coordination with organizations around the world, pursues accessibility of the Web through five primary areas of work: technology, guidelines, tools, education and outreach, and research and development (http://www.w3.org). However, this collective understanding still mainly addresses the issues surrounding the interactive effect of physical impairment and accessibility to information (http://www.w3.org/ 2001, November 13–14).

Problems that have surfaced for the instructional designers wishing to implement interactive courseware with multimedia in education and training, involve knowing where to go for advice and having enough funding to build effective instructional systems. Good work exists in pockets of excellence around the world. However, there is a distinct lack of designers who understand educational pedagogy as well as international best practice. Despite this limitation, there can be no doubt that aspects of Web-mediated instruction or e-learning have emerged as effective tools to bring about a knowledge-sharing culture, linking professional practice and the education sectors (Driscoll, Bucceri, Reed, & Finn, 2001). The increasing demand for effective HCI is forcing courseware providers to think of new ways to understand the social, historical, and contextual nature of learning (Moreno, 2001). However, following the technological advances in instructional delivery media made during the past decade, there can be no doubt that a major dilemma faces the education and corporate sectors this decade. How do we provide cost-effective Web-mediated instruction? Courseware design is problematic when novice designers eagerly develop online learning programs, often assuming that conversion of textual material to a digital format is a relatively simple process.

Argument over Accessibility and Exclusivity

Unfortunately, research is currently ignoring the importance of sociocultural interaction and Web-mediated knowledge exchange. Consequently, there is an expectation that the Web somehow has a natural propensity to facilitate the engagement of people in cognitive processes through collaborative team work (Kearsley & Shneiderman, 1999). Research needs to deal with the complexity of the interactivity between humans and technology (Sims, 2000) and learning intelligence environments (Garner, 2002). Work has commenced to investigate the ontological complexity in Web-mediated collaborative networks (McKay, Garner, & Okamoto, 2002). The Web-mediated learning environment should be about providing open, flexible, and distributed learning environments (Laurillard, 1993). However, without adequate learning management processes embedded within the courseware, this type of distributed learning experience will remain just that, distributed (McKay & Martin, 2002).

Design Aspects with Accessibility and Exclusivity

Instructional design relating to multimedia education for those suffering the effects of inaccessibility due to socio-cultural factors requires commitment from the government and corporate sectors. Moreover, academic researchers also have an important leadership role. As such, they have the opportunity to liaise between funding bodies, providing the investigative means to facilitate well-targeted research projects. Unfortunately, this is not the current state of affairs.

Economic factors dictate how much research is funded for community projects. Instead of increasing accessibility to information and knowledge sharing, it may well be that the machinery required to support interactive multimedia learning platforms is so expensive that the reverse occurs. Although several philanthropic ventures are underway to redress this prospect, much more funded research activity is needed to increase accessibility for those sections of the community in most need. When more is known about how individuals react to multimedia, the current trend to offer generic instructional platforms could diminish.

The Issue of Health and Safety

It is proposed that an HCI syndrome that involves the compulsive overuse of computers is becoming more noticeable since the advent of Web-based technologies. It should not be surprising to note the health and safety issues related to spending many hours in front of a computer screen, often isolated from other people. The amount of research on this issue is limited. However, there are some researchers who have identified that computer overuse can lead to some individuals requiring careful counseling to maintain a lifestyle that involves healthy socio-interaction. While ergonomics issues may be covered well, where are the warnings on both physical and virtual computerized products offered for sale? It could be said that enough is already known about the harmful effects of spending too much time working/playing with interactive multimedia programs. Consequently, the attractiveness of multimedia may outweigh the many negative effects that some individuals experience when concentrating in such a unilateral manner for long periods of time.

The social consequences of computer overuse are being documented. Perhaps it is not surprising to see that interest in the psychological effects of spending long hours in front of a computer screen is emerging from within social science. Problems associated with addictive disorders have been identified, with the Internet cited as the cause. Consider though, how damaging it must be for young children to spend long hours playing with computerized play stations. Perhaps it is only a matter of time before there is a voice rising from the researchers that calls for health warnings to be printed on the packaging of computerized multimedia toys. Much needs to be done to convince the manufacturers of computer games that having a healthy mind and body cannot be achieved by spending many hours in front of a computer. There is also a place for ergonomic lessons to be a functional part of every interactive multimedia module that is presented in an educational or training session.

Design Aspects with Health and Safety

The attractiveness of the visual platforms creates a whole new set of worrisome issues. Strategies that involve awareness of the ergonomic problems of incorrect physical conditions are perhaps more easily put in place than ones that are designed to reduce the dangers of addictive behaviors. Courseware design must take on a holistic framework that includes the delivery mechanisms (ergonomics) and appropriate psychological strategies that deal with the detrimental aspects of spending too much time with interactive multimedia.

The Issue of Mind Over Machine Mentality

Should this discussion on the interactivity of multimedia in education and training include any of the predictions from earlier debates over artificial intelligence (AI) (Koschmann, 1996), and the dire warnings from that debate about machines taking over many of the things people normally do? Furthermore, in looking at the publicity that surrounds the debate on the drive to include multimedia as a significant instructional modality, can the issue of *distributed cognition* also be aligned to this chapter? Distributed cognition may be quite relevant when looking into the effectiveness of interactive multimedia in education and training. This is still a relatively new idiom requiring careful scrutiny. Therefore, it is necessary to clarify the usage of this term in relation to the need for instructional design in this environment. With the rapidly expanding distribution of information through the Web, we have become accustomed to think in mechanistic terms. Is the tendency for some to visualize the importance of machinery over man still as apparent as it was when first recognized by Dreyfus and Dreyfus (1986), long before the Internet? Prior to the evolution of global communication networks, distribution was clearly a human interaction necessary for the sharing of tasks, language, experiences, and cultural heritage (Salomon, 1993). Cognition and ability are certainly inherent internal human processes. As a consequence, distribution cognitions should not reside in a unilateral sense in a Web-mediated environment. Instead, they should be thought of as stretched and jointly existing between each individual engaged in electro-communications (McKay, Okamoto, & Kayama, 2001).

The reliance on machinery may be on the increase. The suggestiveness of interactive multimedia may turn out to reduce cognitive outlay to such an extent that upcoming generations will not have the background knowledge to make sensible judgments. Steps need to be taken now to preserve historical events that have previously been handed from one human being to another (McKay, Nishihori, & Garner, 2003), including the learning process itself.

Design Aspects with Mind Over Machinery

The question must be put forward that asks how much emphasis should be placed on the benefits of engaging with interactive multimedia in education/training, without exposure to the same instructional context devoid of the technological trappings. What are the long-term issues of reducing the cognitive effort required to gain background knowledge? Evidence of the reliance on technological solutions to everyday problems is easy to find. For instance, in the banking sector, it has become mandatory for Internet banking to take precedence over the face-to-face contact expected when visiting the local branch.

Customizable Interactive Multimedia Educational Resources

To see what others are doing in relation to the interactivity of multimedia in education and training, there are few examples of research that make a connection between learning abstract concepts (which forms much of the pedagogical focus of Web-mediated instruction) and graphical representation as an instructional strategy. Consider, for example, a color coding process to trace programming logic flow (Neufeld, Kusalik, & Dobrohoczki, 1997), an interactive system that traces the hidden activities of a computer-programming interpreter (Smith & Webb, 1998), and an interactive learning shell that uses a cognitive-style screening test to direct users to the optimal instructional material for them (McKay, 2000c). In keeping with the notion that first principles of instructional design should always be followed, before there is any more discussion of the effectiveness of multimedia in an educational environment, it is necessary to look at how the literature has dealt with the learners' perceptual differences across a number of instructional environments.

A review of the literature that disseminates current professional practice in Web-mediated courseware reveals an awareness of the importance of following sound design principles (Rosenberg, 2001; Hedberg, Brown, Larkin, & Agostinho, 2001). Moreover, with the advent of the graphical user interface (GUI), it has brought with it a renewed interest in analyzing text and pictures. The GUI has also opened the way for investigations into the many ways of using signs to represent reality (Chandler, 1999). Investigations have emerged into the differing ways people form mental constructs to deal with the GUI environment. There is some evidence relating to how an individual's initial mental construct might take the form of a graphical image (Klausmeier, 1992). It was shown that images could serve as a device for mental recognition only if the actual object was seen earlier. Furthermore, it has been demonstrated that mental constructs include the perceptible and non-perceptible attributes of the concept and the cultural meaning given to the name of that concept.

Therefore, instructional strategies that accommodate different cognitive styles have surfaced. Some learners need help to develop their cognitive skills, while others merely need help in increasing their elaborative skills (Rohwer, 1980). Although there are vast numbers of well-respected theories of intelligence in the literature, opinion is divided according to the personal orientation of the researcher. There are several researchers who proposed new and unsettling explanations about human information processing that completely refute a traditionalist approach (Jenkins, 1980; Baine, 1986; Bruner, 1990). There are several supporters of the notion that contextual considerations play a vital role in the information processing operations of the human mind (Jenkins, 1980). There were others who proposed a purely internal orientation (Scandura & Dolores, 1990), describing the human mind in terms of a closed processing system receiving continual input from the world around us. AI research is driving the focus of instructional science research to find the means to replicate the information processing of the human mind (Tennyson & Spector, 1998). However, there are a growing number of prominent researchers who no longer want to follow the traditional attempts to depict memory as a box in a flow diagram (Ortony, 1979).

Baddeley (1990) has written several interesting and informative books and papers on human memory. He believes it is a collection of interacting systems that combine to store and subsequently retrieve information. It is our capacity to learn and remember that has enabled us to develop tools, communication skills, and technologies. Consequently, it is through this interaction of communication with technology that humans now have an even greater capacity to store and retrieve vast quantities of information. The progression of our ability to communicate through writing, filmmaking, and television, can thus be regarded as an extension of human memory.

Trying to categorize human memory becomes too theoretical (Baddeley, 1982). There are no true answers, only interpretations of available evidence. In organizing information mentally, one of the most common techniques humans draw on is their visual imagery ability. This is implemented with effective use of peg words (Reigeluth, 1983) to recall sequences of unrelated items in an appropriate order.

Conducting research that deals with the interactivity of cognition and instructional format has been problematic. Most of the past research on memory was highly controlled, with results reflecting the contrived experimental laboratory conditions (Baine, 1986). In reviewing memory models and research, Baine warned against generalizing laboratory findings from past research on memory to the natural environment, unless the exact nature of the experimental procedures is known. Mnemonic strategies are practical techniques that have the potential to make information more memorable and easier to retrieve (Baine, 1986). To arrive at this understanding, Baine drew on other well-known research, such as the Rosch *principle of cognitive economy* (Rosch, 1978), in identifying labeling, visual imagery, and maintenance rehearsal as mnemonic strategies. In relation to visual imagery research, Baine referred to numerous studies that involved children. Most of these studies directed the visual imagery behaviors, with participants being instructed to create their own images. However, such instructions have been shown to be an unsuccessful type of self-reporting test (Thompson & Riding, 1990).

As the cognitive approach tackles the great complexities of learning processes (Winn, 1980, 1982a), cognitive theories may offer a more comprehensive account of learning. Because of the extent to which cognitive theories extend into human learning, this, in turn, permits a more complete repertoire of instructional strategies that can be developed for designers to use and refine. Furthermore, Winn suggested that the cognitive approach offers the opportunity for research and practice to move closer together, given that research findings often take some time to filter through as practice. This is due, once again, to the complex nature of learning. The aspects of the learning processes that provide the most influence are instructional strategy or mental skill; knowledge of task (Ausburn & Ausburn, 1978); and the information presentation form, or general ability (Winn, 1982b). However, it was postulated that a factor such as knowledge of task is so important in the learning process that it overshadows other aspects of *instructional strategies*, to the extent that telling learners anything more elaborate than what is expected of them would be a waste of time.

Tennyson and Rasch (1988) described a Learning Environment Model, as an instructional design model to link cognitive processes and objectives to specific instructional methods. This model was proposed to focus on the planning of a learning environment to encourage students not only to acquire knowledge but also to improve their cognitive ability to extend their knowledge acquisition skills. They expanded on earlier research, in which the structuring of concept variables could be divided into two separate learning conditions (Tennyson & Cocchiarella, 1986). The first learning condition was a relational structure within a domain of information; the second was the attribute characteristic, which defines the concept's attribute characteristics, within a schema, along a constant/variable continuum. They suggested that 55% of a learning environment needs to be planned to encourage acquisition of the student's knowledge base (storage to memory), while the remaining 45% of the learning time needs to be allocated to employment and improvement of the student's knowledge base (retrieval from memory).

Future Trends

It would appear that instructional design involving multiple modalities has gone around a full circle. This is due to the intrinsic complexity of the dilemmas that face an instructional designer dealing with interactive multimedia within educational and training settings. At the very least, researchers are asking whether all the hype is worth it (Freeman & Capper, 1999). This is a very good sign; the reality may of course be a very different matter. It will come as no surprise that the corporate giants will try and lead the way. Looking at the amount of corporate dollars spent, it is not difficult to see that short-term cost recovery is not necessarily foremost in their thinking. It certainly will not involve rocket science to uncover the trend toward global corporations investing in their own platforms to enhance profit margins long term. As strong as the push from industry training may be, there will be an equally interested camp that pulls just as hard in the opposite direction, to uncover the best way to gain advantages for those circumstances where access to the educational forum has not been forthcoming. This egalitarian approach is already taking place within the virtual learning communities that are springing up (Miller, 2000; Suzuki, 2000; Ellis, 2000).

We are at a turning point in the design and development of multimodal courseware. There are already collaborative relationships between industry and academic institutions, providing research with excellent models upon which to work. Designers are just beginning to think and design instruction in terms of cognitive processes (von Wodtke, 1993), rather than in terms of overt learner performance (Winn, 1982a). This means that over time, awareness of cognitive research will become commonplace. On the other hand, researchers will still need to deal with learners in natural settings, and because of this, they will need to work more closely with LMS designers. This is because the cognitive approach takes into account things like existing knowledge and interaction with the learning environment, permitting a more comprehensive assessment of learning in the real world (Winn, 1981).

Following the premise that a multisensory approach is beneficial to learning, early LMS are already on the horizon. One such system, called Cogniware, has been developed using an instructional design authoring development tool. It consists of a front-end module to determine the learner's cognitive style (Riding & Rayner, 1998) and a choice of instruction method for the acquisition of programming concepts. Cogniware is multisensory in the sense that the instructional strategies offered provide the learning material in a range of alternative instructional conditions. Figure 4 depicts a typical Cogniware screen interface with three instructional formats or separate viewing areas: graphical, textual, and voice. In addition, there are cueing mechanisms for guided exploration, such as directional icons, a learning module name tag, and an advance organizer screen.

Figure 4: Towards a metaknowledge agent

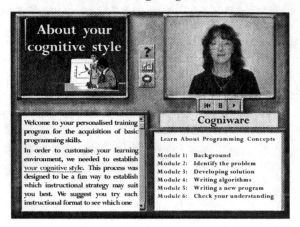

Source: McKay (2000c).

Cogniware provides the background material on different modes of learning in a textual description interface, while at the same time, a voice description can be heard.

Choice of Instructional Format

It is now possible to provide learners with multiple modality learning environments. For instance, Cogniware has three types of instructional formats available—graphical, textual, and voice (see Figure 4)—thereby providing the learner with the format that best suits his or her cognitive style. However, Cogniware is also flexible enough such that a learner can over-ride the default for the chosen format and select any other format.

Textual Modality

There are a number of ways in which we can aid the comprehension of the written word. To overcome one of the central difficulties associated with text processing, LMS developers will provide the reader with the best possible means to select important information from the text (Preece, 1994). Hotwords can be included as pedagogical cues to navigate a novice learner through a new concept. Text should not be considered as a flat structure, where all ideas are expressed with equal importance. For instance, the Cogniware text is a highly structured communication tool, in which ideas are expressed hierarchically, where certain parts of the message can receive more attention than others. As a consequence, particular display techniques enable the reader to focus on the full context of the message by selecting the important issues without being overwhelmed by poorly structured text.

Graphical Modality

In the future, courseware designers will involve carefully chosen graphical metaphors for their recognizable and distinguishing (or salient) features, to depict each concept to be learned. These visual metaphors serve to elicit prior experiential knowledge, enabling the learner to recognize the distinguishing features of the new concept and to interpret the instructional context without specific prior learning (Merrill, Tennyson & Posey, 1992).

Voice Modality

Video clips are another futuristic modality gaining popularity. Audio permits the hearing of verbal descriptions of the learning content. Advice and reassurance are also provided to ensure maximum coverage of the multisensory platform. Voice directions for dealing with the LMS navigation will be designed to reduce the cognitive effort required in dealing with the complexities of multimedia instruction. Reminders can be seen as a useful technique to keep the novice learner on track.

Another important futuristic trend for interactive multimedia is the awareness that corporate training has become a business imperative. Invoking Web-mediated knowledge representation is crucial in the two trillion dollar global education and training industries. Online training and skill acquisition processes, such as collaborative e-learning networks, have not addressed problem-solving and professional practice requirements. Researchers are expending energies to implement linkages between learning investments and professional practice, through an innovative approach to capitalize on a natural desire for lifelong learning. Expected outcomes include an understanding of the ontological complexities involved in online, collaborative learning networks and the contextual-mediation effects of HCI suited to effective knowledge exchange between learners (McKay, Garner, & Okamoto, 2003).

Along with the increased interest in Web-mediated instructional design, and the maturation of thought on the effects of multimodal instructional formats, at some point, researchers must encounter the rich dialogue on semiotics. Semiotics is often encountered during textual analysis (Chandler, 1999). Often it can involve taking a philosophical view on the nature of signs in the construction of reality. Semiotics involves studying representations and the processes involved in representational practice. The time is right for the earlier work on mental models and creativity to be brought to center stage (Schank, 2002). The future looks bright. The hopes are high for customized learning becoming reality. The increased interest in multimodal educational resources will herald the benefits that, until now, were only in some researchers' dreams.

Conclusion

This chapter began by asking whether a WBES can really facilitate cognitive skill acquisition. There are several misunderstandings with common attitudes toward learning that should occur through interactive multimedia. One of the strongest reveals the hope that HCI will activate lifelong learning and knowledge transfer. Sadly, current multimedia courseware reveals the opposite is true. Most of the responsibility for this can be laid at the feet of the LMS providers. That is not to say they deserve being sent to Coventry. The ontological complexity of the interactive multimedia learning context is immense. Even if all the answers to the numerous problems relating to Web-mediated courseware design were known, new problems will continue to arise for the multimodal instructional designer. The pressing problems for implementing interactive multimedia identified in this chapter can, in time, be overcome by newly created resource management strategies. Issues relating to health and safety must be addressed to ensure individuals' minds do not take off into cyberspace, never to return. The common expectations of machine learning have to be engineered such that the humans are returned to the focal point of the HCI environment. A much closer look should be made between the differences of providing the right amount of information to generate an individual's knowledge acquisition (the educational aspect) and providing the right amount of training to generate the correct performance outcomes (the training aspect) (McKay & Martin, 2002). The **Metaknowledge Processing Model** has been put forward as an important tool for courseware designers to use to overcome many of the vexing issues when determining delivery methods, measurable instructional outcomes, and customizing electronic instructional media.

The main purpose of this chapter was to discuss the interactivity of how people think and react to instructional materials in general and how this interaction may be affected by multimedia. Although the amount of research related to how individuals react to traditional learning materials is increasing, not much is known about how people react to multimodal instructional environments. Work has progressed thus far through intuition. The time is ripe for innovative research projects to delve into cyberspace to engineer more effective WBES solutions.

References

Angus, R. (Ed.). (1986). *The Angus & Robertson dictionary and thesaurus in one volume*. Sydney: HarperCollins.

Ausburn, L. V., & Ausburn, F. B. (1978). Cognitive styles: Some information and implications for instructional design. *Educational Communications and Technology Journal, 26*, 336–354.

Baddeley, A. (1982). *Your memory: A user's guide*. New York: Macmillian.

Baddeley, A. (1990). *Human memory*. Hilldale, NJ: Erlbaum.

Baine, D. (1986). *Memory and instruction*. New Jersey: Educational Technology Publications.

Bhattacharya, M. (2000). In S. S. -C. Young, J. Greer, H. Maurer, and Y. S. Chee (Eds.). Collaborative learning vs. cognition (pp. 1496–1503). *8th International Conference on Computers in Education/International Conference on Computer-Assisted Instruction (ICCE/ICCAI 2000): New human abilities for the networked society*, Taipei, National Tsing Hua University, Taiwan.

Bourne, J. (2000). On-line education: Learning effectiveness and faculty satisfaction (p. 288). *Proceedings of the 1999 Sloan Summer Workshop on Asynchronous Learning Networks*, Nashville, ALN Centre, Vanderbilt University.

Brogan, P. (2002). *Using the Web for interactive teaching and learning*. Macromedia Inc. White Paper, http://www.eduport.com/community/kiosk/20002/interactive_teaching_wp.PDF. Accessed February 4, 2004.

Bruner, J. (1990). *Acts of meaning*. Harvard, MA: Harvard University Press.

Bush, M. D. (2002). Connecting instructional design to international standards for content reusability. *Educational Technology, 42*, 5–12.

Cadena Smith, S. R., & Shelley, J. O. (2002). A vision of education in the Year 2010. *Educational Technology, 42*, 21–23.

Chandler, D. (1999). *Semiotics for beginners: The basics*. UK: Routledge (http://www.aber.ac.uk/media/Documents/S4B/the_book.html). Accessed February 4, 2004.

Clements, M. A. (1983). The question of how spatial ability is defined and its relevance to mathematics education. *Zentralblatt fur Didaktik de Mathematik, Sonderdruck, (Ger.Fed.Repub), 1*(1), 8–20.

Dillenbourg, P. (1999). What do you mean by collaborative learning. In P. Dillenbourg (Ed.), *Collaborative learning: Cognitive and computational approaches* (pp. 1–19). Amsterdam: Elsevier Science.

Douglas, G., & Riding, R. J. (1993). The effect of pupil cognitive style and position of prose passage title on recall. *Educational Psychology, 3*(3 & 4), 385–393.

Dreyfus, H. L., & Dreyfus, S. E. (1986). *Mind over machine: The power of human intuition and expertise in the era of the computer.* New York: Free Press.

Driscoll, J. -A., Bucceri, M., Reed, A., & Finn, A. (2001). *Fast path to success with Centra: Best practices, tips and techniques in live Elearning.* Massachusetts: Centura Software, Inc.

Ellis, W. N. (2000). Community lifelong learning centres. In R. Miller (Ed.), *Creating learning communities: Models, resources, and new ways of thinking about teaching and learning* (pp. 14–21). Brandon, VT: The Foundation for Educational Renewal, Inc.

Fredericksen, E., Pickett, A., Shea, P., Peiz, W., & Swan, K. (2000). Student satisfaction and perceived learning with on-line courses: Principles and examples from the SUNY learning network. In J. Bourne (Ed.), *On-line education: Learning effectiveness and faculty satisfaction, Proceedings of the 1999 Sloan Summer Workshop on Asynchronous Learning Networks* (p. 288). Nashville, TN (ALN Center): Vanderbilt University.

Freeman, M., & Capper, J. (1999). Educational innovation: Hype, heresies and hopes. *ALN Magazine, 3*(2).

Fuller, A. (1998). *From surviving to thriving.* Melbourne: ACER Press.

Gagne, R. M. (1985). *The conditions of learning: And the theory of instruction.* New York: Holt/Rinehart/Winston.

Garner, B. J. (2002). In E. McKay (Ed.), Role of solutions architects in learning intelligence (pp. 18–25). Invited paper in *eLearning Conference on Design and Development: International Best Practice to Enhance Corporate Performance,* Oct 21–25, Melbourne, Australia, RMIT Informit Library.

Gay, L. R. (1992). *Educational research: Competencies for analysis and application.* New York: MacMillan.

Gibbons, A., & Fairweather, P. (1998). *Computer-based instruction: Design and development.* New Jersey: Educational Technology Publications.

Gonzalvo, P., Canas, J. J., & Bajo, M. T. (1994). Structural representations in knowledge acquisition. *Journal of Educational Psychology*, *1*[86(4)], 601–616.

Goodman, N. (1968). *The languages of art: An approach to a theory of symbols*. New York: Bobbs-Merrill.

Hedberg, J. G., Brown, C., Larkin, J. L., & Agostinho, S. (2001). Designing practical Websites for interactive training. In B. H. Khan (Ed.), *Web-based training* (pp. 257–269). New Jersey: Educational Technology Publications.

Hoffman, R. R. (1998). AI models of verbal/conceptual analogy. *Journal of Experimental & Theoretical Artificial Intelligence*, *10*(2), 259–286.

http://www.w3.org/ (2004, February 4). Web content accessibility guidelines, Working Group Meeting. Melbourne, Australia.

Hunt, E. (1997). The status of the concept of intelligence. *Japanese Psychological Research*, *39*(1 March), pp. 1–11.

Jenkins, J. J. (1980). Remember that old theory of memory? Well, forget it! In J. G. Seamon (Ed.), *Human memory: Contemporary readings*. Oxford, UK: Oxford University Press.

Kearsley, G., & Shneiderman, B. (1999). Engagement theory: A framework for technology-based teaching and learning, Naval Sea Systems Command: Contract No. N00024-97-4173 (http://home.sprynet.com/~gkearsley/engage.htm, accessed February 4, 2004).

Klausmeier, H. J. (1992). Concept learning and concept teaching. *Educational Psychologist*, *27*(3), 267–286.

Kline, P. (1991). *Intelligence: The psychometric view*. United Kingdom: Routledge.

Koschmann, T. (1996). Of Hubert Dreyfus and dead horses: Some thoughts on Dreyfus "What computers still can't do." *Artificial Intelligence*, *80*, 129–141.

Laeng, B., Peters, M., & McCabe, B. (1998). Memory for locations within regions: Spatial biases and visual hemifield differences. *Memory & Cognition*, *26*(1), 97–107.

Landa, L. N. (1983). The algo-heuristic theory of instruction. In C. M. Reigeluth (Ed.), *Instructional-design theories and models: An overview of their current status* (pp. 163–211). Hillsdale, NJ: Erlbaum.

Laurillard, D. (1993). *Rethinking university teaching: A framework for the effective use of educational technology*. United Kingdom: Routledge.

Loiacono, E. T. (2003). Improving Web accessibility. *Computer: Innovative technology for computer professionals. IEEE Computer Society*, *36*(1), 117–119.

Lowenfeld, V. (1945). Test for visual and haptic aptitudes. *American Journal of Psychology*, *58*, 100–112.

Lukose, D. (1992). *Goal interpretation as a knowledge acquisition mechanism* (p. 426). Faculty of Science and Technology, School of Computing and Mathematics. Deakin University, Geelong, Australia.

Maddux, C. D. (2002). Information technology in education: The critical lack of principled leadership. *Educational Technology*, *42*(3), 41–50.

McKay, E. (2000a). Instructional strategies integrating the cognitive style construct: A Meta-Knowledge Processing Model (contextual components that facilitate spatial/logical task performance). *Com. Sci. & Info. Sys. (Ph.D. thesis)*. Deakin University, Geelong, Australia (3 Volumes).

McKay, E. (2000b). Measurement of cognitive performance in computer programming concept acquisition: Interactive effects of visual metaphors and the cognitive style construct. *Journal of Applied Measurement*, *1*(3), 257–286.

McKay, E. (2000c). In S. S. -C. Young, J. Greer, H. Maurer, & Y. S. Chee (Eds.), Toward a meta-knowledge agent: Creating the context for thoughtful instructional systems (pp. 200–204). Paper presented at the *8th International Conference on Computers in Education/International Conference on Computer-Assisted Instruction (ICCE/ICCAI 2000): New human abilities for the networked society*, Taipei, National Tsing Hua University, Taiwan.

McKay, E. (2002a). Grant submission: *Academic skills evaluation: Enhanced opportunities for young people returning to study or vocation training*. March 2002. Telematics Course Development Fund. Melbourne. (Announced December, 2002). Successful.

McKay, E. (2002b). Cognitive skill acquisition through a meta-knowledge processing model. *Interactive Learning Environments*, *10*(3), 263–291 (http://www.szp.swets.nl/szp/journals/il103263.htm).

McKay, E. (2003). Managing the interactivity of instructional format, cognitive style construct in Web-mediated learning environments. *The 2nd International Conference on Web-Based Learning (ICWL 2003)*, held August 18–20, in Melbourne, Australia, pp.308–319.

McKay, E., & Martin, B. (2002). In B. Boyd (Ed.), The scope of e-learning: Expanded horizons for lifelong learning (pp. 1017–1029). *Conference Informing Science 2002 + IT Education*, Cork, Ireland, Mercer Press/

Marino Books. Refereed article available from: ublisher@Informing Science.org

McKay, E., Garner, B. J., & Okamoto, T. (2002). In Kinshuk, R. Lewis, K. Akahori, R. Kemp, T. Okamoto, L. Henderson, & C. -H. Lee (Eds.), Understanding the ontological requirements for collaborative Web-based experiential learning (pp. 356–357). *International Conference on Computers in Education 2002*, Auckland, NZ, IEEE Computer Society.

McKay, E., Garner, B. J., & Okamoto, T. (2003). Management of collaborative Web-based experiential learning. *Computers and Advanced Technology in Education (CATE 2003)*, June 30–July 2, Rhodes, Greece, IASTED, pp. 409-414.

McKay, E., Nishihori, Y., & Garner, B.J. (2003). Grant submission: Global e-museum system (GEMS): Innovative adult literacy acquisition platform. Category ii. Australian National Training Authority (ANTA). Canberra.

McKay, E., Okamoto, T., & Kayama, M. (2001). In C. -H. Lee, S. Lajoie, R. Mizoguchi, Y. D. Yoo, & B. D. Boulay (Eds.), Ecological design technology in distance learning (pp. 1763–1769). *International Conference on Computer in Education (ICCE/SchoolNet 2001): Enhancement of Quality Learning Through Information and Communication Technology*, Seoul, Korea, Incheon National University of Education.

Merrill, M. D. (2002). Pebble-in-the-pond model for instructional development. *Performance Measurement, 41*(7), 41–44 (http://www.ispi.org/pdf/Merrill.pdf, accessed February 4, 2004).

Merrill, M.D., Tennyson, R.D., & Posey, L.O. (1992). *Teaching concepts: An instructional design guide (2nd ed.)*. New Jersey: Educational Technology Publications.

Merrill, P. F. (1980). Analysis of a procedural task. *NSPI Journal* (February), 11–16.

Miller, R. (Ed.). (2000). *Creating learning communities: Models, resources, and new ways of thinking about teaching and learning*. Brandon, VT: The Foundation for Educational Renewal, Inc.

Moreno, R. (2001). In T. Okamoto, R. Hartley, Kinshuk, & J. P. Klus (Eds.), Contributions to learning in an agent-based multimedia environment: A methods-media distinction (pp. 464–465). *IEEE International Conference on Advanced Learning Technologies (ICALT 2001): Issues, Achievements, and Challenges*, Madison, Wisconsin. IEEE Computer Society, LTTF:IEEE.

Neufeld, E., Kusalik, J., & Dobrohoczki, M. (1997). Visual metaphors for understanding logic program execution. *Graphics Interface '97*, 114–120.

Nonaka, I. (1994). A dynamic theory of organizational knowledge creation. *Organizational Science, 5*(1), 14–37.

Okamoto, T., Kayama, M., & Cristea, A. (2001). In T. Okamoto, R. Hartley, Kinshuk, & J. P. Klus (Eds.), Proposal of a collaborative learning standardization (pp. 267–268). *IEEE International Conference on Advanced Learning Technologies (ICALT 2001)*, Madison, Wisconsin, USA, LTTF:IEEE.

Ortony, A. (1979). Beyond literal similarity. *Psychological Review, 86,* 161–180.

Preece, J. (1994). *Human-computer interaction.* Harlow, England: Addison-Wesley.

Quigley, A. (2002). Closing the gap. *eLearn magazine: Education and technology in perspective* (http://elearnmag.org/subpage/sub_page. cfm?article_pk=2761&page_number_nb=1&title=FEATURE%20STORY. Accessed February 4, 2004).

Raban, R., & Garner, B. J. (2001). *Ontological engineering for conceptual modeling.* KI-2001, Vienna.

Reigeluth, C. M. (1983). Meaningfulness and instruction: Relating what is being learned to what a student knows. *Instructional Science, 12,* 197–218.

Reigeluth, C. M. (Ed.). (1983). *Instructional design theories and models: An overview of their current status.* Hillsdale, NJ: Erlbaum.

Riding, R., & Cheema, I. (1991). Cognitive styles—An overview and integration. *Educational Psychology, 11*(3&4), 193–215.

Riding, R. J., & Rayner, S. (1998). *Cognitive styles and learning strategies.* United Kingdom: Fulton.

Rohwer, W. D. J. (1980). An elaborative conception of learner differences. In R. E. Snow, P. A. Federico, & W. E. Montague (Eds.), *Aptitude, learning and instruction* (Vol. 2; pp. 23–46). Hillsdale, NJ: Erlbaum.

Rosch, E. (1978). Principles of cognition and categorization. In E. Rosch, & B. Lloyd (Eds.), *Cognition and categorization.* Hillsdale, NJ: Erlbaum.

Rosenberg, M. J. (2001). *E-Learning: Strategies for delivering knowledge in the digital age.* New York: McGraw-Hill.

Salomon, G. (2002). Technology and pedagogy: Why don't we see the promised revolution? *Educational Technology, 42*(2), 71–75.

Salomon, G. (Ed.). (1993). *Distributed cognitions: Psychological and educational considerations.* Cambridge: University Press Syndicate.

Scandura, J. M., & Dolores, J. (1990). On the representation of higher order knowledge. Special issue: Cognitive perspectives on higher order knowledge. *Journal of Structural Learning, 10*(4), 261–269.

Schank, R. C. (2002). *Designing world-class e-learning: How IBM, GE, Harvard Business School, & Columbia University are succeeding at e-learning.* New York: McGraw-Hill.

Section508. (2001). Workforce Investment Act of 1998, Electronic and Information Technology (http://www.section508.gov/, accessed February 4, 2004).

Sharpe, L., Hu, S., Crawford, L., Gopinathan, S., Moo, S. N., & Wong, A. F. L. (2001). Multipoint desktop videoconferencing as a collaborative learning tool for teacher preparation. *Educational Technology, 40*(5), 61–63.

Sims, R. (2000). An interactive conundrum: Constructs of interactivity and learning theory. *Australian Journal of Educational Technology, 16*(1), 45–57.

Smith, P. A., & Webb, G. I. (1998). *Evaluation of low-level program visualisation for teaching novice C programmers.* Deakin University, Geelong, Australia: Faculty of Science & Technology: School Computing and Mathematics.

Sonnier, I. L. (1989). *Affective education: Methods and techniques.* New Jersey: Educational Technology Publications.

Suzuki, M. (2000). The International University, Japan: A 25-Year Experiment in Restructuring University Education. In R. Miller (Ed.), *Creating learning communities: Models, resources, and new ways of thinking about teaching and learning* (pp. 80–89). Brandon, VT: The Foundation for Educational Renewal, Inc.

Tennyson, R. D., & Bagley, C. A. (1991). Structured versus constructed instructional strategies for improving concept acquisition by domain-experienced and domain-novice learners. *Annual Meeting of the American Educational Research Association,* Illinois.

Tennyson, R. D., & Cocchiarella, M. J. (1986). An empirically based instruction design theory for teaching concepts. *Review of Educational Research, 56*, 40–71.

Tennyson, R. D., & Rasch, M. (1988). Instructional design for the improvement of learning and cognition. *Annual Meeting of the Association for Educational Communications and Technology,* Louisiana.

Tennyson, R. D., & Spector, J. M. (1998). System dynamics technologies and future directions in instructional design. *Journal of Structured Learning and Intellegent Systems, 13*(2), 89–101.

Thompson, M. E. (1990). In D. G. Beauchamp (Ed.), *The effects of spatial ability on learning from diagrams & text* (pp. 99–103). *Annual Conference of the International Visual Literacy Association,* (22nd), Illinois.

Thompson, S. V., & Riding, R. J. (1990). The effect of animated diagrams on the understanding of a mathematical demonstration in 11- to 14-year-old pupils. *British Journal of Educational Psychology*, *60*, 93–98.

Vanderheiden, G. C. (1990). Thirty-something (million): Should they be exceptions? (trace.wisc.edu, accessed August 2003).

von Wodtke, M. (1993). *Mind over media: Creative thinking skills for electronic media*. New York: McGraw-Hill.

Winn, W. (1981). Effect of attribute highlighting and diagrammatic organization on identification and classification. *Journal of Research in Science Teaching*, *18*(1), 23–32.

Winn, W. (1982a). Visualization in learning and instruction: A cognitive approach. *ECTJ*, *30*(1), 3–25.

Winn, W. (1982b). The role of diagrammatic representation in learning sequenced, identification and classification as a function of verbal and spatial ability. *Journal of Research in Science Teaching*, *19*(1), 79–89.

Winn, W. D. (1980). Visual information processing: A pragmatic approach to the imagery question. *Educational Communication and Technology Journal*, *28*, 120–133.

Chapter XII

Usable and Interoperable E-Learning Resources Repositories

S. Retalis, University of Piraeus, Greece

Abstract

The Web puts a huge number of learning resources within reach of anyone with Internet access. In many cases, these valuable resources are difficult for most users to find in an efficient and effective manner. What makes an e-learning resources repository much more than a portal is the ability to discover a learning object and put it to a new use. The purpose of an e-learning resources repository is not simply safe storage and delivery but the ability of their administration, in terms of updating, identifying, utilizing, sharing and re-using them, which remains a great challenge. Moreover, the various repositories are either closed systems or systems that allow user access only through proprietary interfaces and data formats. In brief, there is lack of interoperability. The aim of this chapter is to present the requirements of an ideal e-learning resources repository that will provide services for covering the aforementioned critical issues. We will also describe such an ideal system could be non-centralized, which is the main difference from all the system that exists today in the WWW. Peer to Peer (P2P) based approaches are more flexible than centralized approaches with several advantages.

Introduction

The Web puts a huge number of learning resources within reach of anyone with Internet access. One can mention a lot of Web sites that hold learning resources, such as Canada's SchoolNet (http://www.schoolnet.ca/), MathGoodies (http://www.mathgoodies.com), or the U.S.-based site maintained by the Educational Object Economy Foundation (http://www.eoe.org/), and many more. The National Governors Association in the United States published a report in 2001 mentioning that "58% of all two- and four-year colleges offered distance learning courses in 1998, while 84% of all colleges expected to do so by 2002" (NGA, 2002). As the number of Web sites continues to grow, search engine retrieval effectiveness is likely to decline, and there is a need to consider alternative resource discovery mechanisms (Milstead & Feldman, 1999).

Apart from the "discovery" problem, the learning resource sharing appears as a major challenge and necessity, because development costs are becoming significant (Zlomislic & Bates, 2002). Since the old days, educators have been reusing learning resources. Textbooks, wall maps in geography classes, periodic tables of the elements in science classes, filmstrips and videos, etc., are resources that appear in many K–12 classrooms worldwide (Downes, 2001). Nowadays, coming into the e-learning era, educators and learners need to have access to as well as to reuse e-learning resources of their interests, needs, and preferences.

This is why e-learning resources repositories or e-Learning Resources Brokerage Systems (LRBS) have emerged. In very generic terms, an online "brokerage system" is an online entity that acts as a one-stop electronic marketplace. A brokerage system has two types of users: those who offer their products for sale (*providers*) and those who buy the products offered (*consumers*). An e-learning objects brokerage system facilitates the exchange of learning objects among organizations and individuals.

The term "learning object" is not intended to be restrictive but refers to any digital asset that can be used to enable teaching or learning (IEEE, 2001). A learning object does not imply some specific size or modularity. It may refer to many different types of objects from simple images or video clips, through complex questions, to collections of objects arranged in one or more sequences. One critical issue about learning objects concerns the ability of their administration, in terms of updating, identifying, utilizing, sharing, and reusing them, which remains a great challenge, as their number continues to grow at a fast rate. The only viable solution proposed to this problem is to define a set of metadata on them, that is, a set of attributes required to fully and adequately describe them (IEEE, 2001). There are several, highly active, standardization initiatives today that are concerned with the definition of specifications for learning resources metadata.

The LRBS usually offer learning objects stored in *digital repositories*. While digital repositories, in the broadest sense, are used to store any digital material, digital repositories for learning objects are considerably more complex, both in terms of what needs to be stored and of how it may be delivered (Duncan, 2002). Digital repositories are not mere portals, i.e., gates of access to learning material. What makes a digital repository much more than a portal is the ability to discover a learning object and put it to a new use. The purpose of a digital repository is not simply safe storage and delivery but also reuse and sharing. In a few cases, LRBS contain digital repositories, but this is not always the case.

An important aspect of LRBS is the categories of users that benefit from them, by performing certain usage scenarios. Users of digital repositories are mostly educators and, in general, authors of learning content. They may produce Web-based courses or classroom courses, face-to-face or distance learning, or full courses or short digital "nuggets." The LRBS should be neutral to the pedagogic purposes of the material, just as a library has no influence over where or when a book is read.

One can mention a lot of e-learning resources repositories. Unfortunately, the various repositories are either closed systems or systems that allow user access only through proprietary interfaces and data formats. In brief, there is lack of interoperability. Interoperability can be defined (IEEE, 1990) as "the ability of two or more systems or components to exchange information and to use the information that has been exchanged." To a user, the lack of interoperability means the following:

•   Applications and their data are isolated from one another.

•   Redundant data entry is common.

On the contrary, interoperability

•   Ensures that data are entered only once in one application and automatically propagates to other applications.

- Allows applications to exchange data more effectively.

- Defines the rules of interaction among software applications.

The aim of this chapter is to present the requirements of an ideal e-learning resources repository that will provide services for covering the aforementioned critical issues. We will also describe how this system could be noncentralized, which is the main difference from the system that exists today in the World Wide Web (WWW). Peer-to-peer (P2P) based approaches are more flexible than centralized approaches and have several advantages. For example, imagine that content consumers, both teachers and students, will benefit from having access not only to a local repository, but to a whole network, using queries over the metadata of learning objects that will be distributed (Nejdl et al., 2002).

The structure of this chapter is as follows. We start by analyzing and comparing the functionalities of various e-learning resources repositories under evaluation. This analysis and comparison lead to the extraction of the tasks and the requirements that an ideal e-learning resources repository should support. We continue by focusing on the special features that an ideal system should present. The special features will be illustrated by using case diagrams and scenarios in order to make them more clear to the reader. In the sequence, we will describe architecture for interoperable repositories. Apart from a central repository where the user can find learning resources, several other repositories located in different places in the Internet can be accessed in order to allow the user to perform a request for specific-learning resources at a network of repositories. The communication among the repositories can be performed via designated interfaces, which can import and export the metadata of their learning resources. The exchange of the metadata can be accomplished through a descriptive and extensive language such as XML.

E-Learning Resources Brokerage System

In this section, we focus on the requirements that an e-Learning Objects Brokerage System must satisfy, after having examined several e-learning objects brokerage systems. The requirements are grouped in tasks that the system has to perform. The type of task analysis we have chosen is hierarchical and borrows ideas from several sources, including Wigley (1985). In a hierarchical task analysis, according to Stammers et al. (1990), each task is analyzed by "breaking it into task elements or goals which become increasingly detailed as the hierarchy progresses." The most general information is placed at the top of the hierarchy, with the more specific information following on lower levels.

Currently, there are several e-learning objects brokerage systems operating on the WWW. Each offers certain functionalities, such as browsing and searching in a catalog of resources, managing an e-portfolio of favorite resources, booking resources, annotating resources, contributing resources, etc. Typical examples of such systems are as follows:

- SeSDL (http://www.sesdl.scotcit.ac.uk)
- LearnAlberta Portal (http://www.learnalberta.ca/)
- CAREO (http://careo.netera.ca)
- COLIS (http://www.edna.edu.au/go/browse/0)
- SMETE (http://www.smete.org/)
- MERLOT (http://www.merlot.org)
- Heal (http://www.healcentral.org/index.htm)
- Universal Brokerage Platform for Learning Resources (http://www.educanext.org)
- European Knowledge Pool System (http://rubens.cs.kuleuven.ac.be:8989/lkptm5/intro.jsp)
- World Lecture Hall (http://www.utexas.edu/world/lecture/)
- Globewide Network Academy (http://www.gnacademy.org/)
- Element K (http://www.elementk.com/)
- Online Learning Network (http://www.onlinelearning.net/)
- DigitalThink (http://www.digitalthink.com/)
- McGraw-Hill Learning Network (MHLN) (http://www.mhln.com/)
- IntraLibrary (http://www.intrallect.com/)

Table 1 summarizes the functionality of all the LRBS that have been examined and gives a comparative view. In Table 1, if a system performs a certain task, it is given a value of 1; otherwise, it is given a value of 0. In the same table, there is a column that illustrates the percentage of systems that perform each task.

Some immediate and useful remarks can be drawn from Table 1. First, almost all the general tasks appear in most LRBS in the sample set. Some general tasks, such as "contribute resource," appear to have a lower percentage. This can be easily explained if we consider that some of the systems in the survey's set are

Table 1: Comparing brokerage system tasks

TASKS	STATS (%)	PLATFORMS														
		UBP	WLH	GNA	ELK	Of n	Dig Th	McGr	SeSDI	IntL	Heal	Colis	Careo	Merlot	Smete	LearnA.
Browse catalog of learning objects	93	1	1	1	1	1	1	1	1	1	0	1	1	1	1	1
View catalog of learning objects	80	1	0	1	1	1	1	1	1	1	0	1	1	1	1	0
Browse learning objects by area/category	93	1	1	1	1	1	1	1	1	1	0	1	1	1	1	1
Search learning objects	93	1	1	1	1	1	0	1	1	1	1	1	1	1	1	1
Simple text search	93	1	1	1	1	1	0	1	1	1	1	1	1	1	1	1
Advanced search	80	1	1	0	1	0	0	1	1	1	1	1	1	1	1	1
Customized query search	7	1	0	0	0	0	0	0	0	0	0	0	0	0	0	0
Sort results	47	1	1	0	0	0	0	1	1	1	0	0	0	1	1	0
View learning object details	100	1	1	1	1	1	1	1	1	1	1	1	1	1	1	1
View learning object metadata	100	1	1	1	1	1	1	1	1	1	1	1	1	1	1	1
View comments, reviews, and ratings	20	0	0	0	0	0	0	0	0	0	0	0	1	1	1	0
View cross-referenced learning objects	13	0	0	0	0	1	0	0	0	0	0	0	0	0	1	0
Reserve learning object	47	1	0	0	1	0	0	0	1	1	1	0	1	0	0	1
Agree with license agreement	13	1	0	0	0	0	0	0	0	0	1	0	0	0	0	0
Book learning object	33	1	0	0	0	0	0	0	1	1	1	0	1	0	0	0
Add to shopping cart	13	0	0	0	1	0	0	0	0	0	0	0	0	0	0	1
Manage reserved learning objects	67	1	1	0	1	0	0	0	1	1	1	0	1	1	1	1
View list of booked learning objects	33	1	0	0	0	0	0	0	1	1	1	0	1	0	0	0
View shopping cart	13	0	0	0	1	0	0	0	0	0	0	0	0	0	0	1
Commit reservation	27	0	0	0	0	0	0	0	1	1	1	0	0	0	0	1
View history of all reserved learning objects	40	1	0	0	1	0	0	0	1	1	0	0	1	0	0	1
Categorize learning objects (e.g., favorites)	0	0	0	0	0	0	0	0	0	0	0	0	0	0	0	0
Comment, review, or rate a learning object	20	0	1	0	0	0	0	0	0	0	0	0	0	1	1	0
Buy learning object (payment)	27	0	0	0	1	1	1	0	0	0	0	0	0	0	0	1
Learning object delivery	100	1	1	1	1	1	1	1	1	1	1	1	1	1	1	1
Connect to system server	60	1	0	0	1	0	1	1	1	1	1	0	1	0	1	0
Connect to another site (provider)	60	1	1	1	1	1	0	0	0	0	0	1	1	1	1	0
Send to customer (via mail)	13	0	0	0	1	0	0	0	0	0	0	0	0	0	0	1

Table 1: (continued)

TASKS	STATS (%)	UBP	WLH	GNA	EL	KOLn	Dig.Th	McGr	ScSDI	IntL	Heal	Colis	Careo	Merlot	Smete	LeamA.
Contribute learning object	60	1	1	1	0	0	0	1	1	1	0	1	1	1	0	0
Upload to system server	27	1	0	0	0	0	0	1	1	1	0	0	0	0	0	0
Provide link to another site	47	1	1	1	0	0	0	1	0	0	0	1	1	1	0	0
Define terms (license agreement)	20	1	0	0	0	0	0	0	0	0	0	0	1	1	0	0
Manage contributed learning objects	47	1	0	1	0	0	0	1	1	1	0	0	1	1	0	0
View list of contributed learning objects	40	1	0	0	0	0	0	1	1	1	0	0	1	1	0	0
Edit/cancel contributed learning object	47	1	0	1	0	0	0	1	1	1	0	0	1	1	0	0
Commit contribution (make available)	27	0	0	0	0	0	0	0	1	1	0	0	1	1	0	0
Personal user account	80	1	0	0	1	1	1	1	1	1	1	0	1	1	1	1
User profile and preferences	80	1	0	0	1	1	1	1	1	1	1	0	1	1	1	1
My library/portofolio of learning objects	60	1	0	0	1	1	0	1	1	1	1	0	1	1	0	0
Site personalization	7	0	0	0	0	1	0	0	0	0	0	0	0	0	0	0
Update notification	80	1	0	1	1	1	1	1	0	0	1	1	1	1	1	1
Mailing list	20	0	0	0	0	1	1	0	0	0	0	1	0	0	0	0
Newsletter	33	0	0	0	1	0	1	1	0	0	0	1	0	0	0	1
What's new/upcoming updates	60	1	0	1	0	0	0	1	0	0	1	1	1	1	1	1
System informative material	100	1	1	1	1	1	1	1	1	1	1	1	1	1	1	1
Help manual	73	1	0	0	0	0	1	1	1	1	1	1	1	1	1	1
F.A.Q.	73	1	1	1	1	1	1	1	0	0	0	1	1	1	0	1
Site map	53	0	1	0	1	1	1	0	0	0	1	1	0	1	0	1
Terms of use	73	1	0	1	1	1	1	1	1	1	0	1	0	0	1	1
Glossary (of technical terms)	20	0	0	0	0	0	0	0	0	0	0	1	1	0	0	1
Company informative material	100	1	1	1	1	1	1	1	1	1	1	1	1	1	1	1
Company profile (about us)	100	1	1	1	1	1	1	1	1	1	1	1	1	1	1	1
Partners and alliances	87	1	0	0	1	1	1	1	1	1	1	1	1	1	1	1
News and events/calendar	67	0	0	1	1	1	1	0	1	1	0	1	0	1	1	1
Contact system personnel	100	1	1	1	1	1	1	1	1	1	1	1	1	1	1	1
E-mail (contact us)	100	1	1	1	1	1	1	1	1	1	1	1	1	1	1	1

Table 1: (continued)

TASKS	STATS (%)	UBP	WLH	GNA	EL.K	OI.n	Dig.Th	McGr	SeSDL	Intl	Heal	Colis	Carco	Merlot	Smete	LearnA.
Support request form	13	0	0	0	1	0	1	0	0	0	0	0	0	0	0	0
Provide feedback form	40	1	0	0	1	1	0	0	0	0	1	1	0	0	0	1
Multilanguage support	73	1	1	0	1	0	1	1	1	1	0	1	1	1	0	1
Multilanguage learning objects	67	1	1	0	1	0	0	1	1	1	0	1	1	1	0	1
Multilanguage system	13	0	0	0	0	0	1	0	0	0	0	0	0	0	0	1
Specialized features	53	0	0	1	1	1	1	1	0	0	0	1	0	0	1	1
Discussion forum	33	0	0	1	1	1	0	0	0	0	0	1	0	0	1	0
Advising services	13	0	0	1	1	0	0	0	0	0	0	0	0	0	0	0
Educational tools/other material	33	0	0	1	1	0	0	1	0	0	0	1	0	0	0	1

actually "providers" of e-learning content and not open "brokers," and thus, they do not support contribution of user material.

Regarding "browsing," there is nothing much to be said, because, as expected, almost all systems support this feature. Regarding the issue of searching the learning content, almost all systems provide some sort of simple text search. However, only about three out of four of the systems provide an option for advanced search and sorting of the results, and even worse, only a small percentage allows for actual customized query-based search. Although "viewing a resource's details" is also implemented by all systems, this feature is limited to viewing a resource's metadata. Only few systems offer "previewing" of the material or an adequate summary. Comments and ratings from other users and cross-referenced resources are also absent from most systems.

As Table 1 indicates, about half of the systems support "reservation of resources." The user is therefore forced to commit to his or her choice and proceed to the resource delivery or payment, without having the option of collectively reviewing his or her choices. Systems that have implemented the resource-reserving feature provide only a limited functionality on managing the reserved resources, by providing an option to view the reserved resources and cancel a reservation. No system provides functionality about viewing all the reserved resources (and not just those of the last transaction), annotating them and categorizing them.

We can, also, observe that some systems that sell e-learning content do not support a very critical feature in the selling process, namely, the "online payment" feature. This should be considered as a drawback for such systems, because it forces the user to interrupt a process and get involved in a separate process in order to achieve his or her goal. "Resource delivery" is implemented by all systems, because this is the ultimate goal of an LRBS. The delivery of the resource can be either by downloading from the system server or by connecting to some external site, depending on the system's architecture and goals. It is also possible that some material may be delivered via mail to the customer.

"Contribution of resource" is a feature that clearly does not refer to all LRBS. But even systems that allow the contribution of resources usually do so partially, because most of them do not allow the user to specify the conditions under which the resource is distributed or do not allow the removal of a contributed resource. Again, the user is forced to commit early to his or her choice. It should be possible for the user to contribute a resource and keep it private, until the user decides to offer it openly.

Although a significant percentage of the systems provide personal user accounts, most of them do not utilize this beyond some basic level. Only few systems allow for personalization based on the users' preferences. LRBS update their content often and should therefore provide some mechanism for notifying their users. Some systems do not comply with this requirement, while others do so in more than one way.

All the systems provide "help" in more than one form, predominantly, the FAQ form. It is, however, surprising that only about three out of four of the systems provide an actual system manual, and that only one out of four systems provide a glossary of technical terms that may be abundant in LRBS. All systems provide an e-mail address so to the user can contact the system's personnel for support or feedback. However, only a small percentage provides more sophisticated and structured ways to submit a support request or provide feedback.

An interesting point is that although nearly three out of four of the systems allow and properly support multilingual content, only a small percentage of the systems account for multilingual support within the system itself. Finally, we see that more than half of the systems provide additional specialized features of some sort, with the ones most popular being the option for discussion forums and educational tools.

Functionality and Services

When examining the functionality and the services offered by the brokers, one can create a superset of these functions and form the ideal functionality. This superset is presented in this section and can be considered the requirements specifications for an "ideal" e-learning objects brokerage system.

The major tasks that LRBS perform are as follows:

1. Browse catalog of resources
2. Search resources
3. View resource details
4. Reserve details
5. Manage reserved resource
6. Buy resource (payment)
7. Deliver resource
8. Contribute resource
9. Manage contributed resources
10. Annotate resource
11. Offer personal user account
12. Update notification
13. Provide system informative material
14. Provide company informative material
15. Contact system personnel
16. Offer multilanguage support
17. Offer specialized features

It is evident that every system should provide some way of *browsing and searching for the offered resources*. It is cleared that a simple text search is not sufficient, and some sorting of the search results should be available. Therefore, we propose that an ideal e-learning objects brokerage system implements the following two general tasks: "browse catalog of resources" and "search resources." Browsing should concern all resources on a specific (easily selected) area/category. As for searching, in addition to the simple text search, an advanced and customized search option should be available. The results should be presented, after being sorted, either alphabetically, by relevance, by category, by last update, or by any other metadata information available for the resources.

When *viewing the details* of a selected resource, it is useful for the user to view, in addition to the metadata available for the resource, some other indicative information. This includes some sample material or a summary/abstract of the resource, depending on each case. Users also seem to find comments and ratings by other users that have used the same resource to be useful. The e-learning objects brokerage system should also offer cross-references to other resources that were also used by users of a given resource. This seems to provide the user with a very focused and high relevancy search option, as illustrated by sites like "Amazon" and "Google" (with the option "Find similar pages").

In the case that an e-learning objects brokerage system requires some form of *resource reservation* (as in brokerage platforms or providers of e-learning content), the system should provide the user with the option to view the "license agreement" under which the reservation (or buying) of resources takes place, at any time (before, during, or after the reservation takes place). The "license agreement" can be either specific to each resource (as in brokerage platforms, where resources have different providers) or common to all resources (as in providers of e-learning content, where the provider offers all resources). The user should have the "Reserve resource" option available, without being forced to commit to his or her choice, until the user is ready to proceed to the next step (resource delivery or payment).

Except for reserving a resource, the user should also be able to somehow *manage the reserved resources*. This option is not limited to viewing the resources reserved during the user's last transaction but may (preferably) include all the reservations (that were actually committed) by the user in the past. This allows the user to manipulate this list by designating his or her favorite resources, recommend a resource for other users, rate a resource, and comment (on usefulness, relevance to some topic, or any other useful criterion). The user can also categorize the resources to custom categories and manage the resources (actually links to the resources). This includes canceling an already reserved resource or committing to the reservation (at which time the resource's provider should be notified, and not prior to that time).

The option to *buy a resource* is critical in LRBS that "sell" e-learning content online. Although the payment stage of a transaction can be carried out via alternative offline methods (e.g., telephone or mail order), we feel that because the rest of the transaction is completed online, so must the payment stage. The subtasks for implementing this requirement are well known and need not be discussed here. We should note, however, that the payment stage should be in accordance with the reservation of resources and the commitment requirement as explained above. Hence, the user should be allowed to reserve and cancel the reservation for any number of resources before committing and paying for them.

Regarding the *delivery of resources*, this can be implemented depending on the resource type, system category, terms of resource sharing (e.g., use once, unlimited use), and its digital rights, in general. This could include presenting the e-learning material onscreen, downloading the material to a local media, or linking to a Web site. In case an e-learning brokerage system contains a digital repository, it will be able to provide access to the e-learning content by itself. In any other case, it should provide only access details that should have already been given by the content provider as an addition to the standard learning object metadata.

Complementary to the resource delivery is the option to *contribute a resource*. This is not required by all LRBS, but it is necessary for digital repositories. When contributing a resource, the user should be able to either provide a link to the resource or upload the material to the system server, according to the desired functionality of the system. In any case, the user should be able to clearly define the intended viewers of the resource and the conditions under which the resource may be used, i.e., the digital rights. The system is responsible to uphold any constraints defined on the resources, provided that these comply with the system's policy.

An assistant functionality to contributing a resource is the *"Manage contributed resources"* feature. In addition to viewing the resources contributed by a user-provider, the user should have the option to edit a contributed resource or even cancel a contribution and withdraw the resource, again given that this complies with the system's policy. Last, the user has the option to make a contribution public and thus commit to his or her contribution.

The user should be provided with an option to *annotate a resource* and store the annotations in an annotation repository. The user should be able to comment on the resource, using either free text or specific notations, e.g., "star system" for rating the quality of the resource. There should be an authentication mechanism for each user, because there can be two kinds of annotations: the private ones and the public ones. Each annotation object should be accompanied by metadata specifying the author, a time stamp, the kind (e.g., "criticism," "praise," etc.). Additionally, other relevant subtasks are to filter and retrieve annotation sets based on their metadata.

The option to create a *personal user account* is almost a necessity in e-learning objects brokerage systems. This allows the system to keep personal user information (e.g., the reserved resources), to contact the user for updates, and to adjust to each user's individual needs. The latter is important in order to provide a personalized and thus efficient and focused use of the system, because each user has unique expectations from the system.

Regarding the *"Update notification"* option, this should be provided upon the user's request only, and the user should be able to terminate it at any time. The information provided should be relevant to the user as possible, something that can be achieved by utilizing the user's personal preferences. The notification should be made both online (e.g., in the home page or some specific news page) and via e-mail (e.g., mailing list or newsletter), according to the user's request.

An important feature of any system is to provide *informative material about the system*. This material can and should take many different forms, including manual, FAQ, site map, and glossary. The user should have the option to select the form with which he or she feels most comfortable with and believes it can most efficiently and accurately provide the needed information. It is also important that the information be presented modularly, starting from help on the basic system functionality and moving to the more advanced functionality upon user request. Lists of steps that guide the user should be used whenever possible, instead of plain text.

The systems should also provide *company informative material* that although not directly related to the system itself, may provide useful information to some users. This information should be clearly marked and accessible but should not interfere with the system's functionality and documentation. The latter will result in confusing the user and blurring the system's intended goals and capabilities.

Besides reading precompiled help material, the system should also provide an option to *contact the system personnel*. The user should have the option to contact (via e-mail, phone, or online live chat, according to the importance of the request) the system personnel and get answers to specific questions or provide feedback about the system. Support and feedback should be preferably implemented via form completion. The structured input guides the user and allows for better processing of information.

The *multilanguage support* feature should be considered among the most important features of an LRBS. A system that provides e-learning content should be able to also address the needs of foreign users that may not master the language of the system. This, of course, is not limited to providing multilanguage resources, which is equally important. The entire system documentation and online information (except contributed resources) should be able to be translated to other languages. A clearly marked way should be provided to toggle between languages, appearing (preferably) on the home page (or every page) through icons (e.g., country flags).

The above covers the basic requirements of LRBS. In addition, some *specialized features* may also be present, depending on the system's goals. Such features include discussion forums, glossaries, etc. Although these features are not considered to be essential, when implemented and integrated correctly, they can advance a system's overall image.

Designing an Ideal
Decentralized System

Most of the existing LRBS are based on a centralized, nondistributed architecture. All the offered learning resources can be found in a central repository of data to which the broker has access. The research and development challenge is to build systems with architectures of distributed data repositories. Apart from a central data repository, where the broker can find its own learning resources, several other data repositories located in different places on the Internet can connect to such a decentralized brokerage system. In particular, each e-learning resources brokerage system or any other independent digital repository can register to this brokerage system. Whenever a user performs a request to the broker for specific learning resources, the broker will search in its digital repository and communicate with the external brokerage systems or digital repositories. The communication with the other systems can be performed via designated interfaces, which can import and export the metadata of their learning resources. The exchange of metadata can be accomplished through a descriptive and extensive language such as XML. Importing the XML representation of metadata, the broker can be informed about the kinds of learning resources that other systems possess. Figure 1 illustrates an overview of the design of a decentralized e-learning objects brokerage system.

Another additional functionality that LRBS should support is the *synchronization* of the metadata descriptions of their learning resources. A *synchronization* process means that a LRBS could decide to provide a replicate of the metadata descriptions of their learning resources to another system, e.g., for

Figure 1: Overview of the design of a decentralized e-learning brokerage system

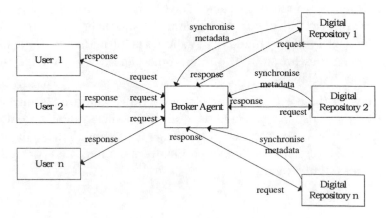

wider dissemination of their resources. In this case, each alteration, creation, and deletion of the metadata description of a learning resource could appear in more than one LRBS. The LRBS will collaborate in order to perform an update or an insert or delete command at their remote metadata repositories.

Following this design principle, a brokerage system can be characterized from an open and interoperable architecture, where various and different delivery systems and repositories that offer learning resources can communicate. The basic prerequisite for enabling interoperability is that each digital repository should fully support the same metadata standard (e.g., IMS LOM, IEEE LOM, etc.).

System Implementation

In order for the above communication to be established, a specific interface for each digital repository must be developed. Each interface is being implemented as a "Java Web Service" and is responsible for the achievement of the

Figure 2: System architecture and application flow

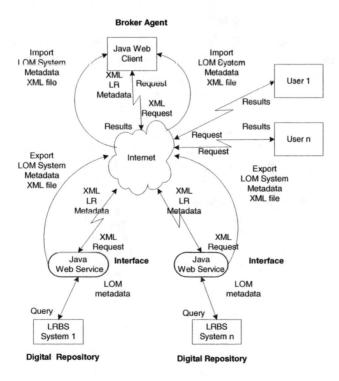

communication between the repository and the broker. This communication will be based on the interchange of metadata files. The broker-agent will compose a Java Web client that will communicate with each Java Web service. Figure 2 illustrates the architecture of the described system, presenting the information flow inside the application.

The first thing that has to be done is the registration process. Through that process, each digital repository registers to our system. The administrator of the repository has to define the information that the search engine needs in order to communicate with the repository. The information contains the IP address or host name of its interface and the port number in which the interface will listen for queries from the search engine. In a future version of the implementation work, the interface will also be able to export the taxonomy of its metadata structure. The search engine will register the repository and provide "guidance" on the communication protocol. Particularly, the search engine will give the method name that each interface must implement in order to be able to provide the requested metadata. It will also give the way it will call that method and the arguments that needed to be passed through the call. That method will be standard for all the interfaces that want to communicate with our system.

The application flow starts from the time a user wants to search for learning resources (Request). After the user enters the selection criteria, the broker agent (or search engine) calls the interface of each digital repository (through the given IP address and port number) and passes, through the predefined method, the user request/query through an XML file (XML Request).

The interface of the LRBS interacts with its LOM subsystem when passing its query (Query). The LOM subsystem responds to the interface returning the LOM Metadata that satisfy the query (LOM Metadata). Once the interface has the requested metadata, it transforms the metadata into an XML format and returns them to the broker agent (XML LR Metadata). Eventually, the broker agent returns the metadata on the user's screen in a readable format (Results). Each one of the LRBS has an interface, which is implemented as a Web service. The interface implementation is based on the LOM System and is independent from the search engine's implementation. The only requirement in order for the search engine–interface communication to be established is the existence of a method that is called "getLRMetadata(XMLQuery)". The method gets as an argument an XML file that contains the query of the metadata that the user requests and returns to the search engine an XML file that contains the LR Metadata that the LOM System returns to its interface/Web service. Figure 3 illustrates a sequence diagram that describes the exchange of the metadata.

Figure 3: Metadata exchange

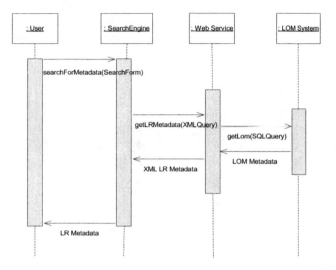

Discussion

The idea of interoperable LRBS is becoming popular. Several groups have started experimenting and standardizing the interoperability process. The IMS Digital Repositories Interoperability (DRI) specification aims to provide recommendations for the interoperation of the most common repository functions. The ultimate aim is to make recommendations that could be turned to implementable services via common interfaces (IMS, 2001). DRI defines a general reference model that captures all instances of possible implementations, such as the following:

- A user searching a repository directly

- A user conducting a search across repositories via a Search Gateway intermediary (acting as a translator)

- A user conducting a search across repositories via a Harvest intermediary (acting as an aggregator)

At technical level Z39.50 (http://lcweb.loc.gov/z3950/agency/), which is widely used for searching at digital libraries, a searcher is permitted to use the familiar user interface of the local system to search the local library catalog as well as any remote database system that supports the standard. While Z39.50 is assumed to be used for searching systems such as digital libraries, XQuery is recommended as the preferred query mechanism for XML-based learning object repositories.

Another group that is working on a test bed for a network of distributed repositories using SOAP-based messaging is the Learning Objects Network, Inc. (http://www.learningobjectsnetwork.com/). Learning Objects Network, Inc. (LON) demonstrated a working model using messaging and metadata search capabilities like that recommended in the IMS DRI specifications at the January 2002 IMS meetings in Cambridge, MA.

Furthermore, The OpenURL is a framework for an open and context-sensitive method of reference linking that is gaining widespread acceptance in the publishing and library communities. Rather than seeking to be independent of physical location, the advantage of OpenURL resolution is finding the appropriate copy or copies of an item that are stored in multiple locations (see http://www.sfxit.com/openurl/openurl.html for more information). Although OpenURL has been developed in the context of scholarly literature, a framework for generalizing the model to other domains has been put forward (the 'Bison-Futé' model—see http://www.dlib.org/dlib/july01/vandesompel/07vandesompel.html). This generalized model could be used as the basis for adoption within the IMS DRI community.

On the JISC-funded OLIVE project, there is ongoing research and development in the distributed querying of learning object repositories. Basically allowing LMS and, in their case, OpenURL resolves to find and retrieve learning objects such as online courses. OpenURL has been fast-tracked by NISO for adoption as a NISO standard (http://www.niso.org/).

Recognizing the fact that learning objects are still a new concept as well as the reusability, exchange, and interoperability of learning resources are significant issues, we have to think of possible obstacles that delay the R&D achievements. These obstacles are as follows:

1. *The lack of consensus about the definition and description of learning objects as well as their granularity.* Perceptions about the nature and size of learning objects differ. One could easily find out that the main learning objects repositories do not conform to the LOM standards. For example, while IntraLibrary (http://www.intrallect.com/) and Merlot (http://www.merlot.org/) are IMS compliant, Belle/Careo (http://careo.netera.ca/) is using the CanCore protocol, which is a simplification and interpretation of the 86 elements of the IMS Learning Resource Metadata Information Model. Moreover, Colis (EdNA) (http://www.edna.edu.au/go/browse/0/) depends on the EdNA Metadata Standard, which is based on Dublin Core Metadata Element Set. Other R&D groups have proposed quite different sets of metadata (in the best case, some of them are extended versions of the IMS standard) in order to describe Web-based multimedia teaching materials in a specific domain. For example, Heal (http://www.healcentral.org/) has developed a standard metadata specification

for sharing medical education multimedia based on the IMS standard. Other ideas come around, like the ones proposed in the UNIVERSAL project (http://www.educanext.org): "LOM does not propose learning resource types, which would be required for categorizing educational activities. At the Universal Brokering Platform, the following educational activity types are introduced: case study, course, course unit, exam, exercise, experiment, group work, lecture, presentation, and project." Furthermore, despite the fact that sites like Math Goodies, which is a free math help site featuring interactive lessons, homework help, worksheets, etc., do not use LOM description, they are very popular. Users prefer resources like lesson plans that do not entirely fit into a LO category.

2. *The lack of clarity on how to reuse learning objects and create new learning resources.* It is evident that learning objects cannot work like Lego. On the one hand, we could affirm that instructional design methods, which could effectively support the process of aggregating course content, do not exist. In fact, there are some ideas similar to that presented by Douglas (2001) that propose a component-based instructional development process, and Douglas argues that we should adopt/adapt object-oriented software design methods. On the other hand, authoring tools and learning content management systems (or even learning management systems) are not advanced enough to create content "on-the-fly" from learning objects. Very few commercial products of this type exist. One prominent example of such a tool could be the Designer's Edge (http://www.allencomm.com/ products/authoring_design/designer/). The unavailability of usable tools is surprising, because research efforts have only started with the European Union DELTA program [e.g., DIScourse project (http://www.itd.ge.cnr.it/ sarti/papers/mispelkampsarti.html)]. The reusability of LOs is still a tacit knowledge.

3. *The insufficient description of the "behavior" of learning objects.* Despite the fact that there are many attributes in learning object metadata description, they do not fully capture the "behavior" of a learning object. A learning object is created with specific learning objectives in mind, holds specific behavior, and interoperates with surrounding learning objects. Isolating a learning object and reusing it means that either this learning object can remain intact, because it might fit well to the new learning context, or this learning object needs changes. In the latter and most usual case, not only do technological problems arise but also instructional. A learning object does not only have its own characteristics and learning value, but its relationship with other learning objects offers additional learning experiences. Descriptive models such as CLEO or educational modeling languages such as EML have been suggested. However, we should also design models for the authoring/aggregation of learning content.

We need to adapt formal design models and methods from the field of hypermedia engineering (e.g., OOHDM, RMM, etc.). Such models will show which learning object consists of a learning application and how these learning objects are interrelated. Of course, these models as well as their formal notations (and bindings) should be compatible with the existing (or the ones that might arise) learning technology standards like the Content Packaging, Learning Design, etc. One approach akin to a modeling notation in education is concept mapping (Gaines & Shaw, 1996), which might be proven valuable if combined by the unified modeling language (UML) (probably extended using its extension mechanisms).

Concluding, the positive answer to the question of whether it is feasible to aim at interoperation of LRBS for the automatic learning resources reusability and recreation depends on progress in conceptual, learning, social, and technological issues. The technological issues are the easiest to be solved. Consensus at conceptual, learning, and social levels is difficult to achieve but not impossible. Standardization can help, as well as research attempts along road maps, as the one published by Duval and Hodgins (2003).

Acknowledgments

The authors would like to acknowledge the support of the European Commission through grants HPRI-CT-1999-00026 (the TRACS Programme at EPCC) and the IST UNIVERSAL project. Many thanks to P. Avgeriou, P. Constantinou, I. Stavrou, and L. Michael for their reviews and valuable feedback on the draft versions of this chapter.

References

Douglas, I. W. (2001). Instructional design based on reusable learning objects: Applying lessons of object-oriented software engineering to learning systems design. *Proceedings of the 31st ASEE/IEEE Frontiers in Education Conference, October 10–13, 2001.* Reno, NV.

Downes, S. (2001). Learning objects: Resources for distance education worldwide. *International Review of Research in Open and Distance Learning,* July.

Duncan, C. (2002). Digital repositories: The back office of e-learning or all learning. *9th International Conference ALT-C 2002: Learning technologies for communication*, September 9–11. University of Sunderland, Sunderland.

Duval, E., & Hodgins, W. (2003). A LOM research agenda. *The 12th International World Wide Web Conference*, May 20–24, 2003. Budapest, Hungary.

Gaines, B. R., & Shaw, M. L. G. (1996). Web map: Concept mapping on the Web. *Proceedings of the fourth international World Wide Web conference* (Vol. 1, Issue 1). Retrieved from the World Wide Web: http://www.w3j.com/1/gaines.134/paper/134.html

IEEE. (1990) *IEEE standard computer dictionary: A compilation of IEEE standard computer glossaries*. New York: IEEE.

IEEE, Learning Technology Standards Committee (LTSC). (2001). *Draft standard for learning object metadata (LOM), Draft 6.4, 2001*.

IMS. (2001). *IMS digital repositories interoperability—Core functions information model*. Revision: January 13, 2003.

Milstead, J., & Feldman, S. (1999). Metadata: Cataloging by any other name... Retrieved from the World Wide Web: http://www.onlinemag.net/OL1999/milstead1.html

National Governors Association. (2001). *The state of e-learning in the states, NGA report*. Retrieved June 6, 2001 from the World Wide Web: http://www.nga.org/cda/files/060601ELEARNING.pdf

Nejdl, W., Wolf, B., Qu, C., Decker, S., Sintek, M., Naeve, A., Nilsson, M., Palmer, M., & Risch, T. (2000). Edutella: A P2P networking infrastructure based on RDF. WWW2002, May 7–11. Honolulu, Hawaii. (ACM 1-58113-449-5/02/0005)

Stammers, R., Carey, M., & Astley, J. (1990). *Task analysis*. In J. Wilson, & E. N. Corlet (Eds.), *Evaluation of human work* (Chapter 6). Bristol, PA: Taylor & Francis.

Wigley, W. (1985). INPO/Industry job and task analysis efforts. *Proceedings of the IEEE Third Conference on Human Factors and Power Plants*.

Zlomislic, S., & Bates, A. W. (2002). Assessing the costs and benefits of telelearning: A case study from the University of British Columbia. Reports from the NCE-Telelearning project entitled "Developing and Applying a Cost-Benefit Model for Assessing Telelearning," Telelearning Networks of Centers of Excellence (http://research.cstudies.ubc.ca/nce/EDST565.pdf).

Part III

Applications and Case Studies

Chapter XIII

Interactive Multimedia and AIDS Prevention:
A Case Study

José L. Rodríguez Illera, University of Barcelona, Spain

Abstract

Using multimedia applications to inform or to train is very different than using them for changing attitudes. The documented and discussed project started with the perspective that a large proportion of young people, despite knowing how AIDS might be contracted, still adopt risk behaviors. A multimedia role play application was designed to include both information and game layers. The game introduces complex situations using video stories, and then lets the users construct different narratives by choosing between behavior alternatives. The result of each narrative is related to contracting the disease or not. A discussion about role playing games follows, on the limits of this approach, as well as the kind of interactivity and the forms of delayed feedback given.

Introduction

This chapter provides a detailed description of a multimedia AIDS prevention project undertaken jointly by research teams in Italy and Spain. The project, "AIDS: Interactive Situations," was funded by the European Union and resulted in the setting up of a Web site and the production of a hybrid CD-ROM, of which more than 40,000 copies were distributed, through both public and private channels, in the two participating countries between 1999 and 2000. The chapter is divided in five parts: a description of the project rationale and an outlining of its objectives; a description of the project's contents; a description of the multimedia technology used and the interactive approach incorporated; a discussion of the project; and conclusions reached.

Project Rationale and Objectives

AIDS prevention is a constant concern of the education and health authorities. Prevention campaigns are frequently mounted, and wide use of the mass media is made in conveying the message. However, interactive media have only rarely been used for this purpose.

At the start of the 1990s, the only software available were HyperCard stacks and similar programs containing AIDS fact files and information about the ways in which the disease might be contracted, and a number of simulation programs based on system dynamics models that demonstrated the evolution of the disease at a time when it was thought to be fatal in a period between 10 and 15 years (González, 1995). Multimedia programs were later developed, but their primary purpose was as a source of medical information (AIDS 2000 Foundation). Other programs included a computer game that allowed the study of epidemics throughout history (Fundació LaCaixa, 1995).

In developing this project, "AIDS: Interactive Situations," the aim was to provide a different focus. In fact, by the mid-1990s, most adolescents (here, and throughout the chapter we refer solely to adolescents in the Western world) had a good grounding in the basics of AIDS prevention, thanks in large measure to the prevention campaigns. Yet, despite knowing how the disease might be contracted, a large proportion of adolescents still adopted risk behaviors. This discrepancy between the information received and the attitudes that guide their behavior is a constant feature among adolescents.

The main aim of this project was, therefore, to focus on the subjects' perceptions of risk situations and the consequences of their behaviors. The other objective of the project involved the provision of decision-making techniques in situations of risk, always exemplified by the failure to use a condom in heterosexual relations.

Contents and Educational Design

The results of the project's psychological and educational analyses indicated the type of contents and transformations required. We concluded that the best approach was to include a purely informative content, offering information about the disease and the ways in which it might be transmitted, plus information describing its psychological and social features. This information serves as a ready reference for schools and can also be consulted on an individual basis. As we shall see later, it serves an additional function, one that we consider to be of considerable importance. This information "layer" is included in a straightforward hypertext format and aims above all to be user friendly. It also incorporates a number of further multimedia tools, including a map of AIDS information centers. The contents are organized in five sections:

1. *The disease*: This section contains information about HIV, how the virus is produced, how it acts on the organism, etc.

2. *Prevention*: This section allows the user to acquire information about how to prevent AIDS, which sexual practices involve the greatest and least risk, and how to use male and female condoms.

3. *The AIDS test*: This section explains when one should take the AIDS test, how to go about taking it, and how to interpret the results.

4. *Ideas and behaviors*: This section focuses on techniques to become more assertive, including negotiation and dialogue at times of conflict, understanding oneself better, etc.

5. *To find out more*: this section lists books, songs, films, and Internet Web sites that contain information about AIDS.

The main content, however, comprises an interactive role-playing game. This format was selected as it was considered the best way to meet the aims of changing attitudes and of simulating the negotiation and dialogue that occurs in situations of risk. In Tonks' (1996) review of techniques for providing information about AIDS and changing attitudes about the disease, role-playing games appear as the basic tool, although not as part of a multimedia application—which in Tonk's review are considered only in their audiovisual format. Role-playing games offer many advantages, above all the possibility of testing the skills that are being learned or developed in a safe environment. Furthermore, role play allows great flexibility in terms of content, and it is typically used without any multimedia components.

The role play is based around the metaphor of a summer trip taken by a group of friends around Europe. In this group, there is a couple in a steady relationship who have to deal with a number of different situations. The program user has to choose at the outset whether to be the male or female character and has to behave in accordance with this choice throughout the journey, as the content varies depending on the role that has been selected. The choice of character does not depend on the sex of the player, given that the game can be played in a group or as part of a class activity within a school, but it conditions the way in which the game develops, presenting a particular point of view in each situation. In fact, we believe that this initial choice constitutes the user's main point of identification with the game, because the player then has to interact in the program as if he or she were one of the characters and to adopt what they consider to be the character's point of view.

The role play is organized around six situations: the first acts as an introduction, the next four present risk situations, and the last tells the user the results of the decisions he or she has taken. Each of the four risk situations is organized in a similar manner: first, a narrative section is presented in which a complex situation is introduced, followed by an interactive section in which decisions are made.

Figure 1: Flow diagram of the game

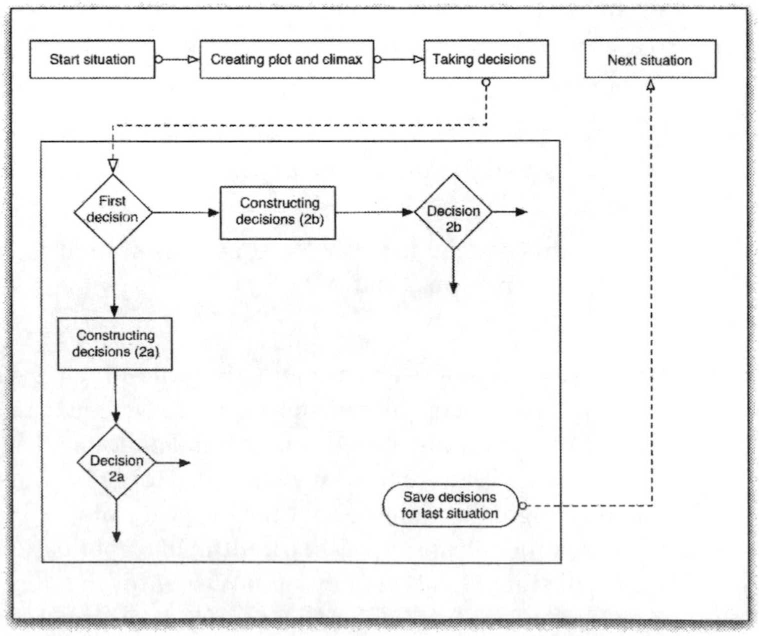

This common format ensures that the main story line in the game is easily followed, as the metaphoric journey is always brought to a halt by a situation that is presented in a similar way, and after the user has made the required decisions, he or she can continue on the journey, whatever happens. Decisions have to be taken: the user cannot proceed with the game if decisions are not made, and the user's results are stored and not shown until the end of the game. Figure 1 shows the overall organization of the game, although the decision-making tree diagram only shows the first two levels.

Each situation involves the use of condoms in heterosexual relationships, but each emphasizes a different ability that we wish to strengthen within the general framework of negotiating condom use: the first is the ability to stand by one's opinions in a dialogue with one's partner, the second is resisting group pressure, the third includes the situations that arise when changing partners, and the fourth includes the decisions that are made under the influence of alcohol and drugs. In addition to these main abilities, each situation presents a considerable amount of informative material contained within the dialogues, both in the video and in the decision-making section. This information, at times debatable as it is presented as the opinion of one of the characters, is contained within the project's hypertext.

The choice of content is important in several respects: first because of the abilities described above, second because of the physical settings in which the story unfolds, third because of the overall credibility of the situations, and fourth because of the language presented within the dialogues.

The Educational Design

Given the complexity of the psychological and pedagogical aspects of the project, it is extremely difficult to find one conceptual framework that can support its educational design. In general, educational multimedia applications tend to use a cognitive theoretical framework or, on occasion, a constructivist one (Duffy et al., 1992; Duffy & Cunningham, 1996). However, in most cases, applications are not designed on the basis of a single theoretical viewpoint but use several to try to resolve a specific instructional problem.

The main feature that distinguishes multimedia projects such as the present one from approaches that seek to automate instructional design is that they are driven both by the problem and by the theoretical frameworks of the designers. That is, inside specific theoretical orientations, instructional and learning strategies are sought that make it possible to resolve the problem—a *bricolage*-type activity. Determining what is most important is only possible if the characteristics of each particular case are taken into account.

For the most part, multimedia role plays such as "AIDS: Interactive Situations" use general educational principles of constructivist type, albeit in combination (*bricolage*) with other related approaches. These principles have been studied on many occasions, though the analysis has been largely generic and has not been applied to specific cases of educational multimedia applications. We can speak of three fundamental principles that guide the educational design:

1. The individual construction of meaning
2. The situated character of cognition and learning
3. The play environment as a construction of the player's identity

The Individual Construction of Meaning

This is the fundamental principle of constructivist approaches and is what distinguishes them from teaching models that are based on the transmission of knowledge. Knowledge is constructed by integrating meaning (or sense) into preexisting, personal structures.

In our case, the content is structured according to the model of interaction discussed above, that is, by allowing the pupils to select their own paths by means of the choices that they make. Participants construct their own path, or narrative, by choosing from the many alternatives that the game allows. In contrast, many of the programs that merely provide information on AIDS, without offering other activities (interesting as they are in their own right) can be considered as merely transmitting a particular type of knowledge (medical, psychological, or social). The construction of meaning requires the involvement of the learner so that the new knowledge is integrated and internalized, even in the case of a simple activity such as deciding how a story is going to develop.

The Situated Character of Cognition and Learning

The concept of "situated learning and cognition" (Lave, 1988, 1990) which is a radical critique of the cognitivist vision, stresses the need to place learners in situations that are meaningful to them. It considers that all learning is linked to the social situation or context in which it is produced. In the case under analysis here, this view of learning has developed into the current notion of "learning communities" and finds its expression in the attempt to make the role play a "situated activity." "Situated activity" is an activity that is both meaningful and credible: meaningful because it focuses on a problem that is important to the subjects and credible because it is life-like (in spite of the inevitable fact that it is presented by means of a computer screen).

Credibility is the main characteristic in each of the situations contained within a role play, because it is impossible to get a subject involved if he or she does not consider the situation to be realistic. This realism is achieved by the careful study and use of three types of factors: physical, linguistic, and narrative:

1. *Physical.* The situations are credible as far as the physical setting and the characters' ways of dressing and moving are concerned. The actors chosen were of ages between 16 and 20 and were encouraged to give their performances as spontaneously as possible. Furthermore, the interactive situations were played out in settings not unfamiliar to young people: a hotel room, a beach after sunset, a discotheque, and a party in the house of friends.

2. *Linguistic.* As in other simulations or pseudosimulations, in role plays such as this, it is the content that conditions the simulation and the realism of the situations, and this is primarily language-based: the game is largely concerned with taking decisions but also with following the reasoning that leads to a decision and, finally, opting between two alternatives that represent opposite, or markedly different, points of view. For this reason, the characters' ways of speaking had to be selected with particular care in order to capture as closely as possible the way young people express themselves.

3. *Narrative.* The game's story line is organized around the metaphor of a journey. To ensure realism, the journey involves a group of friends visiting various European cities one summer by train. At each stop, a new situation can be introduced, and in this way, the journey serves as a narrative thread linking each situation (a thread that would have been difficult to find if the situations had occurred as isolated incidents). Having said this, however, each situation is independent of those that precede it and stands as a separate situation in its own right, with its own problem and solution.

The outcomes of each decision are not revealed, however, until some months after the holiday. On the one hand, it needs to be like this in order to give greater realism to the game, as there exists the so-called "window period" during which infection with the AIDS virus cannot be diagnosed, even when it has occurred. On the other hand, it captures the particular characteristic of the apparent disconnection between the risk behavior and the onset of awareness: when the antibody test can be performed, the subjects have forgotten the practices that have led to the results they are given. In this case, the game indicates the situations and practices of risk during which the infection could have occurred.

The Play Environment as a Construction of the Player's Identity

This aspect is common to games in general, and is particularly relevant in computer games, including role plays. The setting provides a safe environment in which players can experiment with activities that involve a certain risk; they can break the rules in some way, or they can improvise their reactions to an unexpected situation. In role plays, participants represent different personalities and act accordingly but are not liable to suffer from any negative consequences of the decisions they take. The role-play scenario is a safe environment, but it is also a learning environment in which the participants' identities are modified by the ways in which they play the roles of the imaginary characters. This connection between learning and identity has been highlighted by Wenger (1998) and more recently by Gee (2003) with respect to video games.

In the case of AIDS prevention, role play allows participants to create a situation in which they play the parts of adolescents through their identification with their roles, but at the same time without the risk of suffering the negative consequences of the decisions they make. The play environment, the identification with the character, the active choices made in selecting a narrative and constructing meaning, and the "realistic," credible nature of the situations act synergistically in the educational design.

Interactive Multimedia Applications

The decisions taken regarding project aims and content have a direct bearing on several aspects of the multimedia production, as well as the interactive applications.

Multimedia Production

The multimedia production typically includes the graphic interface design, the media, and the programming. The graphic interface was designed following criteria similar to those adopted in the content specifications, which seek to make them suitable for a young end user. The overall design comprises several points of focus that vary as the journey takes its course, and this, in part, reflects the distinctive sections of the project: the hypertext reflects a more conventional presentation of the project's contents, the role play uses a black background combined with a number of innovations (which are described below in the description of the interactive applications), and, interestingly, a small game serves to introduce the various characters, each using a variation in the graphic interface.

The overriding idea in determining the graphic interface was to come up with a product that was as close as possible to the aesthetic design that young people are used to seeing in computer games, multimedia leisure activities, and even in video clips and television. Unlike many adult users, children and young people are particularly critical of graphic interface features, and many educational programs fail to make any attempt to capture the graphic aesthetics that appeal to them. It is also true that the cultural similarity between the two countries in which the CD-ROM was distributed, Italy and Spain, helped unify the graphic criteria used.

The media used included video (nine sequences of around 5 minutes each, bearing in mind that the last sequence had to be divided in four: two depending on the selection of the sex of the character, one showing infection with the virus, and the other showing a situation in which the disease is not contracted), several hundred stills for the simulated dialogues, and music.

The decision to use video, as well as that to use photographs, was made to promote user identification with the characters in the role play. Unlike animated images, which have to be extremely realistic or of high quality, video encourages identification with the characters, and with the story, more easily and more directly. The performances of the actors, and their facial expressions, ensure that in the mind of the user the actors and the characters are inseparable. The stills were taken using conventional photographic techniques, predominantly in close up, with some shots taken at a slightly longer range. The reasons for this are well known in the cinema, as close-ups of the face, capturing the actor's facial expressions and eyes, help the viewer identify with the character.

In short, the choice of the media was based on the need to make the story as realistic as possible, and as such, both video and photography were seen as essential elements in capturing the emotional impact of the story.

The computer technology and programs used were conventional: we used Macromedia Director for the design, given its versatility and the ease with which different media can be integrated, in addition to its multiplatform capacity, linked to QuickTime. A special Internet version was not designed, given the video size (an average of 50 MB), which would have meant it could not even be used on wideband networks. Furthermore, most of the users are secondary schools, or citizen support groups, or young people in general, who typically only have access to an ISDN or ADSL modem connection with a capacity to download video images that is extremely limited.

Interaction

At its most basic, the interaction element is organized around a simple navigational structure in which the user must choose between the information section and the role play. Below we shall see how these two options are interconnected. The information section consists of a hypertext comprising graphics and text, which provide basic information. The text is adapted to the users and is extremely user friendly.

The role play, however, has a more complex interactive format, as it combines a story told in video images with the need to make decisions (stills). The video story is interrupted when a conflict arises between the characters, and the user is left not knowing how it will evolve. The audiovisual story serves, then, to

Image 1: Decision-taking structure in the role-playing game. The video still on the left allows the player to view the whole situation. The small circular images show the previous decisions that have been taken. The player can return to these if he or she wishes to reconsider the decision. The two main images in the middle show the options that the player has to choose between for the situation just viewed: by placing the mouse over each image a text appears summarising the option, while the other image fades out. The small image of the main character at the bottom of the screen reminds the player that they have adopted the role of the female character.

motivate the user and also to present an unresolved problem. The user then needs to respond to this problem according to the role he or she has adopted in the game, which is the character with which the user by now identifies. Therefore, the interaction with the content of the program centers on the choice of various options in a simulated conversation with the main characters—depending on which of two options given is selected, the subsequent options presented will vary.

As described above, once the interaction has been initiated, an internal narrative is constructed in accordance with the options selected: the course taken by the dialogue is determined by the choices that are made. In other words, the application itself constructs the narrative and the course taken by subsequent choices, using a preprogrammed dialogue that is inserted between nodes in the decision tree. This dialogue takes the form of various screens, very much in the style of a photo-novel.

One of the most interesting aspects of this system is that it allows the decisions to be thought through. In other words, there is no time pressure whatsoever on the user, who is free to make his or her decision when they feel fit. This means that the dialogues between one decision and the next can be read and given due thought, as they result in the need for a new choice to be made. The application includes the possibility of returning to the video sequence at any time, as well as changing the choices made, should the user feel he or she made a mistake or wishes to select the other option. The decisions taken are depicted in the form of mini graphic images, so that it is always possible to go back to one of them (although, of course, changing the earliest decisions means that all subsequent decisions are lost).

Interaction during the game enables the more complex decisions, or those that require factual information, to be linked up with the hypertext system in the information section of the program. If the young user wishes to receive information before taking a decision, he or she can launch the information system, although the hypertext capacities of the system are restricted: it is only possible to navigate those screens containing relevant information for the decision that has to be taken at that moment. This is a design choice, implemented so that the user does not cast the net too wide when searching for information and so as to give contextualized support only.

Educational Applications and User Tests

The project was distributed with the national newspapers and was also sent to educational resource centers. This distribution plan ensured a wide audience but made it difficult to conduct any evaluation of its impact. However, an informal method of evaluation was employed by conducting interviews with the users.

The results of this (for a detailed account see Rodríguez Illera et al., 1999) revealed a very high approval rating, while respondents claimed that they had identified easily with the role play. The only criticisms received concerned features of the interface, in particular, in the information section, where some users felt the text was too dense and the letter size too small.

This somewhat limited analysis concerned the programs used in groups with a teacher. For such purposes, the program is accompanied by a detailed guide for educational contexts, one for teachers and another for the end users [http://www.noaids.org]. The latter suggests various activities and means of comprehension for users working by themselves. This possibility was specifically included so as to allow those young people who feel uneasy or who are reluctant to express their opinions in public use the program.

Discussion

We believe that the project demonstrates the means of integrating multimedia capabilities within an instructional design that has clear educational objectives, incorporating elements of interaction to reinforce these objectives within an overall framework that comprises a role-playing game. We would highlight the following aspects of the project:

1. The search for design simplicity at all times: Rather than use multimedia capabilities for their own sake—including animation, audio elements, and music—with little bearing on the educational purpose of the project, we sought to use only those elements necessary to meet the project's specific educational aims. This does not mean that we ruled out the use of more complex interactive capabilities, in particular, given the type of end user we are dealing with. Indeed, the program incorporates a section in which a wide range of multimedia capabilities is used with the primary purpose of entertaining the user: before embarking on the journey, the program allows the user to get to know the main characters of the story better by using a number of short interactive games that differ for each of the six characters. However, this part is clearly isolated from the rest of the program and does not interfere with either the information section or the role-playing game itself.

2. The use of multimedia is designed to facilitate the telling of the story, to create dramatic tension and climatic situations, and to introduce the conflicts. In other words, the features of audiovisual language are used— in this case, features that are more emotive than informative and features that ensure the user identifies with the story's characters.

3. It is true that we do not have an institutionalized means of representing the language of multimedia (Plowman, 1994), and that, therefore, it is difficult to know the significance of certain multimodal configurations (Kress, 2003), such as those that are present in designing complex screens. However, in the case we are concerned with here, the central place of the video in the construction of the story, as well as the absence of the simultaneous appearance of text, means that it can be considered as the dominant component of multimedia, and it can be thought of as being largely responsible for constructing the meaning.

4. The program combines a story, which has its own predefined meaning, with elements of interaction that provide a new meaning and a situation that each user constructs via the decisions that he or she makes, creating a personal narrative along the path that is taken. This format employs interactive multimedia capabilities, while putting them at the service of educational objectives.

The Limits of Role Play

This project description has highlighted what we consider to be its successes, but a subsequent analysis enabled us to see where its limitations lay, in particular, those concerning its instructional design. As indicated, role play is a type of simulation, albeit without any underlying mathematical model, in which it is easy to rehearse certain skills in a safe environment. The strength of the simulation lies in user identification with the characters (and with all the other aspects that are constructed using the multimedia). Once this has been achieved, it becomes virtually independent of the multimedia format that the subsequent interactive program adopts, though not of the logic underlying the choices that are made throughout the program and the story that develops. We believe that this principal feature of the project can be seen in terms of a theoretical construct similar to that present in situated learning and cognition: the attempt to get the young users to see it as something that they have to resolve in a particular way, using the elements that appear on the screen. The "magic" of multimedia applications is in the complete engagement of the user, in a similar way to that in which a book absorbs its reader (Hill, 1999), in other words, its ability to transport the reader or the user to a very high level of cognitive involvement, centered on the activities that they have to carry out. In short, it is the ability to make the user believe that the role play is a real and engaging situation.

The underlying logic of a multimedia role play differs from that of the goal-based scenarios proposed by Schank (1998), which might be considered as another strategy of situated learning. It responds more closely to those cases of ill-defined problems that are so typical of informal teaching and learning situations.

The inadequate definition of the situation or the problem is characteristic of real problems, which, removed from experimental situations, need to be analyzed using multiple perspectives and argumentations and descriptions designed to capture their meanings. In the case of role plays, this need is apparent in the narratives of decision building (Cho & Jonassen, 2002): the characters resituate the choice taken using a simulated dialogue that follows a line of argument until a new decision is made.

If the objective of the role play were to be made explicit from the outset, such as "always use a condom in a risk situation," it would probably lose all interest, in particular for young people. However, if we had to teach skills that had been previously agreed upon with adult subjects, the choice of a scenario based on explicit objectives would be a more recommendable option. Yet, one of the characteristics of games that seek to simulate real situations is that the player does not always know the objective of the game, at least the first time it is played. This gives rise to a certain ambiguity between the objectives of the instructional design (which include a modeling of behavior in risk situations, as well as a set of negotiation skills via the choices to be made and the story that unfolds between the decisions) and those of the player playing the role game for the first time, who does not know very well what it comprises—identify with one of the characters, accompany him or her throughout the journey, and make decisions along the way—but without an explicit objective as to the target that needs to be reached. This ambiguity, or lack of definition as far as the player is concerned, results in a much more situated performance, as the player plays "as if" he or she were one of the characters, making the decisions that they consider to be "normal" whenever required to do so. If the game leads to the player contracting the infection because he or she has engaged in unsafe sexual practices, this simply emphasizes the need for reflection on these practices, reminding the player when and how the behavior occurred but giving the player the opportunity to make mistakes.

The Question of Feedback

Furthermore, as discussed earlier, in the case of AIDS, there is a marked time lag between the occurrence of the risk behavior and the realization of its consequences, which means it is not possible to offer immediate corrective feedback (which would be the most efficient way of doing so).

Several techniques are available for making subjects aware of the anticipated effects of their behavior: one such technique is that used by González (1995), who constructs a graphic simulator of the spread of an infection in a given population (a discotheque) based on sexual relation profiles. The simulator clearly shows how the infection spreads over time and its consequences in the medium and long terms. This technique is very useful for showing the effects on populations or groups and for understanding the epidemic nature of many diseases.

A further didactic technique for individual use, and which was in fact analyzed for use in this project, is that which is used in the application: *If you love me, show me* (Family of the Americas, 1995). Although it does not deal directly with AIDS but rather with sexual relations among young people, it uses an animated narrative to show the ups and downs in a date between a boyfriend and girlfriend. Told from the perspective of the girl, it adopts a highly conservative ideology. This undermines somewhat the veracity of the situation described, and the fact that it has few opportunities for interaction means that it is not of direct interest for us. However, it does introduce a form of behavior modeling that might be considered a form of anticipatory feedback: an imaginary character acts as "the conscience" of the teenage girl, pointing out to her when having to make a decision the hidden intentions of the male character and the consequences of a particular action. What is surprising about the technique is that it operates as an unsolicited source of help before the action occurs.

Both techniques are responses to very different approaches but are not especially applicable to the design of our project: in the first case, the simulator is applied to a group in which the profiles of sexual behaviour determine the consequences. It is not possible for subjects to place themselves within a group and experience the evolution for themselves, as the situation does not depend on their own decision-making skills. Furthermore, the behavior profiles are not necessarily recognizable by the individuals as being their own. In the second case, it is virtually impossible for the user to commit mistakes given its preventive nature, with the result that the type of learning is unlikely to be integrated within the subject's action schema. Schank (1999), following a long tradition of "active pedagogy," insists, rightly we believe, in the need to make mistakes and then to rectify these errors so that the actions committed become true learning experiences and modify our prior schema or scripts.

The solution adopted here is for the role play to reduce the period of real time (in fact, the so-called "window period" extends from three to six months), by using a time step that is resolved in the final situation. This means of representing the passing of time allows the player to receive delayed feedback, though it is in fact given during the same session in which the game is played. Given that the success of the game depends on it being as realistic as possible, this time difference does not have any major effect on the game's realism: first, it is a typical technique of audiovisual media and the language of the cinema; and, second, the final situation is not interactive and is used to reveal to each player the results of the game, depending on the character he or she has adopted. This technique allows us, albeit with some limitations, to overcome the problems of the apparent lack of connection between an action and its delayed consequences, as well as to be able to give feedback on the choices made in a very brief period of time (in the real game time). Furthermore, it does away with the need to introduce other solutions such as those mentioned, which would lead to interactions that are not always cohesive with the educational objectives.

However, any application such as the one analyzed here raises many unanswered questions. To what extent are the skills actually learned? Can we really speak of changes in attitude? Are the skills and attitudinal changes transferred to other situations? Clearly, it is not possible to answer these questions directly, as we are dealing with complex skills. What is required is a longitudinal study, which in this case, as in others before, has been ruled out.

Conclusion

Role-playing games are complex multimedia applications, not just because of the technology they use but also because of the way in which this technology responds to an educational framework design that combines a constructivist approach with other concepts, such as the sociocultural modeling of the action and dialogues of argumentation. It would seem that some of the most recurring and justified criticisms that have been made of educational multimedia packages—namely, their technological and multimedia excesses, combined with a lack of pedagogic underpinnings—can be overcome when the educational design is central to the project and the technologies and the production of various multimedia elements are put at the service of the project.

Perhaps the most general conclusion is that each project requires a specific educational design. Just as different subjects are taught in different ways, multimedia applications should be far more specific in their instructional designs, whether their theoretical backgrounds are cognitivist or constructivist.

Equally, it does not appear that the changes in attitude or the transfers of skills are solely attributable to the use of multimedia tools, however complex or well designed they might be. Rather, they would seem to be the result of more than *one* educational action. From the perspective of health education and, in particular from that of AIDS prevention in the young, it would appear that multimedia role-playing games need to be complemented with more formal instruction techniques backed with a range of additional activities.

Acknowledgment

The project was funded by the EU programme "'Europe against AIDS," and was a joint undertaking between the cooperative group, CLAPS, of Pordenone, Italy, and the University of Barcelona (ICE), Spain. The author wishes to express his gratitude to Carlo Mayer, co-director on behalf of CLAPS, and to the Spanish team of Begoña Gros, Cristina Martínez, and María José Rubio.

References

Andreu, O. A. (1991). Sida y Antropologia social, en *Jano*, Marzo, 1(942), 51.

Bandura, A. (1987). *Pensamiento y acción*. Barcelona: Martínez Roca.

Bayés, R. (1987). Factores de aprendizaje en salud y enfermedad. *Revista Española de Terapia del Comportamiento*, 5(2), 119–135.

Bayés, R. (1994). *Sida i Psicologia*. Barcelona: Martínez Roca.

Brooks-Gunn, J., Boyer, C. B., & Hein K. (1988). Preventing HIV infection and AIDS in children and adolescent. *American Psychologist*, November, 1(11), 958–964.

Cho, K. L., & Jonassen, D. H. (2002). The effects of argumentation scaffolds on argumentation and problem solving. *Educational Technology: Research & Development*, 50(3), 5–22.

Duffy, T. M., & Cunningham, D. J. (1996). Constructivism: Implications for the design and delivery of instruction. In D. Jonassen (Ed.), *Handbook of research for educational communications and technology* (pp. 170–198). New York: Simon & Schuster Macmillan.

Duffy, T. M., Lowyck, J., & Jonassen, D. H. (Eds.). (1992). *Designing environments for constructivist learning*. Heidelberg: Springer.

Fundació LaCaixa. (1995). *Sida. Saber ayuda*. Barcelona: La Caixa.

Gee, J. P. (2003). *What videogames have to teach us about learning and literacy?* New York: Palgrave-MacMillan.

Gonzalez, J. J. (1995). Computer assisted learning to prevent HIV spread: Visions, delays and opportunities. *Machine-Mediated Learning*, 5(1), 3–11.

Green, L. W., Kreute, M. W., Deedds, S. G., & Partridge, K. B. (1980). *Health education planning: A diagnostic approach*. Palo Alto, CA: Mayfield.

Hill, B. (2000). *The magic of reading*. Redmon: Microsoft.

Jonassen, D., Peck, K., & Wilson, B. (1999). *Learning with technology. A constructivist perspective.* Upper Saddle River, NJ: Prentice-Hall.

Kress, G. (2003). *Literacy in the new media age.* London: Routledge.

Lave, J. (1988). *La cognición en la práctica.* Barcelona: Paidós.

Lave, J. (1990). The culture of acquisition and the practice of understanding. In D. Kirshner & J. A. Whitson (Eds.), *Situated cognition* (pp. 17–36). Mahwah, NJ: Lawrence Erlbaum Associates.

Plowman, L. (1994). The "Primitive Mode of Representation" and the evolution of interactive multimedia. *Journal of Educational Multimedia and Hypermedia, 3*(3/4), 275–293.

Rodríguez Illera, J. L., Gros, B., Martínez, C., & Rubio, M. J. (1999). Un software multimedia para la prevención del SIDA en adolescentes. *Multimedia educativo 99.* Barcelona: Universitat de Barcelona.

Schank, R. C. (1998). *Inside multi-media case based instruction.* Hillsdale, NJ: Erlbaum.

Schank, R. C. (1999). *Dynamic memory revisited.* Cambridge, MA: Cambridge University Press.

Tonks, D. (1996). *Teaching aids.* New York: Routledge.

Wenger, E. (1998). *Communities of practice.* Cambridge, MA: Cambridge University Press.

Chapter XIV

Interactive Learning in Engineering Education

Katia Tannous, State University of Campinas – Unicamp, Brazil

Abstract

In the process of teaching and learning, computers as a tool help the students to develop their reasoning and intelligence. In engineering education, computational packages are usual but somewhat didactic and require specific knowledge on the part of the student. Motivation, creativity and autonomy are important for success in chemical engineering courses. This chapter presents novel experience of a chemical engineering education, including a technique and object-oriented programming system applied mainly to undergraduate and graduate students.

Introduction

Technologies as conveyors of information have been used for centuries to "teach" students, whereas interactive technologies began to be introduced early in the 20th century to "engage" students in the learning process. Educational communications and the technologies in which they are encoded are conceived, analyzed, and designed by educational specialists (often referred to as educational or instructional technologists). Historically, teams of educational technologists, including instructional designers, media producers, and media managers, in collaboration with other specialists, e.g., subject matter experts and teachers, have developed educational media. These teams often employ systematic instructional design models to guide their efforts to analyze, develop, produce, and evaluate instruction. Sometimes it is difficult to get in the academic institutions. The teachers still remain the great Masters and the keys to the development of learning processes. Excellent teachers use varying lecture styles that actively engage students in the learning process.

To make this explanation more concrete, it will present in this chapter computed-based cognitive tools and interactive learning environments with chemical engineering examples in different courses.

Computers in the Process of Teaching and Learning

In the process of teaching and learning, computers as a tool help the students to develop their reasoning and intelligence. The progress of computer usage in the teaching and learning process can be observed following this order: programmed instruction, simulation, educational games, programming language, application packages, and intelligent tutorial systems. The components of this evolution are described below (Notare et al., 2003).

Instructional Program

This was the first form and the most widely used. It is also known as CAI (computer-assisted instruction). The instructional program consists, basically, of repetitive exercises, tutorials, or demonstrations. The programs lead the student to carry out a series of exercises with increasing degrees of difficulty. Some information is displayed on the screen, and then the learning is tested. Questions are introduced as multiple choices or with blank spaces to be filled. After each answer, the student is praised for a correct answer or a new change in case of a wrong answer. This kind of instruction can be used at all levels of education. Other types of instructional programs are the tutorials, which make the computer replace the function of the teacher. Usually, a tutorial supplies little information to the students and then suggests questions related to the topic, with possible answers that are known by the system. A good-quality tutorial considers all possible answers. Multimedia-based instructional programs have the potential to appeal to a greater number of senses than traditional instructional programs (Basu et al., 1996). These programs can excite students with animation, sound, and video. They can present complex processes, theories, and facts in a manner that is second only to actual situations. In engineering, the subjects are much more mathematically oriented, and they must contain more graphs, technical drawings, and equations.

Simulations

This is a model that pretends a system, real or not, based on a theory. Today, computers have the ability to simulate very complex systems. With the aid of a computer, a student can test complex hypotheses, manipulate variables, and verify model behaviors under several conditions. It is a powerful tool with which to stimulate reasoning. A good simulation can resort to graphs and animation. A good model should represent well the real behavior, with a considerable amount of detail and without being oversimplified.

Educational Games

These have great educational value, in addition to being fun to promote learning. Some demand logical rules from the players. This makes the student regard reasoning, logic, and language seriously. The student learns to process information and logic and make conjectures.

Programming Languages

For many years, people have theorized that learning to program is an activity that develops higher-order thinking skills. The languages that have most often been taught to learners for developing reasoning and thinking skills are BASIC, PASCAL, and LOGO, and artificial intelligence, Prolog. LOGO is the oldest and most widely known. It is friendly and interactive and emphasizes self-learning. It gradually became the most used language in education. Several studies have indicated that learning through discovery, exploration, and investigation do not only have a special meaning in developing cognitive structures, but also knowledge is retained for longer periods. LOGO was devised to work as an important tool to promote active, dynamic, and meaningful learning. When drawing upon a computer screen, the student is encouraged to think about what he or she is doing, to consider his or her own mistakes, and to change his or her ideas whenever necessary.

Object-oriented programming (OOP) is another procedural language that treats reusable objects combined with a construct in a program. OOP languages can help to promote critical thinking as well as programming efficiency because of their inherent structures and more clearly defined interfaces and usage declarations (Jonassen & Reeves, 2000). OOP may encourage more effective collaboration in defining interfaces, and the skills students learn may be more marketable, because most businesses are using object-oriented versions of popular programming languages.

Rather than procedures and functions as sequences of actions, in OOP, these are treated as reusable objects that can be combined like building blocks to construct a program. The building block approach is especially important in defining screen objects like scroll bars, windows, buttons, icons, and menus in window-type environments that comprise the user interface to the program. So, when the user points and clicks at an icon, the icon object responds depending on its location and program. Languages like Smalltalk were originally designed as OOP environments; however, object-oriented versions of procedural languages like BASIC (Microsoft's Visual Basic), Pascal (Borland Delphi), and C (Borland's C++) are preferred by most programmers today. Another useful language is Java that is in the driver seat of the current trend toward delivering information and services via the Internet.

Software Packages

These are general packages to be used in learning, like word processors, spreadsheets, data bank managers, among others. These packages may have high educational potential. The use of these computational packages, in the chemical engineering courses, has shown potentials and opportunities in the development of new methodologies for independent student learning (Mackenzie & Allen, 1998; Abbas & Al-Bastaki, 2002).

Until now, engineering courses have been applying commercial software packages as teaching aids, such as MathCAD, MatLab, Mathematica, and Maple. MathCAD combines some of the best features of spreadsheets (like MS Excel) and symbolic math programs. It provides a good graphical user interface and can be used efficiently to manipulate large data arrays, to perform symbolic calculations, and to easily construct graphs.

Intelligent Tutorial Systems (ITS)

These are an evolution from the computer-assisted instruction (CAI). ITS computer programs make use of artificial intelligence to represent knowledge and promote better interaction with the student. The main objective of ITS is to make the computer behave cleverly enough to control the student learning process and provide adapted instructions.

Chemical Engineering Education

This section presents some examples of chemical engineering educational techniques and novel experiences applied in interactive learning environments. New educational experiences introduce changes in an established culture by using new procedures. These changes should be carried out through a logical sequence of steps in order to reach definite targets. Motivation, creativity, and autonomy are important for success in chemical engineering courses.

Tannous (2003), Tannous and Donida (2003), and Tannous and Rodrigues (2003) developed some learning techniques applying the authorship system to distance learning in undergraduate courses (Fluid Mechanics) and graduate courses (Momentum Transfer and Fluidization Applications). The courses were adapted to make use of the WebCT software. The software allowed easy access to the contents taught in the classroom, promoting better interactions among the participants.

The courses, introduced virtually, have the following links (www.ead.unicamp.br: 8900):

- General information about the course: instructor information, objectives
- Required disciplines, textbooks
- Calendar of suggested activities
- Course content with texts and complementary texts according to student's answers
- Group work
- Virtual library containing links
- Communication tools (e-mail and chat room)
- Periodic assessment

Figure 1: Activities planning

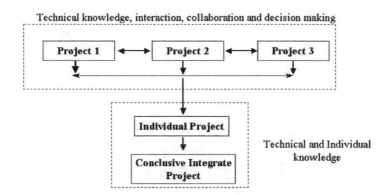

The software allowed the instructor to follow the students' learning through recorded access to the site, acquisition of communication tools, and visits to the sites.

In particular, the courses on "Fundamentals and Applications of Fluidization and Momentum Transfer" involved group work that showed technical/scientific abilities and exercised communication abilities and collaboration among the participants and the instructor.

Figure 1 shows a scheme of the activities undertaken during the course on "Fundamentals and Applications of Fluidization".

Technical Knowledge

At this step, the acquired knowledge and abilities are evaluated. The instructor should master the technical knowledge and tools that are used, including computational ones (FORTRAN, Pascal, MatLab). The tools that might be used to assess this step are as follows:

1. ***Project elaboration***: Students will develop their own technical and computational knowledge through practical assignments, which will be available to all participants. This process may also be carried out in groups.

2. ***Self-assessment***: Students will apply their knowledge to a specific assignment, chosen by themselves, from the course subjects. The students will present their work to the instructor and to other participants in a seminar. A conclusive integrated project ends the assessment of knowledge.

3. ***Chat and discussion list***: The teacher will submit a special topic for discussion between students at the end of every convenient set of chapters.

A deadline is set that provides enough time for discussion among students. The same happens to the chat, with a stricter schedule.

Interaction

The interaction among participants is assessed during the course. Motivation, creativity, and autonomy are observed and marked. Interactivity is associated with the course dynamics. As the students advance in the course, their progress can be observed. The tools used in this step are the chat, the discussion list, and the log-in records. The course required an amount corresponding to 25% of total lectures in which all people involved in the course were together. These meetings provided ground for discussions about the course content to strengthen the acquired knowledge, to develop the communication among participants and instructor, as well as to help to assess the participation of each member.

Collaboration and Decision Making

To assess these features, the students' contributions and suggestions to solve the assignments are taken into account. The students are also evaluated for their participation in the interactive projects and in the individual assignments. These experiences are evaluated considering student profile, software assessment, interactions between student and interface, course content, instructor, and other students.

Engineering Educational Learning Object

Computational packages are didactic and require knowledge of the utilization of software on the part of the student. Another inconvenience of commercial packages is the high price that frequently inhibits their use. Institutional reusability is also important as far as educational software is concerned. OOP systems can help to promote critical thinking, motivation, creativity, and autonomy because of their inherent structures.

Basu et al. (1996) presented the development of a multimedia-based instructional program, for graduate and senior-level classes, in Visual Basic applied to hydrodynamics process and heat transfer. The multimedia developed shows different levels with animation, video, and graphs to explain all that the students' need. Also, they present assessment as an important part of the learning process at the end of most chapters. The quizzes contain yes-or-no questions, multiple-choice questions with a single correct answer, and multiple-choice questions with multiple correct answers. The computer clock controls the time of execution of quizzes.

The Department of Thermal-Fluid-Dynamics in the Chemical Engineering School at Unicamp, in collaboration with undergraduate and graduate students, developed some software based in OOPS. Some of these experiences in the Chemical Engineering courses are described in this chapter.

The object-oriented languages used to develop the software were Basic (Microsoft's Visual Basic) and Pascal (Borland Delphi). The interactive approach adopted was based on the degree of complexity of the topic as well as on the targeted public, mostly undergraduate and graduate students.

Fluid Mechanics Simulator

In order to provide practical application to the students, a course on Transport Phenomena I was developed with a friendly interface (Tannous et al., 2002). The software consists of two independent modules, one applied to pressure drop calculation in industrial pipes and the other to the study of boundary layer on flat sheets. Both modules are simulators.

Head-Loss

The Head-Loss module has access to a data bank in which it is possible to vary the flowing stream and the pipe material and diameter, and it considers many accidents along the pipe. Pressure drop is obtained by classical Bernoulli equation, in which the friction factor is calculated by Colebrook equation (Welty, 1984). When accidents are present, they can be considered either by an equivalent length or by the parameter K (Escoe, 1989). To simulate the flow, the other inputs are flow rate, pipe length, and heights of pipe entrance. The software supplies the Head-Loss, Reynolds number, friction factor, and the equivalent length of accidents.

The visual interface of the software is shown in Figure 2. The software allows for several different operating conditions to be considered, allowing more time for analysis of results, instead of losing time with repetitive calculations, which many times results in loss of attention during the class.

After filling in the mentioned fields on the screen, the pressure drop calculation is made by pressing the button "Calcular" (calculate). The educator invites the student to make a critical analysis of the results.

Figure 2: Visual interface of Head-Loss simulator

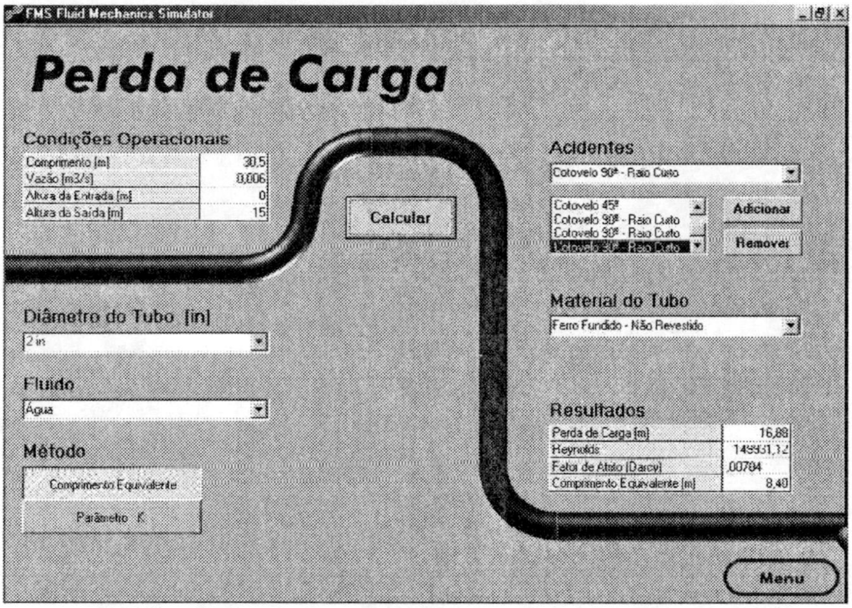

Boundary Layer

The boundary layer module provides visual development of a boundary layer on a plate, allowing for the detection of the change in thickness between the laminar and turbulent conditions. The visual interface for this module is shown in Figure 3.

The input data for this module are the flow speed and the length of the plate. The laminar boundary layer is calculated according to Blasius, while the turbulent one is calculated according to von Karman (Coulson & Richards, 1999). The software allows for the visualization of the laminar sublayer. Furthermore, it allows students to analyze the influence of viscosity on the boundary layer thickness and on the length required to develop the turbulent flow.

It is also possible to change the flow velocity and the plate length to study how these affect the boundary layer. The software produces a graph indicating the boundary layer thickness as a function of the plate length. This plot can be copied and pasted into other documents, such as reports. The case illustrated in Figure 3 considers a 100 cm plate length, with water flowing at 30 cm/s.

Figure 3: Visual interface of Boundary Layer

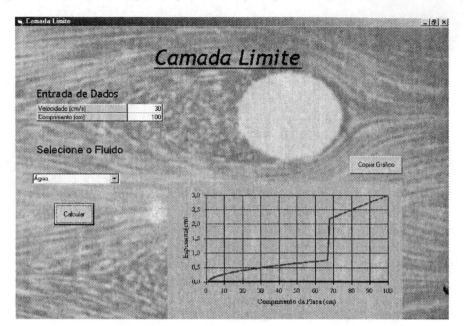

The simulators were used in an experimental condition in 2001. To verify the acceptance of these simulators and computational classes in the theoretical course, feedback from the students was obtained. The students evaluated the following aspects:

- Introduction of computational classes at Transport Phenomena I

- Contribution of classes for learning in the course

- Quality of visual presentation of simulators

- Difficulty of utilization of simulators

- Implementation in other courses

The evaluation of this work revealed that the students considered these simulators as good and excellent, contributing toward relevant learning. The simulators were classified as a good visual presentation with ease of use. Also, it was observed that most of the students recommended the implementation of computational classes in other chemical engineering courses.

Momentum Transport

This experience is from a graduate course on Momentum Transfer (Tannous, 2003), where the constructivism approach is applied in the course, where students conducted a building of software in the graphic interface. Despite the common curriculum among chemical engineering schools in Brazil, student potential are different. Thus, the students were grouped into three groups according to their backgrounds. The dynamics promoted a live interaction among team members, from definition of the project, group organization, group integration, delivery of final project, and assessment of the work after presentation. The result of this technique was the development of a simulator. The software was developed using Delphi language with a graphical interface.

One module focused on the theory and employed text editors (Figure 4), while another employed mathematics (Figure 5). Mathematical expressions and equations are an integral part of any transport phenomena textbook (Bird, 1960). Another developed numerically a solution using FORTRAN language. The student can simulate the velocity profiles for cylinder pipes as a function of time. The simulator (Figure 6) has as input data the following: density and fluid speed, pipe diameter and length, and pressure drop. Two examples can be seen, in Figure 6, considering a flow in the simple pipe and the annular flow between two concentric pipes.

Figure 4: Theoretical approach

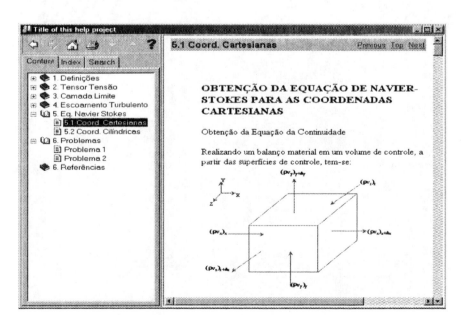

Figure 5: Mathematical approach—Analytical solution

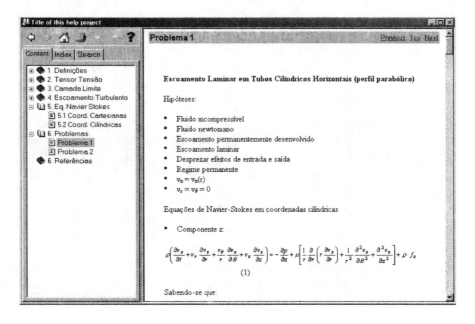

Figure 6: Mathematical approach—Numerical solution (simulator)

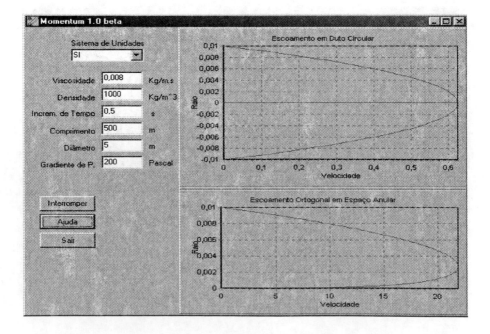

For proper comprehension, a student needs to use the model to arrive at the final result. A parametric study showing the sensitivity of the final result to an input parameter helps the students to understand the model and allows them to explore the model from different perspectives.

Polymer Processing

The software ANAPRO was developed to study the polymerization reactors. It was elaborated using the Delphi language (OOPS). The instruction program allows self-study and considers fluidized-bed and stirrer reactors, including polymer types, stirrer types, chemical reactions, and catalysts. Figure 7 shows the main screen that provides access to several screens of the software (Massa, 2003). There are buttons to access chemical properties, type of reactor, polymerization reaction, suggested exercises, and a help function. This proposal is in development but can show a clear example of an instructional program. We can also evaluate the dimension and the limitation of this kind of software when the subject is large in the Chemical Engineering context.

Figure 8 shows the details of the software for the process components and processes. The process components (distributors and stirrers) are specific for each kind of reactor, as fluidized and agitated bed.

Figure 7: Initial screen of the project

Figure 8: Software details: Process components

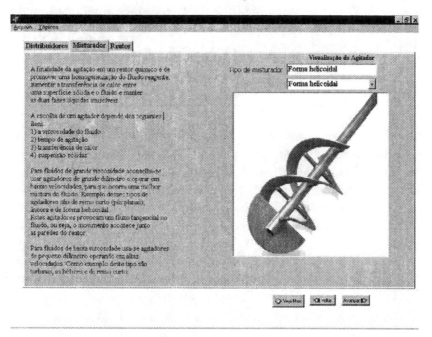

Figure 9: Software details: Process

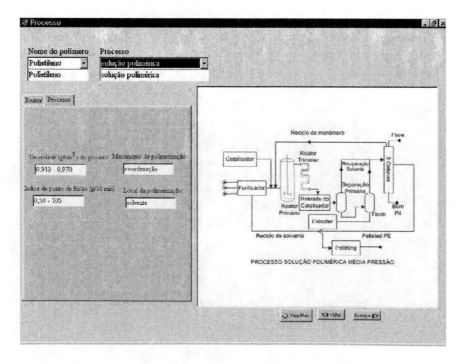

Figure 9 shows an example of software details for the one process between high pressure, solution, slurry, modified high pressure, and gas-phase polymerization.

Conclusion

Information science applied to education in Brazil is still developing. One can find all steps of development of an application within the academic community. The private sector is more advanced than the public schools in the use of information science.

Universities are a step ahead in the development of information science for education. Most virtual environments were developed by universities (TelEduc, Aulanet). Nonetheless, there is still great resistance by academic professionals to incorporate this technology.

In this chapter, we showed and analyzed the following:

- In distance education environments, the choice to employ information science will depend on the instructor objectives. Most used are those programs that provide free access, such as TelEduc/Unicamp. Few systems are not available in Portuguese, making it difficult to use them in Brazil.

- Teaching and learning processes with emphasis on the use of programmed instruction and simulators together with a learning object programming language were discussed.

- Steps involved in programming as a model for future educational projects were discussed.

- Learning techniques and methodologies applying the authorship system to distance courses were presented. The adopted methodology proved of great value for present (or local) and distance courses.

- The goodness of the technology should not disregard the essential role of the instructor.

- The computer has become an integral part of engineering education. The use of multimedia and software packages enhances teaching and learning. The information technology tools have a large number of benefits as invaluable tools for Web-based education and distance learning and training.

Acknowledgment

The author is grateful to the participants in the course IQ 100 Momentum Transfer/2002 for acceptation of the methodology applied.

References

Abbas, A., & Al-Bastaki, N. (2002). The use of software tools for ChE education. *Chem. Eng. Education, 36*(3).

Basu, P., De, D. S., Basu, A., & Marsh, D. (1996). Development of a multimedia-based instructional program. *Chem. Eng. Education, 30*(4).

Bird, R. B., Stewart, W. E., & Lightfoot, E. N. (1060). *Transport phenomena.* New York: John Wiley & Sons.

Coulson, J. M., & Richardson, J. F. (1999). *Chemical engineering—Fluid flow, heat and mass transfer* (Vol. 1). Oxford: Butterworth Heinemann.

Escoe, A. K. (1986). *Mechanical design of process system: Piping and pressure vessels* (Vol. 1). Houston, TX: Gulf Publishing Company.

Horton, W. K. (2001). *Designing Web-based training.* New York: John Wiley Computer Inc.

Jonassen, D. H., & Reeves T. C. (1996). Learning with technology: Using computers as cognitive tools. In D. H. Jonassen (Ed.), *Handbook of research on educational communications and technology* (pp. 693–719). New York: Macmillan.

Mackenzie, J. G., & Allen, M. (1998). Mathematical power tools—Maple, Mathematica, MATLAB, and Excel. *Chem. Eng. Education, 32*(3), Spring.

Massa, R. S. (2003). Development of software in polymerization processes in fluidized and agitated reactors. Scientific report, Laboratory of Particles Technology and Multiphase Processes (in Portuguese).

Moraes, M. C. (2003). Computer education in Brazil: A history lived, some lessons learned (April, 1997). Retrieved from the World Wide Web: http://www.inf.ufsc.br/sbc-ie/revista/nr1/mariacandida.htm

Notare, M.R., Mendes, S.C., & Diverio, T.A.(2000), Historical Overview of Computer Usage in Brazilian Teaching, *Proceeding of Computer of Median Upland*, Passo Fundo/Brazil. In Portuguese.

Tannous K., & Mejoria. (2003). en Calidad de la enseñanza de ingeniería: Transformación de comportamiento entre docente y discente. *3rd Internacional Conference on Engineering and Computer Education— ICECE* (published on CD-ROM, in Spanish), March 16–19. São Paulo, Brazil.

Tannous, K., & Rodrigues, S. (2003). Aplicación de herramienta de educación a distancia como soporte didáctico a la enseñanza en ingeniería química. *Revista de Educação a Distancia* (Online Journal, in Spanish: www.abed.org.br), *1*(2).

Tannous, K., & Donida, M. W. (2003). Evaluation of e-learning engineering graduate courses. *TehKnowLogia—International Journal of Technologies for the Advancement of Knowledge and Learning*, *5*(1), January–March.

Tannous, K., Rodrigues, S., & Fernandes, F. A. (2002). Utilization of computational software directing learning of fluid mechanics. *XXX Brazilian Congress in Engineering Education—COBENGE2002*, September (CD-ROM, in Portuguese).

Welty, R. J., Wicks, C. E., & Wilson, R. E. (1984). *Fundamentals of momentum, heat, and mass transfer*. New York: John Wiley.

Chapter XV

An Embedded Collaborative Systems Model for Implementing ICT-based Multimedia Cartography Teaching and Learning

Shivanand Balram, Simon Fraser University, Canada

Suzana Dragićević, Simon Fraser University, Canada

Abstract

Information and communication technologies (ICT) have created many new opportunities for teaching, learning and administration. This study elaborates a new embedded collaborative systems (ECS) model to structure and manage the implementation of ICT-based pedagogies in a blended learning environment. Constructivist learning, systems theory, and multimedia concepts are used in the model design and development. The model was applied to a third-year undergraduate multimedia cartography course. The findings show that regardless of student background, implementing effective ICT-based learning pedagogies can be managed using the ECS model.

Introduction

Integrating information and communication technologies (ICT)—specifically computers, networks, and the Internet—into higher education has created new opportunities for teaching, learning, and administration. Indeed, the role of ICT in the administration of the higher education process has been reflected in national initiatives such as the 1997 Dearing Committee of Inquiry into Higher Education in the United Kingdom (Dearing, 1997). One of the recommendations of the Dearing Committee was the adoption of national and local ICT strategies to improve the effective and efficient use of resources by U.K. education institutions. Canadian higher education has echoed these strategies and has also increasingly used ICT in the improvement of the quality of distance-education models (Farrell, 1999). The diffusion of information and communication technology into higher education can be attributed to its potential to leverage education processes toward richer and more rewarding learning and management environments (Mitchell, 2002).

In teaching and learning, ICT is a platform on which key learning skills can be efficiently integrated into existing curriculum to boost learner motivation, deepen inquiry, accelerate learning, and widen participation among traditionally isolated groups (Hassell, 2000). Moreover, teaching core ICT skills such as computer operation and programming prepares students to function and succeed in an increasingly information-based society. However, some authors have pointed out that excessive optimism about the micro and mega benefits of ICT in education can develop into broken promises (Selwyn, 2002). These broken promises can adversely influence the adoption of ICT in educational contexts. While most educators agree that ICT has transformed the traditional education process and, hence, demands a new way of thinking, some have pointed out that achieving and verifying useful ICT educational benefits will require strong theoretical evidence, embedded analysis, and research to surmount the associated structural and cultural barriers (Kenway, 1996).

The utility of ICT in providing and retrieving information is of immense value to educators. Instructional designers are now better able to include a range of ICT-based pedagogy into curriculum design and delivery. Many accept that the technology itself does not ensure learning but acknowledge that it enhances traditional instructional systems to deal with modern-day literacy that is a key component of all education goals. Literacy is now generally considered as a multimedia construct (Abbott, 2001). Multimedia improves upon the traditional text and speech formats of interacting with knowledge by integrating other forms of media, such as audio, video, and animations into the learning experience. This has made information more accessible and understandable. But the benefits of multimedia have also come with new challenges. Using multimedia in the classroom is a clear departure from traditional expectations and requires a new mindset and commitment from educators and administrators to ensure effective implementation. Challenges also arise due to the lack of consistent baseline experience to guide the integration of multiple media into the curriculum. Moreover, the wide range of multimedia tools available present a technical challenge to educators who must select instructional technologies to match pedagogical strategies and desired learning outcomes (Abbott, 2001). These challenges demand a flexible and systematic mechanism for managing multimedia tools in traditional learning. Systems theory provides a useful foundation to develop such a management mechanism. In systems theory, the key components of the process are identified and managed separately but as a part of an integrated and functional whole. The resulting systematic structuring ensures that valid models for pedagogy inform the learning process, and that the quality of education is maintained and improved through dynamic interactions between learners and educators.

The utility of ICT in promoting sharing and collaboration among learners is also highly desired. This is reflected in the many content management systems (CMS), such as WebCT (http://www.webct.com), that empower educators to implement synchronous and asynchronous collaborative environments in distance-learning models and in online support for face-to-face instruction or blended-learning models. Socially mediated constructivist learning theory, where learners explore and discover new knowledge, is the foundation for the collaborative learning paradigm. In face-to-face collaboration, individual and group interactions take place to varying degrees, and finding the appropriate balance is one factor that influence teaching and learning effectiveness (Norman, 2002). Mediating these interactions with technology also presents challenges. Research has shown that non-technology learners in traditional learning settings who do not have access to desired levels of technology support are less willing to use and interact with the learning technology (Watson, Blakeley, & Abbott, 1998). This challenges educators to embed the ICT-based collaborative learning pedagogies into the curriculum structure and design.

The goal of this study is to elaborate on a new embedded collaborative systems (ECS) model for structuring and managing the implementation dynamics of ICT-based pedagogies in a blended learning environment. The specific questions addressed are as follows: How can we engage students in more meaningful learning activities to develop multiple skills of relevance? How can we achieve a useful balance between teacher-centered learning and student-centered learning? The literature on constructivist learning, systems theory, and multimedia education provides the theoretical basis for developing the model. The model was applied to a third-year undergraduate multimedia cartography course of 47 students with no prior knowledge of multimedia and with basic computing skills. The results show that regardless of student background, implementing effective ICT-based learning pedagogies can be managed using the ECS model.

Promoting Multiple Skills of Relevance

The focus on the mastery of cognitive and technical skills in the modern-day classroom is a tendency inherited from traditional learning systems. There is now increasing evidence in the workplace to suggest that in the complex problem-solving environment of the real world, the ability to link classroom knowledge with soft skills is a requirement for success. The capability to work in teams, being an enthusiastic and good communicator, infectious creativity, initiative, willingness to learn independently, critical thinking, analytical abilities, self-management, and ethical values are the main soft skills that are highly valued by employers. These new requirements place additional responsibilities on educators to impart knowledge or hard skills together with soft skills in teaching and learning activities so as to prepare learners to function beyond the classroom. This raises the question: How can we engage students in more meaningful learning activities to develop multiple skills of relevance? This question can be examined using a foundation of constructivist learning theory. In this theory, learning is characterized by shared goals and responsibilities, and knowledge is constructed in a discursive environment. Social networking and peer encouragement help motivation and aid individual learning experiences.

Collaborative and cooperative learning have their origins in constructivist learning theory. The goal of collaborative learning is to help learners display individuality and creativity in working with a group toward achieving targets. For collaborative tasks, rewards for achievements are allocated by comparative or normative evaluation systems. In cooperative learning, the focus is on efficiency and effectiveness in achieving a common goal in socially interactive settings (Piaget, 1926; Vygotsky, 1978). In this approach, rewards are allocated based on the quality or quantity of the group product measured against a predefined standard. Although collaborative and cooperative learning share similarities, they differ in their assumptions about competition. Collaborative learning assumes conflict as a part of learning, while cooperative learning tries to minimize this conflict (Bruffee, 1995). One way to resolve this contradiction is to implement the learning approaches in a way so as to extract the positive learning benefits from each.

Balancing Teacher-Centered and Student-Centered Learning

Implementing multiple learning skills activities requires a balance between teacher-centered and student-centered learning within the contact time limitations of the face-to-face classroom. Thus, efficient course management and structuring become important needs with which to keep track of the evolving course dynamics. Norman (2002) outlined a model that defines the interaction space among a set of agents and objects in the learning process. In the model, two sets of agents (instructors and students) and two sets of objects (course materials and course products) overlap to form a complex interaction space. This results in six intersecting areas that form regions where a combination of two or more agents or objects exists. The usefulness of this interaction model is that it shows the variety of interacting elements that require management during the learning process. But while the model provides a comprehensive description of the interactions, it does not deal explicitly with how to balance these dynamic interactions during the learning process. This raises the question: How can we achieve a useful balance between teacher-centered learning and student-centered learning? This question can be examined using a systems theory approach.

Systems theory can be used to manage the instructional tools used to facilitate teaching and learning among the agents. In this way, the theory guides the efforts in balancing the load between student-centered and teacher-centered learning. The theory considers the teaching and learning process to be composed of a set of tightly interrelated pedagogies that can be used to communicate and deliver educational content (Bertalanffy, 1969). Based on the systems approach, together with the constructivist paradigm, a wide range of possible pedagogies can be identified. Examples of these pedagogies include learning contracts, brainstorming, debate, observation, simulation, case study, discussion, and forum. By integrating these approaches systematically, an equitable balance between teacher-centered learning that communicates knowledge and student-centered learning that integrates all levels of Blooms Taxonomy (knowledge, comprehension, application, analysis, synthesis, and evaluation) can be achieved.

Multimedia Cartography Teaching and Learning

The use of computer-based technologies in geography teaching and learning has a long and rich tradition (Gold et al., 1991). This stems from the influence of the quantitative revolution on many areas of the subject. Spatial information studies (encompassing geographic information systems and science, remote sensing, digital cartography, and spatial analysis) are a product of that quantitative influence. Over the last decade, ICT and specialized research software for geography, in general, and spatial information studies, in particular, has caused many changes to the community of research, learning, and teaching practices in these areas. Spatial information studies educators are now battling with how best to balance knowledge transmission with the necessary software practice in the learning process. The "cookbook" approach of traditional lectures and independent student learning of computer skills are two extremes in the learning spectrum of an increasingly computer-driven curriculum. Clearly, any solution must deal with establishing structures for an equitable distribution of the pedagogies across the curriculum and focus the pedagogies on skills students need for success in further studies and the workplace.

Cartography encompasses the art, science, and technology of making maps and requires diverse technical and creative skills for effective practice. The use of multimedia in cartography education serves two interrelated functions: as an instructional tool and as a product development tool. Instructional frameworks to incorporate multimedia-based instruction into the curriculum must be consistent with existing theories of teaching and learning. This has been emphasized by a number of researchers (Alessi & Trollip, 2001; Benyon, Stone, & Woodroffe, 1997; Ellis, 2001; Najjar, 1996). The multiple representation (MR) framework allows the inclusion of knowledge domains within multimedia (Kinshuk & Patel, 2003). The MR approach involves the selection of multimedia objects, navigational objects, and the integration of multimedia objects in the representation of the knowledge domains. Teaching strategies and styles are also important factors in multimedia learning, as they impact learning. The benefits of multimedia education include improved learning retention, portability, modularity, enhanced visualizations, efficiency in instructional design, and learning consistency (Hede, 2002; Yildirim, Ozden, & Aksu, 2001).

The use of multimedia authoring tools in designing course products enables learners to develop and construct enhanced mapping products. This forms the basis of multimedia cartography, in which the paper map is transformed into an enhanced digital map that integrates multiple media to communicate visual and oral expressions of spatial information to the map reader (Cartwright, Peterson,

& Gartner, 1999). These multimedia maps are accessed through CD-ROM, the Internet, or specially designed Web-mapping services. The benefits of multimedia maps include dynamic and multifaceted representation of space and time, superior map production and dissemination, improved information and knowledge transfer, and greater map accessibility.

Embedded Collaborative Systems Model

The embedded collaborative systems (ECS) model is designed based on principles from constructivist learning theory and systems theory. The goal of the model is to improve the quality of student learning in the face-to-face classroom. This is achieved with a focus on the development of multiple learning skills and on independent learning. The model's structure is shown in Figure 1.

The collaborative, knowledge management, and cooperative working spaces are three distinct overlapping interaction spaces that are defined in the model. The overlapping structure strengthens the process and provides connectivity among the stages of focal planning of projects, delivery of course content, and

Figure 1: The embedded collaborative systems (ECS) model

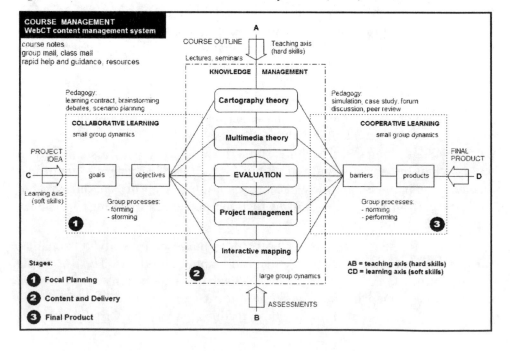

preparation of final course products. The knowledge management workspace occurs in the classroom, where all students receive the same content through lectures and seminars. The collaborative and cooperative workspaces occur during small group laboratory sessions or alternatively in informal meetings among students.

The teaching (AB) and learning (CD) axes serve as both workflow and information flow pathways in the model. These axes control the levels of hard and soft skills that are integrated in the learning experience. The hard skills or teaching axis deals with the substantive course content. This content is normally stipulated by institutional curriculum policies and is implemented using traditional pedagogical tools such as lectures, seminars, and panels. The knowledge management phase of the process is implemented in large groups to encourage critical thinking and discussions. Students develop individual and active learning habits during all stages of the hard skills implementation. The course outline and content together with the assessment requirements drive the nature of the interactions that occur along the teaching axis.

The soft skills or learning axis characterizes the collective and social interaction experiences of students working to achieve targets in a group environment. Examples of pedagogies that can be used involve group projects, learning contracts, brainstorming, simulation, forum, discussions, and case studies embedded in real problem-solving contexts. The intersection of the learning and teaching axes provides an opportunity for formative evaluation. Formative evaluation is an important component of the process, as with it, we are able to establish how students are integrated into the learning experience and how satisfied they are with the learning environment. Formative evaluations include interviews and survey questionnaires, and corrective action is immediately implemented to control any identified imbalances. Evaluations take the traditional form of cognitive assessments using normative testing instruments.

The use of multiple pedagogies provides students with the opportunity to experience deeper learning as they master new concepts by manipulating and refining previous knowledge. The pedagogical tools and the instructional medium appropriate for each stage of the learning process are described and explained in Table 1. The flexibility of ECS model allows students to pursue topics of general interest during the group projects. This supports the assumption that learning is a lifelong process, and learners have a role in designing what they learn.

Achieving a balance between student-centered and teacher-centered learning is inherent in the ECS model. During the initial stages of the model implementation, teacher-centered cognitive learning is at a high level, whereas student-centered learning is at a low level (Figure 2). At the beginning of the collaborative stages, a progression is seen through a fuzzy period of mixed learning toward an equal partnership in learning between teacher and learner. Thereafter, students

Table 1: Pedagogies and instructional media used in the ECS model

Pedagogy	Description of the Pedagogy	Instructional Media	Stage in the ECS Model	Targeted Skills
Presentation	Instructor-centered lecture notes and student-centered communication of project results	Multimedia, videotape, graphic visuals, text	1,2,3	Hard and soft skills
Discussion	Exchange of ideas and opinions among students–students and teacher–students; discussions are guided by reflective questions	Graphic visuals, text	1,2,3	Soft skills
Demonstration	Instructor-centered presentation of example of skills to be learned; use of expert to present case study	Software, the Internet, graphic visuals	2	Hard skills
Drill and Practice	Exercises such as assignments to reinforce skills	Software, text	2	Hard skills
Tutorial	Individual learning through practice and feedback	Software, text, the Internet	1,2,3	Hard and soft skills
Group work	Small group work on defining projects and allocating tasks	Software, graphic visuals, text, multimedia	1,3	Soft skills
Simulation	Experimentation with small version of reality that is to be described and understood	Software, graphic visuals, text, multimedia	1,3	Soft skills
Gaming	A user-friendly environment for testing specific rules and their effects on determined goals	Software, text	3	Soft skills
Discovery	Problem solving through trial and error	Software, graphic visuals, text, multimedia	1,3	Soft skills
Problem solving	Applying skills to find solutions to real problems	Software, videotape, graphic visuals, audio, text, multimedia	3	Hard and soft skills

Figure 2: The dynamic phases of the group learning process

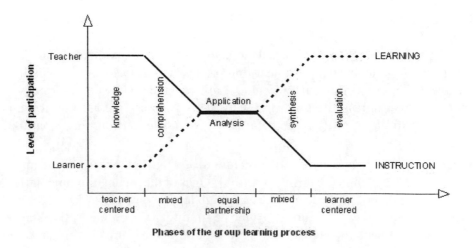

gradually become equipped with the skills and motivation to undertake active and independent learning. Eventually, instruction is replaced with independent learning, as the full spectrum of Blooms Taxonomy is covered. The timing of the introduction of the collaborative and cooperative tasks coincides with the stages of the learning processes shown in Figure 2.

The ECS model is optimized for blended learning environments, where face-to-face instruction is supported and complemented by online instruction. Content management systems (CMS) such as WebCT (http://www.webct.com) offer comprehensive administration tools with which to deploy complex pedagogies that can emerge using the ECS model. The use of systems theory allows the educator to identify the major pedagogical components that will best achieve the desired learning outcomes. In addition, systems theory integrates the knowledge and pedagogy of the process through rigorous alternatives assessments. Each separate component of the process is analyzed for relevance and then integrated to consolidate and expand individual learning. This framework structures the learning environment, provides a mechanism for understanding interrelationships, and provides task balancing and process management benefits among others. The central aspect is that a systematic framework for group interactions is established that allows teams to define roles, define protocols for independent working, and devise strategies for individual accountability.

Application of the ECS Model

Cartography Course Background

The multimedia cartography course used to test the model was at the third-year undergraduate level and consisted of 47 students. The total contact duration was 13 weeks. Two hours of formal lectures and two hours of computer lab work were compulsory, guided sessions each week. The lectures were delivered to all students at the same time, while the computer labs were conducted in three sessions with not more than 20 students attending per session. The rationale for multiple lab sessions was to ensure that students had access to computer resources and were able to receive individualized attention from the teaching assistant. The classroom and lab settings exposed students to both teacher-centered instructions and learner-centered instructions. Students initially had little knowledge of multimedia concepts, cartography theory, or relevant software tools. But this situation was ideal for investigating the ECS model for learning effectiveness among students and the management of the learning process.

Table 2: Motivation of students in the multimedia cartography course

What do you expect to achieve by attending this course?	Frequency of Statements (%) (Number of Statements = 47)
Better understanding of mapping on the Internet	13 (27.7)
Expand my knowledge of cartographic techniques	12 (25.5)
Greater familiarity with the software to be used	7 (14.9)
Academic credits and knowledge	5 (10.6)
Others	10 (21.3)

Designing learning structures that stimulate and promote enhanced student motivation is perhaps the most crucial aspect of learning (Edstrom, 2002). Identifying motivations allows instructors to develop strategies for redirecting student goals toward more meaningful and rewarding learning experiences. A questionnaire survey was implemented at the beginning of the cartography course to determine student motivation and rationale. The open-ended anonymous question: *"What do you expect to achieve by attending this course?"* provided valuable responses (Table 2). Learning about Internet mapping and cartography principles was the most frequent statement given by students who responded. This indicated that student motivation was generally aligned with the course objectives, and hence, more time would be available for the instructor to focus on preparing engaging content. As is expected, some students were interested in software learning to improve their job prospects and others on obtaining the necessary credits toward graduation.

The open-ended anonymous question: *"What can the instructor and teaching assistant do during the lectures and labs to make you learn better?"* indicated that the most frequent expectation was for clearly explained example-based content (Table 3). The information obtained from the two questions guided

Table 3: Students' suggestions for a better learning environment

What can the instructor and teaching assistant do during the lectures and labs to make you learn better?	Frequency of Statements (%) (Number of Statements = 46)
Give clear and concise explanations	8 (17.4)
Provide many examples during teaching	7 (15.2)
Present the materials at a reasonable pace	4 (8.7)
Make the content relevant and interesting	3 (6.5)
Give well-organized lecture notes	3 (6.5)
Make notes available ahead of lectures	3 (6.5)
Others	18 (39.1)

the selection of pedagogical components in the ECS model, so that the learning process was balanced by student expectations and institutional curriculum policies.

Content Structuring and Knowledge Management

The first 4 weeks were dedicated to formal lectures and guided practice on the use of software tools. Moreover, cases were analyzed and best practices extracted such that students became familiar with general practices in the subject area. This forms the knowledge management phase of the model, in which learning proceeds through incremental steps, and individual learning is emphasized. The subsequent weeks were structured so that knowledge management at an individual level and collaborative project at a group level reinforced each other for an enhanced learning experience. Formal lectures included concepts related to cartography, multimedia, Web mapping and project management theory (Figure 1). The focus of the lectures was on case studies, and students were exposed to analytical, application, creative, communication, social, and self-analysis skills (Easton, 1982). Moreover, students were able to discuss their views freely and to listen to the views of peers. The group work and peer support operated both as additional instructions for students and as a forum for wider discussions within the course framework.

Of significance in this stage is the concept of Web-based mapping, which involves some level of computer networking knowledge (Figure 3). In a Web-mapping multimedia application, a digital map, once created, becomes a dynamic index to multimedia content. The map is hosted on a Web server, and a map server provides a dynamic link to a database to allow end users to query and interact with the map in the browser window. Although the learning curve for this particular type of mapping technology is steep, it was surprising to find that students were extremely motivated and committed to learning the software. Informal interviews revealed that the general source of this motivation came from the structuring of the learning outcomes at each stage of the process and the out-of-class support and help provided by the teaching assistant. Students were more committed and motivated when they could control how and when they learned.

Accessing notes and supplementary materials before lectures ensures that students concentrate on synthesis and analysis rather than on note taking. The new electronic media make it easy to provide additional readings based on student needs, and the online environment provides a social space for continuous conversations and support among peers. Optimal learning occurs when students share knowledge among peers in a community of practice where ideas are evaluated and adapted. In order to manage the implementation of the model, the

Figure 3: Levels of use of relevant software

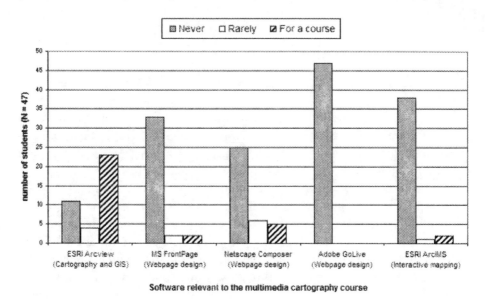

Figure 4: Model implementation using the WebCT content management system

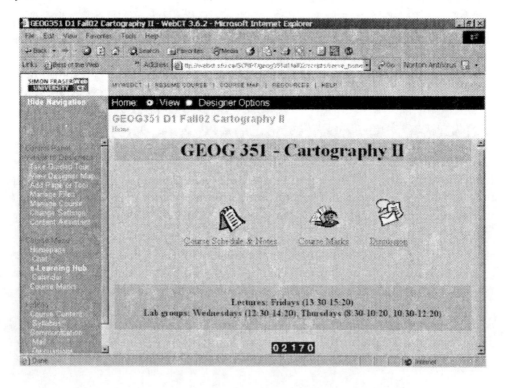

content management tool WebCT was used for managing mailing lists, discussions, and presentation of knowledge content (Figure 4). The real-time facilities of the management tools were useful in fostering the "community spirit" outside of the classroom setting. The final multimedia cartography atlas products developed and implemented by students are documented on the Web (http://www.sfu.ca/geog351fall02/).

Collaborative and Cooperative Learning

In the collaborative learning exercise, learners were divided into nine groups (average of five students per group, some randomly and some based on individual preference), and step-by-step guidelines were given to each group on the final product to be achieved (designing and creating a professional multimedia atlas), and resources (books, journal papers, Internet Web sites) available for unraveling what is to be achieved. Tasks included mastering sets of specific learning objectives and finding ways to transfer that learning to the class as a whole. There was no briefing to students on group roles. Students reported that the first set of group discussions was difficult. This was expected, but students needed to learn how to cope in a new and unfamiliar social and learning environment. The leadership role was usually assigned to the student with much to say. That leader then assigns tasks, facilitates the discussions, and ensures that meaningful results emerge from the discussions. The weekly meetings provided time for critical reflections and perusal of new materials, ideas, perspectives, and further research. Each week, the instructor met with the group to evaluate problems and progress and to offer solutions strategies. Ideas were not imposed on the groups, and this was much appreciated by the learners. Moreover, learners agreed in principle to abide by "moral and ethical" conduct during the course.

Students were involved in the initiation and definition of a relevant project. Support was provided in the form of guidance about the format of the final products to be produced, potential areas for projects, course aims and expectations, time schedules, data resources, and project management information. In the design stage, students were encouraged to develop a concept sketch of their product and to begin the process of tool selection and task allocation. There were many opportunities for students to consult with the course instructor and teaching assistant during this stage and, indeed, for the entire course. All members of the group were encouraged to participate in the creation, assembly, and layout of content so as to ensure a uniform individual learning experience. Internet resources and books were provided to help further the process. Each group identified a member to coordinate their activities and to maintain close liaison with the instructors. The final course products were presented to peers for review, and comments were gathered by the instructor and given to each group.

This feedback was useful in improving the quality of the products and establishing a standardized level. This peer review also introduced critical and reflective practices into the process (Bazeli & Robinson, 2001).

The use of information technology together with communicating and working with peers was identified by students as contributing to the success of the project. There were instances in which some students were more focused on the technological tools and less on the content. The group-learning format ensured that group members provide focus and guidance to individuals. Evidence of this peer learning was reflected in the sophistication of the cartographic products and how these products quickly diffused and were adopted by other groups. The professionalism of the final products helped in motivating students toward greater learning and explorations.

Assessment and Evaluation

Evaluations have substantial gains for individual projects and progress in the field. Moreover, the use of new ICT technology has resulted in curriculum changes and may require new ways of evaluating students. In the collaborative modes of learning, the focus is on teamwork and communication skills, and appropriate measures of these are needed. An interim way of dealing with this is to use outside evaluators and student questionnaires. Also, multiple levels of evaluation can yield richer feedback from external, internal, and peer sources. Logging usage statistics and student interviews is another way to identify features of the course that are good and what improvements can be made so that future refinements of the process can be made.

Assessment materials were returned to students quickly, showing where improvements can be made. The exercise involved students preparing work individually and bringing it to the group. The small groups then integrated the materials using e-mail and face-to-face meetings. The small group work was then shown to the groups in a large-format presentation. The assessment also allows educators to learn about their work in a critical and reflective way so that rapid improvements can be instituted for the benefit of learners (Gerber, 2002). The assessment for the cartography course was comprised of individual assignments, group mini-project presentations, individual participation, examination, and production of a final working group electronic atlas.

All students completed a questionnaire during the formal group presentations, and some students were randomly interviewed at the midway point in the course to obtain feedback toward formative evaluations. In the group presentations, each student was required to judge the presentations of the others on a 5-point verbal scale ranging from poor to excellent. Moreover, reasons for the judgments were also requested. The general trend of the responses was toward the favourable end of the judgment scale and was justified by the respondents on two main grounds—the sophistication of the tools and techniques used for creating the atlases and the non-duplication of these techniques across the groups. Students clearly indicated that these were attributed to the efficient small-group work and the collaborative settings in which they occurred. However, one shortcoming identified was the lack of time. While this was unavoidable given the constraints of the semester and curriculum, techniques and tools for time and project management were again reinforced such that facilities for handling this shortcoming were available to them beyond the course. Another shortcoming identified was the variation in skills within the groups. Although students recognized the difficult logistical problems that this can cause, they nevertheless felt that the group's experience would probably have been more rewarding with balanced skills. One way to deal with this is to make greater use of learning styles and skills inventory to categorize students into the small project groups. However, this will demand a trade-off between efficiency in the course logistics and effectiveness in implementing the ECS model. The two comments below characterize the general attitude of students:

"The projects and presentations overall were very impressive and obviously well thought out. The presentations give an overall view of the work-effort placed within each group."

"In general I would like to say that all the atlas were very different concerning layout and information, but most of them were really very good."

A summative evaluation in the later stages of the course elicited responses on the following questions using a 4-point scale (4 being most favourable):

- The assignments and lectures were [unrelated—well related]; mean score = 2.61 (n = 36)

- The exams and assignments were on the whole [unfair—fair]; mean score = 2.81 (n = 36)

- The marking scheme was on the whole [unfair—fair]; mean score = 2.92 (n = 36)

These results from the summative evaluations are inconclusive. While they indicate a general positive weight to the statements, the aggregations of different student backgrounds and experiences makes any interpretation uncertain. The issue of a learner capability to judge curriculum content and implementation is still unresolved in the literature. Nevertheless, the informal interviews and the level of accomplishment in the final atlas products provide strong indication that the collaborative learning process, as implemented using the ECS model, was indeed effective in managing and task balancing the components toward the intended products.

Future Trends

The further development and integration of ICT into multimedia cartography education is dependent on three factors: access to ICT tools, instructors' knowledge of effective ICT use, and more studies on the benefits of ICT and multimedia in student learning. Access and instructor knowledge are issues best handled from the wider policies and practices of higher education administration. Systematic research is needed to further establish the role of ICT in learning.

The software and hardware needs for geography education are enormous. Centralized servers for demonstrating and hosting Web-mapping services, the multiplicity and constantly changing software tools, and the need to redesign current computer laboratories to accommodate collaborative group learning are some of the central considerations that will influence the wider adoption and diffusion of an ICT in the geography curriculum. A troubling issue for multimedia cartography teaching and learning is software licensing arrangements that can sometimes be a barrier to using certain software tools in the learning process. This, in some ways, dictates the eventual skills that students can achieve. Technology providers will need to seriously consider pricing mechanisms so that academic institutions are better able to afford and maintain basic technological infrastructures to implement core teaching and education programs. There has been some progress in this area, with mechanisms such as university campus licensing that enable widespread use of some software tools for teaching and research.

With the gradual expansion of the home as a center of learning, arrangements for students to use university resources at home promise to be a major issue, especially with respect to copyrights and off-campus licensing agreements. University libraries hold a key position in this regard. Already, electronic books, or e-books, are a common feature of many western university library catalogs, and there has been growing evidence to suggest that some of the more progressive university libraries have already begun to redefine their roles as information gateways to act as the intermediary between the user and information (Dowler, 1997). Electronic data archives, multimedia reuseable learning object databases, subject portals, and continuing skills training for students are ways libraries have begun to accept their changing roles in university teaching and learning. A common thread in all the transformations has been the impact that ICT has brought to the university and classroom with respect to administration, teaching, and learning.

Existing models of multimedia cartography teaching and learning have been mostly descriptive. These models have been useful in understanding the mechanisms in operation and in enabling comparisons to be made across different learning contexts. The results from these studies have enabled educators to generally conclude that ICT and multimedia have positive benefits for learning. However, not much is known about the critical factors and how they influence learning. Systematic investigations of predictive models in diverse contexts provide the next steps for understanding the factors of ICT and multimedia that affect learning. Following along this line will be new learning tools, with which intelligent agents will guide learners through knowledge nodes and learning activities using hypermedia and multimedia in much the same way as the intelligent help assistant acts in the Microsoft Office software products.

Conclusion

The ECS model presented is based on a holistic perspective of learning as complex interactions between multiple agents, physical and social spaces, and instructional technologies. Although the model can be used in hypothesis testing, the main goal is to provide instructional designers and educators with a tool for managing the main factors that need to be considered when designing ICT-based pedagogies. This model provides the framework for good instructional and course-structuring design that takes into account the diversity of learner styles and provides engaging interactions among students.

The use of ICT and multimedia pedagogy in cartographic education is still in the early stages of understanding and development. There are numerous possibilities and pitfalls. But given the early stages of diffusion of multimedia tools in education, the current focus among practitioners is on developing strategies and standardized protocols to produce effective multimedia components that blend engagement and entertainment into a single learning environment. Moreover, collaborative processes aid the pedagogical move toward student-centered learning.

The embedded collaborative systems model was developed to structure and understand the dynamics involved in the implementation of multiple learning skills activities. The implementation involved 47 students in a multimedia cartography course. The course was conducted in a blended learning environment, and discursive group learning was the foundation of the learning experience (Thorne, 2003). Each group defined project content, prepared a proposal, defended their proposal in front of their peers in a formal conference-type presentation, received feedback from peers, and used the feedback to improve their group's project. Also, the other groups judged each group on presentations. This forms the cooperative phase, where individuality and group opinions are merged for consensual learning.

In summary, the issues in this study, namely, how to implement effective (content and experience) multimedia cartography training and education to learners of diverse backgrounds, was addressed by the development and testing of a systems model for integrating the multiple facets involved in the education and training process. Within the systems model, the collaborative and cooperative learning strategies were integrated to promote individual and group development for effective multimedia cartography education and product development. The benefits of the ECS model include the following:

- Improves connectivity among the actors by embedded and continuous interaction

- Cultivates an attitude of independent learning through peer guidance and motivation

- Integrates multimedia information, thereby catering to a range of learning styles

- Provides ownership of the learning process through group and individual project management

- Develops individual social and learning skills and accountability

Acknowledgments

The authors acknowledge the financial support from the following sources: an International Council for Canadian Studies (ICCS-CIES) Scholarship and a Department of Geography (Simon Fraser University) Teaching Assistantship to S. Balram; and a Simon Fraser University President Research Grant to S. Dragicevic. The comments of Dr. David Kaufman, LIDC, Simon Fraser University are gratefully appreciated. The authors thank two anonymous referees for their comments and suggestions toward improving an earlier draft of the manuscript.

References

Abbott, C. (2001). *ICT: Changing education.* London; New York: Routledge Falmer.

Alessi, S. M., & Trollip, S. R. (2001). *Multimedia for learning: Methods and development.* Boston, MA: Allyn and Bacon.

Bazeli, M. J., & Robinson, R. S. (2001). Critical viewing to promote critical thinking. In R. Muffoletto (Ed.), *Education and technology: Critical and reflective practices* (pp. 69–91). Cresskill, NJ: Hampton Press.

Benyon, D., Stone, D., & Woodroffe, M. (1997). Experience with developing multimedia courseware for the World Wide Web: The need for better tools and clear pedagogy. *International Journal of Human–Computer Studies, 47,* 197–218.

Bertalanffy, L. v. (1969). *General systems theory; Foundations, development, applications.* New York: G. Braziller.

Bruffee, K. A. (1995). Sharing our toys: Cooperative learning versus collaborative learning. *Change,* (January/February), 12–18.

Cartwright, W., Peterson, M. P., & Gartner, G. F. (Eds.). (1999). *Multimedia cartography.* Berlin; New York: Springer.

Dearing, R. (1997). *The National Committee of Inquiry into Higher Education.* Retrieved April 10, 2003 from the World Wide Web: http://www.leeds.ac.uk/educol/ncihe/

Dowler, L. (Ed.). (1997). *Gateways to knowledge: The role of academic libraries in teaching, learning, and research.* Cambridge, MA: MIT Press.

Easton, G. (1982). *Learning from case studies.* Englewood Cliffs, NJ: Prentice Hall International.

Edstrom, K. (2002). Design for motivation. In S. Hailes (Ed.), *The digital university: Building a learning community* (pp. 193–202). London; New York: Springer.

Ellis, T. J. (2001). Multimedia enhanced educational products as a tool to promote critical thinking in adult students. *Journal of Educational Multimedia and Hypermedia, 10*(2), 107–123.

Farrell, G. (1999). The development of virtual institutions in Canada. In G. Farrell (Ed.), *The development of virtual education: A global perspective* (pp. 13–22). Vancouver, Canada: The Commonwealth of Learning.

Gerber, R. (2002). Understanding how geographical educators learn in their work: An important basis for their professional development. In M. Smith

(Ed.), *Teaching geography in secondary schools: A reader* (pp. 293–305). London: Routledge Falmer.

Gold, J. R., Jenkins, A., Lee, R., Monk, J., Riley, J., Shepherd, I., & Unwin, D. (1991). *Teaching geography in higher education: A manual of good practice*. Oxford, UK; Cambridge, MA: Basil Blackwell.

Hassell, D. (2000). Issues in ICT and geography. In T. Binns (Ed.), *Issues in geography teaching* (pp. 80–92). London; New York: Routledge.

Hede, A. (2002). An integrated model of multimedia effects on learning. *Journal of Educational Multimedia and Hypermedia, 11*(2), 177–191.

Kenway, J. (1996). The information superhighway and post-modernity: The social promise and the social price. *Comparative Education, 32*(2), 217–231.

Kinshuk, & Patel, A. (2003). Optimizing domain representation with multimedia objects. In S. Naidu (Ed.), *Learning and teaching with technology: Principles and practice* (pp. 55–68). London and Sterling, VA: Kogan Page Limited.

Mitchell, B. R. (2002). The relevance and impact of collaborative working for management in a digital university. In S. Hailes (Ed.), *The digital university: Building a learning community* (pp. 229–246). London; New York: Springer.

Najjar, L. J. (1996). Multimedia information and learning. *Journal of Educational Multimedia and Hypermedia, 5*(2), 129–150.

Norman, K. (2002). Collaborative interactions in support of learning: Models, metaphors and management. In S. Hailes (Ed.), *The digital university: Building a learning community* (pp. 41–56). London; New York: Springer.

Piaget, J. (1926). *The language and thought of a child*. London: Routledge & Kegan Paul.

Selwyn, N. (2002). *Telling tales on technology: Qualitative studies of technology and education*. Aldershot, Hants, England; Burlington, VT: Ashgate.

Thorne, K. (2003). *Blended learning: How to integrate online & traditional learning*. London; Sterling, VA: Kogan Page.

Vygotsky, L. S. (1978). *Mind in society: The development of higher psychological processes*. Cambridge, MA: Harvard University Press.

Watson, D., Blakeley, B., & Abbott, C. (1998). Researching the use of communication technologies in teacher education. *Computers and Education, 30*(1–2), 15–21.

Yildirim, Z., Ozden, M. Y., & Aksu, M. (2001). Comparison of hypermedia learning and traditional instruction on knowledge acquisition and retention. *The Journal of Educational Research, 94*(4), 207–214.

Chapter XVI

Cave Automated Virtual Environment:
A Supercomputer-based Multimedia System for Learning Science in a Science Center

Leo Tan Wee Hin, Nanyang Technological University, Singapore

R. Subramaniam, Nanyang Technological University, Singapore

Sharlene Anthony, Singapore Science Centre, Singapore

Abstract

A multimedia system based on the Cave Automated Virtual Environment is shown to be useful for learning science in the informal setting of a science center. Using the theme of water, concepts such as atomic structure, electron precessing, bonding and phase transformations have been used to provide a framework for scaffolding content in a dynamic manner among students. The high quality visualizations, immersive experiences, interactivity and stereoscopic imagery in this virtual environment also contributes towards experiential learning, and it is suggested that this has constructivist implications.

Introduction

Traditional pedagogical environments such as classroom-based teaching continue to play useful and effective roles in delivering education to students. While it is perceived to have a number of disadvantages, for example, it is teacher-centric, it generally involves the passive assimilation of content by students, and it does not maximize learning efficiency in large groups, it still constitutes the bedrock upon which teaching and learning are premised. In more recent times, the role of science centers in complementing science teaching in schools has become important (Tan & Subramaniam, 1998, 2003a, 2003b, 2003c). By providing a learning environment in which knowledge transmittance occurs informally, considerable scope is afforded for students to expand their mental paradigms through participatory experiences in science exhibitions, large-format theatres, and other mass-based promotional activities. In many of the exhibits as well as in the programs shown in the large-format theatres, there is the mediation of technology to drive the learning experience. The communal dynamics inherent in these informal educational environments also provides a social context for learning.

In using technology to mediate the learning experience, multimedia systems offer tremendous potential. This is based on the recognition that the use of audio, video, and text technologies provide a stimuli-rich initiation into the learning process. Whereas traditional learning is dependent predominantly on oral narratives, the insertion of multimedia permits an expansion of the sensory dimension that is brought to bear on the learning process. And this has cognitive implications. Early versions of multimedia systems were restricted to programs on monitor screens, which provide the necessary audiovisual experiences through computer-generated graphics (Bryson, 1992). In later versions, there was the availability of 3-D images, but these need to be relished using 2-D media, that is, a desktop monitor screen in conjunction with stereographic glasses. While permitting navigation capabilities through the learning worlds generated, they do not have the capability to foster immersive experiences.

Technological advances in computational processing, image rendering, and scientific visualization have contributed immensely to the advent of more complex multimedia systems, notably virtual reality (Bryson, 1996). This has allowed the creation of compelling learning experiences that are participatory in nature. Until recent times, the use of virtual reality interfaces was constrained by factors that precluded their wider use. Initial versions required the use of Head-Mounted Display sets to showcase the visualization of learning scenarios (Teitel, 1990; Chung & Harris, 1990). This had the drawbacks of single-user experience at any one time, use of technical manpower to manage the logistics of the exercise, use of small video screens in the headset, and the fragility of the system. Also, these versions do not permit direct interaction with the artificially generated objects in the virtual world. The use of data glove sets also had similar drawbacks when fostering tactile experiences in various knowledge domains (Burdea, 1996).

A quantum leap in virtual reality technology was attained with the advent of the Cave Automated Virtual Environment (CAVE) (Cruz-Neira et al., 1992, 1993a, 1993b; DeFanti et al., 1993). Comprising a cubic room with multiscreen projection systems that project stereographic (3-D) images, it afforded, for the first time, a generational advance in immersive and participatory experiences for large groups of people at any one time. The wide field presentation permits scaling up of processes and phenomena as well as navigation through these environments to an extent hitherto thought not possible. This navigation can be done without the need for any physical movement by the user. It soon becomes apparent that virtual learning environments for a variety of applications and topics can be built using the CAVE. The level of visualization made possible through the CAVE also helps to simulate virtual representations of complex processes and architectural designs. Compared to Head-Mounted Display systems and data glove sets, the CAVE systems are robust and rugged.

Generally, multimedia systems have the projection plane orthogonal to the viewer, for example, as in conventional theatres. This constrains the utility of the media to a single plane. In the CAVE, the use of multiple projection paradigms affords users new perspectives of the scenario from different positions. This is a key factor that contributes to the feeling of presence in the virtual environment and, concomitantly, greater sensory immersion in the 3-D imagery conjured up in the CAVE.

Because of the cost and technical expertise needed to run CAVE systems, it is found mainly in leading research establishments and universities. Cutting-edge research and sophisticated visualization experiments are done in these CAVEs. More recently, schools have been exposed to the CAVE for their learning needs (Roussos et al., 1997; Moher et al., 1999; Johnson et al., 2000). The Singapore Science Center is the only public access setting in the world to have a CAVE as part of its menu of attractions for students and the public.

In this chapter, the use of the CAVE to learn science in the informal setting of a science center is explored. No previous work on such settings has been reported in the literature. More specifically, the purpose of this chapter is four-fold:

1. To describe the systems architecture of the CAVE used at the Singapore Science Center

2. To briefly review the applications literature related to CAVE

3. To highlight the design and pedagogical aspects of two of the educational programs used in the CAVE for students and the public, respectively

4. To assess the learning efficacy of this new learning environment for one of the programs offered to schools

Systems Architecture of the CAVE

The CAVE at the Singapore Science Center is a cube of dimensions 3 m × 3 m × 3 m, and it comprises the following principal components:

1. *Projection systems*: Three rear projection systems for the walls (front, left, and right) and one down projection system for the floor are used. For the latter, the projector is mounted at the top on a horizontal plane, and the images are projected onto an angularly aligned mirror that reflects them onto the floor. These systems project stereographic images onto the respective screens. Images are projected at a frame rate of 96 Hz. This helps to minimize visual fatigue among users. The multicolor visual fields (1024 × 768 dpi) provide a resolution of about 2000 linear pixels.

2. *Stereo glasses*: When the projectors project the multicolor visual fields onto the screens, the images appear as doublets bereft of stereographic integrity. To resolve these alternate fields as well as to elicit the 3-D effect, the use of stereo glasses (Stereographics' CrystalEyes) by users is necessary. The stereo glasses are battery operated.

3. *Tracking sensors*: The lead user in the CAVE wears a pair of stereo glasses, which has sensors to electromagnetically track the orientation and location of his head. It has six degrees of freedom of movement corresponding to the Euclidean x, y, and z coordinate systems as well as the pitch, roll, and yaw orientations. What the lead user sees is also what the others in the CAVE see. Signals from the sensors are relayed to the computer that constantly auto-adjusts the projection of the images from the lead user's perspective.

    The lead user also holds a wand that comprises a joystick and three buttons. The wand has a sensor based on the Ascension Flock of Birds Tracking System, and it is interfaced by a cable to a serial port on the Onyx supercomputer via a PC. The joystick is used to navigate through the virtual environment in the CAVE, while the buttons are used to trigger modes of interactivity, for example, grabbing an object.

The lead user's stereo glasses and wand are tethered to cables, and this can constrain his mobility in the CAVE to some extent.

4. *Screens*: The display screens used are mounted orthogonally to the plane of projection of the images. They are translucent and of low emissivity.

5. *Sound systems*: Placement of acoustic speakers at the top vertices of the CAVE generates sonification effects that add to the immersive and interactive experience in the CAVE. The sound can be triggered at any speaker so as to make it appear to be coming from a discrete location of the 3-D imagery in the CAVE.

6. *Stereo emitters*: Small stereo emitters placed around the edges of the CAVE have the function of synchronizing the configuration of the stereo glasses to the frame rate used for image projection.

7. *Supercomputer*: The overall operations of the CAVE are directed and coordinated by a supercomputer (Silicon Graphics Onyx 2 Reality Engine).

Figure 1: Schematic of Cave Automated Virtual Environment

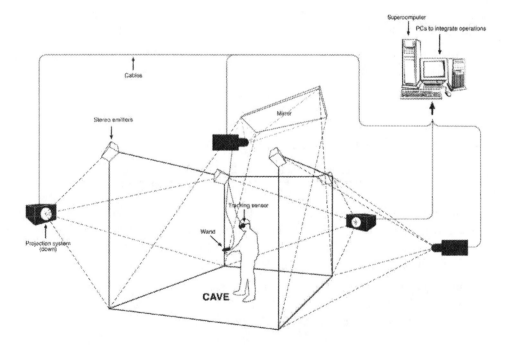

Figure 2: Students inside the Cave Automated Virtual Environment

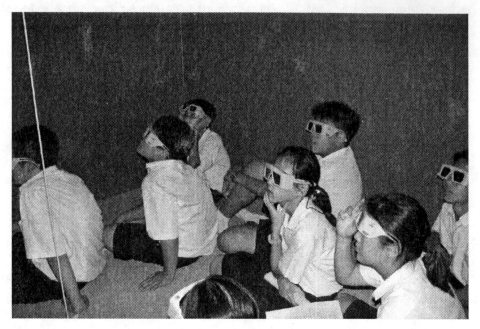

In a typical CAVE program at the Singapore Science Center, up to 12 persons can be comfortably accommodated inside the CAVE. The duration of each program is variable, but it is typically restricted to not more than 15 minutes.

Figure 1 shows a schematic of the setup of the CAVE. In Figure 2, a scene from the CAVE is depicted.

Brief Review of CAVE Applications Literature

The concept of CAVE has its origins in 1991 in the ideas of Thomas DeFanti and Don Sandin of the Electronic Visualization Laboratory at the University of Chicago. An initial prototype based on their ideas was developed by Carolina Cruz-Neir in 1992 (Cruz-Neir et al., 1992, 1993).

Presenting computer-generated and multisensory data as visual sets, the utility of the CAVE was soon recognized by other workers for the simulation of scientific phenomena as well as for the creation of walk-throughs of various virtual environments. Much of the advances in the utility of the CAVE for various learning and training needs was, and is still, being done in the Electronic Visualization Laboratory at the University of Chicago.

Among the numerous applications that have been developed for the CAVE include the following:

1. As a children's activity to collaboratively construct, cultivate, and tend a healthy virtual garden (Roussos et al., 1997)

2. As an activity to explore a large "natural" terrain populated by different plant types (Moher et al., 1999)

3. To provide immersive experiences of distributed data using high-performance networks (Lascara et al., 2002)

4. To study an ant, the interior of the Earth, a volcano, an iceberg, the solar system, and the human heart (Johnson et al., 2000)

5. To prototype a new virtual reality device (Johnson et al., 2002)

6. To educate about cultural heritage (Pape et al., 2000)

7. As a construction, preplanning tool for modeling basic elements of mechanical, electrical, and plumbing systems in buildings (Roy, 1998)

8. To virtually prototype product development, for example, design a ship passenger cabin and build a promenade (Broas, 2001)

The suite of applications that can be developed is limited only by the requirements of the clients and the creativity of the programmer.

CAVE Programs at the Singapore Science Center

Two programs are the subject of this chapter. A brief description of these programs is necessary in order to appreciate the potential of the CAVE for educational needs in the informal setting of the science center.

Molecular Structure of Water

The topic of water is a curriculum requirement in both primary and secondary school science in Singapore (Tan & Subramaniam, 2003d). As it is taught, there are certain problems encountered in getting students to clearly understand its molecular geometry, crystal structure, and dynamics of its phase transformations. It was in this context that the topic of water was specially developed as a CAVE application.

The programming was done at the Institute of High Performance Computing in Singapore based on the brief provided by the Singapore Science Center. The brief calls for specific pedagogical elements and instructional tools to be built into the program in order to meet various teaching and learning needs. In developing the conceptual framework for this program, particular attention was paid to ensure that the relative sizes of the atoms as well as the values of the atomic radii, bond angles, bond lengths, and other parameters were modeled as accurately as possible, within the constraints of the system, in the virtual representations, so that they can stand up to scientific scrutiny. This has been a key factor in dynamically configuring the various structures and processes in the topic and in imposing a coherent format on the program. It was also deemed important that creative interpretations of the ideas as well as game elements be included so as to foster an edutainment experience for students coming for this program. This stems from the popularization philosophy employed by science centers—that is, learning has got to be fun and enjoyable. Initial versions of the program were tested on the CAVE with small groups of users in order to obtain feedback as well as to assess the accuracy of the representations. The feedback was incorporated into later versions of the program.

The program currently being shown allows for the relishing of the following stereographic scenarios:

- Electrons precessing around the nucleus of the hydrogen and oxygen atoms. Visitors also get a chance to navigate into the heart of these atomic configurations in order to view different perspectives.

- Combination of two hydrogen atoms and one oxygen atom through covalent bonding to form a molecule of H_2O, which floats as a 3-D structure in space. A walk-around of this molecule is also made possible, as is the scope for "touching" it.

- Differential aggregation of H_2O molecules to form its three states of matter—solid ice, liquid water, and water vapor

- Crystal structure of ice, including a walk-through to its interior

- Demonstrating phase transformation through temperature-induced changes. For this purpose, there is a virtual transducer that can be manipulated by the lead user to increase or decrease the temperature. As the temperature increases, absorption of heat by the H_2O molecules in the liquid state is cognized through an increase in its freedom of movement. With further rise of temperature, more of the H_2O molecules are seen to break free from the hydrogen bonds that bind them together in the liquid state and escape into the CAVE environment. An increase in temperature further manifests as an increase in the collision frequency of the H_2O molecules in the gas phase. More of these molecules escape into the CAVE environment and "knock" against the visitors inside. Appropriate sound effects are generated during such interactions in order to accentuate the immersive and interactive experiences of visitors.

Walk-through of Virtual Outdoor Field

This program is commonly used to showcase the technological capabilities of the CAVE to a generalist audience. It is recognized that not all visitors would want to be treated to a content-heavy presentation such as the molecular structure of water.

The program, better known as Crayoland, conjures up a scenario of an outdoor field environment, as seen through the eyes of a three-year-old child, using pastel-colored drawings (http://www.evl.uic.edu/pape/CAVE/demos/crayoland.html). The scenery is replete with trees, lakes, flowers, log cabin, streams, and mountains. Users can navigate through the woods and relish the sights along the way. Some of the scenarios in the program include the following:

- Navigating between trees in the woods—if a visitor bumps into a tree, appropriate sound effects are generated

- Disturbing a beehive on a treetop with the lead user's wand, whence the bees disperse among the visitors with a buzzing sound

- "Entering" a log cabin in the woods, either through the door or through the window, and relishing its interior. This sequence tellingly demonstrates to participants that it is the lead user who controls what they see. Others can try to "enter" the log cabin, but it would not be possible, even though it is realistically in 3-D and within reach. It is only when the lead user "enters" the house that others "feel" at home.

- Plucking a flower from the woods and dropping it

- Walking around a well

- Splashing water when wading through a pond

- Encountering buzzing bees, flying butterflies, chirping birds, and quacking ducks in the ecosystem of the virtual environment

At all times, participants can "touch" the 3-D objects in the virtual environment and, thus, add to the grandeur of their experience.

Design of Evaluation Instrument

To assess the efficacy of the CAVE as an educational tool, an evaluation instrument was developed for the program on water. A draft list of 20 statements was first generated, based on the authors' experiences as well as drawing ideas from the literature. These statements covered three categories: learning climate, effectiveness of learning, and educational potential. The statements were edited for clarity, ambiguity, and redundancy. Based on this screening process, the number of statements was pruned down to 16. After obtaining feedback from validators, the 16 statements were slightly refined. For the purpose of this study, it was felt that these 16 statements were adequate. A longer evaluation instrument was not desirable, as it can lead to respondent fatigue.

For ease of administration, the scalability of the statements was set on a five-point Likert-type scale, ranging from Strongly Agree (SA) to Strongly Disagree (SD). The corresponding numerical measures ranged from 5 for SA to 1 for SD. For the negatively worded statements, the numerical measures were reversed.

Two groups of students of mixed gender were used for this study. One group was a class of 35 students (16 males and 19 females) studying in Secondary 3 (Express), while another group was a class of 33 students (16 males and 17 females) studying in Secondary 1 (Express). Both groups were from different schools, and they were exposed to the CAVE program on water on separate days. (The medium of instruction in schools in Singapore is English.) The evaluation instrument was administered to the students after the CAVE experience. Prior to completion of the evaluation instrument, the groups were briefed about the purpose of the study, the scoring used in the instrument, and also provided clarifications on terms such as immersive experience, etc. The evaluation instrument took about five minutes for completion.

Discussion

There is compelling evidence in the multimedia literature that technology-based environments provide good instructional support for meeting learning needs (De Jong et al., 1998; Edelson et al., 1999; Guzdial, 1995; Jackson & Winn, 1999; Johnson et al., 1999, 2002; Taxen & Waeve, 2001). The multisensory experience created in such environments can be contrasted with that prevailing in traditional learning environments, where there is impoverishment of the experiential factor.

The CAVE at the Singapore Science Center was conceptualized as a dual-purpose teaching tool—one that is intended to complement the science curricula in schools and, another, to promote an edutainment experience for the general public. It was recognized that the promotion of both of these aspects is an integral aspect of justifying the investment on the CAVE.

Aligning the program on the molecular structure of water with classroom teaching practice affords a context for reaching out to schools. The topics of electronic structure, bonding, and phase transformations are central to the understanding of a number of basic concepts in chemistry. By integrating these concepts in a unifying theme such as water, a rational framework is afforded for showcasing the capabilities of the CAVE. As the complexity at the microlevel is solubilized by the scaling-up potential afforded in the CAVE, visualization of complex phenomena and geometry at the atomic level takes on greater meaning.

Importance of Lead User

In presenting the CAVE experience on the molecular structure of water, the lead user acts as a pedagogical agent for content delivery in a dynamic environment. The lead user is usually a trained staff member of the science center who has both content knowledge of the subject matter as well as the level of presentation experience expected of science center/science museum professionals. At each stage in the virtual reality excursion, the running commentary by the lead user during gaps in the audio commentary in the program helps to ensure that the CAVE experience does not regress to that of an entertainment session bereft of teaching value but instead fosters the attainment of cognitive goals as well. It may be argued that an on-screen pedagogical agent can as well perform the task. While there are merits in such an arrangement, the use of a human pedagogical interface has a number of distinct advantages. These are elaborated below:

1.   As technical navigating and learning simultaneously imposes heavy cognitive load on users, guided access in a domain of inquiry helps to lessen the dependency on the former factor while augmenting the latter factor.

2.   The show can be temporarily stopped at any time to insert an extended narrative or to clear misconceptions among students on various aspects of the topic.

3.   The program can be rewound to certain sequences so as to recapture salient aspects of the learning.

4.   The participatory elements embedded in the program can be extended to inject further fun elements in the learning experience.

5.   It helps to provide directedness of the learning experience.

6.   It permits dwelling on particular abstractions in the conceptual framework.

7.   Guided access helps to pitch the presentation according to the academic level of the students.

It is the considerable latitude that the lead user brings to the virtual environment that adds to the value of the show experience for students. Both primary and secondary school students come for the CAVE presentation, and the lead user varies the level of abstraction of the presentation accordingly. It needs to be emphasized that the CAVE at the Singapore Science Center is the only system in the world where the lead user inserts a narrative at appropriate gaps in the audio commentary. While the recorded audio commentary is often sufficient for many purposes to comprehend what is happening in the CAVE, the lead user's inputs constitute a value-added enhancement to the learning experience of students. In the case where a trained lead user is not available for some reason, another person can still guide the CAVE participants on a navigational basis with the audio commentary sufficing.

Typically, a 15-minute duration for the virtual reality program on the molecular structure of water is sufficient. Any further extension is not desirable for three reasons: it can affect the user's sense of orientation in the virtual environment; it imposes cerebral indigestion on students; and it affects turn-around time for other student groups in the queue.

Generally, teachers bring student groups to attend the CAVE experience after completing the relevant topics in class. As the nature of the CAVE program on water is organized in a hierarchical manner, the learning journey provides a context for building the concept base of students further.

Evaluation of CAVE

Informal feedback solicited from teachers and groups of students coming for such visits over a period of a year have shown that the CAVE experience helps to complement what is taught in the topic of water in the school science curricula. The verbalization data obtained from this feedback also attest to the fact that the technological mediation afforded in treating the topic of water provides a useful cognitive delivery system for appreciating complex processes and mapping these onto the learners' cognition.

The informal feedback is validated by the more formal study undertaken with the use of an evaluation instrument. Overall, the feedback was very positive on the use of the CAVE as a teaching tool.

For the purpose of this study, our intent has been to show that the CAVE is a viable educational tool. In this context, our emphasis has been on the development of a suitable evaluation instrument as well as the use of simple statistical analyses and reliability analyses of the data. The use of more sophisticated data analysis as well as the exploring of effects such as gender, etc., are not the motivating concerns of this study, and are thus not addressed. Table 1 presents descriptive statistics for each of the 16 statements in the evaluation instrument after analysis of the responses from the Secondary 3 pupils. The means of the statements ranged from 3.57 to 4.40; standard deviations ranged from 0.35 to 0.91. Internal consistency of the evaluation instrument was obtained by extracting the Cronbach Alpha coefficient (Cronbach, 1951). The value of 0.85 is well above the norm of 0.70 recommended by Nunnaly (1978), and thus indicates good reliability of the instrument developed.

Table 2 summarizes the descriptive statistics for the CAVE experience with the Secondary 1 pupils. Again, a similar trend is observed. The means of the statements ranged from 3.75 to 4.36; standard deviations ranged from 0.56 to 0.93. The Cronbach Alpha coefficient of 0.83 for this study further indicates good reliability of the evaluation instrument.

Some of the important findings emerging from this survey are as follows:

- There is strong validation for the philosophy employed by the Singapore Science Center in presenting the CAVE experience on the structure of water. The mean for Item 1 in the survey instrument is 4.40 for the Secondary 3 pupils and 4.27 for the Secondary 1 pupils, the highest among all the 16 statements, thus reiterating the point that learning has got to be fun and enjoyable.

- The CAVE experience not only complements what students learn in school, but it is also more than what they have learned from science textbooks. The effect is especially pronounced for the Secondary 3 pupils (means of 4.14 for Item 9 and 3.71 for Item 8) than for the Secondary 1 pupils (means of 3.81 for Item 9 and 3.94 for Item 8). This could be due to the fact that the Secondary 3 pupils have studied the topic in greater depth than the Secondary 1 pupils.

- The interactive and immersive environment in which the topic was taught has found good support from both groups of students. The mean for Item 5 relating to the immersive environment was higher for the Secondary 1 pupils (4.36) than for the Secondary 3 pupils (4.09). In respect to Item 11 on the interactive nature of the CAVE, again, the mean was greater for the Secondary 1 pupils (4.09) than for the Secondary 3 pupils (3.91). This suggests that younger pupils are more fascinated by the play elements embedded in the interactivity for learning, a finding which needs to be borne in mind when developing more applications for the CAVE.

- The role of technology as a motivator for learning is strongly borne out by the mean of at least 4.0 for Item 16 for both groups. This is of significance, as motivation has long been recognized as an important factor affecting student achievement (Karlsson, 1996). The role of the teacher in exposing students to new learning environments in order to make learning enjoyable is thus of paramount significance (Barry & King, 1993). In Singapore, it is the teacher who makes the decision on what out-of-school learning experiences, such as, for example, the CAVE, their students are exposed to.

- There was a strong expression of interest by both groups of students in wanting to learn other science topics through the CAVE – mean for Item

Table 1: Descriptive statistics for CAVE experience with Secondary 3 students

S/n	Item	Min	Max	Mean	Standard Deviation
1	The CAVE makes learning fun and interesting	3	5	4.40	0.55
2	The design of the CAVE is appropriate for learning	2	5	4.09	0.82
3	The amount of material used in the multimedia presentation in the CAVE was just right	2	5	3.57	0.92
4	The sequence of material shown in the multimedia presentation in the CAVE was logical and systematic	2	5	4.26	0.74
5	I liked the immersive environment in which the topic was taught	2	5	4.09	0.85
6	The way in which information was presented in the CAVE was confusing (R)	1	3	3.83	0.62
7	The use of multimedia technology in the CAVE helped to illustrate concepts in a way that facilitated my understanding	3	5	4.09	0.56
8	I learned more about the structure of water from the CAVE than from my science textbook	2	5	3.71	0.79
9	The CAVE experience on water complements what I learned in class	4	5	4.14	0.36
10	The CAVE builds on my knowledge of water learned from textbooks and in the classroom	3	5	4.11	0.53
11	The interactive environment in which the topic of water was explored in the CAVE contributed to greater learning	3	5	3.91	0.51
12	The guide who led the CAVE presentation facilitated effectively my learning	2	5	4.00	0.64
13	The CAVE is not a good teaching tool to learn science (R)	1	3	3.91	0.61
14	I would like to learn other science topics through the CAVE	3	5	4.23	0.49
15	The CAVE is not an exciting media for learning (R)	1	3	4.06	0.59
16	The use of technology in the CAVE increased my motivation to learn	3	5	4.03	0.66

Notes: Items 1–6 are on learning climate; Items 7–12 are on effectiveness of learning; and Items 13–16 are on educational potential. (R) indicates reversed score item. Cronbach Alpha = 0.85.

14 in respect of this is 4.23 for the Secondary 3 pupils and 3.91 for the Secondary 1 pupils.

Clearly, the learning climate, the effectiveness of learning, and the educational potential of the CAVE are rated positively by both groups of students in this study. This is not surprising, as the CAVE program on water was specifically developed as an application to complement this topic in the science curricula in schools in Singapore. In particular, both groups of students have commented favorably on the use of technology to mediate their learning experience (Item 10 of evaluation instrument). It may be of interest to add that in a previous study of

Table 2: Descriptive statistics for CAVE experience with Secondary 1 students

S/n	Item	Min	Max	Mean	Standard Deviation
1	The CAVE makes learning fun and interesting	3	5	4.27	0.63
2	The design of the CAVE is appropriate for learning	3	5	4.24	0.71
3	The amount of material used in the multimedia presentation in the CAVE was just right	2	5	3.76	0.83
4	The sequence of material shown in the multimedia presentation in the CAVE was logical and systematic	3	5	4.15	0.57
5	I liked the immersive environment in which the topic was taught	3	5	4.36	0.60
6	The way in which information was presented in the CAVE was confusing (R)	1	4	3.97	0.88
7	The use of multimedia technology in the CAVE helped to illustrate concepts in a way that facilitated my understanding	2	5	4.00	0.66
8	I learned more about the structure of water from the CAVE than from my science textbook	1	5	3.94	0.93
9	The CAVE experience on water complements what I learned in class	1	5	3.81	0.88
10	The CAVE builds on my knowledge of water learned from textbooks and in the classroom	1	5	3.91	0.88
11	The interactive environment in which the topic of water was explored in the CAVE contributed to greater learning	1	5	4.09	0.80
12	The guide who led the CAVE presentation facilitated effectively my learning	2	5	4.06	0.75
13	The CAVE is not a good teaching tool to learn science (R)	1	4	3.85	0.83
14	I would like to learn other science topics through the CAVE	1	5	3.91	0.91
15	The CAVE is not an exciting media for learning (R)	1	4	3.85	0.76
16	The use of technology in the CAVE increased my motivation to learn	1	5	4.00	0.87

Notes: Items 1–6 are on learning climate; Items 7–12 are on effectiveness of learning; and Items 13–16 are on educational potential. (R) indicates reversed score item. Cronbach Alpha = 0.83.

the CAVE for simulating science activities for school students, Moher et al. (1999) noted the tremendous scope that technology provides for scaffolding learning as well as broadening the domains of inquiry.

Comprehending the 3-D spatial geometry of atoms, molecules, intermolecular bonding, and the crystallographic structure of ice poses some problems when traditional media and conventional texts are used to teach these topics. The CAVE experience furnishes an alternative platform in rendering accessible these inaccessible phenomena as well as in visualizing molecular geometries. The high quality of the graphics and the level of visualization afforded stereo-graphically are important considerations in this regard. Instructional mentoring by the lead user has also been favorably commented upon by users. All these provide the scaffolding necessary to entrench the concepts in the cognitive psyche of students to a reasonable extent. More importantly, the shared learning experience in the communal setting of the CAVE is a factor that has found support among students coming for such experiences. Teachers have also commented favorably on the realistic portrayal of the various processes and structures.

One drawback that we have found is the penchant for students to fixate attention on the gimmicky elements embedded in the presentation as well as indulging in gestural antics. Though these are necessary to make the presentation interesting in that they afford scope for playful antics, they are recognized to be subservient to the locus of their understanding. Moher et al. (1999) have, in fact, cautioned that the introduction of new technologies such as the CAVE to educational processes has the risk of transforming the nature and focus of the learning, and that this may engender different learning outcomes. We suspect that the veering off of emphasis from content to action, as indicated in our study here, is an example in this regard, even though there was little evidence to show that it has affected the cognitive transfer of knowledge. This could be due to the fact that the CAVE experience was allied to the teaching programs in schools, and that student experiences have been carefully structured to ensure that learning takes place.

The novelty of the CAVE experience has been a factor in drawing school groups. It is the feeling of sense of presence in the CAVE that endears it as a learning medium for students and visitors alike. Several factors contribute to the creating of sense of presence: use of high-resolution graphics, wide field view contributing to immersion, stereographic imagery, and auditory rendering of sonification effects. While not their first experience with virtual reality, because virtual reality arcades and home PC-based VR games are common in Singapore, the feeling of immersion is powerful as is also the stereographic reality of the imagery. It may well be that the novelty factor has a contributory factor in enhancing the learning experience. Moher (1999) contends that the novelty effect can sometimes confound assessment and, that when this wears off, visualization takes center stage in the CAVE and contributes to greater learning. Roussos (1997) has also commented that distraction, fatigue, and cognitive overheads are factors that need to be borne in mind when assessing the influence of learning in the CAVE. To what extent this has implications in our study is not clear but is worthy of further study. We stress that the feedback from teachers and students has been very positive in terms of the learning potential of the CAVE program on water as well as the extent to which it complements their own teaching of this topic.

Constructivist Learning in the CAVE

It is of interest to explore whether the multimedia experience in the CAVE supports constructivist learning. There are several theories of constructivism, but we will focus more on the cognitive constructivist approaches of Bartlett (1932), Piaget (1977), and Taylor (1998), all of whom emphasize responsibility on the part of the individual in constructing knowledge. According to these theories, learning takes place in incremental steps shaped by the preconceived notions of students about a topic. Exposing students to new situations or frameworks for learning, where there are opportunities to build links with their preconceived notions on a topic and thus connect at the intellectual level, meshes with constructivist approaches. Shu (2001) has cautioned that not all multimedia environments meet the learning philosophies of constructivists—the cognitive framework in which the design of the multimedia is built is a crucial consideration for such learning to take place.

In the context of the foregoing, the CAVE can be considered to be a new framework on which to build on the previous knowledge of students on the topic of water. The CAVE program on water drew inputs from educationists, designers, and scientists at the formative stage, with the express aim of complementing the topic as covered in the school science curricula in Singapore and embedding constructivist elements. More importantly, it was conceptualized by cognizing the curricular constructs of the topic and seeing how the potentialities of the CAVE can contribute toward furthering the process of learning. Further support for the constructivist attributes of the CAVE learning is indicated by the high weightage assigned, in particular, for Item 10 in the evaluation instrument as well as for Items 7, 8, 9, and 11. Clearly, both groups of students felt that the CAVE experience builds on their existing ideas on the structure of water. The opportunities presented for resolving cognitive conflicts when the learner's preexisting knowledge construct cognizes new information in the setting of the CAVE are broadly in sync with the requirement that stimulus for learning needs to be provided as a basis for gearing learning toward constructivism

(Piaget, 1977; Fosnot, 1984). Indeed, Shu (2001) has commented that "learning is a series of encounters with cognitive conflicts and the process of restoring cognitive equilibrium, leading to the construction of understanding." The fact that hypermedia, of which CAVE is an example, has been shown to act as a vehicle for stimulating learners to think (Barrett, 1989) and reflect (Zimmerman, 1989) is also of significance in furthering the constructivist potential of the CAVE.

At each learning opportunity in the program in the CAVE, students' existing ideas are reformatted in light of new knowledge gained, eventually leading to the entrenching of a firmer concept base on the topic. The immersive experience in the knowledge environment of the CAVE is also an additional factor in formatting the knowledge construct of students in constructivist ways. Additionally, the mediation of the learning experience by the pedagogical agent in the form of the lead user provides opportunities for students to attain a firmer grasp of the scientific principles following their initiation into the topic by their school teacher.

CAVE Experience for the Public

For the public, the CAVE program generally focuses on the virtual field experience. It facilitates a good introduction to the capabilities of the system without the need to embed traditional pedagogical elements in the presentation. The latter can, in fact, be heavy going for the general public—another reason why the program on the molecular structure of water is generally not screened for them. There is no audio commentary for this program, and the lead user provides navigational assistance to participants as well as demonstrates the capability of the system in this environment.

The intent behind the offering of the CAVE experience to the public on a showtime basis is to put in place an additional attraction on top of the regular offerings at the Singapore Science Center. With the mushrooming of new attractions, competition from existing attractions and the lure of home entertainment programs, institutions such as science centers face a constant challenge in increasing visitor numbers. The availability of a leading-edge research tool, found only in research establishments and universities, has been found to be a strong selling point in drawing people to a public domain in order to experience the hi-tech attraction for the cost of an admission ticket; there is no extra cost imposed for the CAVE experience.

Affective Dimension of Learning in the CAVE

In a science center environment, the affective dimension of learning is generally more important because of the informal approaches used. Examples of affective processes include play experiences, increased level of engagement, and enhanced scope of interactivity. There is support in the educational literature on the need to also foster affective gains in the learning process in the overall educational development of students (Koran, 1984). The use of the CAVE in contributing toward affective enhancements in the learning process among students can be seen from the high weightage assigned by both groups for Item 1 in the evaluation instrument. In fact, the mean for Item 1 is the highest among all items for both groups—4.40 for the Secondary 3 pupils and 4.27 for the Secondary 1 pupils.

Conclusion

The creation of new user interfaces to aid conceptual and functional understanding of a scientific concept among students contributes significantly to the attainment of cognitive outcomes of the learning process. Empowerment through the mediation of technology can augment the traditional pedagogical approaches in this regard.

The addition of a CAVE to the Singapore Science Center has enabled it to offer a new and exciting science-based program that leverages the attributes of creativity and innovation in order to make learning fun and enjoyable. By tying with schools for the offering of this program, an opportunity is afforded to complement the traditional learning approach and further cement links with the education system.

There is no doubt that multimedia technologies present tremendous potential for use in educational and training settings. Permitting visualization of complex phenomena and simulation of discrete processes on a variety of topics and subjects, the scope for interactivity and immersion in the 3-D environment of the CAVE is a novelty factor that has been capitalized to good effect in extending its educational potential. Immersion in the virtual environment has the advantage that students connect with the knowledge representation more purposefully and, in the process, cognize some of the epistemological connotations inherent in these environments more effectively.

The present study adds to the growing body of literature supporting the educational potential of the CAVE for school students, for example, the studies by Roussos et al. (1998) on using the CAVE as a learning medium in biological domains with high conceptual and social content; the work of Moher et al. (1999) in using the CAVE to promote collaborative investigations in biology among students; and the research of Johnson et al. (2000) in using the CAVE for teaching the solar system and the human heart.

Our study further reiterates the point that for technology to mediate the learning experience, it has got to be embedded in a pedagogical framework, where the learning outcomes and educational goals are clearly articulated from curricular considerations. Without this requirement, there is the possibility of the session degenerating to an entertainment session bereft of educational value.

Recognizing the success of the CAVE program on water with schools, plans are underway to develop an extensive range of programs on various topics in order to aid the efforts of schools—an immediate priority is the topic of DNA. Students have expressed positive feedback on their desire to learn more science through the CAVE.

Our experience shows that for the CAVE to be used as an educational facility for schools, it is desirable to locate it in a science center or even a science museum. Such institutions make natural partners with schools because of the convergence of aspects of their mission objectives. Given the cost and technical expertise needed to man such hi-tech facilities, it is neither viable nor desirable for schools to have such facilities. The placement of this facility in a public access setting contributes to better utilization as well as helps the host institution serve the needs of schools more effectively.

References

Barrett, A. (1988). Introduction: A new paradigm for writing with and for the computer. In E. Barrett (Ed.), *Text, context and hypertext*. Cambridge, MA: The MIT Press.

Barry, K., & King, L. (1993). *Beginning teaching*. Sydney: Social Science Press.

Bartlett, F. C. (1932). *Remembering*. Cambridge, MA: Cambridge University Press.

Broas, P. (2001). Advantages and problems of CAVE: Visualization for design purposes. *Virtual Prototyping Seminar*, Otaniemi, Finland.

Bryson, S. (1992). Virtual reality takes on real physics applications. *Computers in Physics, 6*(4), 346–352.

Bryson, S. (1996). Virtual reality in scientific visualization. *Communications of the ACM, 39*(5), 62–71.

Burdea, G. (1996). *Force and touch feedback for virtual reality*. New York: John Wiley & Sons.

Chung, J. C., Harris, M. R., Brooks, F. P., Fuchs, H., Kelley, M. T., Hughes, J., Ouh-young, M., Cheung, C., Holloway, R. L., & Pique, M. (1989). Exploring virtual worlds with head-mounted displays. *Proceedings of the SPIE Conference on three-dimensional visualization and display technologies*, 1083 (pp. 42–52).

Cronbach, L. J. (1951). Coefficient alpha and the internal structure of tests. *Psychometrika*, *16*, 297–334.

Cruz-Neira, C., Leigh, J., Papka, M., Barnes, C., Cohen, S., Das, S., Engelman, R., Hudson, R., Roy, T., Siegel, L., Vasilakis, C., DeFanti, T. A., & Sandin, J. (1993b). Scientists in wonderland: A report on visualization applications in the CAVE virtual reality environment. *Proceedings of the IEEE Symposium on Research Frontiers in Virtual Reality* (pp. 59–66).

Cruz-Neira, C., Sandin, D., & and DeFanti, T. (1993a). Surround-screen projection-based virtual reality: The design and implementation of the CAVE. *Proceedings of ACM SIGGRAPH '93* (pp. 134–142).

Cruz-Neira, C., Sandin, D., DeFanti, T., Kenyon, R., & Hart, J. (1992). The CAVE: Audio visual experience automatic virtual environment. *Communications of the ACM*, June, 64–72.

DeFanti, T., Sandin, J., & Cruz-Neira, C. (1993). A room with a view. *IEEE Spectrum*, October, 30–33.

De Jong, T., van Joolingen, W., Swaak, J., Veermans, K., Limbach, R., King, S., & Gureghian, D. (1998). Self-directed learning in simulation-based discovery environments. *Journal of Computer-Assisted Learning*, *14*, 235–246.

Edelson, D., Gordon, D., & Pear, R. (1999). Addressing the challenges of inquiry-based learning through technology and curriculum design. *Journal of Learning Sciences*, *8*, 391–450.

Guzdial, M. (1995). Software-realized scaffolding to facilitate programs for science learning. *Interactive Learning Environments*, *4*, 1–44.

Jackson, R., & Winn, W. (1999). Collaboration and learning in immersive virtual environments. In C. M. Hondley, & J. Roshelle (Eds.), *Proceedings of Computer Support for Collaborative Learning '99* (pp. 260–264).

Johnson, A., Moher, T., Cho, Y. J., Lin, Y. J., Hass, D., & Kim, J. (2002). Augmenting elementary school education with VR. *IEEE Computer Graphics and Applications*, March/April, 6–9.

Johnson, A., Moher, T., Leigh, J., & Lin, Y. J. (2000). Quickworlds: Teacher-driven VR worlds in an elementary school curriculum. *Proceedings of ACM SIGGRAPH '00 Education Program* (pp. 60–63).

Johnson, A., Moher, T., Ohlsson, S., & Gillingham, M. (1999). The round earth project: Collaborative VR for conceptual learning. *IEEE Computer Graphics and Applications*, *19*(6), 60–69.

Johnson, A., Sandon, D., Dawe, G., DeFanti, T., Pape, D., Qiu, Z., Thongrong, S., & Plepys, D. (2000). Developing the PARIS: Using the CAVE to prototype a new VR display. *Proceedings of IPT 2000: Immersive Projection Technology Workshop*, Ames, Los Angeles.

Karlsson, M. R. (1996). *Motivating at-risk students*. Westminster, CA: Teacher Created Materials.

Koran, J., Morrison, L., Lehman, J., Koran, M., & Gandara, L. (1984). Attention and curiosity in museums. *Journal of Research in Science Teaching*, *21*(4), 357–363.

Lascara, C., Wheless, G., Cox, D., Patterson, R., Levy, S., Johnson, A., Leigh, J., & Kappor, A. (1999). Tele-immersive virtual environments for collaborative knowledge discovery. *Advanced Simulation Technologies Conference*, San Diego, California.

Moher, T., Johnsoon, A., Yongjoo, C., & Ya-Ju, L. (1999). Observation-based ambient environments. In B. Fisherman, & S. O'Conno-Divekbiss (Eds.), *Proceedings of the Fourth International Conference of the Learning Sciences* (pp. 238–145).

Nunnaly, J. (1978). *Psychometric theory*. New York: McGraw Hill.

Pape, D. (1996). A hardware independent virtual reality development system. *Computer Graphics and Applications*, *16*(4), 44–47.

Pape, D., Anstey, J., Carter, B., Leigh, J., Roussous, M., and Portlock, T. (2000). Virtual heritage at iGrid 2000. *Proceedings of INET 2001*, Stockholm, Sweden.

Piaget, J. (1977). *The development of thought: Equilibration of cognitive structures*. New York: Viking.

Roussos, M., Johnson, A., Leigh, J., Vaslakis, C., Barnes, C., & Moher, T. (1997). NICE: Combining constructivism, narrative and collaboration in a virtual environment. *Computer Graphics*, *31*(3), 62–63.

Roy, M. (1998). Using virtual reality modeling and CAVE technology as a construction pre-planning technique with a focus on building system integration design coordination. M.Sc. thesis, Virginia Tech., USA.

Shu, C. Y. (2001). Synergy of constructivism and hypermedia from three constructivist perspectives—social, semiotic and cognitive. *J. Educ. Comp. Res.*, *24*(4), 321–361.

Tan, W. H. L., & Subramaniam, R. (1998). Developing nations need to popularize science. *New Scientist*, 2139, 52.

Tan, W. H. L., & Subramaniam, R. (2003a). Science and technology centers as agents for promoting science culture in developing nations. *Int. J. Tech. Management*, *25*(5), 413–426.

Tan, W. H. L., & Subramaniam, R. (2003b). Virtual science centers: Web-based environments for promotion of non formal science education. In A. K. Aggarwal (Ed.), *Web-based education: Learning from experience* (pp. 308–329). Hershey, PA: Idea Group Inc.

Tan, W. H. L., & Subramaniam, R. (2003d). Earth systems science and global science literacy: The Singapore experience. In V. J. Mayer (Ed.), *Implementing global science literacy* (pp. 167–186). Ohio: Earth Systems Education Program, The Ohio State University Press.

Tan, W. H. L., Subramaniam, R., & Aggarwal, A. K. (2003c). Virtual science centers: A new genre of learning in web-based promotion of science education. *Proceedings of the 36th Hawaii International Conference on System Sciences*, Hawaii, January 6–9, 2003. California: IEEE Computer Society.

Taxen, G., & Naeve, A. (2001). CyberMath: Exploring open issues in VR-based learning. *Proceedings of ACM SIGGRAPH '01 Education Program* (pp. 49–51).

Taylor, P. (1998). Constructivism: Value added. In B. J. Fraser, & K. Tobin (Eds.), *The international handbook of science education* (pp. 1111–1123). Dordecht: Kluwer Academic Publishers.

Teitel, M. (1990). The eyephone: A head-mounted stereo display. *Proceedings of the SPIE Conference on Stereoscopic Displays and Applications*, 1256 (pp. 168–171).

Zimmerman, B. J. (1989). Models of self-regulated learning and academic achievement. In B. J. Zimmerman, & D. H. Schunk (Eds.), *Self-regulated learning and academic achievement: Theory, research and practice*. New York: Springer-Verlag.

Chapter XVII

Multimedia Learning Designs:
Using Authentic Learning Interactions in Medicine, Dentistry and Health Sciences

Mike Keppell, Hong Kong Institute of Education, Hong Kong

Jane Gunn, The University of Melbourne, Australia

Kelsey Hegarty, The University of Melbourne, Australia

Vivienne O'Connor, The University of Queensland, Australia

Ngaire Kerse, University of Auckland, New Zealand

Karen Kan, The University of Melbourne, Australia

Louise Brearley Messer, The University of Melbourne, Australia

Heather Bione, The University of Melbourne, Australia

Abstract

This chapter describes the learning design of two multimedia modules which complement a problem-based learning health sciences curriculum. The use of student-centred, authentic learning design frameworks guide academics and instructional designers in the creative pedagogical design of learning resources. The chapter describes the educational context, learning design of two multimedia modules and suggests a number of strategies for improving the design and development of multimedia resources.

Introduction

This chapter examines the instructional design of two multimedia modules that utilize authentic learning interactions to teach medical, dental, and health science concepts. Interactive multimedia modules complement the broader goals of a problem-based learning curriculum and enrich the health science curriculum by addressing conceptually difficult content areas. It is essential that the learning design (Koschmann, Kelson, Feltovich, & Barrows, 1996) of self-directed learning modules "should be informed from its inception by some model of learning and instruction" (p. 83). The use of student-centered learning approaches is becoming increasingly popular in medicine, dentistry, and health science curricula as the teaching of problem-based learning and case-based learning assure a close match with real-world clinical cases. This chapter outlines the educational context and then examines two multimedia modules that utilize a case-based learning design. As educators, it is essential that we articulate our learning design for educational interventions from the earliest stages so that we are able to integrate the module into the educational setting and also provide a framework for evaluating the innovation (Koschmann, Kelson, Feltovich, & Barrows, 1996).

Educational Context

The medical course at the University of Melbourne had traditionally been taught using a discipline-based approach. Internal review mechanisms and student feedback in recent years had highlighted a number of deficiencies in the traditional course. In broad terms, these included insufficient integration between the basic and clinical sciences, insufficient attention to teaching communication skills, problem-solving skills, and social aspects of health, and an overload of biomedical detail that was duplicated in subjects originating from different departments. In an effort to remedy these deficiencies and also to incorporate current theories of medical education, a new medical curriculum was introduced in 1999. The pedagogical model for the new medical curriculum incorporates elements of problem-based learning (PBL) and self-directed learning (SDL) (Koschmann, Kelson, Feltovich, & Barrows, 1996). The primary focus of learning in semesters 2 through 5 is through medical problems (known as problems of the week), which are presented to students in small group tutorial settings. A key feature of the new curriculum is the horizontal integration across disciplines and the vertical integration of clinical situations with basic scientific material (Keppell, Kennedy, Elliott, & Harris, 2001).

The transformation of a medical course by the faculty involved considerable analysis, planning, investment of resources, staffing, and fundamental changes to teaching and learning approaches. Changing a traditional teaching and learning approach to a PBL approach represented a major pedagogical shift for academics within the faculty. In addition to this fundamental change, the curriculum also placed considerable emphasis on Web-based and multimedia teaching resources. This major departure from a traditional medical curriculum required support from academic staff across a wide range of diverse disciplines. A number of researchers have examined the importance of context in supporting major change like the faculty's curricular transformation. According to Altschuld and Witkin (2000), the following was found:

> ...implementation of innovations required awareness on the part of and strong support from administrators, a dedicated and critical mass of staff working with the change, communication channels that were frequently used by that staff to promote change, and a climate that makes nonadopters feel as though they are "out of it" unless they begin to adopt or move forward (p. 182)

These factors will make or break the implementation of the innovation.

Use of Information and Communication Technology in the Curriculum

The use of information and communication technology (ICT) is an important feature of the problem-based learning curriculum. ICT is utilized to deliver medical content in two ways. These include the use of the Web-based problem of the week embedded in the TopClass learning framework and stand-alone, computer-facilitated learning modules. The TopClass learning framework provides a central access point for students to enter the online course work, complete self-assessment tests, view class announcements, participate in discussion groups, and send and receive messages from teachers or peers. In the first three years of the medical curriculum, the medical student needs to complete 60 problems of the week. Approximately 120 problems of the week will be required for the entire curriculum. Self-directed learning resources, in the form of computer-facilitated learning modules, are also required to support the core content of the problems. Approximately 70 modules are in use or are currently under development within the faculty, and it is envisaged that 100 modules will be required to support the curriculum in its entirety.

Self-directed learning resources have a unique role in the curriculum. These resources are often initiated by clinicians who teach conceptually difficult content areas. A conceptually difficult content area (usually one to two hours) is often identified and developed by academics and multimedia teams. For instance, a module on pediatric dentistry focusing on a diabetic child complements a dental curriculum; a module on sensitive examination technique (SET) cervical screening is used to complement the teaching of cervical cancer. These resources may be used independently of the PBL curricula or they may be developed to complement the content within a problem of the week. Often, these computer-facilitated learning modules support the core content of the problems. Figure 1 portrays the use of ICT in the curriculum and the use of computer technology to complement, enhance, and support teaching and learning in the curriculum. The focus of this chapter is on the self-directed learning component of Figure 1.

Figure 1: Use of computer technology in the medical curriculum

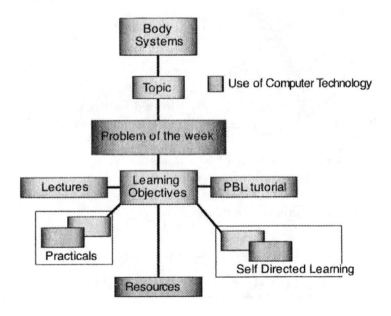

Figure 2: Multimedia and online modules utilized within the faculty

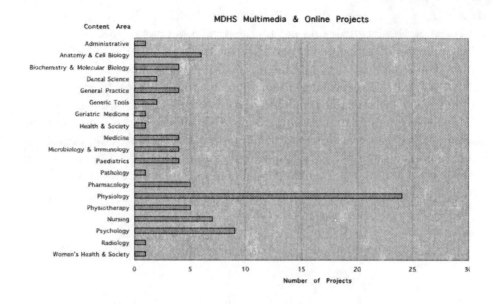

Multimedia and Online Modules

Figure 2 shows the variety of modules developed by the faculty as of December 2002. Each content area is outlined with the number of modules per discipline area. This graphic provides an overview of the diversity of content areas that utilize multimedia to enhance teaching and learning. Many modules utilize student-centered teaching and learning approaches. In some instances, instructional designers have worked with the academics to develop their module utilizing constructivist teaching and learning principles, including case-based learning. The following aspects of this chapter examine the application of these principles to the design of two multimedia modules.

Student-Centered Learning

There has been a trend away from teacher-directed instructional approaches to student-centered learning environments. Jonassen and Land (2000) compare the two methods in Table 1. In particular, in student-centered learning environments, contextualized, authentic, and situated learning interactions are emphasized. These principles have been adopted in the learning design of the two specific

Table 1: A comparison of instructive and student-centered learning environments

Instruction	Student-Centered Learning Environments
Transmission, acquisition	Interpretation, construction
Mastery, performance	Meaning making
External reality	Internal reality
Abstract, symbolic	Contextualized, authentic, experiential
Individually interpreted	Socially negotiated, coconstructed
Individual	Collaborative
Encoding, retention, retrieval	Articulation and reflection
Symbolic reasoning	Situated learning
Psychology	Anthropology, sociology, ethnography
Laboratory	in situ
Well-structured	Ill-structured
Decontexualized	Embedded in experience

Source: Adapted from Jonassen and Land (2000).

modules that will be discussed in this chapter, which utilize authentic learning interactions.

Learning Design

Although, as stated in Herrington, Oliver, and Reeves (2002), "it is impossible to design truly authentic learning experiences" (p. 60), we attempted to develop learning experiences that would complement and enhance the professional practice of doctors and dentists. We considered a range of factors including the intent of the curriculum, lecturer teaching style, and learning outcomes in designing the multimedia modules. Authentic learning experiences, according to Jonassen, Mayes, and McAleese (1992), are "those which are problem- or case-based, that immerse the learner in the situation requiring him or her to acquire skills or knowledge in order to solve the problem or manipulate the situation" (p. 235). And, according to Young (1993), "Authentic tasks enable students to immerse themselves in the culture of the academic domain, much like an apprentice" (p. 43). Authentic learning contexts such as the virtual dental clinic and cervical screening module may have a number of advantages over more decontextualized teaching and learning settings. The authentic nature of the technology-enhanced, student-centered learning environment may anchor knowledge in authentic contexts. An effective learning environment enables learners to use its resources and tools to process more deeply and extend thinking (Jonassen, 1996; Jonassen & Reeves, 1996; Kozma, 1987).

In order to create realistic learning experiences for the students, it was essential that we immerse the student in authentic cases to guide our creation of the two modules. Herrington, Oliver, and Reeves (2002) outlined 10 characteristics of authentic activities. These comprise the following:

- Authentic activities have real-world relevance.

- Authentic activities are ill-defined, requiring students to define the tasks and subtasks needed to complete the activity.

- Authentic activities comprise complex tasks to be investigated by students over a sustained period of time.

- Authentic activities provide the opportunity for students to examine the task from different perspectives, using a variety of resources.

- Authentic activities provide the opportunity to collaborate.

- Authentic activities provide the opportunity to reflect.

- Authentic activities can be integrated and applied across different subject areas and lead beyond domain-specific outcomes.

- Authentic activities are seamlessly integrated with assessment.

- Authentic activities create polished products valuable in their own right rather than as preparation for something else.

- Authentic activities allow competing solutions and diversity of outcome.

Two modules will be analyzed to demonstrate how the above principles have been utilized to design authentic learning interactions. In the first instance, Tables 2 and 3 outline an overview of the principles and their concrete applications.

Table 2: Authentic learning design principles and their concrete applications within the design of the virtual dental clinic (see Figures 3 and 4)

Principle (Herrington, Oliver, & Reeves, 2002)	Concrete Application (Virtual Dental Clinic)
Authentic activities have real-world relevance.	• The clinical case on diabetes was developed in conjunction with experts from medicine and dentistry. • The virtual dental clinic was designed using photographs of the actual clinical setting. Photographs of the clinic were used to build the setting in order to keep the real-world relevance. • Actual case information from real-life patients was used to develop the scenario. This clinical information included actual photographs, radiographs, and medical case information in relation to a child with diabetes.
Authentic activities are ill-defined, requiring students to define the tasks and subtasks needed to complete the activity.	• The diabetes scenario is presented to the students as an actual case. They complete sections on pathophysiology, medical management, and dental management and then apply their knowledge in a realistic case. • There is no step-by-step sequence to completing the clinical case. Students are expected to determine the most appropriate strategies and sequence for completing the treatment plan. • The case information is accessible in any order. The students must make a decision as to the information they require at a particular point in the clinical case.
Authentic activities comprise complex tasks to be investigated by students over a sustained period of time	• The clinical case requires students to concentrate their energy toward the case for a period of approximately 45–60 minutes. • It is expected that the student would return to the case over a period of time as their knowledge is elaborated in the area.

Authentic activities provide the opportunity for students to examine the task from different perspectives, using a variety of resources.	• A wide variety of resources assist the student in obtaining an in-depth examination of the case.
	• These resources include the following:
	  o Seven clinical photographs
	  o Three radiographs
	  o Patient history
	  o Medical history
	  o Dental history
	  o Height/weight
	  o Social history
	  o Expert opinions from a teacher, psychologist, and endocrinologist.

Authentic activities provide the opportunity to collaborate.	• This module was created as a self-directed learning activity that is used by the professors in a lab setting. • Students complete the module and are provided with expert assistance as required. • Collaboration with other students is not explicit, although teaching staff could complete collaborative group activities at certain points in the tutorial.
Authentic activities provide the opportunity to reflect.	• Explicit reflective activities have not been included in the design of the module. • The use of questions immediately following the presentation of the virtual dental clinic may encourage students to backtrack and re-examine information. • The use of an electronic reflective journal at appropriate points would foster reflection. This feature may be considered at a future time.
Authentic activities can be integrated and applied across different subject areas and lead beyond domain-specific outcomes.	• This case is focused on dental students who will learn generic case-based strategies. • Generic skills of observation, analysis, synthesis, and professional practice would be fostered.
Authentic activities are seamlessly integrated with assessment.	• This is a major strength of the virtual dental clinic. • Students complete a treatment plan that contains all treatment procedures used by an Australian dentist. • The treatment plan encourages the students to re-examine the clinical information (case information, photographs, radiographs) and complete a legitimate treatment plan for the diabetes child. • Students submit their treatment plan and compare their plan to an expert treatment plan. • Students can confirm their treatment plan or re-examine the clinical photographs and radiographs to determine where they may have been incorrect in their initial judgement.
Authentic activities create polished products valuable in their own right rather than as preparation for something else.	• This module is valuable in its own right as a clinical case. Future cases may be developed around the virtual dental clinic. • The clinical case is also the fundamental interaction utilized by the dentist in clinical practice.
Authentic activities allow competing solutions and diversity of outcome.	• Students examine the clinical information and create a treatment plan based on their clinical judgement. • Students may clearly perceive all relevant clinical information and complete the case successfully. However, the design of the case encourages the student to backtrack and re-examine the clinical information and to adjust their treatment plans after submitting to obtain an expert treatment plan.

Table 3: Authentic learning principles and their concrete application in the design of the SET module (see Figures 5, 6, and 7)

Principle (Herrington, Oliver, & Reeves, 2002)	Concrete Application (Cervical Screening Module)
Authentic activities have real-world relevance.	• The clinical case on cervical screening was developed in conjunction with experts in medicine from three different universities in Australia and New Zealand. • State health departments involved in cervical screening also participated in the design of the module. • Topic 1 examines five cases from different cultural and ethnic backgrounds and the barriers that differ across these cultures. • Topics 2, 3, and 4 follow one woman into the communication, examination, and follow-up stages. • The virtual clinic was based on an actual clinical setting. Photographs of the clinic were used to build the setting in order to keep the real-world relevance. • Actual case information from real patients was used to build the scenario. This included actual photographs and video and case information in relation to medical history.
Authentic activities are ill-defined, requiring students to define the tasks and subtasks needed to complete the activity.	• The cervical screening cases presented in Topic 1 require the student to examine the different types of barriers of different women from different ethnic and cultural backgrounds. • Students should begin to understand the influence of personal factors, previous experience with cervical screening, and cultural norms in relation to treating different women in the clinical setting. • Questions are open-ended, which requires the student to examine a variety of information resources to determine appropriate responses. • The case information is available for students to access as needed. A glossary and library provide additional resources for examination.
Authentic activities comprise complex tasks to be investigated by students over a sustained period of time	• The clinical case requires students to concentrate their energy toward the case for a period of approximately 3–4 hours. • It is expected that the student would return to the case over a period of time as their knowledge is elaborated in the area. • The video examples of communication and examination provide a means for the student to view best-practice examples before clinical practice and as revision after clinical practice. Used in these two ways, the student should be able to reflect on appropriate strategies for improving the clinical practice of this sensitive area.

Authentic activities provide the opportunity for students to examine the task from different perspectives, using a variety of resources.	• A wide variety of resources assist the students in obtaining an in-depth examination of the case.
	• These resources include the following:
	  o Clinical photographs
	  o Video of ideal communication between the doctor and the woman
	  o Video of ideal examination procedures
	  o Patient history
	  o Medical history
	  o Social history
	  o Expert opinions from practicing doctors
	  o Definitions of key words in the glossary
	  o Extended information in the library
	  o Expert feedback

Authentic activities provide the opportunity to collaborate.	• This module was created as a self-directed learning activity and as an adjunct to the cervical screening program in Victoria. • It is expected that participants in the clinical screening program will discuss key issues and concerns using aspects of the module as a trigger for activities. • Collaboration with other students is not explicit at this point in time, although teaching staff could complete collaborative group activities at certain points in the tutorial.
Authentic activities provide the opportunity to reflect.	• Explicit reflective activities have been included in the design of the module. • A reflective notebook allows the students to document reflections and ideas throughout the module. This can be saved as an electronic file or printed out at the end of the session. The use of an electronic reflective journal at appropriate points would foster reflection. • Open-ended questions require the student to complete a detailed response before proceeding. This can be saved as an electronic file for future examination. • The use of questions immediately following the presentation of the video segments may encourage students to backtrack and re-examine information.
Authentic activities can be integrated and applied across different subject areas and lead beyond domain-specific outcomes.	• The module examines a difficult and sensitive area in which students may experience some awkwardness. • It is hoped that students will begin to learn skills in empathy and improve communication skills that can be applied to other sensitive areas in medical clinical practice, such as breast examinations. • Generic skills of observation, analysis, synthesis, and professional behavior would be fostered.
Authentic activities are seamlessly integrated with assessment.	• Formal assessment has not been determined. Future implementation will determine this assessment. • Self-assessment activities are embedded throughout the module. Students are asked to complete activities after viewing each video segment.
Authentic activities create polished products valuable in their own right rather than as preparation for something else.	• This module is valuable in its own right as a clinical case. • The clinical case is also the fundamental interaction utilized by the medical doctor in clinical practice.
Authentic activities allow competing solutions and diversity of outcome.	• Students examine the clinical information and create a schema for future medical consultation. • The design of the case encourages the student to backtrack and re-examine the clinical information.

Authentic Activities have Real-World Relevance

In designing the two modules, we considered the "real-world tasks of professionals" (Herrington, Oliver, & Reeves, 2002, p. 62) as a basis for the module. For instance, in the field of pediatric dentistry, there are concerns that dental students are not competent in combining preventive and restorative management philosophies while integrating diagnosis and treatment planning (Suivinen, Messer, & Franco, 1998). Declining patient numbers and a need to focus on integration suggested that the use of multimedia case simulations were a viable alternative, as they replicate the dental clinic without requiring live patients. A module on diabetes and its implications for dentistry provides an opportunity to develop and consolidate the concept of integrated patient care. The diabetes case created unique challenges for the design team. A virtual pediatric diabetic patient was created in order to address the difficulty of obtaining relevant patient photo-

Figure 3: Virtual dental clinic

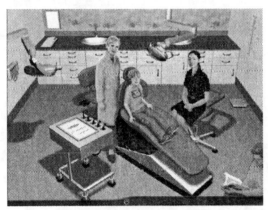

Figure 4: Virtual dental office

graphs. Our explicit learning design focused on increasing the level of student engagement with the content by contextualizing the scenario content within a virtual dental clinic (Keppell, Kan, Messer, & Bione, 2002).

The SET project attempts to examine a real-world clinical case of cervical screening so that medical students can decide which women should be screened on the basis of evidence-based screening recommendations. It also discusses the barriers to cervical screening from the patient's and doctor's perspectives and effective communication skills to explain how a Pap test is performed. Videos are sequenced to explain and demonstrate the steps involved in taking a Pap test and how to communicate the results to a woman. Currently, medical students have few opportunities to observe or perform Pap tests, and current literature documents negative screening experiences by women as a major barrier to participation in the cervical screening program. Participation in a cervical screening program has been shown to prevent most cases of cervical cancer (Keppell, Gunn, Hegarty, Madden, O'Connor, Kerse, & Judd, 2003).

Figure 5: Situated learning environment utilized for the SET Project—1

Figure 6: Situated learning environment utilized for the SET Project—2

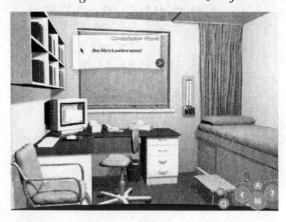

Figure 7: Situated learning environment utilized for the SET Project—3

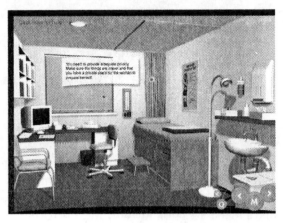

Authentic Activities are Ill-Defined, Requiring Students to Define the Tasks and Subtasks Needed to Complete the Activity

In the SET project, we specifically attempted to engage the students by providing cases that the student would need to examine from a clinical perspective. Topic 1 examines five mini-cases and provides perspectives on the barriers of cervical screening from the woman's different cultural background. Learners may have insufficient knowledge and will need to examine additional clinical information in the form of a glossary of key medical terms and the library that provides detailed information about cervical screening. This additional information may assist the student in interpreting and analyzing each case more effectively. Students can

Figure 8: Glossary utilized in the SET module

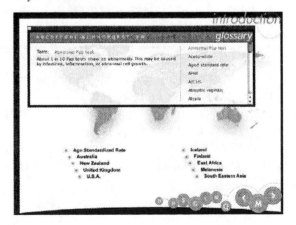

identify their own knowledge deficiencies and supplement their ideas via the additional resources provided (see Figure 8).

Authentic Activities Comprise Complex Tasks to be Investigated by Students over a Sustained Period of Time

SET will be used by universities in Australia and New Zealand to introduce the concepts of cervical screening and intimate examinations in a consistent way that emphasizes the importance of sensitive communication and examination skills. It should be noted that many students are nervous about performing intimate examinations, and the SET module will attempt to demystify the clinical process. Because the module focuses on communication skills in conjunction with clinical skills, students will need to examine the module over a period of time. Initially, students may obtain an overview of the cervical screening pathway before undertaking clinical practice. They may also revise certain sections after clinical practice. While practicing as a general practitioner, the doctor may revisit appropriate sections of the module and examine best-practice processes and procedures in the field. For this reason, the four to five hour module will require sustained attention over a period of time and for different purposes. Specifically, the SET module will be utilized in different ways in the medical program of Melbourne, Queensland, and Auckland. The module will be used to compliment face-to-face teaching as well as allow students to explore the "learning loops" provided on SET both in the tutorial and self-directed learning (SDL) setting. The SET module will be available for students to use in the computer labs/PBL rooms at each site.

Authentic Activities Provide the Opportunity for Students to Examine the Task from Different Perspectives, Using a Variety of Resources

The use of different cases provides the students with an ability to examine different barriers that may affect cervical screening. The library resources also provide additional information and a variety of resources that should assist the student (Herrington, Oliver, & Reeves, 2002) to "examine the problem from a variety of theoretical and practical perspectives, rather than allowing a single perspective that learners must imitate to be successful" (p. 281) (see Figures 9 and 10).

Figure 9: Clinical visuals and radiographs that can be enlarged for further detail within the virtual dental clinic

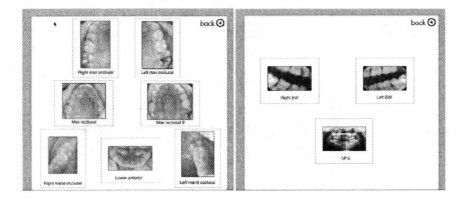

Figure 10: Library resources utilized by the student for additional clinical information about cervical screening

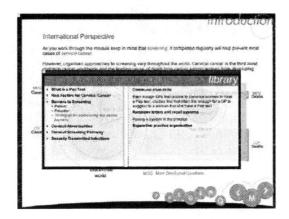

Authentic Activities are Ill-Defined, Requiring Students to Define the Tasks and Subtasks Needed to Complete the Activity

Both modules examine complex content areas in the areas of dentistry and medicine. Due to the complexity of the content, a range of resources provides definitions of key terms and more elaborate content in the library. Key dental, medical, and physiological concepts are defined in a glossary. Users can choose to browse all glossary terms or select specific terms that require clarification at the relevant point in the module. In addition, resources are provided in a library section in the SET module. The virtual dental clinic has a range of clinical images and case information available within the clinical setting, allowing students to access as required in the examination of the dental case. We specifically attempt to engage the students by providing cases that the student will need to examine from a clinical perspective. This means that they may need to search for relevant content in other sections of the module to achieve a deep understanding of the content.

Authentic Activities Comprise Complex Tasks to be Investigated by Students over a Sustained Period of Time

Each module focuses on 1 to 3 hours of difficult dental, clinical, and physiological content that is used to complement face-to-face teaching. The modules will also be used to support lectures by allowing lecturers to recommend that students examine the self-directed learning module located in a lab setting. The students may also be asked to utilize the modules as a revision tool before examinations. Because the modules focus on conceptually difficult content, they will require multiple exposure and viewing by the students. For example, students can review communication practices before they complete cervical screening in a clinical setting and then after clinical practice to review their communication and examination methods. Dental students can reinforce clinical treatment protocols in treating a pediatric dental patient by working through a legitimate case on diabetes.

Authentic Activities Provide the Opportunity for Students to Examine the Task from Different Perspectives, Using a Variety of Resources

Within the virtual dental clinic, we provide multiple entry points into the clinical information. This allows the user to explore the clinic and obtain the necessary clinical information about the patient. We wanted the student to "criss-cross the landscape of knowledge" in order to obtain information that will enable them to complete the relevant treatment plan (Young, 1993, p. 46). The user can navigate around the clinic and find information in two ways. By traveling around the clinic, they will find hotspots that provide clinical information. A site map also provides clinical information enabling the student to access patient records (patient information, medical history, height and weight, dental history, and social history), seven clinical slides, three radiographs, and expert information from a teacher, psychologist, and endocrinologist. By providing the necessary scaffolding for the novice learner, we attempt to move the learner toward expert case management (see Figure 11–14).

The use of different cervical screening cases provides the students with an opportunity to examine different barriers that may affect cervical screening. The library resources also provide additional information and a variety of resources

Figure 11: Student response to an open-ended question with an expert answer within the SET project

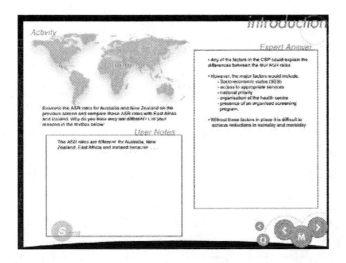

Figure 12: Reflective notebook utilized in the SET project

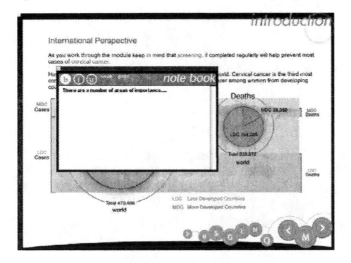

Figure 13: Electronic treatment plan utilized for the diabetes clinical case

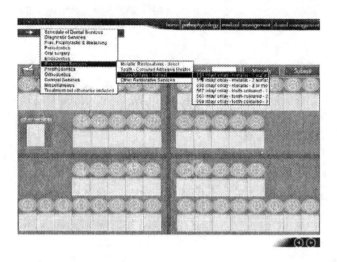

Figure 14: Expert answers for the diabetes treatment plan

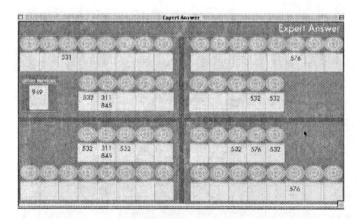

that should assist the student (Herrington, Oliver, & Reeves, 2002) to "examine the problem from a variety of theoretical and practical perspectives, rather than allowing a single perspective that learners must imitate to be successful" (p. 281).

Authentic Activities Provide the Opportunity to Collaborate

Within the virtual dental clinic, the learning context allows the student to learn within an expert-supported learning environment. Lab sessions have been scheduled in which students interact with the module and were supported by pediatric dentists. According to Young (1993), "From the perspective of situated cognition, the teacher's role should be to 'tune the attention' of students to the important aspects of the situation or problem-solving activity, specifically those attributes that are invariant across a range of similar problems and therefore will transfer to many novel situations" (p. 47). The advantage of utilizing expert support is that some information about the case can be clarified and explained by the expert tutors. Their roles in the learning process are as a coach, collaborator, and mentor for student learning. According to Choi and Hannafin (1995), coaching focuses on "directing learner attention, reminding of over-looked steps, providing hints and feedback, challenging and structuring ways to do things, and providing additional tasks, problems, or problematic situations" (p. 62). The SET module will also be used in a collaborative setting.

Authentic Activities Provide the Opportunity to Reflect

Many of the activities embedded throughout the SET module ask the student to type in extended responses to questions. These responses are then submitted, and the student is provided with expert feedback. In addition, these typed responses can be saved by the student and referred to at a later point in their study. This approach was adopted to encourage students to engage with the content and synthesize ideas in their own words. Students are also encouraged to write their own notes and ideas in their personal notebook that can be printed or saved as a Microsoft Word file for review at a later point in the semester.

Authentic Activities can be Integrated and Applied Across Different Subject Areas and Lead Beyond Domain-Specific Outcomes

Students will be able to view the cervical screening cases from different perspectives. Medical students, nurses, and other health professionals should become aware of different disciplinary approaches and roles in cervical screening. Students should begin to see the cervical screening process from the woman's perspective as opposed to the clinical perspective.

The case-based approach utilized in the virtual dental clinic allows students to examine a process for examining other similar cases in dentistry.

Authentic Activities are Seamlessly Integrated with Assessment

Young (1993) suggested that traditional forms of assessment in situated learning may prove to be inadequate. Authentic learning tasks must be assessed using methods that best align with the task. Within the virtual dental clinic, we attempted to do so by asking the students to develop a treatment plan using an electronic version of the protocols utilized in a traditional clinic. Our aim in developing this method of assessment was to foster higher-order thinking skills. We were also conscious of providing a method of formative assessment that allowed (Choi & Hannafin, 1995), "generation of ideas and the presentation of problem-solving processes such as planning, implementing, and revising" (p. 65). In order to simulate the use of the treatment chart, an electronic dental chart was created to allow users to create treatment plans. The electronic dental chart allows the trainee dentist to select a category of dental services and allocate a specific treatment for individual teeth. This chart also allows the user to complete cases and submit information to obtain expert feedback. The expert feedback provides precise information about the treatment protocol for each tooth. The students can compare their treatment plans to the experts' plans and then reenter the virtual clinic to rectify any inaccuracies and misconceptions. This concept of authentic assessment tasks is essential in the instructional design of authentic learning tasks. As stated in Young (1993), "Assessment should be a seamless, continuous part of the activity (a learning/assessment situation)" (p. 48). The final exam paper also mirrors the authentic learning task in the multimedia package by utilizing a case-based learning approach.

Although not a formal part of assessment, the SET module will be gradually utilized in all parts of the medical curriculum. Activities have been embedded that reflect real-world decisions and clinical encounters. Students will be given the opportunity to complete a number of on-screen sequencing and clinical interpretation tasks. To assess whether they are able to identify the barriers to cervical screening, they will be required to respond to a number of questions relating to the video sequence. Student assessment will be via the above self-assessment activities and tutor feedback during the tutorial setting. As the assessment is developed, we will utilize principles as outlined by Young (1993).

Authentic Activities Create Polished Products Valuable in Their Own Right rather than as Preparation for Something Else

Both modules are polished products in their own right, which focus on specific content relevant for treatment in dentistry and cervical screening. By studying each of the modules, the students will learn in-depth knowledge about the topic. Because the modules focus on a difficult content area, they act as stand-alone modules or complement other aspects of the curriculum. For instance, the SET module will be utilized to complement the existing forms of teaching cervical screening, which include face-to-face settings, video, pelvic models, observation, and clinical practice.

Authentic Activities allow Competing Solutions and Diversity of Outcome

The virtual dental clinic focuses on the examination of clinical information to develop a treatment protocol, whereas the SET module emphasizes communication, process, and procedures in relation to cervical screening. In examining the SET module, students should be able to learn about communication practices that can be transferred to other clinical areas, particularly, of a medically sensitive nature. Students should be able to interpret content in a diversity of ways and begin to assimilate some of these concepts into their own process of completing cervical screening.

Evaluation

An initial evaluation was undertaken to determine user perceptions in relation to the virtual dental clinic. Three practicing pediatric dentists participated in a focus group. A number of insights were gained into the design of the virtual clinic and its authenticity. We examined the match between the actual clinical setting and the virtual dental clinic. It appeared that presenting all relevant clinical information in one session may overwhelm the student:

> *If we think about the diabetes case and ... the virtual clinic, what do you think about that case in terms of how realistic it was...*

It would be quite different. You would probably have more than one appointment and that was quite tricky deciding—on the first day I probably wouldn't do all these things. You could put them under general anaesthetic. Apart from that it was quite difficult if you had to write the whole lot out on the same day you would probably do something after the general anaesthetic get them back two weeks later and say okay, how's the toothbrush going.

Navigation also appeared to be an issue in the virtual clinic. We provided two methods of navigation. These included a site map and hotspots in the clinical setting. Although we provided a brief tutorial for the students, all three students still failed to utilize the hotspot information.

When I moved the mouse it came up and I didn't realise what I could click. I think if you want us to get the picture on the top of the menu, you should have it flashing or something like that. So that it shows up.

Further design work is being undertaken to address this misunderstanding. An animation will be utilized instead of the existing help screens to highlight relevant information in the virtual clinic. Our design attempted to provide an open exploration of the clinic. However, this proved too advanced for the users. Although we provided flexible access to the resources to solve the clinical case, the students still utilized the site map in a traditional top-to-bottom and left-to-right reading pattern as opposed to clicking on information that they considered relevant at that point in the case:

When you went into the office?

I went back to the menu and went to help. I couldn't understand. So then I went back to the other picture and found it by accident. I clicked on the telephone or something.

The sequence of information was also important to the user:

Did you actually read about the teacher; the specialist information?

Don't you think this information should go before the examination? You are talking about the medical history and social history. It should go before the examination.

If it was a referral, you would get a note from a doctor before she actually comes in, which gives you the whole..., and you don't have to look for anything.

Our goal of designing the module so that students would need to revisit some clinical information appeared to be successful in some instances:

Did you go back to the visuals when you were completing the treatment plan?

Did you need any other information at that point?

Patient file, complaints and history. I did use it, but I did go back to the pictures quite a lot. How many times? Three, five times. I think I wrote it down which made it a bit easier. I don't know the numbers so it made it a lot harder.

However, it appeared that the students had difficulty providing a treatment number from the electronic treatment plan as opposed to the usual paper-based booklet. It also appeared that obtaining expert feedback could have been optimized:

Did you all submit and get the expert answers? I didn't get the answers. I went to next. That's why I didn't find the expert.... Maybe it's a good thing to put the expert under next. Down the bottom. So you go to the next phase.

Further evaluation with a subsequent group should also inform the design and provide feedback to the development team. However, it appears that there is a fine line between authentic myth and reality.

Although the SET module has not been formally evaluated, our next step in the process is to complete extensive evaluation on the module from different perspectives. In the first instance, we will evaluate the module with clinicians experienced in the process. Some formative evaluation has already been undertaken with this group. In the second instance, a number of multimedia experts will be asked to evaluate the learning design of the module. Student evaluation will be undertaken over the next 12 months. We are also examining the evaluation of the module in cross-cultural settings to determine its applicability for different international usage. The module examined one woman's journey through the cervical screening process. In the future, we intend to examine modules for different ethnic groups.

Major Problems Encountered

The examination of the two modules within this chapter demonstrates a student-centered approach to their design. They represent rich teaching and learning resources that address conceptually difficult content areas. However, there are also cases of projects that have not been successful in developing viable educational resources. We cannot assume that design and development processes adopted by many development teams are sufficient to assure the success of a project. Burford and Cooper (2000) support this view and suggested that "most academics are not skilled in interface design, multimedia, selecting appropriate technologies for online teaching, nor project management" (p. 207). For this reason, they suggested that "whatever the developmental model, it must be achievable within the confines of established practice and available resources" (p. 209). However, it is important to remember that online and multimedia design and development are highly creative processes. Design and development models help to minimize potential difficulties in projects, but they never eliminate all constraining factors. According to Burford and Cooper (2000), "Whatever the model used, however well defined the process, the development process itself is a diffuse and difficult one. From its first conception to a final product, a development process is fraught with undefinable influences and unpredicted contributing factors" (p. 210). This section examines some of the consistent problems encountered in the transformation of a curriculum with multimedia and online learning:

- A consistent problem encountered in designing and developing multimedia modules is that academic staff members are over ambitious with their goals. Through a process of coaching and educating academic staff, it is possible to change this perception. Because it often requires 300–800 hours of development per course hour, multimedia should only be used for areas where it is appropriate. The virtual dental clinic and the cervical screening module represent conceptually difficult content that warrant the above time and effort on the part of the development team. The first two questions we ask are as follows: Can this be completed using another teaching method? And why multimedia? Technology must enhance the teaching and learning process and should be used for addressing learning misconceptions and complex and difficult content that cannot be easily explained in another form.

- Another common problem is that many academic staff members apply their traditional teaching styles in designing and developing multimedia and online learning. Academic staff often focus on instructivist teaching models in developing their online or multimedia modules. The challenge in this situation is for the instructional designer to provide other pedagogical perspectives and suggest alternative approaches such as case-based reasoning, PBL, and authentic learning environments. There are a number of factors that need to be considered in this situation. For instance: What are the learning outcomes of the module? What pedagogical methods best suit the attainment of these outcomes? It is important to always take an eclectic approach to the teaching and learning process and suggest methods of teaching best suited to the entire learning context. There is a delicate balance between implementing the content expert's approach and coaching the academic in other pedagogical possibilities, which may enhance the learning of the content by the user.

- It is important not to underestimate the time required to design and develop online and multimedia products. As suggested by the above formulas, there must be an excellent pedagogical reason for justifying the resources required for multimedia and online learning.

- Working in teams is both a rewarding and challenging experience. It is important to employ a dedicated manager who can coach the design and development team in appropriate processes, and who has the ability to harness creative energy and deal with the inevitable tensions that arise in creative teams. By focusing on the goal as opposed to personal ownership, tensions can often be dissipated.

A potential bottleneck exists between the content expert and design and development staff (instructional designers, graphic designers, programmers, etc.) in terms of translating content into a form that embodies sound educational design. A process or strategy is required to streamline the interaction between the instructional designer and subject matter expert (Keppell, 2001). One of the most important principles in any project is to clarify the roles and expectations of the client/SME. Many projects fail due to an inappropriate consideration of what the client/SME expects from the project. According to Coscarelli and Stonewater (1979–1980), "An understanding of client psychological types and an ability to differentially respond to various types is a particularly effective designer strategy for relationship building and managing" (p. 16). It is therefore essential to establish a successful working relationship with an SME by determining philosophical assumptions of the SME before beginning the instructional design (Davies, 1975), as "a great deal of what is accomplished depends on the quality of the client–consultant relationship" (p. 351).

Conclusion

Learner-centered approaches emphasize problem-based and case-based learning, which attempt to create realistic learning interactions in order to replicate professional practice. The above discussion demonstrates how authentic learning multimedia modules have been used to complement a medical, dental, and health science curricula. The learning design for each module is carefully articulated in order to provide an insight into the process of instructional design that can be transferred to other learning settings and other content areas. The articulation of the learning design also demonstrates the explicit instructional design decisions that were made in the two modules, each of which are based on a constructivist teaching and learning model. It is also suggested that interactive, media-rich multimedia modules are relevant for difficult content areas or areas where misconceptions may be prevalent in the curriculum. The articulation of this model of teaching and learning allows other designers and researchers to examine the applicability of these designs for their own setting and circumstances.

Acknowledgments

The author wishes to acknowledge the graphic designers on both projects: Jennifer Kirk, Avril Martinelli, Jacqui Jewell, Andrew Bonollo, and Carolyn Casey from the Biomedical Multimedia Unit.

References

Altschuld, J. W., & Witkin, B. R. (2000). *From needs assessment to action: Transforming needs into solution strategies.* Thousand Oaks, CA: Sage Publications, Inc.

Burford, S., & Cooper, L. (2000). Online development using WebCT: A faculty managed process for quality. *Australian Journal of Educational Technology, 16*(3), 201–214.

Choi, J.-I., & Hannifin, M. (1995). Situated cognition and learning environments: Roles, structures, and implications for design. *Educational Technology, Research and Development, 43*(2), 53–69.

Coscarelli, W. C., & Stonewater, J. K. (1979–1980). Understanding psychological styles in instructional development consultation. *Journal of Instructional Development, 3,* 16–22.

Davies, I. K. (1975). Some aspects of a theory of advice: The management of an instructional developer–client, evaluator–client, relationship. *Instructional Science, 3,* 351–373.

Herrington, J., Oliver, R., & Reeves, T. C. (2002). Patterns of engagement in authentic online learning environments. In A. Williamson, C. Gunn, A. Young, & T. Clear (Eds.), *Winds of change in a sea of learning. Proceedings of the 19th Annual Conference of the Australasian Society for Computers in Tertiary Education* (pp. 279–286). Auckland, New Zealand: UNITEC: Institute of Technology.

Jonassen, D. (1996). *Computers in the classroom: Mindtools for Critical Thinking.* Englewood Cliffs, NJ: Merrill.

Jonassen, D., & Land, S. M. (2000). Theoretical foundations of learning environments. Mahwah, NJ: Lawrence Erlbaum.

Jonassen, D., & Reeves, T. (1996). Learning with technology: Using computers as cognitive tools. In D. Jonassen (Ed.), *Handbook of research on educational communication and technology* (pp. 693–719). New York: Scholastic.

Jonassen, D., Mayes, T., & McAleese, R. (1993). A manifesto for a constructivist approach to uses of technology in higher education. In T. M. Duffy, J. Lowyck, & D. H. Jonassen (Eds.), *Designing environments for constructive learning.* Berlin: Springer-Verlag.

Keppell, M. (2001). Optimising instructional designer—Subject matter expert communication in the design and development of multimedia projects. *Journal of Interactive Learning Research, 12*(2/3), 205–223.

Keppell, M., Gunn, J., Hegarty, K., Madden, V., O'Connor, V., Kerse, N., & Judd, T. (2003). Using authentic patient interactions to teach cervical screening to medical students. In D. Lassner, & C. McNaught (Eds.), *Proceedings of ED-Media 2003 World Conference on Educational Multimedia, Hypermedia and Telecommunications* (pp. 1431–1438). Honolulu, Hawaii, Association for the Advancement of Computing in Education.

Keppell, M., Kan, K., Brearley Messer, L., & Bione, H. (2002). Authentic learning interactions: Myth or reality? In A. Williamson, C. Gunn, A. Young, & T. Clear (Eds.), *Winds of change in a sea of learning. Proceedings of the 19th Annual Conference of the Australasian Society for Computers in Tertiary Education* (pp. 349–358). Auckland, New Zealand: UNITEC: Institute of Technology.

Keppell, M., Kennedy, G., Elliott, K., & Harris, P. (2001, April). Transforming traditional curricula: Enhancing medical education through multimedia and web-based resources. *Interactive Multimedia Electronic Journal of Computer-Enhanced Learning (IMEJ)*, *3*(1). Retrieved March 2002 from the World Wide Web: http://imej.wfu.edu/articles/2001/1/index.asp

Koschmann, T., Kelson, A. C., Feltovich, P. J., & Barrows. H. S. (1996). Computer-supported problem-based learning: A principled approach to the use of computers in collaborative learning. In T. Koschmann (Ed.), *Computer supported collaborative learning: Theory and practice in an emerging paradigm.* Mahwah, NJ: Lawrence Erlbaum.

Kozma, R. B. (1987). The implications of cognitive psychology for computer-based learning tools. *Educational Technology, 27*(11), 20–25.

Suivinen, T., Messer, L. B., & Franco, E. (1998). Clinical simulation in teaching pre-clinical dentistry. *European Journal of Dental Education*, (2), 25–32.

Young, M. (1993). Instructional design for situated learning. *Educational Technology Research and Development, 41,* 43–58.

Chapter XVIII

Using an Interactive Feedback Tool to Enhance Pronunciation in Language Learning

Felicia Zhang, University of Canberra, Australia

Abstract

This chapter focuses on the effect of a learning environment in which biological, physical and technological ways of perceiving Mandarin Chinese sounds have been used. One of the most important tools of this environment is the use of a speech analysis tool for audio and visual feedback. This is done by way of incorporating a visual representation of student's production that can be easily compared to the speech of a native speaker. It is the contention of this chapter that such an interactive feedback tool in conjunction with other feedback mechanisms can provide opportunities for increasing the effectiveness of feedback in language learning.

Introduction

This chapter reports on an experiment of restructuring the learning environment using a variety of computer-enhanced language tools with the explicit aim of training students to perceive Mandarin (hereafter referred to as "MC") sounds. It focuses on the effect of creating a learning environment in which biological, physical, and technological ways of perceiving MC sound have been taught to students. It is hoped that access to these different approaches to perception will help students to know how to better perceive MC sounds outside the classroom context. One of the most important parts of this environment is the use of a speech analysis tool for offering audio and visual feedback by way of incorporating a visual representation of student's production that can be easily compared to the speech of a native speaker. It is the contention of this chapter that an interactive feedback tool such as this can provide opportunities for increasing the effectiveness of feedback in language learning. It is hoped that through the exploration of the results of this research, clearer directions on how this technology can be generalized to other learning contexts with other languages can emerge.

Critique of Various Ways of Teaching Pronunciation

Practitioners of both "traditional" and "modern" approaches of language teaching have generally acknowledged good pronunciation as a very important objective in learning a second language (L2). As perception is intricately connected to speech production, training to perceive sounds necessarily becomes an important part of language acquisition and good pronunciation acquisition. However, in the history of foreign language instruction, pronunciation has not always been regarded in this light.

The grammar translation method, which focuses almost entirely upon written texts, has always considered pronunciation nearly irrelevant. The cognitive code approach also de-emphasized pronunciation in favor of grammar and vocabulary, because it was thought in the late 1960s and early 1970s that native-like pronunciation could not be taught anyway (Scovel, 1969).

Subsequent approaches, however, put more emphasis on oral communication. For example, the direct method has claimed that pronunciation is very important and presents it via teacher modeling. This methodology assumes that sounds practiced in chorus or even individually will automatically be transformed into "correct" production by the students. Similarly, the immersion method assumed that students would acquire good pronunciation through exposure. In the audiolingual approach, pronunciation is also very important. In this approach, the teacher models and the students repeat, usually with the help of minimal pair drills. However, by making students "improve" their pronunciation through a set of minimal pair drills suggests that every learner will make a particular error through a particular trajectory. For example, if an English as a foreign language (EFL) learner makes an error with the word "beach," it will inevitably be that he or she will say it as "bitch." This predetermination of what kind of errors students will make when learning a L2, not only denies a student's individuality, it also excludes many other possible causes that may lead a learner to make that particular error.

Even in the teaching approaches that focus on oral communication cited above, relatively scanty attention has been paid to the complex nature of phonation and auditory perception in a L2. In fact, teaching people to perceive in a L2 is considered so difficult that most teaching methodologies have based their approaches for teaching pronunciation on the teaching of elements that are relatively easy to define (e.g., vowel and consonant sounds). Elements that are relatively unstable and hard to define, such as intonation patterns, are usually left out of the teaching process. The teaching of intonation and rhythm has hardly been explored. The logic behind this is easily understood: one must first put together the elements of language and then, later, somehow add the intonation. These methods of teaching pronunciation have been widely used in language teaching. However, they have not yielded particularly useful results, for instance, in the field of teaching English as a second/foreign language. This led Jenkins (Jenkins, 2000) to argue that in the case of the English language, as many nations in the world use a variety of English as their own native or official language, rather than measuring native-like pronunciation or intelligibility against any particular form of the English language from say, the United Kingdom or the United States of America, it might be worthwhile to set up an international core for phonological intelligibility for the English language. It suffices to say that within this core for phonological intelligibility for English, prosodic features such as intonation were the least important according to Jenkins' reasoning. Yet this might, in fact, be approaching the problem from the wrong direction entirely.

Moreover, one cannot possibly dismiss the relationship between good pronunciation and social power. If one wants to be accepted and respected in the target language culture, the first testament of one's worth is one's pronunciation and fluency in that particular target language. Thus, mastery of intonation patterns of that L2 is actually an integral and crucial part of language proficiency.

Finally, research by Hinofotis and Bailey (Hinofotis & Bailey, 1980) has demonstrated that "there is a threshold level of pronunciation in English such that if a given non-native speaker's pronunciation falls below this level, he or she will not be able to communicate orally no matter how good his or her control of English grammar and vocabulary might be." It is then reasonable to assume that there might also be a similar threshold level of pronunciation in MC for non-native speakers of MC. Tones in MC, as an indispensable part of intonation, perform the function of differentiating word meaning. The importance and endurance of tones in MC is such that native speakers will still find your speech intelligible, even if the vowels and consonants are unintelligible (Chao, 1972). This is why recognition bestowed upon a non-native speaker's mastery of MC is almost entirely based on native speakers' perceptions of their tones. In other words, intelligibility of non-native MC is based very much on the speaker's correct tonal production. For this reason, mastery of tone proves to be one of the most worthwhile tasks in learning spoken MC. This is true not only of a tonal language such as MC; it is also true of a nontonal language such as French (James, 1976).

In short, it is maintained that instead of focusing on the easily definable and discrete elements that make up speech, perhaps a worthwhile experiment would be to start with the intonation and the melody of a language and the process of training L2 students to perceive sounds in a L2. The study described in this chapter reports on an experiment based on this orientation of pronunciation training.

Objectives of Feedback

Getting good-quality feedback is an important aspect of language learning (and learning in general). For many educationalists, feedback is important, because it is essential for learning and can play a significant role in students' development by providing knowledge required for improvement (Hinett, 1998; Hyland, 2000). The objectives of providing feedback are as follows:

1.   To enable students to understand feedback and to make sense of it;

2.   To establish a common understanding of how this feedback may be implemented or acted upon by students between students and teachers.

Toohey (2000, p.154) gave a model of a learning process involving feedback: initially the student encounters or is introduced to an idea, this is followed by the student becoming aware of the idea, the student then tries the idea out, receives feedback and then reflects and adjusts the implementation of the idea. Feedback as described in this model takes place in a language teaching classroom on a daily basis. In a communicative classroom, students are frequently called upon or volunteer to try out a new sentence, conversation, or structures. The student then receives feedback from the teacher or his or her fellow classmates almost instantly in many ways. In the classroom, many channels are used for communicating feedback, through error correction and other channels, such as body language, nonverbal behavior, facial expressions, gestures, tone of voice, and so on. Such feedback is usually instantaneous, involuntary (from the feedback provider), episodic, and disappears very quickly from the memory of everyone involved. So in a traditional classroom, while we receive a huge amount of feedback on our production, the feedback received seldom becomes guidance or long-term learning in a real, face-to-face communicative interaction outside the classroom.

First, can we expect the classroom situation to provide feedback that is able to achieve the objectives listed above? Clearly, the episodic nature of the feedback offered in the classroom can have minimal effect on student learning. Second, understanding what the feedback contains and how to act on it are not as easy as they seem. The feedback offered in a L2 language classroom does not only contain information on the correct way of pronouncing or writing something. In some cases, error correction offered can be as detrimental as not offering any feedback at all. An excellent example is in the teaching of MC tones. In a character-based language such as MC, each character has a lexical tone that is stable when it is isolated from other words. However, in a sentence situation, a lexical tone of a character is influenced by other characters and their tones before and after it. In other words, a character might lose its stable lexical tone in a larger stretch of discourse. In the MC language, changes in tones across sentences and longer stretches of discourse are very hard to predict and describe. Yet, in every classroom in the world where students are learning MC as a foreign language, teachers are constantly pulling students up on their tones by demonstrating the right tones for individual characters and telling them the tone for a particular character is a fourth tone not a first tone and so on. The problem is that such corrective effort is usually ineffective, as the immediate context (influence of words left and right to the character in question) of the correction for that particular character is ignored, and the effect is usually short-lived and transitory.

The Contribution of Computer Technology in Feedback Provision

The advent of computer technology in language learning has added a very interesting dimension to the role of providing feedback. Computer technology can provide an environment in which certain memory traces that work for a particular learner can stay longer in that students' consciousness or sometimes unconsciousness. In a real-life situation, such memory traces can be called upon to help facilitate the communication involved. The advantages of feedback offered by a computer are that the feedback is constant; it can be repeated over and over; and it allows students to control their own learning.

However, the design of CALL tools for providing feedback still depends on the theoretical framework that conceptualizes the tools. For instance, in a Speech-Recognition-Based pronunciation training experiment conducted by Tomokiyo et al. (2000), the feedback offered still follows the model of offering explanation using diagrams of articulatory position and minimal pair practice. Many CALL tools still tend to focus on the production side of pronunciation rather than on exploring how students perceive sounds. Thus, the criticisms that are put forward against the various approaches of teaching pronunciation in language teaching are equally pertinent here as well. The present study proposes that instead of conducting research based on the more stable aspects of pronunciation (i.e., vowels and consonants) that are constrained by particular theories of linguistics, it might be more productive for students if we conduct research based on sound theories of learning. The speech tool we developed, and which will be discussed in more detail shortly, is based on verbo-tonal system of phonetic correction, developed by the late Professor Guberina in connection with his work with people whose hearing was impaired (Renard, 1975). This is a system that brings the human brain and the human body as a whole to the forefront of the study of auditory perception. The computer software is used in a language learning environment that has been designed to use all the sensory organs of the body to facilitate auditory, visual, and other perceptions and to contribute to the brain's realization of every perception.

Most of the feedback that is currently offered in computerized multimedia environments is focused on the product of student's performance rather than upon the process. For instance, we are familiar with many language-teaching exercise makers that allow you to offer feedback such as "try again" or "well done." However, such feedback is pointless, and students are unlikely to benefit from it if they do not change their actions during the process of production. In the case of getting better pronunciation in any language, this amounts to getting students to try to say a sentence differently. Most feedback mechanisms, while offering feedback in terms of judgment, do not offer any feedback that contributes to the process of production. The speech tool we developed, by contrast, is designed to offer feedback that is nonjudgmental and allows students to explore and reflect during the process of learning, not just at the end of the learning process. Reflection occurs when students can observe visually the differences between their productions and the native speaker model. When this is combined with the biological and physical memory traces built up in the classroom context, students can act upon their reflections and change the processes of production. It is the contention that this way, students will be able to turn feedback to students into learning in the long run.

Providing Feedback Using Sptool

A few attempts have been made to teach melody and intonation in a new and original way by displaying the melodic contours on a screen. The students hear a model sentence and, at the same time, they watch the melodic pattern form on the screen where it is "frozen." They then attempt to match the model melody by speaking. As their melodic pattern is also "frozen," they can compare their productions with the model. Students can then employ auditory and visual stimuli for assistance in the comparison process. Such methods, overall, have had good results (James, 1976). In the past, this kind of feedback machine was relatively expensive and, as only one person could be trained on any single machine at any one time, not really feasible for widespread educational use. However, computer technology has made it possible that such a feedback mechanism can be provided at the click of a button. The Sptool (Zhang & Newman, 2003) used in this research is such a feedback mechanism.

The Sptool program is produced with a windows component called dotnetfx.exe; it is 20 megabytes in size. It is most stable for Windows 2000 and XP; a bit unstable for Windows 98. When you open the program, you can see the open icon, which allows you to import any other prerecorded audio file saved in the .chwav, .mchwav, or .wav formats. If you have a prerecorded sound file, saved in Windows .wav format, you should be able to open it and run through the program. If you record a male voice in Cooledit (Syntrillium, 2002) or any other recording software, save it under the Windows .wav format to .mchwav. If you record a female voice, save it to .chwav, and then Sptool should play and measure your recorded sentence. At the moment, the program is not able to work with large files over 10 megabytes due to the limitation imposed by the Microsoft component.

Other Speech Analysis Tools

There are other speech analysis tools on the market. The commercial product Winpitch (Martin, 2003) is such a speech analysis tool. Praat (Boersma & Weenink, 2003) is free and also available. However, these software programs are far too complex for beginning language students to use. As the students involved in this research are zero-level beginners of MC with varying computer literacy levels, the complexity of the programs described above made the creation of a more user-friendly speech analysis tool integrated into the teaching material a necessity.

The Tell-Me-More series (Auralog, 2000) of language-learning programs also have built within them a speech comparison tool. However, the speech comparison chosen by the creator of Tell-Me-More is using phoneme matching. In other words, while the sentences contained in the language program can be verified by the speech comparison tool attached to the program, it cannot verify any other sentences outside the program. This means the usefulness of their speech tool is really limited.

Theoretical Framework Underpinning the Current Research

The use of Sptool is embedded in a larger learning theory based on the theory of the verbo-tonal system of phonetic correction. This theory is mainly concerned with the way students perceive sounds of a L2. The starting point of this theory is the complex nature of phonation and auditory perception of a language. From the verbo-tonal point of view, auditory perception develops synchronously and synergistically with the development of the motor, proprioceptive, and visual abilities (Guberina, 1985). One of the senses in audition is through the ears. A person with normal hearing in his mother tongue will behave, in a foreign language, as though he or she were hard of hearing. Each language sound carries all frequencies from about 50 Hz to about 16,000 Hz (albeit at various intensities). Theoretically, at any rate, each sound can be heard in many different ways. The ear seems to have a "choice" as to what to hear, in practice, depending on the way in which the ear has been trained. L2 students tend to make "choices" in the target language based on what they are familiar with in their mother tongue. Each sound has a particular "optimal" frequency (i.e., the frequency band, or combination of frequency bands, at which a native speaker best recognizes and perceives the sound in question). This is what Troubetzkoy (1969) referred to as the mother tongue "sieve."

Students who experience difficulty with a particular foreign language sound are considered as not having recognized its optimal. Hence, they are unable to reproduce the sound correctly. One of the ways in which students can be made to perceive the optimal of each sound is to remove (e.g., through electronic filtering) any interfering frequencies that might prevent it from being perceived. In this way, it is possible, in theory, to bypass the mother tongue "sieve" (Troubetzkoy, 1969). Once this has been achieved, students will be able to perceive, for the first time, the specific quality of the troublesome sound.

However, exposing the students to the native speaker optimal may still be insufficient. A set of "corrective" optimals then needs to be determined. These will be such as to direct a student's audition away from its natural tendency to structure as it has always done.

Verbo-tonalism postulates that the articulation of sounds poses relatively little difficulty once the specific quality of the sound has been heard. Consequently, the determination of corrective optimals for any one student will be established on the basis of his or her pronunciation. It is through exposure to corrective optimals, followed by intensive articulatory practice, that students will carry with them valid acoustic models constituting the normal range for the phonemes of language. The intense exposures to the sentences in this course via the Sptool plus the intensive articulatory practice carried out in the two-hour lecture provide students with such valid acoustic models of the phonemes of the L2.

Audition is a form of total behavior that occurs on the level of the body as a whole. In the present course, nine steps in the lecture sequence have been designed to integrate phonation and expressiveness that occur in the space between the lungs and the nasal cavity, with the breathing, moving, feeling patterns of a person in entirety so that a multitude of memory traces will be retained in different parts of the body.

Given the complexity of the various processes involved in perception and phonation, an intellectualization of these processes is unlikely to be successful. Learning processes must therefore operate at the "unconscious" level. Rather, it is essential that proprioceptive powers be called into play in the development of good pronunciation so that students might become conscious and perceptive of the rhythms and stresses of the target language. The fact that translation into English, romanization in Pinyin, etc. are not emphasized or used at all in this course suggests that the course is especially designed to allow new language to be processed "unconsciously"—or perhaps *intuitively* would be a better word— first and foremost. In other words, we are not really talking about unconscious learning but the more intensive utilization of the language centers through the exploitation of different parts of the nervous system, such as the parts that are concerned with proprioception and bodily sensation.

The elements described in the following lecture sequence and the audiovisual materials contained in the teaching materials represent the pedagogic measures that integrate the senses of the body with movement with the process of ear training through working on a system of errors rather than isolated elements of the language. It is proposed that starting an audition process from intonation would result in the proper training of several systems at once in MC. These pedagogic measures also are designed to instill in students certain memory traces by physically "marking" on their brains so that these memory traces can be reactivated once feedback either from Sptool or from any other sources has been received.

These memory traces are essential in enabling students to act upon the feedback received. This is the second important objective of any feedback system: to create a set of memories that are not merely cognitive records but feelings of relaxation and muscular tension that are distributed through the students' experience of his or her bodily sense. What follows is a brief description of a teaching method that, in helping to create such somatic traces, provides an environment suitable to the inclusion of the Sptool and assists students in the exploitation of that resource.

A New Method of Teaching Mandarin Chinese Pronunciation to Beginners

It is 5:30 pm on a Tuesday afternoon, in a large room capable of holding up to 50 students; the lecture chairs with attached arms have been pushed to the perimeter of the room. The students are randomly slouched on their chairs relaxing after a tired day of either work or lectures.

The teacher walks into the room carrying the necessary computer gear, CD-ROMs and so on. She greets the class cheerfully with "ni3men hao3" (hello, everyone) and puts the CD-ROM in the computer. "Now, leave your seat and lie comfortably on the floor and listen." Then the following audio file is played:

> *"Imagine that you are lying on your back on the grass on a warm summer day and that you are watching the clear blue sky without a single cloud in it (pause). You are lying very comfortably, you are very relaxed and happy (pause). You are simply enjoying the experience of watching the clear, beautiful blue sky (pause). As you are lying there, completely relaxed, enjoying yourself (pause), far off on the horizon you notice a tiny white cloud (pause). You are fascinated by the simple beauty of the small white cloud against the clear blue sky (pause). The little white cloud starts to move slowly toward you (pause). You are laying there, completely relaxed, very much at peace with yourself, watching the little white cloud drift slowly toward you (pause). The little white cloud drifts slowly toward you (pause). You are enjoying the beauty of the clear blue sky and the little white cloud (pause). Finally the little white cloud*

comes to a stop overhead (pause). Completely relaxed, you are enjoying this beautiful scene (pause). You are very relaxed, very much at peace with yourself, and simply enjoying the beauty of the little white cloud in the blue sky (pause). Now become the little white cloud. Project yourself into it (pause). You are the little white cloud, completely diffused, puffy, relaxed, very much at peace with yourself (pause). Now you are completely relaxed, your mind is completely calm (pause), you are pleasantly relaxed, ready to proceed with the lesson (pause)."(Step 1)

"Now, get up and stand in a circle." The teacher joins the circle.

The teacher says "I will hum to the rhythm of the sentence and please hum with me while walking slowly in a circle." This is done five times. (Step 2)

"Now, I will clap to the rhythm of the sentence and then you can clap after me." (Step 3) Again, this is done five times.

"Notice the high sounds and the low sounds in the sentence? With your palm up, push your hands above your head as high as possible for the high sounds. For the low sounds, stamp your feet done as hard as possible. Now let's hum the sentences again." (Step 4) This is again done five times.

"Continuing with the movements, now mouth the sentences while I say them out loud." (Step 5) Of course, at every lesson, at this stage, one or two people always end up repeating the sentences rather than mouthing them. This is again done five times.

"Now repeat after me, and then add words to the intonation." This again is done five times. (Step 6)

Now the teacher instructs each individual to repeat the sentence by themselves; checking that each student is reproducing the sentence correctly. (Step 7)

"Now what is the meaning of the sentence?" Students enthusiastically volunteer the meaning in English, and the meaning of the sentence is usually established in seconds. (Step 8)

In each two-hour lecture sequence, every sentence is presented and practiced using the above procedure. At the end of each lecture, the whole class engages in a pair or group work conversation activity using the materials covered in the lesson. (Step 9)

At the end of the lesson, students are instructed to sit and write the meaning or whatever notes they want to make themselves.

In the lecture sequence described, several rather unconventional elements make an appearance. For instance, relaxation exercise, humming, mouthing to the words, body gestures, and mouthing the words and then repetition, are all present in the learning sequence. How are these related to each other? How do these elements relate to the Sptool under discussion?

Focusing on the Rhythm and Intonation of the Language

The activities described in the above lecture sequence all have to do with focusing on the rhythm and intonation of the language. Intonation is a universal feature of all languages. Melody (which includes tones and intonation) holds the units together and arranges them with respect to one another. It is a very special kind of glue. Attempting to arrange the sounds with the wrong "glue" is like building structures of the wrong kind.

The smallest unit of the language being presented is a sentence rather than individual words or compounds. This is because in MC, the acoustic characteristics of the words change when they are in a sentential environment. For instance, when a word is read in isolation, the frequency of the word is different from when the word is part of a sentence. So concentrating one's effort in mastering the tones of individual words or compounds does not guarantee success in producing the sentences containing those words. This is true of MC as well as other nontonal languages.

Step 1: In this step, the imagery of the "little white cloud" is used to relax the students and the teacher. This constitutes the *relaxation* phase. This sets up a relaxed atmosphere for learning for the rest of the lesson. Stevick (1986) has stressed the usefulness of working with imagery in language teaching. In education, visualization can facilitate the interiorization of knowledge by creating a more receptive state of awareness, permitting the affective and creative functions of a more holistic nature to participate in and strengthen the learning experience (Murdock, 1987). According to Neville (Neville, 1989), "the fragmented, dispersed, chaotic energies of our organism are aligned, harmonized and made purposive by the imagined experience, just as they would be by a 'real one', possibly leading to important changes in our 'self-image, attitude and behavior' (p. 95).

Step 2: This step involves humming along to the rhythm of the sentences without the vowels and consonants (five times). This is used to highlight the intonation and tones of MC.

Step 3: Clapping to the rhythm allows students to experience the rhythm of the sentence and observe different groupings of the words in a sentence. This also allows the students to observe how stress, realized by length and loudness in MC, is tied to meaning. This also allows them to observe the key words in a sentence and realize that not all words are of equal value and that in making oneself understood, one only needs to get the key words right. This training is essential in training them the strategy of prediction and advanced planning in listening comprehension.

Step 4: In this step, walking about with feet coming down on every syllable is practiced in order to get the body used to producing a tense downward tone that is also loud. Raising or stretching upwards as though attempting to touch the ceiling to experience the tenseness of the body in producing the first high level tone is also done. Instruct the students to adopt a forward lumping of the shoulders for the second and third tones in MC that need a relaxed posture.

Research shows that Chinese speakers have a much wider voice range when speaking MC than English speakers speaking English (Chen, 1974). As the first tone starts at a higher frequency than what most Australian speakers are used to, extra physical efforts need to be made to remind one that one must start high. To stretch one's muscular system to express these MC tones, one must not slouch in seats. By asking students to stand up straight and walk in a circle with various gestures, students are experiencing the coordination and synchronization of various muscles with the sounds uttered.

Steps 5 through 9 are steps that further highlight the melody of the sentences involved. Notice that throughout the learning sequence, translation and writing down the sentences are not needed until the last moment. By the time students come to write down the meaning, they will have already internalized the melody of the sentences.

The nine steps of the lecture sequence offer students a range of physical ways for remembering tones beyond the set contact hours every week. These measures set up a series of learning steps that can be used for self-access learning at home.

Role of the Speech Tool and the Course Data CD and Audio CD

Course Data CD

Each new vocabulary item, new sentence, or new phrase in the teaching materials is linked to a normal sound file. Only the sentences are linked to both a normal sound file and a filtered sound file.

All the sound files in the materials can be passed through the Sptool (Figure 1). Once passed through the Sptool, the learner can listen to the teacher's model pronunciation by clicking on the "teacher" icon. With one click, the student can hear the model sentence, and the pitch curves of the model sentence are displayed. If the learner wants to hear a smaller chunk of the sentence, then he or she can select that bit of the curve by dragging the cursor over the portion they want to hear. After listening to the sentence numerous times, the learner can decide whether he or she wants to record his or her own production.

Before clicking on the record button, however, it is necessary for the student to tell the program whether he or she is female or male. This is necessary because

Figure 1: Picture of the teaching material

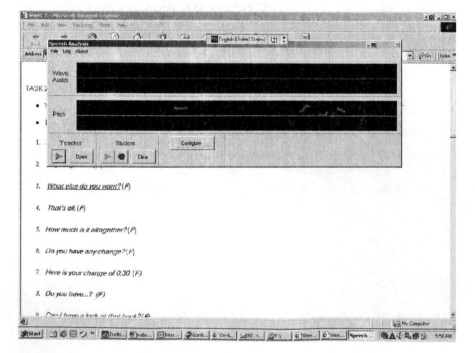

females generally have higher fundamental frequencies than males. The difference is sometimes as much as over 100 Hz. If the program is configured to measure a female voice, the pitch curve of a male learner will not be able to be displayed. However, once configured correctly, the pitch curve of the learner's recording will then be displayed properly.

The course data CD also contains teaching materials in html format; all the associated sound files, the Speech tool, and short video skits with which students can test their comprehensions of the new language can be learned by watching these video skits. An audio CD of the sound files is also provided with the course materials. In 2003, a weekly compulsory class using computer-enhanced teaching materials was arranged. Other computer-enhanced learning materials such as Tell-Me-More (Auralog, 2000), VCDs, movies, and videos with similar content are also available in the computer center.

The Role of Sptool

Steps 2 to 7 in the lecture sequence are duplicated in different forms through the use of the Sptool. While the classroom sequence is more or less teacher driven and physical, the Sptool allows the lecture sequence to be experienced in a different way. It also allows other choices to be made:

*   The beat, stress, word groupings, key words, and sentential intonation are all indicated in the speech curve and the sound file. In the sample sentence, zai4 nar3 you3 mai4 bi3 de0 (Where can one buy some pens?) shown in Figure 2 on the next page, "zai4 nar3" is the key word and the curve clearly shows that the three characters are in a group together and should not be separated.

*   The height (related to the muscular tenseness of the body) of both first and fourth tones is indicated clearly with respect to other tones. The height of the first and fourth tones reminds the students of the need to stretch their voice range beyond their normal voice range. This information is very useful in enabling students to change their ways of producing the target sentences after observing the differences between the native speaker's production and theirs.

*   Comparison of the pitch curves of individual words in the vocabulary section with the same words used in sentences is possible.

*   Students can select any portion of the sentence for listening practice and repetition.

*   The links between words are easily observable. For instance, in the sentence,

Wo3 sheng1yu2 yi1 jiu3 wu3 ling2 nian2.

I was born in the year 1950.

The production of "sheng1yu2" requires the body to be tense and to be kept tense in order to produce the next "yi1: one." Students can select the three syllables "sheng1yu2yi1" in order to explore how physically one has to keep one's body tense in order to produce this group of words using the physical gestures practiced in the classroom.

The use of Sptool encourages students to reflect on and explore the process of learning. Many of the explorations are usually impossible to be predetermined by a teacher, as most teachers, even the most able, do not have an extensive list of rules about how the different combination of words are produced physically in MC. Many of the things that can be done using the program may not be initiated by teachers but are being explored by the students through use. Furthermore, being able to experience each sentence repeatedly through the Sptool creates an environment in which students can totally immerse themselves consciously and unconsciously in the language.

Figure 2: Picture of the Sptool showing the sample sentence: Where does it sell pens?

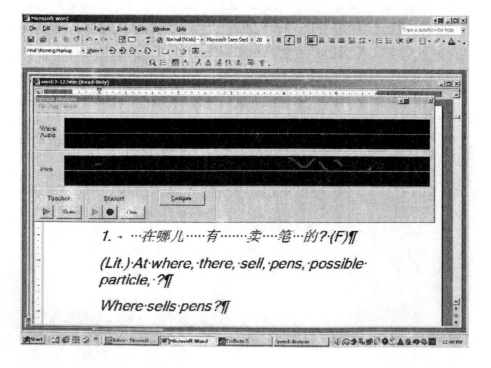

The Study

Sample

The progress of three groups of beginners of Mandarin Chinese has been followed. The first group (hereafter referred to as "Group 1") consists of two other groups of total beginners from 1995 and 1996 who were taught pinyin (the Chinese romanization) from the beginning of their MC study. The oral test data collected from this group represent the baseline data.

The second group (hereafter referred to as "Group 2") of beginners finished their two semesters of study in Mandarin in 2001. These participants were students enrolled in *Chinese 1a: Language and Culture* and *Chinese 1b* of the first-year Chinese course at the University of Canberra in 2001. By the end of the experiment, they had completed 130 contact hours of lectures and tutorials over two semesters.

The third group (hereafter referred to as "Group 3") consisted of students who studied MC in the first semester, 2003. Students in Group 3 were zero-level beginners when they started and were taught exclusively by the use of the Sptool. These participants in this study were 15 students enrolled in *Chinese 1a: Language and Culture* in 2003. There were three students from Japan, one student from Korea, and 10 Australian students. By the end of the experiment, they would have completed 65 contact hours of lectures and tutorials over one semester. They were all zero-level beginners of MC at the beginning of the course.

Data Collection Methods

A configuration of data methods was used to explore the experiences of Groups 2 and 3 students as they learned MC through this technology-rich learning environment. The configuration of methods is as follows:

Qualitative:

*   One-to-one oral tests (four of them for Group 2; one for Group 3)

*   Self-scripted video segment done in small groups (four for Groups 1 and 2; one for Group 3)

*   Written examination tests (four for Group 2; and one for Group 3)

Quantitative:

- Computer-technology-related questionnaires from Group 2 students
- One-to-one interviews with Group 2 students

Results and Discussion

Qualitative Data

Group 2:

Data collected from the 2001 group of students were compared with two other groups of total beginners from 1995 and 1996. The fundamental difference between the groups was that the 2001 group of students was not taught pinyin from the very beginning. Analysis of students' oral performances revealed that the rate of acquisition of MC initials (consonants) and finals (vowels) was faster for these students. For instance, in the data from students in Group 1 (the pinyin group), a large number of errors with palatals [x] and [j] and [q] were present. While the Group 2 students made some errors with [x] and [q], errors with [j], after only six weeks of instruction, did not occur. Furthermore, by the time the second oral (after 65 hours of instruction) was conducted, no errors were made with respect to these initials.

Group 3:

Students in Group 3 started learning Mandarin only since the end of February 2003. This group is the only group that benefited with a verbo-tonal-theory-driven teaching methodology combined with a fully developed software package that included course data and audio CDs and the speech tool. By the end of May 2003, this group of students had completed their first written and oral tests.

Oral test:

The first oral performances of eight students in Group 3 had been analyzed. Out of 1827 words (MC characters) uttered, 77 errors were made with consonants and vowels. In other words, only 4.2% of errors were made. Out of the 77 errors, students from a non-Australian background, i.e., one Korean, one Thai, and one

Cantonese speaker of Chinese made the majority of the errors. In terms of consonants, only one Australian student made two errors with "zhi3." He pronounced it as "zi3." Again, errors with palatals [x] and [j] and [q] were not present. After only 30 hours of face-to-face instruction, all the Australian students had gained complete control of the initials of MC. Similar to previous groups of students, pinyin and non-pinyin groups, the problematic errors were with the vowels and diphthongs rather than with consonants.

The faster rate of Mandarin sound system acquisition can be attributed to the removal of romanization and the availability of sound files on CDs and the speech tool. The combined effect of both tools appeared to have helped to reduce the transfer effect from the students' mother tongue—English. A close examination of the audio recordings of Group 3 students' oral also suggests that Group 3 students were more fluent. Though they still had tone problems, the rhythm of their speech was much more natural when compared with a native speaker's rhythm.

Furthermore, anecdotal reports from students suggested that students were confident with their listening comprehension ability, citing that the use of humming, clapping, and so on in class combined with the use of Sptool, allowed them to hear and remember more distinctly the rhythm and stress of the language. This meant that they were able to hear familiar key words that enabled them to predicate what was coming up more accurately. Evidence of this came in the form of the ranking of students in different parts of their written tests. For this group, the top three ranks were occupied by Australian zero-level beginners overall. For the entire group, for the listening comprehension section, even the weakest student (the student who scored the lowest for the entire written test) scored well for this section. This was very different from the results of previous years. As one student remarked, this course was more like an immersion language program in which students were expected to use the whole body in the process of learning.

Quantitative Data

Group 2: Results of the Computer Technology Questionnaires:

The reaction to the computer-based materials was extremely positive with this group of students. Many, 85%, of the students regularly used the audio and data CDs for at least one to three hours per week in an evaluation survey conducted at the end of the first semester in 2001. At the end of the first semester, students requested that in the written text on the data CD, each line of each dialogue be linked to its corresponding sound file, thus making the practice of the target language, line by line, easier.

A similar technology-oriented questionnaire was also administered at the end of the second semester. All students used the course data and audio CDs regularly to prepare and review the materials covered. Two out of six students requested each item of the vocabulary each week to be linked to its own audio file. Two students requested more regular use of VCD, and some requested more regular use of the Tell-Me-More CD in class.

Group 3:

No quantitative data had been collected from this group of students at the time of writing this chapter. Both questionnaire and interview data have been collected in late June of 2003 but are yet to be analyzed. A brief glimpse of the questionnaires completed by Group 3 students suggests that, on average, these students spent around 10 hours per person outside class contact time on their Chinese learning. This kind of devotion to the learning of MC has not been experienced by the researcher in her entire teaching career.

The availability of such an array of computer-enhanced learning materials encouraged students to engage in more autonomous learning behavior. As pronunciation could only be obtained either through looking in the dictionary or listening to the accompanying course CDs, all students spent time on a regular basis to listen to the CDs to prepare for the week's materials. This autonomous learning pattern actually forced students to open their ears to the target language in and outside of class, thus enormously increasing exposure to the target language. Autonomous behaviors happen every time each student listens to a string of sounds in Mandarin, as each student has to perceive the sounds according to his or her individual perception and translate them in a way that is recognizable to each student, individually.

Future Directions

It is important to note that Sptool can be used with any language, whether mother tongue, L2, or languages in danger of becoming extinct. It can be used with languages or any sound wave. Therefore, it can be used to enhance the teaching of the prosodic aspect of any language. For instance, in the teaching of English, the Sptool described in this chapter makes it possible for different models of native English sentences to be made available to teachers and students.

The Sptool used in the learning process is by no means perfect and, therefore, can be further improved in several aspects:

1. At the moment, it can only work with preproduced sound files of a fairly small size. This means that a sound file has to be prerecorded before it can be run through this tool. It will be a huge improvement if as soon as someone speaks, the speech is recorded and automatically analyzed with the pitch wave displayed on the screen instantly. In other words, this tool should be able to process speech in real time.

2. Another icon called "filtered" can be built into the program to display the filtered version of any sentences.

3. This program should be able to talk to other programs, such as a video database, so that the sound file from any movie can also be measured and displayed instantly.

4. Band passes can be built into the program so that students can investigate the "optimal" frequency of a particular consonant or vowel.

5. A Web-version of the course should be created, and flash technology should be used so that once students point on a sound file, the speech tool opens automatically.

While Improvements 1 through 3 will not make the program too complicated to use, a large amount of research needs to go into investigating the possibility of Improvement 4. Improvement 5 is also possible, but the use of the World Wide Web itself already restricts its use. However, a Web version of the Sptool is being planned.

One of the most promising research directions at the moment with regards to this program is further improvement of the program and then testing of the tool with a larger group of students in different languages.

Conclusion

Limited findings described in this article demonstrated that a well-thought-out and properly implemented curriculum involving computer technology can make feedback to students more effective. This kind of environment is instrumental to produce students with better pronunciation in a L2 and can increase students' motivation for learning the language and culture of an L2. One significant consideration of creating this environment is the fact that the technology chosen is of a *"low-tech"* nature, utilizing mainly CD-ROM technology. While it has been acknowledged that adding the Net to this learning process may also be beneficial for students, at the beginning stage of language learning, the use of the Net only serves to increase the cognitive load on students.

Another significant characteristic of this environment is its *modularity*. I would like to refer to all the elements within the environment metaphorically as "machines." The "machines" used in the environment are easily accessible and user friendly and adaptable. The non-technology-driven elements such as one's body, voice, movement, and gesture are already available to every student. The technological elements, such as the sound, video, text files, and filtered sound files, are not hard to produce. The frequency of interaction and ease of access afforded by the Sptool and other sound files have been extremely motivating for students. Through the use of various machines in this environment, feedback, offered through physical, biological, and technological means, has acted in concert to motivate students and convert feedback in learning.

Acknowledgment

The investigation described in this chapter is sponsored by a University of Canberra research grant, 2002–2003 from the University of Canberra, Australia. I would like to thank Professor Michael Wagner for participating in the grant and offering me useful feedback and advice throughout the grant.

I would also like to thank Kate Wilson and two anonymous reviewers for helpful feedback on a previous version of this chapter. I am, however, entirely responsible for the good and bad herein.

References

Auralog. (2000). Tell Me More (Asian). Auralog S.A.

Boersma, P. A., & Weenink, D. (2003). Praat. Institute of Phonetic Sciences, Institute of Phonetic Sciences, University of Amsterdam.

Chao, Y. R. (1972). *Mandarin primer: An intensive course in spoken Chinese.* Cambridge, MA: Harvard University Press.

Chen, G. T. (1974). The pitch range of English and Chinese speakers. *Journal of Chinese Linguistics, 2*(2), 159–171.

Guberina, P. (1985). The role of the body in learning foreign languages. *R. P. A., 73, 74, 75,* pp. 38–50.

Hinett, K. (1998). *The role of dialogue and self assessment in improving student learning.* British Educational Research Association Annual Conference, The Queen's University of Belfast.

Hinofotis, F., & Bailey, K. (1980). American undergraduates' reactions to the communication skills of foreign teaching assistants. In J. C. Fisher, M. A. Clarke, & J. Schacter (Eds.), *TESOL '80* (pp. 120–133), Washington, DC, Teachers of English to speakers of other languages.

Hyland, F. (2000). ESL writers and feedback: Giving more autonomy to students. *Language Teaching Research*, *4*(1), 33–54.

James, E. F. (1976). The acquisition of prosodic features using a speech visualiser. *International Review of Applied Linguistics in Language Teaching*, *14*, pp. 227–243.

Jenkins, J. (2000). *The phonology of English as an international language.* New York: Oxford University Press.

Martin, P. (2003). Winpitch. Pitch Instruments Inc.

Murdock, M. (1987). *Spinning inward.* Boston, MA: Shambhala.

Neville, B. (1989). *Educating psyche: Emotion, imagination and the unconscious in learning.* Victoria: Collins Dove.

Renard, R. (1975). *Introduction to the verbo-tonal method of phonetic correction,* Didier.

Scovel, T. (1969). Foreign accents: Language acquisition and cerebral dominance. *Language Learning*, *19*(3,4), 245–254.

Stevick, E. W. (1986). *Images and options in the language classroom.* Cambridge: University Press.

Syntrillium. (2002). *Cooledit 2000.* Syntrillium software.

Tomokiyo, L. M., Le Wang, et al. (2000). *An empirical study of the effectiveness of speech-recognition-based pronunciation tutoring.* Proceedings of ICSLP, Beijing.

Toohey, S. (2000). *Designing courses for higher education,* Buckingham: The Society for Research into Higher Education and Open University.

Troubetzkoy, N. S. (1969). *Principles of phonology (Grundzuge de Phonologie, Travaux du cercle linguistique de Prague).* University of California Press.

Zhang, F., & Newman, D. (2003). *Speech tool.* Canberra: University of Canberra, Australia.

About the Authors

Sanjaya Mishra holds a Ph.D. in Library and Information Science in the area of library networks. He has been a teacher of communication technology to distance educators. He has been involved in successful implementation of many multimedia and Internet-based courses, including a multimedia CD on multimedia. With professional training in distance education, television production, and multimedia, he is actively involved in collaboration at the international level. Currently, he is a senior lecturer at the Staff Training and Research Institute of Distance Education (STRIDE) at Indira Gandhi National Open University (IGNOU), New Delhi (India). Previously a programme officer of the Commonwealth Educational Media Centre for Asia (CEMCA) at New Delhi, he was engaged in conducting training programs in the application of multimedia in education in the Asian region. He has served as consultant to UNESCO, UNESCAP, and the World Bank. He was book review editor of the *Indian Journal of Open Learning* (1997-2000) and also edited a few special issues of the same journal. He is author/editor of five books and has contributed more than 60 research papers in reputed professional journals. He is on the editorial advisory boards of many reputed journals including *Distance Education, Malaysian Journal of Educational Technology, International Review of Research in Open and Distance Learning, Educational Technology and Society,* and *PUP Journal of Distance Education*. He is founder editor of the *Asian Journal of Distance Education*.

Ramesh C. Sharma holds a Ph.D. in Education in the area of Educational Technology and is currently working as regional director in Indira Gandhi National Open University (IGNOU) (India) (since 1996). Before joining IGNOU, Dr. Sharma was a senior faculty in a Teacher Training College for nearly 10 years and taught Educational Technology, Educational Research and Statistics, Educational Measurement and Evaluation, and Psychodynamics of Mental Health Courses for the B.Ed. and M.Ed. programs. He has conducted many training programs for the in- and pre-service teachers on the use of multimedia in teaching and instruction. He is a member of many committees on implementation of technology in the Open University. His areas of specialization include ICT applications, computer networking, online learning, student support services in open and distance learning, and teacher education. He is on the editorial board of referred and international journals in distance education. Dr. Sharma is on the editorial board of many reputed journals like *Distance Education, International Review of Research in Open and Distance Learning*, and *PUP Journal of Distance Education*. He is an editor of the *Journal of Information Technology Education* (Informing Science Institute, USA). He has co-authored one book on distance education research and contributed articles to referred journals. He is founder editor of the *Asian Journal of Distance Education*.

*   *   *   *   *

Sharlene Anthony is a senior scientific officer in the Life Sciences Department of the Singapore Science Centre. A marine biologist by training, she previously worked with marine mammals at Underwaterworld Singapore, with sea turtles at the Universiti Putra Malaysia, and with sea urchins at Dalhousie University, Canada. Currently, she is pursuing a master's degree at the Nanyang Technological University, Singapore, where she is exploring the linkages of the Singapore Science Centre with the formal education system.

Shivanand Balram is a lecturer in the Faculty of Natural Sciences, University of Guyana. At present, he is a researcher in the Department of Geography, Simon Fraser University, Canada. His nearly 12 years of academic, industry, and consulting experience have focused on geographic information systems and science, university teaching and learning, and physics. Shivanand has published in these areas and has developed "the embedded collaborative systems model for cartography education," "the 18i interactions model for blended learning," and "the collaborative spatial Delphi methodology for group learning and decision-making." His other interests include constructivist learning and Web-based instruction.

Ashok Banerji is an electrical engineer, who integrated management science and then multimedia computing to his professional attainments. His interest in e-learning, simulations, and just-in-time skill support led to one of the earliest Ph.D. research on Electronic Performance Support Systems (EPSS) at the University of Teesside, UK. He was director of Performance Consulting with a company based in Virginia (USA). As senior lecturer at the Education and Staff Development Department in Singapore Polytechnic in Singapore, he introduced courses on Educational Technology and Multimedia for Business and had R&D

funding for several projects on EPSS and multimedia-based training for semiconductor, marine industry, and virtual laboratory development. Currently, he is an adjunct professor in multimedia computing in Calcutta, and as a member of a philanthropic organization, he is working toward promotion of education leveraging technology. He was a consultant for International Telecommunication Union for a project on ICT for development.

Heather Bione is a dentist with a MDSc (Melb), who became interested in computer-assisted teaching and learning while working in research with the Department of Restorative Dentistry, The University of Melbourne (Australia). In 1999, she developed seven treatment planning cases for restorative dentistry using the Pathfinder program. Since that time, she has been involved as a content expert, in all four modules, for the pediatric multimedia project developed by the Department of Pediatric Dentistry, The University of Melbourne.

Alfred Bork is professor emeritus of Information and Computer Science at the University of California, Irvine (USA). His degrees are from Georgia Tech and Brown University. Dr. Bork has been at the Dublin Institute for Advanced Studies, the University of Alaska, Reed College, and Harvard University. He directs the Educational Technology Center, a research and development group, in highly adaptive technology-based learning. He is vice president of A Bork Endeavors. Recent projects include production systems for highly adaptive learning, learning about the methods of science, improving reasoning capability, voice input to computers, learning Japanese, and education for all. The Scientific Reasoning Series and Understanding Spoken Japanese are commercially available. Bork is interested in the effective use of highly interactive multimedia technology to make order of magnitude improvements in learning at all levels. He has published hundreds of papers and books about these issues. The most recent book, with Sigrun Gunnarsdottir, is *Tutorial Distance Learning* (Kluwer).

Loreen Marie Butcher-Powell is an assistant professor of Business Education and Office Information Systems at Bloomsburg University of Pennsylvania, USA. Within the last two years, she has presented or published more than 15 publications on security and pedagogical techniques. She is NASA's International Advanced Spaceport Technology Working Group (ASTWG) Education and Outreach Committee board member, an international board of editors for the *Journal of Information Technology and Education*, a program committee member and international reviewer for the Informing Science and IT Education Conference in Pori, Finland (June 24-27, 2003), and an expert panelist for the AECT Project for the Pennsylvania State University at University Park, Pennsylvania (USA). Loreen has received the 2002 Teaching Academy Grant from the Pennsylvania State University at Hazleton, Pennsylvania, and was a 2002 committee member for the $100,000 Common Wealth College Networking Mini-Grant at Pennsylvania State University.

Vassilios Dagdilelis is assistant professor in the Department of Educational and Social Policy, University of Macedonia, Greece. With a Ph.D. in Applied Mathematics, Dr. Dagdolelis's current interest area includes use of computers in education and training, didactics of informatics, and e-learning.

Peter E. Doolittle is an assistant professor and current head of the Educational Psychology Program in the School of Education at Virginia Tech, Blacksburg, VA (USA). He is also co-director of the Metacognition and Multimedia Project (MMP) at Virginia Tech. His research focus includes the investigation of the development of cognitive and metacognitive strategies within multimedia environments.

Suzana Dragićević is an assistant professor in the Department of Geography, Simon Fraser University, Canada. She has 16 years of academic, governmental, and industry experience focusing on geographic information systems and science, geodesy and surveying, and university teaching and learning in multiple language settings. Her research and teaching interests include spatial data analysis and modeling, fuzzy sets, multimedia cartography, and Web-based GIS. She has published widely on technical and teaching aspects in her research areas. In addition, she has organized special issues for reputable journals, bringing together experts in her field of research.

Patrick J. Fahy is associate professor, Centre for Distance Education, Athabasca University (Canada). His career began with teaching in the public schools of rural Western Canada. From there, he moved to the Alberta college system, spending 20 years in teaching, administration, and research positions ranging from adult basic literacy to graduate-level programs. During this period, he served as newsletter editor and president of both the Movement for Canadian Literacy, and the Alberta Association for Adult Literacy. In the 1990s he moved to the private sector, spending over five years in a multinational technology-based training company, where he managed regional activities in maritime and western Canada. He has engaged in private consulting in the areas of program evaluation and project management across North America for over 25 years. Presently, in addition to developing and teaching educational technology courses in Athabasca University's Master of Distance Education program, Pat coordinates the MDE's Advanced Graduate Diploma in Distance Education (Technology) program, and the annual MDE Distance Education Technology Symposium. He is a former president of the Alberta Distance Education and Training Association (ADETA).

Lisa Gjedde is an associate professor at the Danish University of Education (Denmark), where she is affiliated with the Research Programme for Media and ICT in a Learning Perspective. Her background includes a Ph.D. in Communications and Narrative Research, from the Department of Communications, Computer Science and Educational Research, University of Roskilde, Denmark. She has been a visiting research fellow at the University of Sussex, UK. She has done extensive research and development work in the areas of narrative learning processes, creative learning, and digital storytelling.

Jane Gunn is associate professor and research director in the Department of General Practice, The University of Melbourne (Australia). Jane is involved in women's and mental health research and teaching in addition to working as a general practitioner one day a week.

Kelsey Hegarty is a general practitioner and part-time senior lecturer responsible for postgraduate activities in the general practice department of The University of Melbourne, Melbourne. Her research and teaching interests are in women's health and, in particular, women's emotional well-being (partner abuse, depression, counseling). Her research experience includes a doctoral thesis on measurement and prevalence of partner abuse in general practice. She has had extensive teaching experience at undergraduate and postgraduate levels in the areas of communication skills, procedural skills, and management of common clinical problems. She has practiced as a general practitioner for over 15 years.

Leo Tan Wee Hin has a Ph.D. in Marine Biology. He holds the concurrent appointments of director of the National Institute of Education, professor of Biological Sciences in Nanyang Technological University (Singapore), and president of the Singapore National Academy of Science. Prior to this, he was director of the Singapore Science Centre. His research interests are in the fields of marine biology, science education, museum science, telecommunications, and transportation. He has published numerous research papers in international refereed journals.

Karen Kan is a specialist paediatric dentist in private practice in Melbourne, Australia. She completed her Bachelor of Dental Science (1992) and her Master of Dental Science (1996) at The University of Melbourne and gained her

Fellowship to the Royal Australasian College of Dental Surgeons in 1997. Karen has been a clinical research fellow in the Department of Dentistry, at the Royal Children's Hospital in Melbourne (1996), and an assistant professor in the Division of Pediatric Dentistry, School of Dentistry, University of Minnesota, USA (1997). Her current university involvement includes teaching and developing multimedia-assisted learning in pediatric dentistry.

Fusa Katada (Ph.D., Linguistics, University of Southern California) is professor of Linguistics and English at Waseda University, School of Science and Engineering, Tokyo, Japan. Dr. Katada has Teaching Credentials for Mathematics (Tokyo Metropolis Educational Committee) and Certificate in Teaching English as a Second Language (California State University, Long Beach). Dr. Katada was a linguistic programmer at SYSTRAN Inc. in the early 1980s for its English-Japanese machine translation system and was acknowledged as a Scientific Linguist by the U.S. Department of Labor. She had worked for Applied Computer Technology in Education: Upgrade directed by Robert Hertz at the California State University, Long Beach, and Understanding Spoken Japanese directed by Alfred Bork at the Educational Technology Center of the University of California, Irvine. Dr. Katada received her Ph.D. for her work on anaphoric relations in Logical Form. She specializes in formal linguistics: phonology, morphology, and syntax, with allied interests in biological foundations for language, atypical language, and dynamics of linguistic diversity.

Paul Kawachi has been teaching at universities for more than 20 years and is currently at the Department of Informatics, Kurume Shin-Ai Women's College, Japan. He has recently been awarded Doctorate of Education by the University of Hawai. An award-winning author, Dr. Kawachi is founder editor of the *Asian Journal of Distance Education.*

Mike Keppell joined the Hong Kong Institute of Education (HKIEd) as principal lecturer and head of the Centre for Integrating Technology in Education (CITIE) in January 2003. He was the former head of Biomedical Multimedia Unit, Faculty of Medicine, Dentistry and Health Science, The University of Melbourne (Australia). The CITIE is a design, development, evaluation, and research-based center that has a focus on enriching teaching and learning through educational technology. He is also the Information Technology Academic Development Coordinator for the HKIEd and coordinates the implementation of the e-learning platform—Blackboard. The research interests of Dr. Keppell cover four areas: student-centered learning (problem-based learning, case-based learning, project-based learning, and online communities); multimedia design (conceptualizing, concept mapping, design processes); processes involved in optimizing the instructional designer–subject matter expert interaction; and knowledge management (project management, systems and processes). His current interests at the Institute focus on technology-enhanced authentic learning environments, online communities, problem-based learning, and learner-centered assessment.

Ngaire Kerse is a general practitioner at the University of Auckland, New Zealand. Her Ph.D. from the University of Melbourne was an evaluation of a comprehensive education program for doctors, and her continuing research interests aim to improve education for doctors, improve primary care of older people, and inform innovation in primary health care.

Elspeth McKay is a senior postdoctoral research fellow on Human-Computer Interaction (HCI), at the School of Business Information Technology, RMIT University, Australia. Elspeth has extensive industry-sector experience in computer systems. Her Ph.D. (Computer Science and Information Systems) thesis breaks new ground for effective learning from multimedia with innovative approaches to visual instruction. She also has a Bachelor of Business, with distinction (Business Information Systems), a Graduate Certificate of Applied Science (Instructional Design), and a Graduate Diploma of Education (Computer Studies). Her doctoral research identified that not all individuals cope effectively with graphical learning. Elspeth's research findings clearly identify the complexity of the visual learning environment, and outline prospects for customizing e-learning shells, based on ontological requirements. The prospect of customizing e-learning shells tailored dynamically to the requirements of individual learners has stimulated contemporary research into knowledge mediation, and the associated ontological strategies, of actual learning contexts with Web-enabled asynchronous learning frameworks, design and development of enhanced accessibility through touch screen technologies. Elspeth's continuing commitment to mentoring scholastic achievement is also evident in the number of her international invited Editorships.

Andrea L. McNeill is a doctoral student in the Instructional Technology Program in the School of Education at Virginia Tech, Blacksburg, VA, USA. Her research interest lies in the development of multimedia learning environments designed to enhance learners' cognitive and metacognitive skills.

Louise Brearley Messer holds a Ph.D. in Nutrition from the University of Minnesota, USA, and is currently Elsdon Professor of Child Dental Health, and Director of Graduate Studies at The University of Melbourne, Australia. She is responsible for the teaching of undergraduate dental students and postgraduate students in all aspects of pediatric dentistry. Much of this teaching today is done using interactive preclinical lab activities and currently developed multimedia modules such as those described in the chapter written by her in this book.

Alastair Milne has a B.Sc. in Computer Science from the University of California, Irvine (USA). He is an adjunct faculty member at California State University, San Marcos. Mr. Milne worked for more than 10 years with the UC Irvine project at the Educational Technology Center, and later with the CUI Geneva group, working on such areas as middleware support for programmers (especially in computer graphics); implementation of scripts; consultation with design teams on scripting procedures and strategy; and later with the incorporation of multimedia into Irvine's middleware support. He has authored and coauthored a number of documents on the system, some for programmers and some for pedagogical audiences. He has led the porting of the entire middleware system into a new operating system and the programming of prototype material using live video on digital videodisc. His current work includes consulting with Rika Yoshii at CSUSM on evolution of the whole strategy to improve scripting automation and to provide development for, and delivery by, the Web.

Vivienne O'Connor is an obstetrician and gynecologist at The University of Queensland, Australia.

S. Retalis is associate professor at the Department of Technology Education & Digital Systems, University of Piraeus, Greece. He holds a diploma of Electrical and Computer Engineer from the Department of Electrical and Computer Engineering studies, National Technical University of Athens, Greece, an MSc degree in Information Technology-Knowledge Based Systems from the Department of Artificial Intelligence, University of Edinburgh, Scotland, and a Ph.D. from the Department of Electrical and Computer Engineering, National Technical University of Athens, Greece. His research interests lie in the development of Web-based learning systems, design of adaptive hypermedia systems, Web engineering, and human-computer interaction. He has participated in various European R & D projects. He serves on the editorial board of international journals such as *Computers in Human Behavior*, *Educational Technology and Society*, *ACM Computing Reviews*, and *Journal of Information Technology Education*. He participates in the ACM Web Engineering special interest group, the IEEE Learning Technologies Standardization Committee, and CEN/ISSS learning technologies workshop.

José L. Rodríguez Illera is the director of the Research Center on Virtual Learning of the University of Barcelona (Spain), where he also teaches courses on Educational Multimedia at the Faculty of Pedagogy. His recent publications include books on *Multimedia Technology for Teaching and Learning in Higher Education* (2003), *Virtual Learning* (2003, in press), as well as articles on "Electronic Reading," "Collaborative environments and task design in the University," and "Multimedia Learning." His work is also focused on research and development. During the last 15 years, he and his group have developed both educational multimedia applications and open tools addressed to teachers, many of them related to language learning. Current interest is on the study of comprehension strategies of digital multimodal texts.

Michael Sankey currently works at the University of Southern Queensland (USQ) in Australia as an instructional designer at the Distance and eLearning Centre and a teacher of Web Design in the Faculty of Education. Michael's current doctoral research is in the areas of the multiple representations of concepts when utilizing multimedia technologies and how the use of these electronic environments can enhance the learning opportunities for students, particularly for those students studying at a distance. With a background in art and design, Michael is passionate about the way in which aesthetically enhanced learning environments can better transmit information and concepts to be communicated to students of all backgrounds. He believes that the use of the Internet and online education hold wonderful possibilities for the future of education, particularly higher education.

Glenda Rose Scales is the assistant dean for Distance Learning and Computing in the College of Engineering at Virginia Tech (USA), where she provides leadership for implementing a world-class distance-learning program. She earned her bachelor's degree in Computer Science from Old Dominion University, her master's degree in Applied Behavioral Science from Johns Hopkins University, and her doctorate in curriculum and instruction from Virginia Tech. Dr. Scales began her career working for the Department of Defense in Fort Meade, Maryland, as a computer analyst. After completing her terminal degree, she accepted a major leadership position at North Carolina A&T State University, where she, along with the distance-learning team, launched the University's virtual campus. She has presented her research in Electronic Performance Support at national conferences and, most recently, a market research study on graduate distance-learning programs for working engineers at the American Society for Engineering Education national conference.

Stephanie B. Scheer is an assistant professor and instructional designer in the School of Continuing and Professional Studies at the University of Virginia, Charlottesville, Virginia (USA). Her research interests include examining the potential of various distance-learning modalities to create rich learning communities for distance learners.

R. Subramaniam has a Ph.D. in Physical Chemistry. He is an assistant professor at the National Institute of Education in Nanyang Technological University and Honorary Secretary of the Singapore National Academy of Science. Prior to this, he was acting head of Physical Sciences at the Singapore Science Centre. His research interests are in the fields of physical chemistry, science education, theoretical cosmophysics, museum science, telecommunications, and transportation He has published several research papers in international refereed journals.

Katia Tannous is associate professor of Chemical Engineering at State University of Campinas, Brazil. Working closely with undergraduate and graduate students, fellow faculty members, and other research associates, Dr. Tannous has studied a wide range of problems that are fundamental in nature but that have practical applications. Dr. Tannous has interest in educational technology, particularly the application of multimedia and the Internet for teaching and learning.

Krista P. Terry is the director of Instructional Design and Technology and assistant professor in the College of Education at Troy State University in Troy, AL (USA). Her research interests include designing and evaluating multimedia, visual literacy, and designing instruction for distance-learning environments.

Geraldine Torrisi-Steele is currently a lecturer in multimedia technologies at Griffith University (Australia) Gold Coast Campus in the School of Information Technology. Against a practical experience in the design, authoring, and delivery of educational multimedia materials especially for remote communities, she has developed a special interest in the application of multimedia and associated new technologies to learning environments. Until recently, she worked as an educational designer within Griffith University assisting tertiary educators with the design and development of flexible learning online materials.

Rika Yoshii (Ph.D., Computer Science, University of California, Irvine) is associate professor and Department Chair of Computer Science at California

State University, San Marcos (USA). Dr. Yoshii received her Ph.D. for her work on machine translation from Japanese to English. She had worked with Alfred Bork at the Educational Technology Center of the University of California, Irvine, where she was the project manager of the Understanding Spoken Japanese project. She specializes in computer-aided instruction of languages and development of authoring tools for conversational tutoring systems. She has developed computer-based tutoring systems for mathematics, ESL (articles and noncountable nouns), and programming. In recent years, she has been leading the development of authoring tools in Java. She has published many papers on these topics in conference proceedings and journals.

Felicia Zhang has a B.A. (University of Queensland, Australia), Graduate Diploma in Education (University of Melbourne, Australia); Certificate in Teaching English as a Foreign Language (TEFLA) granted by the Royal Society of Arts, United Kingdom; and Master of Arts in Applied Linguistics (Honors) (University of Melbourne, Australia). Ms. Zhang has had more than 10 years of teaching and research experience in the area of language teaching and learning. Since 1994, she has been researching ways of incorporating computer technology into the classroom and teaching curriculum. Ms. Zhang is currently a Lecturer in Chinese and Applied Linguistics at the University of Canberra, Australia. She is currently doing her Ph.D. in the area of pronunciation teaching in Mandarin using a methodology that combines the use of audiovisual materials with a number of computer-enhanced learning software. One of her major concerns in utilizing technology in teaching is the need to cater to a wide range of student needs, i.e., from students with advanced computer skills to students who do not have access at all to technology.

Index

D

intending 2 teach or give instruction

E

verbal-thinking 219
verbo-tonal system 384
verbo-tonalism 385
video 5
virtual classroom 55
virtual dental clinic 369
virtual education vi
virtual environment 328
virtual pediatric diabetic patient 359
virtual reality 27, 328
virtual university 55
visual representations ix
visual thinking 140
visualization 139
voice modality 239

W

wand 330
Web Access Initiative (WAI) 230
Web-based educational systems
     (WBESs) 214
Web-based multimedia viii
Web-based training 55
WebCT 308
WebCT software 293
"window period" 277
working memory 148, 186
working memory model 186
World Wide Web (WWW) 252
written examination tests 393

X

XML 262